# THE
# ROMAN
# ARMY

# — THE —
# ROMAN ARMY

A Social and Institutional History

PAT SOUTHERN

A B C  C L I O

Santa Barbara, California  •  Denver, Colorado  •  Oxford, England

Library of Congress Cataloging-in-Publication Data
Southern, Pat, 1948–
The Roman army : a social and institutional history / Pat Southern.
p. cm.
Includes bibliographical references and index.
ISBN 1-85109-730-9 (hardback : alk. paper) — ISBN 1-85109-735-X (ebook)
1. Rome—Army—History. 2. Sociology, Military—Rome. I. Title.
U35.S625 2006
355.00937—dc22
2005030389

Production Team
    Acquisitions Editor: Simon Mason
    Senior Media Editor: Sharon Daugherty
    Media Resources Manager: Caroline Price
    Production Editor: Cisca Louise Schreefel
    Editorial Assistant: Alisha Martinez
    Production Manager: Don Schmidt
    Manufacturing Coordinator: George Smyser

Text design: Jane Raese

09  08  07  06   10  9  8  7  6  5  4  3  2  1

This book is also available on the World Wide Web as an e-book.
Visit http://www.abc-clio.com for details.

ABC-CLIO, Inc.
130 Cremona Drive, P.O. Box 1911
Santa Barbara, California 93116-1911

This book is printed on acid-free paper. ∞
Manufactured in the United States of America

# CONTENTS

# PREFACE AND ACKNOWLEDGMENTS

IT HAS BECOME CUSTOMARY nowadays to start with an apology for "yet another book on the Roman army," but this author, who would be the first to admit to a very strong bias toward the subject, feels that no apologies need be made for any amount of books on the Roman army. Not everyone has access to large libraries in the various educational institutions in the United States and Europe, so it is only students and lecturers who can view in one place most of the past and present corpus of books on the Romans and their armies. For the interested general reader, reliant upon public libraries and bookshops, the range is more limited. Books go out of print, and the older ones do not necessarily turn up in quantity on the Internet or in second-hand bookshops. There was a time, about thirty to forty years ago perhaps, when you could read everything there was available in the English language on the Roman army, but thankfully that has changed. The plethora of modern books, some of them translated from other languages, each have something extra to say, viewed from a different angle, and many of them do what books should do, which is to make you *think*. As for this book, it may just be the first one that a reader picks up about the Roman army, and then he or she may want to read other books to take the subject further. No serious-minded study on armies can afford to ignore the tremendously successful army that established a presence over so many parts of Europe and the Middle East, and survived far longer than any other.

My first debt, a very old one now, is to the BBC, which broadcast history programs for schools on Wednesdays, when I suppose the teachers were glad of the opportunity to assemble us in our small village school, all twenty-eight of us, to listen to the radio, where it has been said "the pictures are better." My second debt is to those wonderful epic films that they used to do so well and still make now and then. It doesn't matter whether they get all of it right, if the films foster and develop an interest that is already there. You can learn a lot by trying to find out if the Roman soldiers were dressed correctly, if they did put their shields over their heads and call it a tortoise, if chariot races really were like that, if there was a slave revolt crushed by the armies of Marcus Licinius Crassus, and if Marcus Aurelius fought the German tribes from a base on the Danube. My third debt is to colleagues from the Department of Archaeology at the University of Newcastle upon Tyne, to the late Charles Daniels who discussed things and listened, to Karen Dixon who first suggested writing, and without whom I probably would never have written anything, to Lindsay Allason-Jones for encouragement and ready wit, to Dr. Kevin Greene for the discussions in the Refectory on Friday afternoons, to Dr. Julian Bennett ditto, to Dr. Jon Coulston ditto, and to Carole Riley for all the ice creams and coffees.

# MAPS

# THE
# ROMAN
# ARMY

# CHAPTER 1

# Introduction

Tʜᴇ ʜɪsᴛᴏʀʏ ᴏғ ᴛʜᴇ Rᴏᴍᴀɴ ᴀʀᴍʏ embraces more than a thousand years, from the foundation of the city-state of Rome, traditionally placed in the eighth century ʙᴄ, until the fall of her Empire, traditionally placed in the late fifth century ᴀᴅ. While these traditional dates are not absolute truths innocent of scholarly dispute, the time scale is indisputably vast, and it is true to say that the army was an important factor at every stage of Rome's development. The lives of the citizens and soldiers were so closely bound together that it is sometimes difficult to differentiate between the civilian, political, and military history of the Roman Republic, and quite impossible to conceptualize the Roman Empire without the army. The Romans were never far removed psychologically from the army or from awareness of it, and until the later Empire any rising young man from the upper echelons of society almost universally combined a political and military career, passing from civilian magistracies to army commands and back again, in a variety of locations across the Empire.

The very longevity of the Roman army places it unequivocally in the category of one of history's greatest armies. During its long history there were several changes, some of them minor, some of them deeply penetrating, some of them gradual, some of them sudden as a result of pressing needs. The continuous evolution of the army over several centuries should not be taken to imply that the Romans constantly honed their military forces to improve upon them until at last they arrived at the final definitive version. Indeed, it cannot be said that there was ever a final version, only a series of adaptive stages that suited the circumstances of the time. The army of one period of Roman history cannot be judged better or worse than the army of any other period; the only criteria that mattered to the Romans themselves were first whether the army was successful, and second, if it had proved unsuccessful, whether it could be adapted to become successful.

Adaptation was one of Rome's strong points. Over the years, the military system underwent revisions and changes in order to keep up with the times, as certain practices became outmoded. As she expanded, Rome continually met new adversaries, who fought with different tactics and different weaponry. Old enemies learned new ways and adapted their fighting methods and their equipment. The Roman army was organic, constantly adapting to circumstances, both internal and external, and also adapting to the geographical constraints imposed by the widely different locations where troops were stationed. The Empire at its fullest extent covered most of Europe, the Near East, and North Africa, comprising many diverse peoples, several varied climatic zones, and some seriously challenging geographical features.

The vast territorial extent of the Roman Empire and the immense time scale of its history must be continually emphasized in any study of the Roman army. The sources are abundant, but they are spread over several centuries and derived from several regions of the ancient world. Although it is true that there was an overall unity in the Empire in many respects, there were also divergences in the detail. Therefore, in using these sources it must be borne in mind that what was valid for one period or for one region may not have been valid for other periods or other regions. It is impossible to present a complete picture of the Roman army at any one time across the Empire or for any one place for the duration of Roman history. We can merely reconstruct snapshots of it here and there and from time to time. Some of these snapshots are very detailed, and we can extrapolate from them, cautiously, to fill in the gaps in our knowledge of other areas and other periods where the army operated. Like the Roman army itself, the study of it is organic, changing as new discoveries are made and as new thinking points the way to different conclusions. The fact that we do not yet know all there is to know is at one and the same time the most irritating and the most fascinating aspect of the history of the Roman legions and auxiliary troops, their forts and their battles, their dress and their routines, their private lives and their conduct. Future scholars can rest assured that there is ample room for thought and speculation, and for addition and subtraction of facts, theories, and ideas.

Throughout its early years, the Roman army was brought under arms annually in each campaigning season in order to train and prepare for the defense of Rome and her growing territorial interests. During her very early history Rome was ruled by kings, who were evicted, according to a deep-seated Roman tradition, at the end of the sixth century BC. Thereafter, the Roman state took the form of a Republic, governed by a pair of magistrates called consuls, who were elected each year. Annual election and the collegiate principle were adopted in order to preempt the arrogation of power into the hands of one man.

The new Republican political system that replaced the rule of the kings was carefully thought out, owing nothing to its regal antecedents. Leaving aside detailed discussion of the purely political setup, the main effect on the military life of Rome was that the two chief magistrates, the consuls, combined civil and military duties, their principal duty being to take command of the army, for the year that they were in office. As Rome extended control over more widely distributed territories, there could be several armies in the field simultaneously. Since the troops took an oath of loyalty to their commanders, and sometimes those commanders and their armies were far away from the influence of Rome, the inherent dangers in the system soon became problematic. Unscrupulous generals could refuse to disband their armies once the campaigns were over, and then they could use the menacing presence of their troops to blackmail the government. Civil wars resulted from this practice, and Roman soldiers under one general's command showed themselves perfectly willing to fight other Roman soldiers under a rival general's command. Especially during the late Republic, command of armed forces was vital to politicians who wished to rise to prominence and remain there, culminating in the struggle between Gaius Julius Caesar and Pompey the Great, and then shortly afterward the civil wars between Mark Antony and Octavian. Numerous armies were raised during this period, and at the end of it all when Octavian defeated Antony and Cleopatra in 30 BC, he took over many thousands of troops, totaling more than sixty legions. It was these seasoned soldiers who formed the basis of the Imperial Roman army, whittled down eventually to some twenty-five legions. The Roman historian Tacitus, writing in the late first century AD about the recent events of the civil wars of AD 69–70, described the support of the troops as the secret of Empire, but it had never been a secret, and it had been known and understood for many years before Tacitus took up his stylus.

The early Roman soldiers understood that their duty was to fight for and on behalf of the city of Rome, and they never traveled very far away from their familiar surroundings. Romans fought for the survival of their city, and the Republican army was much more homogeneous and much smaller than the army of the Empire. Many of the soldiers of the Imperial armies who joined the units stationed in their own provinces had probably never even seen Rome, and therefore they fought for an ideology rather than an actual city-state in the middle of the Italian peninsula. Perhaps the most remarkable aspect of the Empire is that the Romans were able to impress this ideology upon so many people and to perpetuate it for so long.

During the Empire, the army fulfilled multiple roles. Its prime directive was to fight enemies of the Roman world in defensive wars, or in aggressive campaigns and preemptive strikes into enemy territory, but at the same time the army combined several other roles apart from that of defense and attack. Many of the uniformed officials who are familiar to us in modern life were united in the Roman army. In addition to its military functions, the army also acted as the equivalent of the modern police force with a duty to keep the peace. There was no distinction between civilian and military police in the Roman army; there was just the multifunctional military body, responsible for and performing anything and everything concerned with attack and defense, law and order, crowd control, courier duties, convoy patrol, protection and escort of the emperors and the provincial governors, and more besides. Soldiers also acted as customs guards and frontier police, collecting taxes and tolls on goods being transported across the boundaries between provinces, and watching and regulating what was carried into and out of the Empire across its frontiers. On occasion, military commanders acted as regional governors in remote parts of some provinces, where the populace turned to the army in order to obtain justice over the settlement of disputes and assistance in local affairs.

Several salient characteristics made the Roman army great. The Romans generally displayed a tremendous organizational flexibility, combined with a penetrating analysis of a particular enemy's methods and a willingness to restructure if necessary, perhaps not instantaneously, but gradually over a period of time. The Romans made mistakes, but they acknowledged them and they were usually ready to admit that things did not work properly. On the other hand, they were reluctant to acknowledge that they were beaten. Where contemporary city-states would fight a war, lose a few battles, win a few battles, then make terms and go home, Rome would never yield, refusing to stop until she had emerged the undisputed victor (Goldsworthy, 1996, 2003). In order to achieve victory, Rome instilled stern discipline in the troops, and it was this discipline that gave Rome the victories she desired. Punishments for transgressions such as falling asleep on sentry duty, deserting a post, fleeing from a battle, and throwing away or losing weapons were clearly prescribed and rigorously carried out, with the result that they did not have to be imposed very often. On the other hand, rewards for valor were also clearly prescribed and were bestowed and received with pride.

Once she had won her victories, Rome did not necessarily crush her opponents completely. In the early days, Rome was not so interested in acquiring territory by outright annexation, but preferred to convert former enemies into "friends and allies of the Roman people" as the formula ran. One of her most enduring methods of controlling conquered tribes and states was her ready assimilation and Romanization, by example rather than force, of the vanquished peoples, who were usually obliged to provide recruits for the army in return for certain privileges. This system provided her with ever greater manpower to replenish her armies, and it unified the Empire on many levels without totally obliterating regional and tribal differences. Last but not least, one of the most pertinent features that categorizes the Roman army among the greatest that the world has ever seen is the establishment under Augustus and his successors of the standing army consisting of sequentially numbered legions composed of Roman citizens, and auxiliary infantry and cavalry units composed of noncitizens, the whole with a properly organized recruitment system, pay structure, and pension scheme (Keppie, 1984). It had been feasible for soldiers to pursue a more or less continuous military career during the Republic, since there were several prolonged wars, sometimes simultaneously on more than one front. This meant that troops were in the field for many seasons, often being retained under arms over the winter as well as the summer season. But the Republican armies were usually disbanded when the wars were over, with the result that soldiers then had to seek further employment in other units in other wars. The Republican soldier's career was sporadic and uncertain, without the firm promise of any reward at the end of it all, but military life during the Empire was more secure. Imperial soldiers signed up for a standard period with a guaranteed pension when they retired.

## SOURCES

The source materials for the study of the Roman army are vast and varied but not always cohesive or coherent. One of the main sources of information about how the soldiers appeared, where and how they lived, and about the tools and artifacts they used, derives from archaeological investigations. Archaeological data is supplemented by a corpus of other sources. The Romans left behind an array of archival records concerning the administration of their armies, and these are to be found on papyrus, stone slabs, and wooden writing tablets. There are even rough daily records written on potsherds, the Roman version of scrap paper, presumably for copying up later in the unit offices. These records, together with tombstones, altars, and building inscriptions, are all used in conjunction with the literary record to assemble the history of the Roman army. There are now several compilations in English of literary and epigraphic sources relating to the Roman Empire (Cherry, 2001; Lewis and Rheinhold, 1955; Shelton, 1998) and specifically to the Roman army (Campbell, 1994).

### Archaeological Sources

In addition to the ancient literature, there is a growing mass of information about military equipment and installations, all derived from archaeological investigations as more and more forts, fortresses, marching camps, and civilian Roman sites are studied and excavated. The study of military equipment has always attracted a wide audience. Museums all over Europe, the Near East, and North Africa display examples of Roman swords, daggers, javelins, shields, helmets, body armor, boots, and belts. Different types of horse armor have come to light from places as far apart as Dura-Europos in Syria and Straubing in Germany. Much of this material has been studied and made accessible by H. Russell Robinson (1975), Bishop and Coulston (1993), Connolly (1998), and Feugère (2002). The mundane aspects of military life are reflected in the letters to relatives asking for socks and underpants, and in the cooking pots and drinking vessels, hand mills for grinding grain, and the remains of ovens found in the rampart backs. In recent years specialist journals, books, and international congresses have grown up devoted purely to the subject of Roman military equipment. Several reenactment societies have been established in different countries, with the main purpose of re-creating the arms and armor of particular legions or auxiliary troops. Their contribution is valuable since the practical demonstrations of military maneuvers and the manufacture of equipment and armor all add to our knowledge. It is useful to know if armor can be comfortably worn, and whether sandals and boots reconstructed from actual examples wear out after a few marches. Practical experiments show whether or not it is possible to draw the *spatha,* the long cavalry sword, while seated on a horse, and if it is possible to stay in the saddle after receiving a body blow. Reconstructions of different types of Roman artillery have been made by several people, who base their attempts on surviving sections of original artillery pieces, sometimes combining these with the information from literary accounts and to some extent from sculptural reliefs. The results can be formidable, not to mention lethal.

Roman forts have been studied all over the Empire with the preponderance of excavations in western Europe (Johnson, 1983), but the study of the military remains of the eastern and North African Roman provinces has not been neglected. Dating evidence from pottery, coins, and inscriptions helps to establish the context of a particular fort or camp, and if there are sufficient finds it is usually possible to document the broad general history of these excavated forts. Archaeology can establish the size and number of barrack blocks, the internal alterations that may have taken place, and sometimes it can be established which unit garrisoned the fort at certain times. In many older books on the Roman army, it is frequently stated that all forts across the Empire were built more or less to the same standard pattern, but as more sites are investigated in more depth, an increasing number of anomalies are discovered, revealing that although the Romans adhered to a broad general plan, they also adapted to circumstances and did not slavishly follow the pattern book. Archaeology is a fairly new and very exciting tool, but it is not one of pinpoint accuracy. Other corroborative information must be brought in to complement and augment the archaeology of a site, and there is always the problem of mistaken or misinterpreted evidence, as is occasionally revealed by further investigation and research.

## Papyrus Records and Writing Tablets

The Roman army was efficiently organized to the point of extreme bureaucracy. Fortunately for posterity, a considerable quantity of administrative records survives, covering various aspects of the day-to-day concerns of the legions and auxiliary troops. The chief categories of administrative records are to be found on papyrus, on wooden writing tablets, and in inscriptions on stone. Most of the papyrus evidence comes from Roman provinces such as Syria or Egypt, where the dry climate is conducive to the preservation of such items. There are several notable collections of papyrus records distributed among the museums and libraries of the world. Two of the largest collections with considerable interest for the Roman army are those from Oxyrhynchus, 200 kilometers south of Cairo in Egypt, and from Dura-Europos on the Euphrates. The Oxyrhynchus papyri are diverse in content, covering private documents, official civilian material, and also much of military interest. The Dura-Europos papyri (Welles, 1959) cover a much narrower field with regard to time scale and content, but they are of considerable importance for the study of the army, since they contain the duty rosters of *cohors XX Palmyrenorum,* the auxiliary unit that was stationed there in the early third century AD. Some individual papyri have been intensively studied and have acquired long bibliographies of their own. For instance, the British Museum example known as Hunt's *Pridianum* (a yearly strength report) has been examined and questioned by many scholars, some of whom have doubted whether it qualifies as a *pridianum* at all, since there is no mention anywhere in the document of this particular title, and likewise there is no firm evidence that it was in fact an annual return. Whatever its true classification, it is definitely a strength report of some description (Fink, 1971), and it is a fascinating document. It is probably to be dated to the first decade of the second century, and it concerns the *cohors I Hispanorum Veterana* stationed on the lower Danube in the province of Moesia. The text reveals, among other items, that many of the soldiers of the unit were absent from their fort for many different reasons. One cavalryman had been killed by bandits, someone had been drowned, some men were absent in another province procuring clothing, and others had been sent to find grain. Two groups had been detailed to bring animals for the unit: one had been sent to get horses, which possibly involved crossing a river (the text is uncertain), and a second group had been sent to the mountains to bring cattle. Some men were on a scouting expedition with a centurion in command, and several soldiers had been posted in different locations on guard duty over the crops and the draft animals. This and the many other papyrus records concerning the army are invaluable; no other source so readily brings to life the daily routine of Roman soldiers nearly two thousand years ago.

Some administrative records have been preserved even without the aid of hot, dry weather. The persistent damp climate and the particular soil conditions of northern England have preserved a collection of wooden writing tablets from the fort at Vindolanda (modern Chesterholm), just south of Hadrian's Wall. These tablets throw much light on the day-to-day lives of soldiers at the extreme northwestern edge of the Empire at the end of the first century AD (Birley, 2002;

Bowman, 1983; Bowman and Thomas, 1983). A selection of these tablets have become justly famous, such as the party invitation from the commander's wife, the letter inquiring about the supply of hides, and the complaint that has such a modern ring to it—that the roads were very bad. It is a portrayal that would surely have been recognizable in broad general terms to other Roman soldiers stationed in other provinces, and perhaps also to soldiers of many other periods of history.

## Epigraphic Records

Throughout the Empire, the Romans faithfully adhered to the epigraphic habit of recording significant events on stone, an ingrained practice that is useful to archaeologists and historians in reconstructing the lives of Roman soldiers and in the study of the army as a whole. Thanks to the labors of eminent nineteenth-century scholars there are collections of Latin and Greek inscriptions that are indispensable to Roman military historians, such as the vast *Corpus Inscriptionum Latinarum (CIL),* which was begun in 1862 and comprises many volumes, arranged roughly by regions of the Roman Empire. A smaller but no less useful assemblage is H. Dessau's collection *Inscriptiones Latinae Selectae (ILS).* This was begun in 1892, and the inscriptions are classified by subject, so that all the inscriptions of military origin are grouped together under subheadings. For Greek inscriptions with relevance to Roman history there is the *Inscriptiones Graecae ad Res Romanas Pertinentes (IGRR),* begun in 1906. These collections cover the whole Empire. Useful adjuncts to these are the collections from individual countries, approximating to Roman provinces. Several of these are from frontier provinces such as *Roman Inscriptions in Britain (RIB),* now in several volumes covering not only inscriptions on stone but also graffiti and other mediums. For Syria there is the *Inscriptiones Latinae et Graecae Syriae (ILGS),* and for Hungary *Die Römische Inschriften Ungarns (RIU).* This is by no means a complete list of all the available collections of primary epigraphic sources.

There is a great variety of inscriptions concerning the Roman army. Simple military tombstones reveal much about the individual named on them, giving information about the name of the soldier, the unit or units in which he served, his age at death, sometimes his age at enlistment, and more rarely the cause of death. The tombs of more important individuals often give more information about their entire careers and can be used to document the mobility of the officers throughout the Empire. Some men moved in successive commands from unit to unit and from province to province. On occasion, wealthy time-served veterans conferred great benefits on their hometowns or cities, or on the communities where they chose to live in retirement. Their achievements were often recorded on building inscriptions, religious dedications, or honorary monuments, together with a useful summary of their entire careers in several different military units and in several civilian administrative posts.

One of the most famous career inscriptions comes from the province of Numidia in North Africa, where the town councillors of Diana Veteranorum (modern Zana, Algeria) set up a long text in honor of the distinguished soldier Marcus Valerius Maximianus, one of the generals promoted by Marcus Aurelius in the Danube Wars of the AD 180s (Pflaum, 1955). Maximianus was an anomaly of sorts, being an officer of equestrian status who was elevated to the Senate and rose to become consul. He lived through a time of great upheaval and frontier wars, when social mobility was dramatically increased and soldiers of merit could be promoted, especially if they came to the notice of the emperor. In the case of Maximianus, the Emperor Marcus Aurelius, the man of peace who spent most of his life at war, entrusted him with special independent commands, and by way of reward for his services he eventually promoted him to the Senate. The career inscription from Diana Veteranorum documents Maximianus's many exploits and military tasks. He saw service all over the Roman Empire, in the Danube provinces of Pannonia, Moesia, and Dacia, in the east in Parthia, in the provinces of Macedonia and Thrace, and in North Africa. This rise in social status and succession of posts is not untypical of that of some other officers, but Maximianus's movements are better and more fully documented than most, since he is known from several other inscriptions besides the famous example from Diana Veteranorum (*CIL* III 1122; *CIL* VIII 2621; 2698=18247; 2749; 4234; 4600). He is mentioned on another equally famous example dating to the Danubian Wars of Marcus Aurelius. The text (*CIL* III 13439=*ILS* 9122) is carved directly into a rock face at Trencin (Czechoslovakia), and can be viewed but not closely examined from the rear window of a hotel that backs onto the cliff. This interesting and important inscription reveals that Roman troops were operating 125 kilometers north of the Danube on the river Vag or Waag. Maximianus was serving as legate of *legio II Adiutrix,* and was temporarily in command of a legionary detachment on an expedition beyond the main theater of the war. The value of evidence such as this cannot be overestimated.

When the Romans built forts and fortresses, or helped to construct civilian buildings, walls, and gates, they usually declared who the builders were on inscriptions prominently placed over the gates. The most significant information for modern dating purposes derives from the custom of noting the full titles of the emperor, together with the number of his consulships and the number of years that he had held tribunician power. Sometimes the builders also noted who were the consuls of the year when they worked on the buildings. Since these dates are fully documented, the building dates are easy to establish.

These corporate inscriptions inform us which army units were active in which areas and at what times, sometimes filling the gaps in unit history and in the overall picture of each province. Another form of epigraphic record, from both corporate and personal sources, is the dedication of altars to the multiplicity of gods to be found in the Empire. Several altars are often found outside forts, usually around the parade ground, but some military dedications have come to light from towns and cities, as soldiers passed through or were stationed there for a variety of reasons. Generally speaking, it was not until the late Empire that soldiers were billeted in towns, but a military presence was not totally excluded from civilian locations. For instance, some soldiers were detailed to guard markets and keep order, whereas others were attached to the governor of the province as part of his entourage. A personal dedication can sometimes provide information on the movements of the soldier's unit, though caution should be exercised since individuals could operate on personal business or official orders without the implication that the whole unit was involved. Similarly, a few soldiers on patrol could set up an inscription far from their bases. One such example has been quoted above in connection with the military career of Valerius Maximianus, and another example is known from Africa, where a few soldiers on patrol a long distance from their base left behind a stone inscription. Single inscriptions unassociated with any other finds should not be taken as an indication of the presence of a whole unit in garrison or a fort somewhere in the vicinity, but only of the presence of a body of troops for a short time on a special mission. But in particular when several altars are discovered around a fort naming the same unit, archaeologists can be certain that the unit was stationed at the fort for some time.

## Sculpture

Artistic representations of individual soldiers and the army in action are found in the corpus of sculptural evidence from the Roman Empire. Most Roman military tombstones display a portrait of the deceased, not to be interpreted as an accurate depiction of the soldier, but stylized according to an accepted, Empirewide pattern. Cavalry tombs from a wide variety of regions all over the Empire usually show the horseman with full gear and horse trappings, spear in hand, and a crouching barbarian tribesman under his horse's hooves. Legionary tombs usually display great detail about military dress and equipment. One of the most famous examples is the tombstone of Marcus Caelius (*ILS* 2244), the fifty-three-year-old senior centurion of the Eighteenth legion (*legio XIIX*) who was killed in AD 9 in Germany, in the infamous disaster of Quinctilius Varus when three legions were annihilated in the Teutobergerwald. Marcus Caelius had a brother called Publius who survived him and set up his funerary memorial. The text indicates that if the remains of Caelius were ever found, his bones could be interred at the spot where the stone was set up (*ossa inferre licebit*).

Legionary tombs usually display great detail about military dress and equipment. Pictured here is one of the most famous examples—the tombstone of Marcus Caelius (*ILS* 2244), the 53-year-old senior centurion of the Eighteenth legion (*legio XIIX*). (Rheinisches Landesmuseum, Bonn, Germany/Bildarchiv Steffens/Bridgeman Art Library)

Perhaps by way of compensation for being unable to cremate his brother with due ceremony, Publius chose to depict Marcus with all his military decorations, his *phalerae* or metal discs denoting battle honors, held on leather straps across his chest, and on his head the *corona civica,* awarded for saving the life of a Roman citizen. Marcus Caelius is depicted in a lively fashion from the hips upward as though he is standing behind a low wall. In his right hand he holds his centurion's vine stick protruding over and partly obscuring the initial C of his name on the inscription below him. Another centurion's tombstone from Colchester in Britain (*RIB* 200) depicts its subject full-length, resting his right hand on his vine stick as though it were a modern walking stick. This is the centurion of the Twentieth legion (*legio XX*), Marcus Favonius Facilis, who died not long after the Claudian conquest of Britain. His armor and military dress are shown in great detail, including the straps holding his sword on his left side, and his dagger on his right.

The accuracy of the details of the infantry and cavalry arms and armor, and of the horse trappings on military tombs, has been much debated. It is known that the portraits and the lettering of the tombs would have been brilliantly painted, so it is probable that some details that were difficult to depict in a carved relief were probably made much clearer in paint. But in general the sculptured reliefs of soldiers give us more information than any amount of words, and they can be favorably compared to the archaeological finds of weapons and armor from all parts of the Empire.

Besides the many funerary monuments there are several relief sculptures that are worthy of close study in documenting the Roman army. These vary tremendously in quality and content, and the usual cautionary remarks must be made about the unquestioning acceptance of all that they offer. In particular, all the monuments set up by the emperors had a statement to make, disseminating very positive messages about Imperial rule and military successes. A natural propensity for idealization obscures the truth, and even if the distortions are only minimal, it must be asked how much has been sacrificed to artistic license, or even ignorance on the part of the artists. Attempts have been made to identify specific military units in sculptural representations, based on the different styles of weapons or shield types, or helmet types, but the artists had not necessarily seen the troops in action and might simply have redesigned the swords, helmets, and shields to fit them into the available spaces or to improve the composition.

Despite these obligatory cautions, there are certain significant sculptural remains that contribute to the study of the Roman army at various stages of its development. For the early Republican army, two ivory plaques were discovered a few miles southeast of Rome at the ancient town of Praeneste (modern Palestrina), depicting hoplite warriors armed with long spears and protected by a circular shield. Each soldier's armor consists of greaves, a cuirass molded in the appearance of a muscled torso, and a magnificent crested helmet. Under the cuirass they each wear a sleeved tunic, and over it a draped cloak. These two splendid if stylized warriors are not necessarily Roman soldiers, but the images show how they might have looked in the very early period of Rome's history.

For the later Republic, one of the major pictorial sources is the altar of Domitius Ahenobarbus, found in the city of Rome, probably in the vicinity of the Campus Martius. It probably belongs to the late second century BC, but the date is disputed. The altar was four sided, with carved panels on each side. Three of them are housed in the Glyptotek in Munich, while the fourth panel with representations of late Republican soldiers now resides in the Louvre in Paris. A cavalryman and four infantry soldiers are shown as part of a procession at a sacrifice of an ox, a sheep, and a pig (a ceremony called the *suovetaurilia*). The chain armor of the infantry is clearly shown, and all the soldiers wear swords on their right sides, carry oval shields, and wear helmets with crests, but one helmet differs in style, so it is debatable whether this difference indicates anything of significance about the various types of soldiers, or whether it represents the situation before equipment was standardized.

The Imperial army is well documented in sculpture, both public and private. For the ordinary soldiers of the northern provinces there are the stylized portrayals on two column bases from the Landesmuseum, Mainz, showing short squat soldiers, one intended to portray a legionary, the other an auxiliary. They are both depicted behind shields that almost obscure them, but the visible details still convey useful information, from the sharply defined draped clothing of the legionary soldier to the bootstraps of the auxiliary infantryman. Their helmets alike display neck guards and cheek pieces, but their arms and armor are different; the legionary protects himself with a curved oblong shield and wields a short stabbing sword, and the auxiliary soldier carries an oval shield behind which he clutches two spare javelins, in addition to the spear in his right hand. Similarly, the famous portrayal of the Praetorian Guardsmen, now in the Louvre in Paris, reveals elaborate detail about their military dress and equipment. The sculpture is probably to be dated to the reigns of either Trajan (reigned AD 98–117) or Hadrian (reigned AD 117–138). It has been suggested that the soldiers are really legionaries in their finest parade armor, but this suggestion has not been universally accepted, since the soldiers simply exude wealth and privilege of the sort attributed to the Praetorians. Two of the heads have been restored, but the restorers faithfully adhered to the style of the soldiers in the rear of the panel, which are original. The Praetorians' helmets in particular are shown in all their plumed and crested finery, probably providing the template for many a Hollywood costume department in the days of the great epics.

One of the traditional Roman methods of celebrating military victories was to erect a triumphal arch depicting the campaigns of particular individuals. Some of these have been lost and are known only from their remains or from literary references, but many survive to the present day and have been inten-

The inner panels of the Arch of Titus show the triumphal procession after the Jewish campaign of the first century AD. (Library of Congress)

sively studied. Still standing at one end of the Forum in Rome, the panels of the Arch of Titus show the triumphal procession after the Jewish campaign of the first century AD, and at the opposite end of the Forum the Arch of Severus near the Senate House is adorned with representations of the campaigns of Severus and his two sons Caracalla and Geta. There are four main panels depicting scenes from the wars in the east against the Parthians, one of them showing Severus addressing his troops, with military standards in the background and the cloaked soldiers in the foreground all gazing up at him on the tribunal. The reliefs are very worn, so much detail is lost, and the whole monument is perhaps of more interest for its blend of military history and Imperial propaganda than for its accurate depiction of soldiers and their equipment. The arch that Severus built in his native city of Leptis Magna in North Africa is adorned with panels depicting the Romans besieging a city, while other panels are concerned with the triumphal processions and religious ceremonial.

Outside the Forum in Rome, standing next to the Colosseum, is the Arch of Constantine, but this arch is not of great use in documenting Roman military history. Since Constantine (AD 309/10–337) had arrived at sole power in the Roman world in AD 324, via unacceptable civil strife rather than approved foreign wars of conquest, he made certain that the military elements received little or no emphasis on this arch. Besides this deliberate suppression of too much martial propaganda, the sculptural evidence is more misleading than ever, since the roundels and sculptured figures were taken from other, older monuments, chiefly from Trajanic and Hadrianic buildings of the late first and early second centuries AD. Therefore, the sculptures do not necessarily depict the contemporary presentation of Constantine's fourth-century achievements, or his enemies, or his troops.

Perhaps the most intensively and extensively studied monuments concerning the Roman army are the columns of Trajan and Marcus Aurelius, with their continuous sculptured spirals documenting the Danubian Wars of these two emperors. These relief sculptures have been labeled strip cartoons, but it is probably more pertinent to compare them, at least in terms of political and military propaganda, with the Bayeux tapestry, wherein William the Conqueror presented his pictorial narrative of the Norman conquest of England in 1066.

Every scene on these columns is worthy of study, and there is a large corpus of modern work describing every aspect of them from artistic, social, political, and military viewpoints (Lepper and Frere, 1988). Trajan's Column commemorates the Dacian Wars of the early second century AD, which ended with the annexation of Dacian territory and its conversion to a Roman province, more or less coterminous with the boundaries of modern Romania. The column was dedicated in AD 113. The reliefs spiral upward from the base in a continuous pictorial narrative, showing various scenes from the wars that presumably could be authenticated by the men who took part in the events. The many scenes on the column show the army on the march, loading ships, disembarking from ships, crossing a river on a bridge of boats, building forts and camps, felling trees, fighting battles, besieging cities, having their wounds dressed, taking animals to religious sacrifices, listening to addresses by the Emperor Trajan. The reliefs show the details of military dress, armor, shields, a variety of weapons, standards, and soldiers carrying their kit on poles. Different types of troops are included, possibly in stylized form. Not only legionaries and auxiliary infantry and cavalry are shown, but also there are scale-armored Sarmatians, scantily clad Numidian horsemen, and club-wielding, trousered, long-haired native troops fighting on the Roman side. Attempts have been made to recognize specific units known to have been in Trajan's army. In particular, the native troops fighting with clubs have been equated with the *numeri,* small units not strictly classified as the usual *auxilia,* which are attested on the German frontier and elsewhere, but it has to be emphasized that there is not enough evidence to identify any of the troops represented on Trajan's Column so closely as this.

Another monument that commemorated the Dacian Wars of Trajan was set up in Romania itself, at Adamklissi. There are three monuments on this site— one a mausoleum that may not be of Trajanic date; an altar that commemorates

Trajan's Column commemorates the Dacian Wars of the early second century AD. The reliefs spiral upward from the base in a continuous pictorial narrative, showing various scenes from the wars. (Library of Congress)

a Dacian war, but because the name of the emperor is missing it is not securely dated; and the *Tropaeum Traiani*, or trophy of the Emperor Trajan. This is not a single column like the monument in Rome. The trophy was mounted on a flat-topped cone situated on a large drum, with fifty-four reliefs in panels, or metopes, all around the drum. Although it is indisputably connected with Trajan, no one knows for certain whether it predates or postdates the column in Rome. The sculptures are much more crudely executed than the sharply detailed scenes of the column, and may have been carved by provincial sculptors. One scene shows a Roman soldier in chain armor battling against a Dacian, who is armed with the notorious *falx,* a sword with a curved tip like a large billhook, that could slice off arms with appalling ease. For protection against this fearsome weapon, the Roman soldier has clearly defined overlapping armor on his sword arm, perhaps derived from the style of arm-guard that some gladiators adopted, made of articulated metal cylinders that allowed for movement but was intended to divert downward blows that theoretically glanced off without damaging the arm.

Many years after the Trajanic Wars, the Emperor Marcus Aurelius spent much of his life fighting tribesmen of the Danube region, and he too commissioned a commemorative column, clearly modeled on that of Trajan. It was finally dedicated by the Emperor Severus in AD 193. The relief sculptures are easily distinguishable from those of Trajan's Column, the individual soldiers being slightly more squat, and carved in greater relief than the relatively flat figures of the earlier monument. Chain armor is represented by drilled holes, and the segmental armor (*lorica segmentata*) is distinguishable by deeply carved divisions between segments, but the whole effect is one of stylization rather than an accurate portrayal. As a historical narrative, the scenes on the column document the events of the Danubian Wars. Several of these events are corroborated by the ancient literature, and while this fact alone cannot be used as proof of total veracity, the column attests to the version of military history that the Romans themselves accepted.

## Diplomas

Another important source of information about the auxiliary troops of the Imperial Roman army derives from the various diplomas that have come to light in many provinces. These have been studied by several authors all over the world, and these studies have been collated with commentaries by Margaret Roxan (1978, 1985, 1986, 1994) and Roxan and Holder (2003). The name "diploma," describing the two-leaved bronze plaques, is a modern convention, and no ancient source uses this label. Beginning in the reign of Claudius (AD 41–54), diplomas were issued when the non-Roman auxiliaries had served for the statutory term, usually twenty-five years; with the issue of the diploma, the recipient and his children became Roman citizens, with all the privileges that this entailed.

Diplomas are commonly called discharge certificates, but this term is misleading, because it was not necessarily the case that the soldiers in receipt of a diploma had been discharged and had left the ranks. The information to be gleaned from diplomas reveals much about the troops that were stationed in the provinces. It seems that the Roman authorities waited until there were time-served soldiers in several auxiliary units in a province and then issued diplomas for all of them together. Consequently, diplomas usually carry a list of several units stationed in the province, not necessarily a complete list, but sufficient to build up a picture of the provincial garrison. Comparison of diplomas of different dates from the same province shows whether there was stability in troop deployment or whether there was a turnover of different units. Other historical sources can be brought to bear to explain the stability or the change of units. For instance, serious wars sometimes necessitated the transfer of troops from their home bases to the theater of war in another province. In rare cases, units that disappear from the record of one province turn up in the archaeological evidence, or the epigraphic record, or on diplomas from another province, allowing archaeologists and historians to reconstruct the movements of army units and to document the military history of the provinces concerned.

## Coins

The most authoritative English language studies of Roman coins are to be found in the multiple volumes of *Roman Imperial Coinage* (*RIC*), and the catalogue volumes published by the British Museum in London (*BMC*), edited by H. Mattingley (1923–1950; 1976). Other more accessible studies include those of Sydenham (1952); Sutherland (1974), and Kent (1978). The Romans used their coinage to disseminate political and military propaganda, a practice that gained considerable popularity during the civil wars of the late Republic, when the generals issued their own coinage to pay their troops. Favorite motifs were the military standards of various legions and units, and displays of armor with shields and weapons. The emperors followed the precedent, especially in times of stress, when the legends running round the coins often praised the "fidelity of the army" (*Fides Militum*) or the "fidelity of the cavalry" (*Fides Equitum*).

The study of coins can impart much information about a particular emperor's military policies. The find spots of multiple coins can sometimes reveal the presence of troops during wars, especially when there was a special issue to pay troops. For instance, in the late first century BC, Mark Antony's legionary coinage was intended for payment of his soldiers, not for general circulation. Much later, in the third century AD, when he was hemmed in and threatened on all sides, the Emperor Gallienus likewise issued special coinage to pay the legions. The coins indicate that troops were operating in a particular location, but cannot answer the questions as to precisely when they were there or why. In order to answer these questions, historians must turn to the ancient authors.

## Literary Sources

A sizable quantity of ancient literature gives information about the Roman army, covering a very long time span from the end of the Punic Wars of the late third century BC to the transitional Roman/Byzantine armies of the late fifth and early sixth centuries AD. The written sources range from very detailed accounts of military procedure to garbled, cursory, and tantalizing notices about various armies in late Latin and Greek works. Some of the literature is worth its weight in gold, whereas other literary sources must be used with extreme caution. Some ancient writers had axes to grind just as much as modern authors do, and some of them were necessarily biased, either because of the restrictive political climate in which they worked or simply because of their natural predisposition. Some ancient writers researched their subjects properly, delving into the archives, using official documents and carefully checking their facts, while others reported that they had not been able to verify the source for their tales but then included the narrative anyway, for what it was worth.

One of the most misleading facets of ancient literature concerns the anachronisms that have crept in, possibly arising from the author's lack of understanding. Ancient authors who described what they themselves had witnessed did not necessarily report everything they saw with the utmost accuracy, but they can generally be considered more reliable than those who wrote retrospectively of the distant Roman past. Greek and Roman historians did not always know or acknowledge how much things had changed over the years, and therefore they sometimes judged by the contemporary practices of their own times. This has led to the occasional unwitting misuse of military terms, confusing to the unwary modern scholar. It is always useful to ascertain the background to ancient literature, to find out who the author was, under which Roman emperor or political system he worked, why he wrote, how the work survived, who copied it, and how old is the most authentic copy. All these factors can help to evaluate the accuracy and worth of an ancient source.

### Authors with Personal Experience of the Roman Army

There are a few invaluable works by ancient authors who had personal experience of the Roman army at different times in its history; one or two of them were even on the receiving end of Roman military action. Although eyewitness accounts are not always absolutely reliable in all aspects and must not be accepted without due consideration, there is no better alternative, and at a distance of over two thousand years the contemporary personal descriptions that have been preserved are matchless.

**Polybius: *Histories.*** Polybius (c. 200–c. 118 BC) was a Greek historian whose major theme in the forty books of his *Histories* was to explain the rise of Rome from a small city-state to the dominant power in the ancient world. He had seen this phenomenon for himself, living as he did through the last decades of Greek freedom and independence in the 170s and 160s BC, which Rome had guaranteed, but then found that she could guarantee it only by outright annexation and direct administration. There is no certain evidence as to the date of Polybius's birth, perhaps at the end of the third century BC, or the beginning of the second. His home was Megalopolis in Arcadia, part of the Achaean League in which his father played an important political role. Polybius was probably destined for a political career and may have already written works of history when he came into contact with Rome after the battle of Pydna in 168 BC. This battle was the culmination of Rome's third war with Macedon, and the victory signified the end of autonomy not only of Macedon, but of all the Greek states. Anti-Romans began to make some efforts to resist, but it was too late. The Romans made a point of rewarding those who were well disposed to them, and they were powerful enough to punish those who obstructed them. One method they used to ensure cooperation was to remove the leading men and important individuals of an area and take them to Rome, where they were in effect held as hostages. Polybius was among the thousand men taken from the Achaeans. He was lodged at the house of the Scipio family, where he became a close friend of their adopted son, Scipio Aemilianus, the natural son of the victor of Pydna, Aemilius Paullus.

Polybius has been accused of a strong bias in favor of the Scipio family. Although he did overemphasize the military exploits and political prominence of the Scipios, it cannot be denied that this family did play a very large part during the Punic Wars, and Polybius's saving grace is that his work is still the best source we have for the Republican army, which he saw firsthand. He accompanied Scipio Aemilianus on his military service in Spain in 151 BC and may have been among Scipio's entourage at the siege of Numantia nearly two decades later. Thus, he was better qualified than most to write about the Roman army. He used older sources, some of which he acknowledged, and he weighed the evidence presented by the various authors, occasionally pausing to express his opinion that certain well-worn theories were rubbish, and then going on to give his own considered version. He was not an active serving soldier, but he was far from being an armchair historian—he made a point of traveling through the Alps in order to find out what it was like for Hannibal when he crossed with his army and his famous elephants.

In chapters nineteen to forty-two in the sixth book of his *Histories,* Polybius describes in minute detail how the army was assembled, how the officers were appointed, how the men were armed, how the military camps were laid out, how the watch was kept, the nature of offenses, punishments, training, decorations and awards, and how the Romans struck camp and organized the march. Writing in Greek for a Greek audience, Polybius devoted great attention to those aspects of the Roman army that he thought his readers would not immediately understand, so it is usually assumed that the things he did not describe minutely were already familiar to the Greeks of his day. This allows modern historians to apply Greek models to explain the more obscure passages in Polybius's work.

**Julius Caesar:** *Gallic War; Civil War; Alexandrian, African, and Spanish Wars.*
Gaius Julius Caesar produced three main works: one on the Gallic War, another on the civil war with the Pompeians, and one on the Alexandrian, African, and Spanish Wars against the sons of Pompey. Some of his work was finished off by his officer and friend Aulus Hirtius, but it is probable that Hirtius worked from notes left by Caesar himself. Therefore, the authenticity of the works is not too much in doubt, but the prime purpose of Caesar's writings was self-advertisement, to present his own point of view, or rather to manipulate how he wanted to be seen by contemporaries and by posterity. While he was busy conquering Gaul, creating a military reputation and making a political name for himself, he was only too aware that in recent years Pompey the Great had failed to advertise himself sufficiently. Pompey's reputation and self-evident achievements ought to have carried all before him, but when he returned to Rome, the senators, especially those whose toes he had crushed in his efforts to obtain the eastern command, blocked his every move. Caesar intended that the people of Rome and Italy, and also the Senate, should not forget about him or ignore him while he was absent in Gaul, and that they should know more of him when he returned home.

Caesar's description of the battles in Gaul are vivid and detailed, and the period when his army marched and fought is close enough to Imperial times for some of the details to be valid for the army of the Empire as well as the later Republic. The translator of the Loeb edition of *The Gallic War* considered that the work had been compiled from the information contained in Caesar's dispatches to the Senate, which in turn would have incorporated the dispatches of the various subordinate officers sent to Caesar at his headquarters. This would account for the immediacy and vigor of the accounts of military operations, which is enhanced by Caesar's adherence to the present tense and the third person when describing his actions. Never did he say, "I did this" or "I achieved that," but rather "Caesar does this" or "achieves that." Much of Roman literature, especially of this type, was meant to be read out loud, or almost performed as a dramatic work, just as modern raconteurs lapse into the present tense when telling their stories. Lacking television and other modern media coverage of his achievements, Caesar produced the next best form of self-advertisement.

After the civil war, Caesar needed to justify his actions in the run up to the political struggles. He gives much information about what the army did but does not include much about how the army was organized. Whereas modern audiences must glean these details from between the lines, his contemporary audiences would not have needed such explanation. His narratives of maneuvers and battles are probably trustworthy, and the value of his works is not in doubt, not least because there is nothing else by any other author that covers the same period. Historically, there is very little detail concerning topography for the accounts of the various civil wars, and the chronology is sometimes questionable, but this should not detract from the overall worth of the military details. For the Gallic War in particular, Caesar's narrative shows his army in action. It was a very personalized army by this time, loyal to Caesar first and Rome second. Like most of his contemporaries, Caesar had never had any formal training as a military commander, but he had perhaps studied the former battles of the Scipios and of the generals of his own day. He was a hard taskmaster, demanding severe discipline, unquestioning obedience, initiative where appropriate, incredible speed of operations, willing self-sacrifice, and more—and he got everything he asked for. He would have made an excellent psychologist, as far as the command of men was concerned.

Caesar's books show the Roman army on the march and in battle. The troops were multiskilled in other military necessities; they constructed bridges and built transport ships, war galleys, camps, and forts; they conducted sieges as well as fighting battles; they guarded routes, and they organized and protected their food supply and communications. In some instances, Caesar's officers were placed temporarily in independent commands and acted on their own initiative. He could not keep the whole army together at all times because he needed to hold down several areas at once, and he could not easily feed the whole army if he kept it in one place in the winter. As a result, he appointed legates (*legati*) to command some of his legions or groups of legions. Since communications were desperately slow by modern standards, subordinate commanders could not afford to wait for instructions from the great man himself. Credit was given where it was due in Caesar's narrative for the good sense and successes of his legates, and especially for those officers and men he had personally observed performing great feats during battles or on campaigns. No doubt he also derived some of his information from the reports his officers sent to his headquarters.

One of Caesar's officers, Aulus Hirtius, wrote the eighth and last book of the account of the Gallic War. Hirtius and Cicero both regarded the commentaries on the Gallic War as materials for the historian rather than history proper. As literary works, they are simple, clear, and easy to read, lacking only the merit of polished style, but it is possibly a distinct advantage that they were *not* polished and rewritten by a historian, who could have distorted the narrative for the sake of a turn of phrase. Probably for political reasons, the books were written up very quickly, which enhances the impression of immediacy and vigor. Most important, Caesar presents a rounded picture of the Roman army as the Republic was transformed into the Empire. The fighting methods did not undergo vast changes, and the methods of recruitment, administration, pay, supplies, and discharge of time-served soldiers were already extant in embryo, to be gradually standardized only a few decades later by Caesar's great-nephew and adopted son Octavian, who became Gaius Julius Caesar Augustus.

**Flavius Josephus:** *History of the Jewish War.*  Josephus, like Polybius, started out in opposition to Rome and then wrote of what he witnessed for himself of Roman politics and military organization. He was an aristocratic Jewish priest, with some experience of Rome, which he had visited as part of a delegation in AD 64. He saw at first hand the immense power of the Roman Empire, and on his return to Judaea he perhaps tried to dissuade his countrymen from going to war with the Romans, but to no avail. He was ultimately forced into compliance with the rebels against Rome, and for a while he championed Jewish religion and culture, but when war with Rome finally came he seemingly had little hesitation in defecting after he was captured at the siege of Jotapata. Since the safest place for him was in the Roman camp under the eye of the General Flavius Vespasianus, he was in a prime position to observe the Roman army closely. When Vespasian traveled to Alexandria, where he was proclaimed emperor, Josephus accompanied him, but then returned to his homeland with Vespasian's son Titus and remained with him in the military camp while Jerusalem was besieged. He berated the revolutionary groups and tried to persuade the rebels in Jerusalem to give up, but failed. At the end of the war he was made a Roman citizen, and he wrote an account of the Jewish War in Greek. The first books give a brief survey of Jewish history, while the rest of the work consists mostly of his own contemporary observations of the Roman army. Given that Vespasian and Titus looked upon him very favorably, he may even have been allowed access to their commentaries and notebooks. Certainly, they endorsed what he had written as a reliable record, and while they were probably much more closely concerned with their own reputations and how they were portrayed in Josephus's narrative, it is to be expected that if there were gross misjudgements and misperceptions of the army in Josephus's work, they would have pointed them out and had them corrected. Like Caesar's commentaries, Josephus's work provides a snapshot view of the Roman army at one point in time, describing its appearance and its ethics, how it conducted sieges, how it made and broke camp, and its daily routine.

**Sextus Julius Frontinus:** *Stratagems.*  We know more about Frontinus's career than about his origins. He may have been born in Gaul, possibly around AD 30 or 40. He followed the typical Roman career, taking up a succession of posts as an army officer and moving on to civilian magistracies and provincial governorships. He helped to suppress the revolt of Civilis in Gaul in the early 70s, then served as consul in AD 72 or 73 and was appointed governor of Britain from 74 to 77 or 78. This was a very senior, militarily important post because Britain was only partially subdued, and the army had suffered considerable reverses in the rebellion of Boudicca in AD 60. Frontinus's main task in Britain was to subjugate the tribes of south Wales, and possibly he saw some action among the tribes of the Pennines or at least sent his officers to deal with the area. He may have served in Domitian's German Wars of the early 80s and then went on to govern Asia, another very prestigious post. In his next appointment in AD 97, he was put in charge of the aqueducts of Rome (his post was called *curator aquarum*) and as a result of the experience he gained in this post and the efforts that he contributed to it, he wrote a useful book on the Roman water supply.

Frontinus's other writings included a military manual, called *De Scientia Militari,* or *De Officio Militari,* which is unfortunately lost. It is mentioned by Flavius Vegetius Renatus, who says that Trajan much admired this work. Frontinus's surviving work is his *Stratagems,* which describes historical examples of military techniques, ploys, and deliberate deceptions. The work is divided into four main parts, the first three dealing with events before battle, then during battle, and after it. Frontinus employs examples from Greek and Hellenistic historians, as well as from Roman history. The fourth book consists of a collection of maxims on generalship. Writing under the Emperor Domitian, Frontinus inevitably includes several references to the stratagems of Domitian's German campaigns, but these stories may not be related purely from a desire to flatter, since Frontinus may have accompanied the emperor.

It is not sure who the intended audience was for Frontinus's *Stratagems.* It has been suggested that he intended to write a textbook for generals because there was no formal training scheme for officers, except for the hands-on experience they gained while actually serving. Together with his lost work, the *Stratagems* would have given young officers a good theoretical grounding that might have helped them when it came to putting theory into practice.

**Lucius Flavius Arrianus (Arrian):** *Order of Battle Against the Alans; Essay on Tactics.* Arrian was born c. AD 86 in Nicomedia in Bithynia. He became a friend of the Emperor Hadrian, who was in Greece from AD 108 to 112. Arrian perhaps accompanied Hadrian on some of his journeys and was certainly favored by the emperor. He was made consul and governor of Cappadocia, where he repulsed an attack by the Alani, or Alans, in AD 135. The border was fortified, but pastoralist nomads frequently made attempts to cross the Caucasus, so Arrian produced a dossier in Greek on how to deal with these invasions. Based on his own experiences, he wrote a work called *Order of Battle Against the Alans* (*Ektaxis contra Alanos*). His other works include the *Circumnavigation of the Black Sea* (*Periplus*) and *Essay on Tactics* (*Tactica*). *Tactica* concerns exercises for the cavalry and therefore has great importance for the study of the Roman army, though it should be remembered that this work concerns the practices and established procedures with which Arrian was familiar in the second century AD. Thus, extrapolation backwars or forwars in time may not be wholly relevant.

**Ammianus Marcellinus.** Ammianus, a Roman military officer serving on the staff of Ursicinus, was commander of the cavalry (*magister equitum*) from AD 349 to 359 and commander of the infantry (*magister peditum*) from 359 to 360. He was dismissed from his post after the fall of the besieged city of Amida to the Persians. The mid- to late fourth century was a time of constant military activity, which took Ammianus to Gaul, Germany, Italy, Illyricum, and Mesopotamia. He served under the Emperor Julian in Gaul, and came out of retirement to follow him to Persia, where Julian conducted a disastrous campaign that ended in his defeat and death. Ammianus can be fairly accused of a bias toward Ursicinus and to Julian, but this does not necessarily detract from his worth as a historian. He witnessed some of the peaks and troughs of the Roman army's performance and was able to combine this personal knowledge with research into other sources when he wrote his history of Rome in Latin, in thirty-one books. His work is a combination of narrative history compiled from different sources, and accounts of those events in which he had partaken, so although his agenda was wide and his work was dependent on other sources, he deserves to be ranged alongside Polybius, Josephus, and Caesar rather than with historians such as Livy and Appian. Ammianus started his history of Rome with the Emperor Nerva, perhaps consciously picking up the thread where Suetonius left off in *The Twelve Caesars,* but the first thirteen books are lost. From book 14 onward Ammianus recounts events from 353 to his own day. He covers the siege of Amida in 359, the battle of Adrianople in 378, and Julian's disastrous Persian expedition; for the military history of the later fourth century there is no better source.

*Narrative Historians*

Much information about the Roman army is derived from those authors who wrote about Roman history in general, covering periods of time remote from their own day. Some of these authors are less reliable than others, depending on the sources available to them and their own particular motive for writing. There was a central records office in Rome (the *Tabularium*) where official reports and correspondence were filed, and very likely similar record deposits were kept in provincial headquarters all over the Empire. It is not known how much access writers would have been allowed to these archives. It is said, for instance, that when Suetonius was writing *The Twelve Caesars,* he used the official archives until he fell out with the Emperor Hadrian, and then he had to resort to gossip and hearsay because he could not verify his facts. This theory is far from proven, but it accounts for the relative sobriety of the lives of the first few Caesars and the more frivolous biographies of the remainder.

**Titus Livius (Livy):** *History of Rome.* Livy, the great historian of Augustan times, was born in the mid-first century BC and died just after the end of Augustus's reign, probably in AD 12 or possibly five years later. Livy covered the whole of Roman history from the foundation of the city to 9 BC, in 142 books. Only 35 complete books exist. Some of the sections of the missing books can be reconstituted from quotations in other works, in particular from the Oxyrhynchus epitome from the early third century AD, and the *Periochae,* a summary of all the books except 136 and 137, possibly compiled in the fourth century. By using these two very much condensed versions, a more or less comprehensive version of Livy's history can be reconstituted.

Livy's account of the progress of Rome from her foundation to the latter years of Augustus's reign naturally dealt with the military history of Rome, but the relevant material about the army has to be gleaned from his narrative. Since he was not a soldier, Livy's military details are not always reliable, and his audience would not necessarily have required such pinpoint accuracy. His purpose was the glorification of Rome, and his subject matter was truly vast, so it is not surprising that he produced a work of synthesis. He relied on the works of earlier historians, without checking original records for himself. One of his sources may have been Fabius Pictor, whose history of Rome, written in Greek, dates to about 200 BC. There may have been a Latin translation of this work. Livy may not have used the original books, since he appears to know only certain quotations. He also used Polybius for much of his history of the army and some other unidentified sources. He occasionally misinterpreted military terminology, and since he was steeped in the Augustan worldview, he described some things anachronistically. His aim was to document the rise of Rome, and in this he was patriotic but not wholly biased toward the Roman ethos—he describes adversaries as far as possible from their own point of view.

**Dionysius of Halicarnassus:** *Roman Antiquities.* Dionysius was a Greek historian of the late first century BC who came to live at Rome, working as a teacher of rhetoric. He was a contemporary of Livy, and some of his work corroborates that of Livy, perhaps because he used the history mentioned above by Fabius Pictor. Dionysius's work on Roman history was a literary assemblage of Roman legends combined with attempts to assess historical accuracy. There were twenty books in the original, of which eleven have survived, together with some fragments of the missing volumes, but in the main Dionysius's history is valid only as far as the mid-fifth century BC.

**Cornelius Tacitus:** *Annals; Histories; Agricola; Germania.* The life of Tacitus spanned the mid-first to the mid-second centuries AD, covering the reigns of Nero, Galba, Otho, Vitellius, Vespasian, Titus, Domitian, Nerva, Trajan, and Hadrian. He witnessed great events and changes, one of the most important being a serious civil war when he was a teenager in AD 69, when four emperors came to power in one year, and the first three were killed in quick succession. The feature of Roman rule that made the most impression on Tacitus was living through the dreadful and uncertain later years of Domitian's reign, when no one of the senatorial class felt safe, largely because the emperor himself did not feel safe and was therefore deeply suspicious of everyone.

Tacitus's two main historical works, the *Annals* and the *Histories,* deal successively with the history of the Roman Empire from AD 14, when Augustus died, to the assassination of Domitian in AD 96. Since there was a great deal of military activity during these years, Tacitus is an invaluable source for the wars themselves and the politics behind them. His other works that have relevance to military matters are the *Agricola,* the life of his father-in-law Gnaeus Julius Agricola, governor of Britain from AD 77 or 78 to 84 or 85, and the *Germania,* a description of the land and the tribes that Rome encountered beyond their northern boundaries. The *Agricola,* dealing with the seven seasons of Agricola's campaigns in Britain, is the only source (apart from a fragmentary inscription and a lead pipe from the legionary fortress at Chester, inscribed with Agricola's name) that tells us who was the provincial governor during this enigmatic period of Romano-British history. The narrative informs us about the activities of the Roman army for each of the seven campaigning seasons, the first of them in north Wales and the rest in northern Britain. The main theater of the war for the last five years of Agricola's governorship was in Scotland, but locations and place names are only grudgingly given by Tacitus, who was writing for an audience far away in Rome, where exact place names would mean nothing and the action would mean everything. The major problem has always been to marry the archaeological record from Scotland and northern Britain with the literary record, and make sense of it. Much ink has flowed, for example, over the unknown site of the last major battle of Mons Graupius, where Agricola won his final victory.

The *Germania* describes the various Germanic tribes that the Romans had fought with mixed success from the late Republic onward. There is much ethnic detail in this work, concerning tribal structure, customs, and ceremonial, with emphasis on the warlike character of the tribes, whose whole ethos revolved around the warrior culture and valor in battle. Tacitus probably had no first-hand knowledge of the Germanic peoples or their lands, but his sources are generally accredited and accepted as reliable. One of them may have been the Syrian author Posidonius, who was interested in ethnography as well as history. Other sources available to Tacitus no doubt included personal accounts of the men who had fought and negotiated with the German tribes, from the time of Marius in the late Republic through Julius Caesar's brief encounter on the north bank of the Rhine, the disaster under the Governor Varus in AD 9, to Tiberius's and Domitian's wars. From the latest campaigns under Domitian, there would be several contemporaries from whom Tacitus could have gained information. None of this is firmly documented, and Tacitus does not reveal his sources, but his work provides those details that many other authors fail to supply about the nature of the enemies that the Roman army was called upon to fight.

**Appian:** *The Civil Wars.*  A native of Alexandria in Egypt, Appian was born in the early years of the second century AD. He developed a great admiration for Rome, eventually acquiring Roman citizenship and moving to the city, where he wrote a history of Rome in twenty-four books, in Greek. Appian's main work was as an advocate, and he had a consuming interest in the details of administration and finance. When he died in the 160s, he had started to write a manual on the military and financial organization of the Empire.

Using many other sources to compile his history, Appian preserves information from historical works that are now unfortunately lost. The surviving sections of his books deal with the civil wars that ended the Republic and founded the Empire, and as such they cover military events rather than presenting a history of the army, though he does preserve details of military administration.

**Dio Cassius:** *Roman History.*  Dio's history of Rome, written in Greek, filled eighty books, covering a vast time span from the earliest years to AD 229. He adopted the annalistic tradition, recounting events as they occurred, inserting discussions here and there but without breaking the chronological narrative. About twenty-five books of the original eighty survive, but many of the gaps can be filled by the epitomes of his work that were compiled by different Byzantine historians. Through these other sources it is therefore possible to discern at least the main thrust of Dio's argument.

Dio was born in Nicaea in the province of Bithynia, possibly in AD 155. He lived most of his life as a Roman senator, but retired and went home to Nicaea in AD 229. The date of his death is not known. His career was varied and distinguished. He reached the consulship twice and held posts in several provinces. His experience of the Roman army was not favorable. As governor of Upper Pannonia, he met with troublesome and undisciplined soldiers. He dealt with the problems but at a personal cost. When he was about to take up his second consulship, he met with opposition from the Praetorians in Rome, who indicated to him that his measures as provincial governor had been harsh, and they would be rather displeased if he attended the inauguration ceremony in person. Dio's view of the Roman army was therefore perhaps distorted; he certainly thought that it cost too much and did not give value for money.

### Specialist or Theoretical Military Manuals

There is evidence that the Romans had access to Latin and Greek military manuals that were written and published from the earliest years of the Empire, but only a few of the texts survive intact. Some of the known works are attested only in the writings of other authors, either by casual references that merely list the author and the title, or by direct quotations that give some idea of the scope and purpose of the lost work. It is known, for instance, that the Elder Cato wrote a book called *De Re Militari,* but it has not survived except in a few fragmentary references in other books, such as those of Frontinus and Vegetius. There were one or two authors such as Asclepiodotus and Aelian who devoted themselves to the study of the Greek phalanx, a formation that would have held antiquarian interest for the commanders of the Imperial legions and auxiliary troops. The practical value of the military manuals to prospective or actual Roman officers is not known, though modern authors such as Gilliver (2000) have examined the recorded performance of the army with reference to the information in the handbooks.

**Hyginus:** *De Munitionibus Castrorum,* or *De Metatione Castrorum.* The authorship of this work, written in Latin, is not fully established. In the past it was attributed to Hyginus Gromaticus, since the author was probably a military surveyor (*gromaticus*). Unfortunately, this theory cannot be substantiated, so the work is usually listed as that of Pseudo-Hyginus. The authorship is not the only unsolved problem. More pertinent to the history of the army is the fact that the date of the work is not established. It concerns the layout of a military camp and the army on the march, but doubts have been expressed as to whether it concerns a real campaign or a hypothetical one. Even if it has a definite historical context, it is not possible to date it closely, since it concerns a campaign when the emperor was present with the army on the Danube, and this could be Domitian at the end of the first century AD, Trajan at the beginning of the second century, Marcus Aurelius toward the end of the second century, or even the emperors of the third and fourth centuries who conducted punitive campaigns across the Danube. Arguments have been put forward for all these solutions, but no one has proved any theory conclusively.

The work is incomplete, but for all the inherent problems in using it, there is little else that covers the subject in so much detail. Some of the information seems to corroborate the evidence from archaeological excavations. For instance, Hyginus indicates that the number of men in the first cohort of the legion was double that of the other cohorts, a feature that can be seen in the excavated barracks at the legionary fortress of Inchtuthill in Britain. Not every scholar agrees with this interpretation, however, and it is possible that the double first cohort did not apply to all legions or to all historical periods. Tantalizingly, Hyginus's text mentions troops other than the legions and auxiliaries, such as the *nationes* and *symmachiarii,* about which there is no firm knowledge and only speculation. Attempts have been made to recognize these troops in archaeological and historical research, but there is no solid proof. The work of

Hyginus cannot be ignored altogether in a study of the Roman army, but until more evidence comes to light, it must be used with caution.

**Flavius Vegetius Renatus:** *Epitoma Rei Militaris.* This work is a manual on the Roman army comprising four books, classified by subject, on recruitment and training, army organization and administration, the army on the march and in battle together with strategy and tactics, and sieges and fortifications, with a section on the naval forces. The author Vegetius worked in the finance department of one of the later emperors, perhaps as *comes sacrarum largitionum,* an official in charge of taxes, the mints, and mines. He was not a military man, but he was fascinated by the history of the army. Although the date of his work is disputed, it is generally agreed that Vegetius lived and wrote at the end of the fourth century and the beginning of the fifth, and he dedicated his work to an unnamed emperor, who may have been Theodosius the Great (reigned AD 379–395). Whatever his precise dates, Vegetius worked at a time when the military reforms of Diocletian and Constantine had changed the army of the high Imperial period almost out of recognition, but he ignored the contemporary state of affairs and wrote about the army as it stood before the end of the third century. His agenda, which he explains was demanded from him by the emperor himself, was to summarize the military works of the authors of the Imperial period, and he names some of the authors whose writings he had used. In some cases, quotations and references in Vegetius's work provide the only knowledge that has come down to us of other military manuals. Clearly, Vegetius did not give a complete list, and one of the problems facing modern scholars is that he used many different sources without necessarily evaluating them or differentiating between the possible political or geographical bias of the authors, or their chronological place in history—all of which could have cast an anachronistic or overemphasized political slant on his own accounts of the army. In part, Vegetius had a hidden agenda, which was to write about the army as he thought it should operate, so he searched the military works of the past to produce an amalgam of procedures and practices which in his own day probably did not feature in army organization. Nonetheless, despite its chronological vagaries, its possible misinterpretations, and its fourth- or fifth-century viewpoint, Vegetius's military manual is as good as it gets for the study of the Roman army, both because it is so detailed and there is nothing to rival it in all the other surviving literature.

**The Emperor Maurice:** *Strategikon.* The authorship of this military manual is not definitely established beyond doubt, but it is almost universally attributed to the Byzantine Emperor Maurice, who ruled from AD 582 to 602. There is much of common sense in this manual that can be retrospectively applied, with the usual cautionary remarks, to the Roman army of the first to the fourth centuries AD. It is full of practical advice, such as the importance of collecting suffi-cient fodder for the horses in advance, in case of blockade or retreat, and how to keep water fresh by constantly running it from one vessel into another. Maurice recommended storing water in large earthenware jars, pierced at the bottom so that the water could run into another jar and then be poured back into the first jar. He also recommended watering the horses by bucket if the only available stream was small and narrow, in order to avoid congestion and fouling of the supply—a practice that presupposes that the troops concerned had enough time on their hands for this labor-intensive method. Maurice was also very em-phatic about the need for constant training, particularly for horse archers, who should be born in the saddle and be able to shoot rapidly to the front, the rear, the right, and the left. He preferred sustained rapid arrow fire to perfect aim, no doubt for the psychological effects.

### Law Codes

The collections of laws that were produced in the Byzantine period have a great deal of relevance to the Roman army. In the fifth century, the *Codex Theo-dosianus* was compiled from a variety of earlier laws and enactments (Pharr, 1952), and in the first half of the sixth century, *Digest of Justinian* was issued covering a very broad range of subjects (Watson, 1998) and collating not just laws but also legal opinions with a bearing on application of the laws. The mate-rial in these compilations was by no means restricted to the later Roman period, since several sections of the codes date from the first and second centuries, par-ticularly in the *Digest of Justinian,* where the useful habit was adopted of at-tributing the legal opinions to their original author, so that the chronological context and their long-term relevance can be evaluated.

In a military context, one of the most commonly quoted passages from the *Digest* is that of the second-century military officer and lawyer, Tarruntenus Pa-ternus, alternatively Tarrutenius, or more likely Taruttienus. He may be the same Paternus who is mentioned by Dio in more than one passage, first as *ab epistulis Latinis* (secretary for Latin correspondence) to Marcus Aurelius, then in an inde-pendent military command in AD 179 perhaps as Praetorian Prefect, finally exe-cuted by Commodus. Taruttienus wrote a military manual now known only by its title, *De Re Militari* or *Militarium,* but the *Digest* attributes to him a list of *im-munes* in the Roman army, or those specialists who were excused fatigues. The list provides a revealing insight into Roman military administration.

Another compilation of laws with much more direct value for the Roman army is the book attributed to Ruffus, whose real identity is unknown, but it is speculated that he may have been Sextus Ruffus (or Rufius) Festus, who was a provincial governor under the Emperor Valentinian II, who reigned from AD

371 to 392 (Brand, 1968). If this is so, then Ruffus could have written from direct experience of the army, gained while he was in office; he may have started out as a soldier himself. On the other hand, some modern scholars consider that Ruffus was the author of the *Strategikon* attributed to the Emperor Maurice, and in this case it is thought that Ruffus may have held some military post under that emperor. This wide diversion between speculative dates does not necessarily detract from the usefulness of Ruffus's military laws, which seem to have been culled from sources other than those used by the two great law codes, since in those cases where there is a similarity in the intent of the law, the wording is different. Ruffus's laws are clear about who could and could not join the army: slaves, those convicted of adultery or other public offenses, and those who had been exiled were all excluded. There was never any doubt about the obligation to serve in wartime, or the punishment for evasion when the Empire was under threat being enslavement. Any misdemeanors that threatened the safety of colleagues or could influence the outcome of a battle were usually dealt with by execution, flogging, or mutilation. Running away from a battle, striking or wounding an officer, open insubordination, and inciting men to mutiny, all fell within the category of capital punishment. The penalty for stealing baggage animals was to have both hands cut off, and for a rapist, it was recommended that the nose of the offender should be detached. Some crimes resulted in loss of pay, or dishonorable discharge, which deprived auxiliary soldiers of the privileges of citizenship that they normally gained when honorably discharged. Punishments were harsh in Roman times, but due consideration was given to length of service, conduct, and war record. Drunkenness, for instance, did not always result in corporal punishment, and was sometimes dealt with merely by transfer to another service. It was recommended that when a soldier who had gone AWOL eventually returned to his unit, there should be an inquiry as to why he had done so, in case he faced personal or family problems. The military laws demonstrate that the high officers and administrators of the Roman army, not generally noted for their kind humanitarian principles, understood the ancient equivalent of battle fatigue and shell shock.

### Maps and Itineraries

Knowledge of Roman surveying is fairly extensive, but the study of maps is limited to the surviving examples of which there are very few (Dilke, 1985). The discovery of fragments of the marble plan of the city of Rome, the *Forma Urbis Romae,* demonstrates that the Romans could produce accurate and detailed plans of their cities and individual buildings. The larger view is demonstrated by a thirteenth-century copy of a world map, the original version of which possibly dates to the second century AD. This is the so-called Peutinger Table, a Roman map showing most of the inhabited world ranging from the far west, including Britain and Spain, to the furthest known eastern parts, reaching as far as India. The routes and the places named on them are accurately depicted, though there is no attempt to draw the whole map at the same scale. For the study of Roman military history, the map shows that the high command had access to information about major routes, rivers, mountains, and other geographical features across the whole Empire.

It is not known whether the military authorities used maps to follow provincial routes and boundaries, or to guide them on expeditions beyond the frontiers of the Empire. The Romans drew up lists of routes, noting the forts, towns, settlements, and posting stations along them and the distances between the various named features. One of these lists, probably military in origin, is the *Itinerarium Provinciarum Antonini Augusti,* better known as the Antonine Itinerary. In combination with other sources that also provide the names of certain cities, towns, and military features, this itinerary greatly assists archaeologists and historians in establishing routes and tracing Roman roads. Occasionally, it has been possible to fill in the gaps in our knowledge by applying the place names of the Antonine Itinerary to some of the settlements for which there is no other source. Vice versa, scholars have been enabled to speculate as to the likely locations of the towns named on specific routes but hitherto unknown in the archaeological record.

The primary sources outlined here form the basis of the study of the Roman army. Many of them are accessible to the general reader, especially since the rate of translation has increased in recent years. For the ancient texts, the Loeb classics are the best source because they give the Latin or Greek text on one page and the English translation on the accompanying page, with footnotes to explain the more obscure details. Besides the Loeb texts, there are several other translations of ancient works with helpful commentaries to accompany them. For the epigraphic and papyrus collections, there is a vast corpus of collated works that was begun by indefatigable nineteenth-century scholars. These works are either out of print or so vastly expensive that only the wealthiest of students could afford to collect even a small number of them, so recourse must be had to academic libraries whose managers had the foresight to start collecting when the works were first published.

Secondary sources on the Roman army abound, as will be seen from the bibliography appended to this volume. Many of these books are out of print, and some of them are restricted in scope, if not in depth, in that they set out to deal with only one aspect of the army. In addition, these works are often limited to a particular historical period, such as the Republic, the early Empire, or the later Empire, excluding the other periods. There are now many specialist studies on such topics as forts and camps, arms and armor, military decorations and awards, the social aspects of military service, military law, religion in the Roman army, frontiers and frontier policy, and studies of the army in one particular province. Specialist studies of a broader nature are also important for the study of the army. For instance, the careers of many officers can be traced in the volumes of *Prosopographia Imperii Romani (PIR)* and *Prosopographia Militiarum Equestrium* (Devijver, 1976–1980), where evidence from all sources, including literary, epigraphic, and miscellaneous secondary works, is gathered together to construct the biographical details of thousands of individuals of the Roman world.

There has been a profusion of collected works covering all aspects of Roman history, such as the ongoing series *Aufstieg und Niedergang der Römischen Welt (ANRW)*, which draws contributions in various languages from scholars all over the world. Periodicals have also grown in number to add to the already large collection of vital journals such as *American Journal of Philology, Classical Quarterly, Journal of Roman Studies, Germania, Historia, Comptes Rendus de l'Académie des Inscriptions et Belles Lettres,* and the many museum-based archaeological and classical publications from round the world. The subject is limitless, because of the widespread interest in the Romans and their armies, and because new discoveries and new thinking occasionally add to knowledge and necessitate the revision of older works.

This book covers the Roman army from its obscure beginnings through its thousand-year history, ending with a chapter on the army of the late Empire. It brings together information from the variety of sources outlined above to examine many aspects of the army besides its development and use. Rome was a militaristic and Imperialist state, attributes that invite opprobrium and disapproval today, but generations of people lived in peace and prosperity over the Empire, which was kept intact for a long time by the efforts of the emperors and the soldiers at his disposal. It is worth noting that while some armies may perhaps have been greater, better organized, and more successful, none of them lasted as long as the army of Rome.

### REFERENCES AND FURTHER READING

Birley, Anthony R. 2002. *Garrison Life at Vindolanda: A Band of Brothers.* Stroud, Gloucestershire: Tempus Publishing.

Bishop, Michael C., and Coulston, Jon C.N. 1993. *Roman Military Equipment from the Punic Wars to the Fall of Rome.* London: Batsford.

Bowman, Alan K. 1983. *The Roman Writing Tablets from Vindolanda. London:* British Museum.

Bowman, Alan K., and Thomas, D.J. 1983. *Vindolanda: The Latin Writing Tablets.* London: Society for the Promotion of Roman Studies. Britannia Monographs Series No. 4.

Brand, C.E. 1968. *Roman Military Law.* Austin: University of Texas Press.

Campbell, Brian. 1994. *The Roman Army 31 BC–AD 337: A Sourcebook.* London: Routledge.

Cherry, David (ed.). 2001. *The Roman World: A Sourcebook.* Oxford: Blackwell.

Connolly, Peter. 1998. *Greece and Rome at War.* London: Greenhill Books. Rev. ed.

*Corpus Inscriptionum Latinarum.*

Dessau, Hermann (ed.). 1892–1914. *Inscriptiones Latinae Selectae.* Berlin: Weidmann Verlag. 3 vols., 2nd ed., 1955.

Devijver, H. (ed.). 1976–1980. *Prosopographia Militiarum Equestrium Quae Fuerunt ab Augusto ad Gallienum.* Leuven: Universitaire Pers Leuven.

———. 1980–. Supplementary volumes to *Prosopographia Militiarum Equestrium Quae Fuerunt ab Augusto ad Gallienum.* Leuven: Universitaire Pers Leuven.

Dilke, Oswald A.W. 1985. *Greek and Roman Maps.* London: Thames and Hudson.

Feugère, Michel. 2002. *Weapons of the Romans.* Stroud, Gloucestershire: Tempus Publishing.

Fink, Robert O. 1971. *Roman Military Records on Papyrus.* Cleveland, OH: Case Western Reserve University for the American Philological Association.

Gilliver, Catherine. 2000. *The Roman Art of War.* Stroud, Gloucestershire: Tempus Publishing.

Goldsworthy, Adrian K. 1996. *The Roman Army at War 100 BC–AD 200.* Oxford: Clarendon Press.

———. 2003. *The Complete Roman Army.* London: Thames and Hudson.

Goodman, Martin. 1997. *The Roman World 44 BC–AD 180.* London: Routledge.

Grenfell, B.P., et al. 1898–date. *The Oxyrhynchus Papyri.* London: Egypt Exploration Society for the British Academy.

*Inscriptiones Graecae ad Res Romanas Pertinentes.* 1906–1927. Paris: E. Leroux. Reprinted 1975. Chicago: Ares. 4 vols.

Johnson, Anne. 1983. *Roman Forts.* London: A. and C. Black.

Kent, John P.C. 1978. *Roman Coins.* London: Thames and Hudson.

Keppie, Lawrence. 1984. *The Making of the Roman Army: From Republic to Empire.* London: Routledge.

Le Bohec, Yann. 1994. *The Imperial Roman Army.* London: Routledge.

Lepper, Frank, and Frere, Sheppard. 1988. *Trajan's Column.* Gloucestershire: Alan Sutton.

Lewis, Naphtali, and Rheinhold, Meyer. 1955. *Roman Civilization: Sourcebook II: The Empire.* New York: Columbia University Press.

Mattingly, H., and Carson, R.A.G. (eds.). 1923–1964. *Coins of the Roman Empire in the British Museum.* London: British Museum. 6 vols. Reprinted 1976.

Pflaum, H.-G. 1955. "Deux carrières equestres de Lambèse et de Zana." *Libyca* 3, 123–154.

Pharr, C. (trans.). 1952. *The Theodosian Code and Novels and the Sirmondian Constitution.* New York: Greenwood Press.

*Prosopographia Imperii Romani.* 1933–1998. Berlin: de Gruyter.

Robinson, Harold R. 1975. *The Armour of Imperial Rome.* London: Arma and Armour Press.

*Römische Inschriften Ungarns.* 1972–1984. Amsterdam: Hakkert, and Bonn: Habelt.

Roxan, Margaret. 1978. *Roman Military Diplomas 1954–1977.* University of London, Institute of Archaeology Occasional Publication no. 2.

———. 1985. *Roman Military Diplomas 1978–1984.* University of London, Institute of Archaeology Occasional Publication no. 9.

———. 1986. "Observations on the reasons for changes in formula in diplomas circa AD 140." In W. Eck and H. Wolff (eds.). *Heer und Integrationspolitik: die Römischen Militärdiplome als Historische Quelle.* Cologne and Vienna.

Roxan, Margaret. 1994. *Roman Military Diplomas 1985–1993.* Occasional Publication University College London Institute of Archaeology no. 14.

Roxan, Margaret, and Holder, Paul. 2003. "Roman Military Diplomas." *Bulletin of the Institute of Classical Studies* Supplement 82.

Shelton, Jo-Ann. 1998. *As the Romans Did: A Sourcebook in Roman Social History.* Oxford: Oxford University Press. 2nd ed.

Southern, Pat. 2001. *The Roman Empire from Severus to Constantine.* London: Routledge.

Sutherland, C.H.V. 1974. *Roman Coins.* London: Barrie and Jenkins.

Sydenham, E.A. 1952. *The Coinage of the Roman Republic.* London: Spink.

Wacher, John (ed.). 1987. *The Roman World.* London: Routledge. 2 vols.

Watson, A. (ed.). 1998. *The Digest of Justinian.* Philadelphia: University of Pennsylvania Press. Rev. ed., 4 vols.

Watson, George R. 1969. *The Roman Soldier.* London: Thames and Hudson.

Welles, C.B., et al. (eds.). 1959. *Excavations at Dura-Europos: Final Report V, Part I: The Parchments and Papyri.* New Haven, CT: Yale University Press.

# CHAPTER 2

# Historical Background

## GEOPOLITICAL CONSIDERATIONS

The city of Rome began as an insignificant collection of thatched huts, situated at a convenient crossing point of the river Tiber. From these inauspicious beginnings this small city-state eventually expanded to rule most of the western world, not for a short-lived flash of unstable political and military dominance, but for many centuries, outliving several lesser empires.

The settlers of early Rome were predominantly of Latin stock, and the Romans and the communities of Latium in central Italy shared a common heritage, language, and religious customs. Pre-Roman Italy was inhabited by many different peoples, speaking a variety of languages, observing different customs, and governed by different political systems. The Etruscans lay to the north of Rome, and beyond them were the Umbrians; to the south were the Campanians and the ferocious Samnites. There was a long-standing Greek influence in the south of Italy and in the coastal areas, where colonies had been established many years before and where the first language was still Greek (Potter, 1987).

Rome was one state among many, and initially her rise was slow. Contrary to the relentless advance that loyal historians such as Livy promoted, Rome did not sweep through her adversaries like a hot knife through butter. Her armies were defeated, sometimes disastrously, but despite many setbacks, the Romans always survived and eventually emerged supreme, thanks to their excellent political and military organization. The Romans were a pragmatic and down-to-earth race, not great philosophers like the Greeks, but strong in administration and law, staunchly conservative and proud of hallowed tradition, but also appreciative of new concepts when they understood their practical worth, and therefore much given to plagiarism of other people's ideas. Cicero endorsed this duality when he said that the Romans always followed precedent in peacetime, but expediency in wartime (*de Imperio Pompeii* 60). Polybius (*Histories* 6.25) admired the adaptive qualities of the Romans, declaring that no people were more ready to adopt new ideas when they saw that others performed better than they did themselves.

Rome was founded in a country still notable today for its geographical diversity. Italy comprises several distinct regions with different climatic zones, offering variable agricultural potential. It is divided into two unequal parts by the chain of mountains called the Apennines running down the length of the peninsula. The mountains are closer to the eastern seaboard than to the western coast, with the result that while there is only a narrow lowland zone facing the Adriatic, the most extensive and most fertile lands are to be found on the western or Mediterranean side. Furthermore, the Mediterranean coast is better equipped with natural harbors, and enjoys a more regular water supply than the Adriatic coast, which in Roman times was less fertile, less populous, and less wealthy than the western side of the Apennines (Cornell and Matthews, 1982).

The river Tiber marked the border between Latium and Etruria, and was navigable up to and beyond Rome, though this was sometimes a dangerous undertaking, because of the fast current and the possibility of floods. The position of Rome afforded several advantages that were quickly recognized and appreciated by the inhabitants. The city enjoyed a mild climate, not too uncomfortably hot in summer, and warm without being too wet in winter. The fertile plains that surrounded Rome enabled the early settlers to sustain themselves by growing barley, wheat, peas, and beans, and by raising pigs and goats (Cornell and Matthews, 1982; Frayn, 1979). The Tiber was a highway for the transport of food and other produce from inland regions, and also from the western coast of Italy. Rome was near enough to the sea to facilitate maritime trading, but far enough away to avoid hit-and-run raids by pirates.

Archaeological evidence shows that around the turn of the seventh and sixth centuries BC the thatched huts of early Rome were replaced by stone houses with tiled roofs, and the Forum was laid out with temples and other public buildings surrounding it (Cornell and Matthews, 1982; Masson, 1973). Urbanization had begun, and it is possible that as tradition states, one of the kings, the Etruscan Tarquinius Priscus, initiated the process of transforming the groups of villages into a city. The cultural influence of the Greek colonies and of the Etruscans, who were more advanced than the Romans, probably accelerated the growth of the city through trading contacts.

The early Republican Romans were not interested in territorial acquisition for its own sake but were primarily concerned with protecting their borders. This was a process that inevitably led to fear and suspicion of neighbors, then wars and absorption of neighboring lands and their occupants, and next the creation of new borders with new neighbors, and so the process began all over again. At first, this took place in Italy itself, where many different tribes were gradually brought into the Roman hegemony after the founding of the Republic. The total conquest of Italy occupied several centuries. Even in Augustus's day, there were some remote Alpine tribes who were not fully incorporated into the Empire. Communications were much improved as the Romans took control

Surfaced portion of Appian Way in Rome, the oldest and most famous road built by the ancient Romans. The Roman Empire's road network is one of its most abiding legacies. (Library of Congress)

of more and more territory and began to establish their road network throughout Italy, and eventually into Gaul and Spain, and then into other provinces as the Empire expanded (Chevallier, 1976). The mountainous terrain of the Italian peninsula hindered travel and transport, as well as engendering and fostering regional variations. In the north there was the extensive barrier of the Alps, which the Romans tackled in their typical workmanlike manner, once they had gained partial control of the Po valley, the most fertile of all the Italian plains. Friendly relations with the Greek trading center at Massilia, and later the wars with the Carthaginians, ensured that Republican Romans became familiar with the land route to the south of France, and from there into Spain; expansion to the Rhine and Danube required other routes through the Alps. The road network is one of the most abiding legacies of the Roman Empire.

Internal and external trade was always of importance to the survival of Rome (Garnsey et al., 1983), though some scholars deny the importance of commerce, emphasizing the indifference of the aristocracy to trade, the predominance of agriculture as the basis of wealth, and the difficulties of long-distance transport. If trade in goods was unimportant, the transport of food supplies was vital, and much of this was seaborne, utilizing the ports of the west coast such as Ostia at the mouth of the Tiber and the port of Puteoli (modern Pozzuoli). According to Roman tradition, Ostia was founded by King Ancus Marcius in the seventh century BC. While archaeological evidence cannot support this claim to such an early date, it is certain that the city was established as a fortified maritime colony at some time in the fourth century BC. Despite its description as the port of Rome, Ostia had no harbor, and transshipment of goods was difficult until the Emperor Claudius created an enclosed harbor at Portus, two miles to the north. Trajan improved upon the original design by adding an extra inner harbor. A large proportion of the grain bound for Rome came through Ostia. The port of Puteoli was originally founded by Greek colonists, and by the second century BC was handling much of the trade with the east. Like Ostia, much of the imported grain passed through Puteoli. Rome's early connections with Sicily enabled her to supply her growing population from the agricultural produce of the island, and later the establishment of provinces in North Africa and the acquisition of Egypt vastly increased the grain shipments across the Mediterranean.

After the absorption of many of the tribes and states around her own territory, Rome came into contact with the major Mediterranean power, Carthage, a city originally founded by the Phoenicians, traders par excellence. The Carthaginians monopolized maritime trade in and beyond the Mediterranean, and initially Rome was content with the situation. Treaties were arranged between the two powers in 508 and 348 BC, and for many years Rome did not disrupt Carthaginian activity in the Mediterranean, while Carthage refrained from interference in Roman activity in Italy. When the question of domination of Sicily arose, the conflicts that followed, known as the first, second, and third Punic Wars, were perhaps the most influential of all previous or subsequent wars in shaping both Rome and her army. It could be said that the wars with Carthage laid the foundations of the Roman Empire. The first provinces of Sicily and Sardinia were annexed in the aftermath of the first Punic War, and after the war with Hannibal the Romans took over Spain. The battles of the Punic Wars were not confined to Italy itself, so the Romans learned how to fight and to sustain their armies in other countries. Nor did the wars involve only land battles, so the Romans rapidly learned how to fight at sea, not very expertly at first, since they assembled and lost three fleets in quick succession. They built some ships of their own, but in the main they relied on the supply of ships and crews contributed by their allies on the Italian coast, who had greater experience of naval matters. During the first Punic War, the Romans started to build a navy in earnest. Without control of seapower, the Empire would have been inconceivable.

The conclusion of peace with Carthage after the defeat of Hannibal in 202 BC did not bring about a return to the old Roman way of life. Rome had become

Trajan, emperor of Rome, on horseback with spear, hunting wild boar. The Roman Empire started to grow in the third century BC and reached its furthest extent under the Emperor Trajan in the early second century AD. (Library of Congress)

a world power and had begun to notice, and was noticed by, other people beyond Italy. Roman influence spread, and several states turned to her for military assistance against their enemies. Rome made a few experimental forays into other lands and at first brought her troops home after fighting, but it soon became clear that the direct administration of territory was a more attractive and less troublesome way of dealing with other powers, especially those that seemed to be internally unstable or externally threatened. The Empire started to grow in the third century BC and reached its furthest extent under the Emperor Trajan in the early second century AD. Trajan's successor Hadrian gave up some of the newly conquered territories in Arabia, and Dacia (modern Romania). Abandonment of territory was never a popular move at Rome, but Hadrian decided that expansion had gone far enough and had perhaps outstripped the ability to govern the Empire effectively, so he began to enclose it within clearly defined boundaries, some of which were demarcated routes, and others were physical barriers like the German earth and timber frontier, and the stone wall that bears Hadrian's name in northern England.

North
Sea

ATLANTIC
OCEAN

Britannia

Germania
Inferior

Belgica

Lugdunensis

Aquitanica

Germania
Superior

Raetia

Noricum

Alpes Poeninae

Panno

Alpes
Cottiae

Narbonensis

Alpes
Maritimae

Dalma

Lusitania

Tarraconensis

Corsica

Italia

Baetica

Sardinia

Mediterranean Sea

Sicilia

Mauretania
Tingitana

Mauretania
Caesariensis

Africa

| 0 | 300 Miles |
| 0 | 300 Kilometers |

Map of the Roman Empire in the mid-second century AD showing the provinces
and the limits of Roman control. (Drawn by Graeme Stobbs)

Geographically, the Empire was extremely diverse. The Romans adapted to several different types of terrain, which was subject to widely differing climates and inhabited by a variety of peoples, ranging from tribal societies in the west and along the Rhine and Danube to sophisticated eastern city-states with long experience of urbanization. Although Latin was the official language of government and the law, Greek was widely used in the east, and many different languages, customs, and religious practices were allowed to flourish under Roman rule. For over three centuries, Rome welded together this large extent of territory with its regional differences.

With the steady acquisition of new territories from the third century BC onward, the mechanics of provincial government were developed on an empirical basis. The political and administrative systems that had evolved to govern a small city-state had to be adapted to meet the needs of the Empire and its several different provinces. In order to provide sufficient manpower to control and protect the growing number of territories, the structure of the army gradually changed from the Republican system of an annual levy of Roman citizens and their Italian allies to the Imperial standing army of legions and auxiliary troops, which by the second century AD were stationed in permanent forts on the frontiers and at strategic points within the provinces. During the history of the Empire, the Romans responded to changing political and military needs sometimes by transferring troops on a temporary basis into the war zone and at other times by permanently increasing garrisons.

Rome's relations with her neighbors were mostly watchful and opportunistic. The tribes and states beyond the Imperial frontiers were fully aware of Rome, and the Roman presence did not cease abruptly at the boundaries, even when the frontiers were established under Hadrian and his successors. Expeditions were mounted into non-Roman territory, and embassies were exchanged; soldiers were recruited from beyond the Rhine and Danube and from Africa and the east, and Roman goods traveled beyond the frontiers, even as far as India. Many of these Roman items could have reached non-Roman peoples as booty captured in wars, or as a result of long-distance trade, but it is equally possible that some of the finer items were part of the gift-exchange culture, where the Romans cultivated the elite classes beyond the provinces just as they did among the provincial populations. In this way, the Romans befriended and promoted native leaders and their warriors to encourage them to keep their own tribesmen under control, and also to facilitate a watching brief on events and political developments among the tribesmen of more remote regions. The subsidies were paid in prestige gifts, cash, and sometimes in the form of food, enabling the tribal leaders to share the largesse with their chiefs and keep them under control.

The most profitable relationship with the tribes was large-scale recruitment into the Roman army. The use of native troops had a long history from Repub-

## PROVINCIA

The term *provincia* did not originally define a territory but denoted a specific task allocated to a magistrate. With the acquisition of a growing Empire and the consequent need for a regular supply of governors to administer the new lands, the word *provincia* began to be applied not only to a specific duty or task but also to a territory, thus acquiring the sense in which the word is used today. The *provinciae*, or individual tasks, could be quite flexible, routine or novel, short or long term. They could involve such things as repairing roads, managing the forests, attending to the grain supply, or any other assignment that the Senate decided upon, some of which could have military duties attached, and some of which were administrative. In the early and middle years of the Republic, the serving magistrates took up their *provinciae* during their year of office. The consuls and sometimes the praetors commanded the armies in times of war, and in times of peace all magistrates attended to the tasks they had been allocated. Later, when the increase in administrative duties necessitated more personnel, the pro-magistracy was established and it became more normal for magistrates to attend to duties in Rome while in office. They would then take up the various *provinciae* at the end of their year, when they became proconsuls and propraetors. The Senate decided on the tasks that were necessary and also those that were to be given to praetors or consuls. By various means, certain politicians could bribe and insinuate themselves into lucrative or prestigious *provinciae*. To counteract this development, the tribune Gaius Sempronius Gracchus passed a law in 123 BC to ensure that the Senate decided upon which *provinciae* were to be allocated to the consuls before the elections were held, so that it would not be possible to plan an election campaign by swaying the voters on the issue of the tasks to be performed. When Julius Caesar made it clear that he intended to stand for election as consul for 59 BC, the Senate tried to block his rise to power by allocating the mundane duty of caring for the woodlands and paths as the *provinciae* for the retiring consuls of that year—the last thing that anti-Caesarians wanted was Julius Caesar in a *provincia* that gave him a territory and command of troops. The ploy failed miserably. Caesar's consular colleague Calpurnius Bibulus was no match for him in popularity, audacity, or ruthlessness, and the people of Rome dubbed the year 59 BC as the consulship of Julius and Caesar. It was with little difficulty that Caesar changed the *provinciae* for 58 BC and arranged that he should be allocated Gaul as a territorial province with himself as proconsul in command of several legions. He held this post for the next ten years.

The Romans did not attempt to impose a rigid uniformity in the government of the provinces but varied their approach according to local circumstances. When territory was annexed after military conquest, there was much work to do in organizing the province, establishing the legal framework, the taxation system, the constitutions of the various towns and cities, and fixing the boundaries. This work was summed up in the *lex provinciae*, which was ratified at Rome by the Senate and the people, and formed the basis of government of the province from then onward.

lic times, when they were engaged for the duration of a war, usually in their own territory or in lands neighboring their own, and then released when the wars were concluded. In Imperial times, when the army was established on a permanent basis, more and more native recruits were levied, sometimes by accepting volunteers and sometimes by treaty arrangements when large numbers of men were recruited all at once. The more unruly recruits were sent to other provinces, removing them from their homes so that they could not incite their kinsfolk to make trouble. For instance, under Trajan or Hadrian, numbers of British tribesmen were sent to the frontier forts of Germany, and Marcus Aurelius sent 5,500 Sarmatians from the Danube regions to northern Britain.

The northern tribes beyond the Rhine and Danube were relatively stable in the first two centuries of the Empire, but then a combination of climatic changes and political developments altered the balance. In what is now northwestern Europe, prolonged and unusually high rainfall rendered primitive agricultural methods untenable, and in the absence of sophisticated drainage techniques, whole settlements disappeared. The sea levels rose and ruined the farmlands of the western coast and the mouth of the Rhine, resulting in food shortages on a grand scale. Further north, in Denmark and Jutland, there is evidence of serious warfare starting around AD 200, which is thought to have displaced whole populations as more aggressive tribal groups took over their lands (Southern, 2001). Hunger and the need for land caused large-scale movements of tribesmen who turned toward the Roman Empire, where many of them hoped to be allowed to settle. Absorption of thousands of tribesmen had been organized in the past, starting with Augustus who brought in 50,000 settlers from across the Danube into the province of Moesia, and later Tiberius allowed 40,000 Germans to take over land in Gaul. The status of the new settlers may have varied, but they provided a source of recruitment for the army. The problems of displaced peoples continued into the following centuries. In the midsecond century AD Marcus Aurelius settled 3,000 Naristae within the Empire, and in the third century Probus was said to have brought in a staggering 100,000 Bastarnae. If the figures are suspect, at least the process is authenticated, and for the first two centuries of the Empire it worked reasonably well. During the third century the pressure mounted as the movement of tribes became more violent, and successful attacks were made on the frontiers, which were never designed to withstand assaults on a grand scale. Political evolution among the tribesmen resulted in the emergence of tribal federations of men from various tribes, with new names such as the Alammani, which simply means "all men," or the Franks, which may mean "fierce warriors" or alternatively "free men." There was no distinct homogeneous or racial connotation in the new tribal names. The tribal groupings evolved as a result of the tribesmen's conscious political decisions, and these decisions directly affected the Roman Empire. The third century Roman army was neither large enough nor mobile enough to deal with all the attacks at once, especially as there was another threat in the east, from the new dynasty that had taken over the Parthian Empire.

Parthia was the only state that rivaled Rome at the same level of sophisticated political and military organization, but most of the wars were preemptive strikes by the Romans rather than serious invasions by the Parthians. The major problem with Parthia was its territorial extent, together with the fact that, like the Roman Empire, it was a composite entity comprising many different peoples and dependent kingdoms. Much of Rome's wealth and political energy was devoted to attempts to stabilize the eastern frontier, but the Romans never achieved more than pushing the boundaries a little further east and then securing them for a while, and in this respect Trajan, Severus, and Diocletian were successful. None of the Roman emperors achieved lasting peace on the eastern frontier because they could never subdue the whole of Parthia. An attempt to do so would have been the ancient equivalent of the disasters incurred by more recent western rulers from Charles XII of Sweden through Napoleon to Hitler, who all invaded but signally and catastrophically failed to conquer Russia.

At around the same time that the attacks of the tribesmen intensified in the western half of the Empire, in the east the Parthian rulers entered into a revolutionary phase during which the royal house of the Parthian Arsacids, founded by Arsaces about five centuries earlier, was obliterated and replaced by the Persian Sassanids, founded by the energetic Iranian prince Ardashir. The Parthians had been steadily weakening at the end of the second century AD, a situation that was welcome to Rome, but in the third century the new dynasty of Ardashir proved strong and aggressive, and therefore a perceived threat to the security of the eastern provinces. A Roman expedition under the Emperor Valerian in AD 260 ended with the capture and surrender of the emperor himself and his army.

In the same year all the other frontiers were breached or fell, and Roman territory was invaded. Rome was now threatened on two long and important fronts and was not dealing with either threat successfully. The Empire began to disintegrate. Breakaway states were formed, one in the east under the Palmyrene ruler Odenathus and another in the west where the military leaders declared independence and formed the Empire of the Gauls (*Imperium Galliarum*). This division was made in an effort to protect themselves from attacks that the central government under Valerian's son Gallienus was in no position to halt. After only a few years, the Empire was reunited under the strong leadership of Aurelian, but significantly Rome ceased to be the single center from which emanated all control. The city was too far away from the war zones, and communications were too slow to cope with the rapidly changing, fluid situations on and beyond the frontiers. The emperors required several different bases in addition to Rome, where they could assemble troops and also carry on the government of the Empire. Regional centers began to appear, designed to accommodate the emperor or his deputies, their bodyguards, and the more mobile mounted troops, within easy reach of the theaters of war. Imperial headquarters were set up in northern Italy at Milan, in northern Gaul at Trier, on the Danube at Carnuntum, and in the east at Antioch, among other cities. Ultimately, the most important of these Imperial residences was Byzantium, where Constantine founded his rival capital and renamed it Constantinople after himself. The Empire was split into two halves at the beginning of the fifth century AD, the eastern sector enjoying a long existence and surviving as the Byzantine Empire, but the venerable city of Rome declined in importance, and the western Empire declined with her.

## DEMOGRAPHY

The demographic material from the Roman world has been studied by Parkin (1992) and Scheidel (1996), but since complete population statistics for the Roman Empire are nowhere fully attested, historians must rely on estimates. Although births had to be registered in all provinces of the Roman Empire, the records have not survived. Even though there is an impressive collection of data from funerary inscriptions, the information is not necessarily useful for demographic purposes. Ages at death are often included, but it is only rarely that the cause of death is revealed in inscriptions, and since the Romans generally cremated their dead, forensic evidence is unobtainable. Only in the Christian era did people start to bury their relatives, giving archaeologists a chance to glean evidence of ailments, life spans, and possible causes of death. This is why the skeletons discovered at Pompeii, and more recently at Herculaneum, hold such enduring interest for historians.

For population statistics generally, we are a little better served by census figures. In ancient Rome responsibility for conducting the census was vested in the kings, then the consuls, until in the middle of the fifth century BC two new officials were created, appropriately called censors. These men were usually ex-consuls and were elected every four years (later every five years) to take up office for eighteen months. The data collected included the full name of the person concerned, the name of his father, the place where he normally resided, what he did for a living, and how much property he owned. This information decided the individual's place in the Republican army.

As the Empire expanded, the Romans conducted census surveys in the provinces, primarily to record those people who were liable to pay taxes. Despite all this activity, the picture that emerges after 2,000 years is a little patchy. Even if figures can be obtained for an individual city, or a province of the Roman Empire, the basis on which the surveys were carried out is not known, and therefore the use of such statistics without the attendant discussion can present a distorted image. A documented rise in the Roman population could be attributed to several different causes, especially as the inhabitants of some regions could be granted Roman citizenship en bloc. Thus a vast increase was created between one census and the next that was totally unrelated to the birth rate or the average life span. It is not known if or when women and children were counted, and this is one of the factors that must be taken into account in explaining why the census figures for Roman citizens in 70 BC were given as 910,000, whereas the census conducted under Octavian Augustus in 28 BC reported over 4 million people. Another factor is that the late Republican and early Imperial census figures may be restricted to a count of the adult males of a certain property qualification, omitting the very young and the lower classes altogether.

For military purposes, there is the evidence of Polybius, in the context of the invasion of the Gauls in 225 BC. The Romans and the Italians had met the Gauls before and had been badly mauled. Polybius (2.23–24) describes how the Italians readily cooperated with Rome, as every tribe and city sank their differences, and the Romans conducted a census of all the men capable of bearing arms, a total of 700,000 infantry and 70,000 cavalry. Of these, the Romans and their nearest neighbors contributed 250,000 infantry and 23,000 cavalry, and the rest came from the Latin and Italian tribes and cities. The value of this passage has been debated, but there is neither supporting evidence nor any contemporary contradictory claim, so it has to be taken at face value without knowing the nature of Polybius's sources.

Italian and provincial population figures are harder to estimate than those of Roman citizens. The cities for which some figures exist are predominantly in the eastern provinces, where there was a long-standing urban tradition, but even these statistics are not fully elucidated because, in addition to the people who lived in the city, the surrounding rural population attributed to city administration may also have been included. The population of Rome itself during the Empire is usually estimated at one million, kept relatively stable by a high birth rate negated by a high death rate. The same stability is postulated for the major cities of the Empire. As for the non-Roman inhabitants of the provinces, there is no information except for what can be deduced from archaeological evidence. For instance, aerial photography combined with excavations suggest that there was an increase in the population of northern Britain in the second century AD in the hinterland of Hadrian's Wall, where the assurance of peaceful conditions promoted prosperity and growth.

An attempt to enumerate the vast number of replacement troops that were required by the army is one aspect of the demography of the Roman Empire, and this problem has been examined by MacMullen (1980) and Le Bohec (1994). The total number of legions and auxiliary units can be demonstrated, or at least closely estimated, for most periods of Imperial history from the reign of Augustus to the late third-century reforms of Diocletian, and some estimate can be made of the number of men retiring and the number of recruits that would be necessary each year. The main problems are that losses in battles and natural wastage from accidents and disease are not known, except in literary sources where the numbers of troops killed in wars or the numbers of replacements are given but are highly suspect.

## POLITICS, DOMESTIC AND INTERNATIONAL

The history of Rome embraces three distinct forms of government. From the foundation of the city by Romulus, traditionally in 753 BC, Rome was ruled by kings, whose regime lasted until the late sixth century BC when the Republic was established. For five centuries the Republic, which was not a democracy but rule by an aristocratic minority, survived political crises and military disasters. Then in the first century BC the system began to founder, and the Romans turned full circle from rule by kings to rule by emperors.

The ancient regal period is shrouded in mystery, and even though there is more historically reliable information about the last seven kings, it appears that not even the Romans themselves had all the information at their disposal about this era. It is impossible now to disentangle the personal histories of the individual kings and their dynastic squabbles. The fact that some of the kings were Etruscan does not necessarily mean that Rome was groaning under the oppression of a foreign tyranny. Throughout their long history, the Romans welcomed other peoples into their city and integrated them into their society, and the influence of the Etruscans was always very strong in Roman culture. The symbols of power of the Roman Republic and Empire were Etruscan in origin. The most enduring of these was the *fasces,* from which the modern term Fascism is derived. The *fasces* consisted of bundles of wooden rods containing a single headed axe, symbolizing the power of the magistrates to inflict punishments and even the death penalty. The Roman triumph and the gladiatorial games were also Etruscan imports.

Traditionally in 509 BC, the Roman aristocracy rid themselves forever of their kings and turned themselves into a Republic, governed by the Senate and annually elected magistrates. The exact date and even the nature of the event is not clarified—was it just a peaceful and natural transition, or was it a violent revolution? There was great political instability in Italy during the sixth century BC, and the birth of the Republic coincided with the decline of Etruscan influence and power. The expulsion of the kings did not necessarily entail the eviction of all the Etruscans from Rome. It was a political matter and not a racial problem. Trading contacts and aristocratic associations would have been maintained, and it is also likely that the Roman army still contained many soldiers of Etruscan origin.

Republican government was far from being a democratic institution. Unity and equality were not strong features of Roman social and political organization, which was heavily weighted in favor of distinction of birth and wealth. The aristocrats, known as patricians, formed the ruling classes, while the rest of the population, the plebs, had little or no political voice. In the early Republic, a vast personal fortune without aristocratic ancestry was not sufficient to earn distinction, so however rich the leading plebeians became they were at first excluded

## THE FOUNDATION OF THE REPUBLIC

Ancient sources for the regal period of Rome are hazy and possibly include a certain amount of fictitious detail interpolated by later authors. While the same could be said for most of the historical accounts of the very early years of the Republic, there may be a firm basis of archival records documenting the names of the first consuls, the laws that were enacted, and the treaties that were made with other states and powers. Around these documents, coupled with the traditional tales handed down by successive generations of the aristocratic families, historians could hang a fairly credible narrative, but the earliest sources that have come down to us are Livy's history and that of Dionysius of Halicarnassus, both of whom wrote in the first century BC.

The lurid details of the fall of the monarchy portray the last kings as tyrants, whose evil deeds so enraged the aristocratic clans that they rebelled, forcibly expelled the kings, and set up their own system of government. The tales that have been preserved represent the last king of Rome, Tarquinius Superbus, or Tarquin the Proud, as a usurper who seized the throne without the approval of the Senate and the people. He has been claimed as the son of the previous king but he was more likely the grandson of the elder Tarquin; his origins do not really count for or against him, since the monarchy was elective, not hereditary. Tarquin ably defended Rome and ensured her supremacy at the head of the Latin League, and he is credited with embellishing the city with fine buildings. At home, however, he ruled without reference to the Senate, inflicting capital punishment arbitrarily and taking over estates and properties of his victims. The crucial moment came when Tarquin's son Sextus gave in to his passion for a young woman called Lucretia. Although she was married, he blackmailed her into a liaison with him by threatening to spread the story that he had caught her in an adulterous relationship with a slave. Lucretia submitted but then confessed all and committed suicide. Angered beyond endurance the Romans looked to the stern Lucius Junius Brutus to lead them in revolt. They expelled Tarquin, subverting his troops in the process. It was not quite the end for Tarquin, since he kept coming back with his friends and more troops to try to regain his position. Thwarted by the famous defense of the bridge by the Horatii, the Etruscans under Lars Porsenna failed to take Rome. Although Tarquin did eventually rally the Latins to his cause, he had to wait for several years for the battle, which occurred at Lake Regillus in 496 or 497 BC. The Romans won, Tarquin was wounded, and he retired, renouncing his ambitions, and from then on the history of the kings of Rome was at an end.

from government. In 494 BC, the plebs went on strike and removed themselves from the city, refusing to serve in the army, a ploy that they used on more than one occasion to obtain what they wanted (Brunt, 1971; Mitchell, 1990). The prolonged struggle of the orders between plebs and patricians resulted eventually in a rise in status for the plebs, as they gained political power and were finally admitted to the Senate provided that they could demonstrate sufficient wealth. A new nobility was formed from a blend of the diminishing numbers of patrician families and the growing number of plebeian notables.

The constitution of the Republic was not written down, and in the strict modern sense of the term it was not a constitution at all. As such, it was most likely the result of cumulative experience and experimentation, or at least of political maturity (Lintott, 1999). Republican government operated by means of custom and tradition but changed according to circumstances, and was always firmly tied to military requirements. Consequently, it is necessary to describe much of Roman history and politics in order to study the army. For several centuries after the formation of the Republic, the Romans literally fought for their survival, then for dominance and supremacy, and then to remain in that position. Their collective political and military experiences created a determined and intransigent national character. In Roman ideology, occasional defeats were acceptable, but ultimate capitulation was not an option (Goldsworthy, 1996, 2000).

Attention to international politics scarcely featured at all in Rome's early history. The conquest of the Italian peninsula occupied the Romans for many generations, as wars were fought with individual tribes and cities, bringing them gradually into the Roman federation of citizens and allies. The invasion of southern Italy by Pyrrhus and the defeat of two Roman armies at his hands in 280 and 279 BC altered the balance and ultimately brought Rome and Carthage into conflict. The islands of Sicily and Sardinia were annexed, first to keep the Carthaginians out, and second to obtain profit from the grain that was grown in the new provinces. After the second Punic War with Hannibal, Spain was annexed and divided into two provinces, called, respectively, *Hispania Citerior* and *Ulterior* (Nearer and Further Spain). Having entered the politics of the Mediterranean and eastern worlds, the acquisition of Empire accelerated. The great powers watched each other for signs of weakness, ready to execute their territorial imperative. In 200 BC Rome went to war against Philip V of Macedon, using as an excuse his aggressive policy toward Attalus, king of Pergamon. Roman troops were dispatched to Greece under the consul Sulpicius Galba in 200, and then under the more energetic Titus Flamininus, who defeated Philip at the battle of Cynoscephalae in 198. Two years later, Flamininus made his famous proclamation that Greece was now free, meaning that the Greek cities were classified as client states, with definite and specific obligations to Rome that he did not sufficiently underline. The Greeks interpreted freedom more literally, under the illusion that they were free to formulate their own foreign policies. The Romans soon corrected them. This episode typified the Roman attitude to international politics for the rest of her existence.

The annexation of Greece followed. The Aetolians were made allies of Rome, with obligations to support the Romans against their enemies, and the Macedonians were decisively defeated by Aemilius Paullus at the battle of Pydna in 168 BC. The Achaean league was subdued without fighting, the Rhodians were compelled to give up their territorial possessions in Asia Minor, and Antiochus IV of Syria was persuaded to abandon his invasion of Egypt simply by the threat that Rome would declare war if he refused. The Romans had discovered that annexation was quicker and easier than withdrawing and fighting again,

Pompey's Pillar in Alexandria, Egypt. Although the pillar is associated with
Pompey the Great, it was actually built in honor of the Roman Emperor
Diocletian around 300. (Library of Congress)

and that setting an example of success in war coupled with militant determination could sometimes achieve results without fighting at all. Another welcome
discovery was that war was profitable; after the third and final Macedonian War,
the income flowing into Rome was sufficient to enable the Senate to abolish the
direct taxation of Roman citizens.

The decades from the 160s to the 130s BC were marked by repeated wars, sometimes on two or more fronts. Rebellions in Spain involved Roman armies in bloody and cruel wars that strained manpower resources. Levies to replace troops became very unpopular. This was quite unlike the war with Hannibal, where Rome and the allies were under threat from an invader on their own territory, and willingly made sacrifices to provide soldiers to protect their homelands. The foreign wars represented no immediate threat to Rome, and there was not even a promise of cartloads of booty to compensate for the unpopularity of service. Roman commanders were not chosen for their military talents, but appointed as their turn came. For the most part they failed to act with either ability or nobility, contributing to the prolongation of the war and waste of manpower.

While the Spanish wars dragged on, Rome also dealt with Carthage, completely destroying the city in 146. In the same year, Corinth was also destroyed. The province of Africa was created from the most fertile lands around the site of Carthage. Crete and Cyprus were annexed to help to control piracy in the Mediterranean and to provide grain for Rome, and Syria was taken over after the eastern campaigns of Pompey the Great. In the west, Julius Caesar spent ten years subduing the Gauls, and then territorial expansion ceased while the Romans fought each other for nearly two decades.

### Recurrent Themes in the Political Agenda of the Late Republic

The army and politics were inextricably interrelated as the Republic turned into the Empire. The burden of military recruitment had always fallen mainly upon the rural population. When the soldiers eventually returned home, their small farms were often in ruins or mortgaged in order to support their families. Some soldiers remained in the provinces, and some of the small farmers migrated, while others were simply displaced and their lands absorbed by the owners of the large estates, the *latifundia*. Many of the dispossessed joined the urban mob in Rome. In the mid-second century BC the disappearance of the farmers from the land became a serious political issue, because of the consequent reduction in the pool of Roman citizens and Italian allies eligible for army service. Resettlement on the land was a perennial feature in the political programs of the reformers.

Tiberius Sempronius Gracchus, tribune of the plebs in 133, introduced a land bill designed to replace the small farmers on plots of public land that they could not give away or sublet, and for which they were to pay an affordable rent to the state. This scheme would thus reconstitute the class of smallholders who provided recruits for the Roman army. The main problem was that the public land had gradually been encroached upon by landowners who had ignored the laws that restricted the size of their holdings. Thus, the plots destined for the displaced farmers and landless Romans and Italians would first have to be reclaimed from the cultivators, who had come to regard the plots as their own. The law was passed amid bloodshed and rioting in which Tiberius Gracchus was killed, but the land commission was established and the reforms went ahead.

The political program of Tiberius Gracchus was revived ten years after his death by his younger brother Gaius, who was twice elected tribune, for the years 123 and 122. Gaius proposed laws designed to remedy a wide range of problems, including attempts to prevent the exploitation of the provincials and to improve the efficiency of the courts. Gaius Gracchus also attended to small details of army service, providing an insight into the practices that were current in his day. He passed laws to prevent the recruitment of soldiers younger than seventeen and to prohibit deductions from military pay for arms and clothing. Gaius also attempted to curb the punishments that commanders could inflict and to reduce the length of continuous service. In 122 Gaius stood for election as tribune for the third time, but he had lost the confidence of the electorate, and in 121 he was killed.

Another recurrent theme in the late Republic concerned the enfranchisement of the Italian allies. For many years the Senate resisted this project. One of the Gracchan land commissioners, Fulvius Flaccus, was elected consul for 126 BC and proposed a law to grant Roman citizenship to the Latins and the Italians. It failed, but the idea remained on the political agenda for some time to come. In 91 BC the tribune Marcus Livius Drusus took up the dual theme of land distribution and the enfranchisement of the allies, but he met with dogged opposition from the Senate as well as from the Roman people, and he was assassinated. For the allies it seemed that there was no hope of achieving their aims by peaceful means, so they chose war. The Social War (from *socii*, allies) lasted from 91 to 87 BC. Neither the majority of the Latin colonies nor the Greek cities of southern Italy joined the revolt, and they were rewarded in 90 BC with the grant of citizenship, as were the cities of Etruria and Umbria in a successful attempt to win them over. The next political ploy was to offer citizenship to all Italian allies, with a sixty-day limit on staking a claim to the grant. This undermined allied resistance, and the war came to an end.

A notorious aspect of Republican government was the opportunity for all provincial governors to exploit the inhabitants whom they were supposed to govern and protect. Many rising politicians borrowed incredible amounts of money to finance their careers, in the usually realistic expectation that once they reached the post of provincial governor they could line their pockets on a sufficient scale to repay their loans and also lay the foundations of a personal fortune. Some governors achieved this without overstepping the rules, but others such as Verres, who governed Sicily as though it was his own personal domain, stripped their provinces of anything that they could remove. Jury courts (*quaestiones*) were set up to deal with these cases of extortion (*repetundae*), but the composition of these courts was subject to political wrangling. The courts that were set up to try cases of extortion were the preserve of the Senate until Gaius Gracchus replaced senators with equites, or middle classes. The term *equites,* from *equus,* Latin for horse, literally means horsemen and derives from the cavalry of the very early Roman army. As time passed the Romans recruited cavalry from among their allies, and the original equites no longer served as horsemen, but as a class they retained their title. Only a couple of decades after Gracchus's reforms, in 106 BC, senators and equites were mixed. This was followed by a new scheme that ousted senators altogether. In 91 BC Livius Drusus proposed to give the courts back to senators, and Sulla actually did so, but soon afterward Pompey restored the balance by readmitting equites.

The political shenanigans that killed the Republic are too lengthy to describe in detail, but an outline of the turmoil that brought Augustus to power serves to demonstrate the links between the Republic and Imperial rule. The late Republic was characterized by the growth of wide-ranging military commands to deal with specific problems that could not have been dealt with in any other way. Pompey's rapid campaign to round up the Mediterranean pirates provides an example. The seaborne grain supply of Rome was threatened, and piecemeal attempts to control the pirates had failed. Pompey's command gave him control of all provincial territory around the Mediterranean up to 50 miles inland, so that he could use combined land and sea operations against them even when they retired to their strongholds. The pirate problem highlights the dilemma of the late Republic. Rome was a world power with world-embracing problems and required commanders with extensive powers to deal with them, but the political eminence and military supremacy that accrued to these few commanders created further problems in Rome.

One aspect of military command that accentuated this supreme power was the creation of armies that were loyal to their commanders and not primarily to the state. The original oath that the Republican soldiers swore was to obey their generals, but since the generals were the annually elected consuls it was probably not foreseen that one day the oath would be misused. The first signs of trouble occurred when Lucius Cornelius Sulla decided to force the Senate into granting him the eastern command against Mithradates by marching on Rome with his troops. Some of his officers refused to follow him. The law stated that a general at the head of an army should not cross the city boundary (*pomerium*), and Sulla's success in flouting this law set a dangerous precedent.

The bond between soldiers and commanders was considerably enhanced by the lack of provision for veterans when the troops returned to Rome. Inevitably, the men looked to their generals to obtain allotments for them. Pompey's struggle to provide for his men dragged on for a few years after he returned victorious from the eastern campaign in 62 BC and were not ended until Caesar forced

Lucius Cornelius Sulla issued this coin in 81 BC. The obverse shows the head of the goddess Roma, and on the reverse, an equestrian statue of Sulla is depicted. He names himself as L[ucius] Sulla Feli[x] Dic[tator]. Sulla was the first general to use the army to coerce his own countrymen to give him what he wanted. He marched on Rome to force the Senate to appoint him to the command against Mithradates in the east. (Drawing courtesy of J.T. Taylor)

through the necessary legislation during his consulship in 59 BC. This legislation simply solved the problems of the moment, without establishing a permanent system for veteran settlement. Caesar went on to conquer Gaul, which took him a decade to achieve. In the meantime Pompey had built up a power base of his own, governing his provinces of Spain via deputies, without leaving Rome.

From this time onward it was clear that command of troops and success in foreign wars was the only way to achieve and maintain political preeminence. In Caesar's case, command of an army was of paramount importance, since he wished to proceed from provincial governorship to a second consulship without hazard, and he had high ambitions to reform and streamline Republican government. Pompey could not tolerate such a powerful rival, and the situation escalated into civil war. It started before Pompey was ready, and it ended with his defeat at Pharsalus. He escaped to Egypt, where Caesar followed him to prevent him from borrowing money and raising another army. When Caesar arrived in Alexandria, the young Ptolemy XIII presented him with Pompey's head. Thus ended the first act in the drama of the civil wars, but at the same time the foundations were laid for the next one. Ptolemy XIII and his sister Cleopatra VII were involved in a struggle for the throne of Egypt, and Caesar was drawn into the fighting, eventually installing Cleopatra as ruler of the country with Roman backing.

The battles against the remnants of the Pompeian armies took Caesar to Africa and Spain, and finally back to Rome, where he was assassinated in 44 BC,

Head of Gnaeus Pompeius Magnus (Pompey the Great) showing his characteristic hair style. Pompey began his career under Sulla, but used his influence much more subtly, building up more power and retaining it for longer than his erstwhile master, and he set the precedent for Augustus by commanding troops in Spain without actually going there as governor. (Photo Courtesy of the Ny Carlsberg Glyptotek, Copenhagen)

precipitating another round of civil war. The Liberators, as the conspirators called themselves, were soon in conflict with Caesar's right-hand man, Mark Antony, and his teenage great-nephew and heir, Gaius Octavius, who was now entitled to call himself Gaius Julius Caesar Octavianus. Antony and Octavian settled their differences and pursued the Liberators, defeating them at Philippi in 41 BC. The third act of the civil wars was about to begin. Antony and Octavian divided up the Roman world between them, Octavian eventually taking control of the west, and Antony of the east, including Egypt. Antony's famous association with Cleopatra gave Octavian all the excuse he needed to go to war, persuading the Roman people and Senate that the Egyptian queen represented a mortal danger to Rome. At the naval battle of Actium, Octavian's admiral Marcus Vipsanius Agrippa made short work of Antony's fleet, and Antony and Cleopatra sailed away to Alexandria, where they committed suicide as Octavian approached the city with his troops.

On the Ides (13) of January 27 BC, three years after the defeat of Antony and Cleopatra and the restoration of peace, Octavian made a speech in the Senate, ostensibly restoring the Republic and giving back to the Senate the government of the Empire. In that year Octavian was consul for the seventh time, and he needed to avoid any hint of perpetual power such as had been bestowed on Julius Caesar. The full text of Octavian's speech has not been preserved, despite the attempt by Cassius Dio to reconstruct it in his history written in the third century, but the exact words are not as important as the result. The senators shrank from government of the whole Empire, and a compromise was arranged. For the next ten years Octavian would govern Egypt, which he always intended to keep to himself, as well as Gaul, Spain, Syria, Cilicia, and Cyprus. The Senate would be responsible for the remaining provinces. The ten-year term avoided any suggestion of permanence, but in effect the temporary term was easily renewed, and Octavian kept direct control of most, but not quite all, of the armies, governing his provinces via legates, and choosing the commanders of all the legions. One of the responses to this "restoration of the Republic" was that Munatius Plancus proposed that the honorary title Augustus should be bestowed on Octavian, who accepted with good grace and passed the title on to his successors. The outcome of Octavian's actions in 27 was interpreted by later Latin and Greek authors as the true foundation of the Empire.

## Imperial Politics

Valuable precedents for Imperial rule had already been set in the later Republic, such as the development of wide-ranging special commands and the appointment of legates answerable to the military leaders and governors of provinces rather than the Senate. The Mediterranean command bestowed on Pompey in the 60s BC covered almost all the Roman world and necessitated the appointment of deputies, each with a territorial sphere of influence. While these areas were not provinces, the principle could be applied to provincial government, and again Pompey had shown the way by governing his Spanish provinces via legates. Julius Caesar regularly appointed legates to legionary commands, and though these postings were only temporary, it pointed the way to the creation of the longer term association of legate and legion.

Imperial administrative methods and terminology did not spring into place fully fledged in January 27, but after a gradual evolution, governors of the Imperial provinces were called *legati Augusti pro praetore,* regardless of whether the candidate had held the praetorship or the consulship. Ex-consuls governed the provinces with two or more legions, but if there was only one legion, the governor was usually an ex-praetor, and he commanded the legion as well as governing the province. In all provinces, the commanders of the legions were usually ex-praetors, called *legati Augusti legionis.* The governors of the senatorial provinces were appointed by the Senate from the pool of ex-praetors and ex-consuls. They had the title proconsul but did not have access to troops.

The political priorities of the emperors were first and foremost to remain in power, which effectively meant controlling the army without blatantly advertising this dominion. The army had to be kept loyal and eager to serve, and all benefits, payments, privileges, and senior promotions must be in the gift of the emperor. The Republic had been threatened by great commanders who could buy the loyalty of the army, but in the Empire there must be only one man who could do this, and no others could be allowed to raise themselves to the same position. Through the potential coercive force of the army, the emperor controlled everything else, but Republican traditions were respected in order to remain within the law and to soften the harsh reality of rule by an individual.

During the Republic, the political machinery that conferred the necessary military powers on the consuls and other magistrates was the formal grant of *imperium,* ratified by a law passed by the curiate assembly (*lex curiata*). The concept of *imperium* embraced, but was not confined to, command of the army. The word is related to the Latin *imperare,* meaning to command or give orders, and to the title *Imperator,* an honorific salutation spontaneously given by the soldiers to their commanders. The title *Imperator* was eventually adopted permanently by the emperors, who also fostered and encouraged these military salutations and assiduously kept a count of them, expressing the number of such occasions as part of their titles on inscriptions, usually in the abbreviated form IMP III, or IMP IX, or however many times it had occurred.

A decree of the Senate was necessary to bestow power on new emperors, a formality that was more than ever necessary if there was no family connection with the previous emperor. The only text that has survived for this procedure concerns the powers of Vespasian (*CIL* VI 930) who was declared emperor by the troops in Alexandria in July AD 69. His accession took place during the civil war that followed the death of Nero, known as the Year of Four Emperors, and he had no connection at all with the dynasty that had just expired. Once installed in Rome, it was necessary to establish himself as undoubted emperor, so his powers were confirmed by law (*lex de imperio Vespasiani*). There was a clause in this law that ratified all his acts from his proclamation in summer AD 69 until the law was passed in January AD 70.

A predominant concern of all emperors was the succession. Augustus's efforts to secure the transfer of power to a member of his family were thwarted by the early deaths of all his designated heirs, so his step-son Tiberius succeeded him, and after Tiberius the infamous Caligula became emperor. When Caligula was murdered, the Imperial German bodyguard followed by the Praetorians chose another family member as emperor: Claudius. This set the precedent that the soldiers, especially the Praetorian Guard, could make or break emperors.

The problems of the succession were never satisfactorily solved, except perhaps for the relatively brief period when the so-called adoptive emperors designated their successors in advance to preempt a general scramble for power as soon as they were dead. Even this declaration of intent did not ensure a smooth transfer of power. Hadrian was faced with the harsh necessity of executing a handful of rebellious senators after the death of Trajan. He began his reign under a cloud that was never dispersed, and Antoninus Pius had to remind a vengeful Senate that if he allowed them to abolish all of Hadrian's acts as they wished to do, then the adoption of himself as successor would be rendered invalid.

Sharing power with a colleague was one way of trying to ensure the succession. Marcus Aurelius shared the Empire with Lucius Verus, and then when Verus died, he made his son Commodus his Imperial colleague, but though this ensured the succession, the reign of Commodus was far from what Marcus intended. After the assassination of Commodus and then the removal of his short-lived successors, Severus repeated the process of sharing power with his son Caracalla, who was also assassinated. From this time onward it was military men who wielded supreme power, but not one of them ruled for prolonged periods or died peacefully in bed. Diocletian tried to solve the problem of the succession by instituting the Tetrarchy, with four emperors ruling a quadrant of the Roman world, two of them seniors with the title of Augustus and two juniors with the title Caesar. The experiment did not secure the succession and failed to avert civil wars.

## The Components of Roman Political Organization

### The Senate

The advisory body of the kings, composed of the members of the council or Senate, survived the transition to the Republic and was retained as the advisory body of the annually elected magistrates. Membership of the Senate was based on wealth. In the Republic the property qualification was 400,000 sesterces (*sestertii*), increased under Augustus to 1 million sesterces. Although the leading senators were predominantly drawn from a few illustrious and mainly landowning families, the Senate was not necessarily a totally aristocratic institution, nor was membership purely hereditary. The collective experience of the senators qualified them for the supervision and administration of all aspects of government, including domestic and foreign policy, the law, and religion. It was the Senate that dealt with foreign embassies coming into Rome, and delegated and dispatched embassies to other countries outside Italy (Talbert, 1984). The Senate also presided over public trials for serious crimes, such as treason, conspiracy, and assassination, and by the third century BC the Senate could even interfere in the affairs of the Italian states under these headings. The Senate was responsible for the administration of income and expenditure and therefore held the purse strings even in the matter of supplies for the army, since only the Senate had the power to authorize the provision of food, clothing, and pay to the troops. Commanders of Republican armies could fall at the first hurdle if the Senate chose to obstruct them.

After the establishment of the Empire, membership of the Senate was modified and regulated. The numbers varied from 300 in the second century BC, to 900 under Julius Caesar and 1,000 at the end of the civil wars. In 18 BC Augustus

Statue of Augustus, who was born simply Gaius Octavius but took Caesar's name
when he became his adoptive heir in 44 BC. More patient and subtle than either
Pompey or Caesar, he became supreme commander of nearly all the armed
forces of the Empire while appearing to share power with the Senate. The
Imperial Roman army was established by Augustus, but founded on Republican
forms. This famous statue was found at Prima Porta, Italy, and shows him in
military dress. His elaborate breastplate commemorates his diplomatic coup
when he organized the return to Rome of the military standards lost by Marcus
Licinius Crassus in Parthia. (Bettmann/Corbis)

set the total at 600, a figure that remained constant until the third century AD. During the Empire, an aspiring young man from a senatorial family usually served as one of the twenty junior magistracies known as the *vigintivirate* and then for a short term as military tribune of a legion. After this apprenticeship, he would stand for election as *quaestor,* a post that was primarily concerned with financial duties and qualified him for entry to the Senate. Thereafter a career that combined military and civilian posts lay open to him, leading to command of a legion, perhaps the *consulship* and one or more tours of duty as a *provincial governor.* In the Imperial era, the functions of the Senate were restricted to the exercise of certain legislative powers and the right of conferment of power on the emperors. As the Empire widened and opened its doors to new peoples, the membership of the Senate changed. In the reign of Augustus, nearly all the senators were Romans or Italians. Then in the first century AD some of the enfranchised Gauls became senators, and Africans and citizens of the eastern provinces followed in the second century. By the early third century, only half of the senators were of Italian origin.

Although the direction of military affairs and financial policy was taken over by the emperors, membership of the Senate was still the gateway to an administrative and political career during the Empire. Some of the provinces were directly administered by the Senate, and there were senatorial duties to be undertaken in Rome and Italy. The posts were hierarchical and progressive, culminating in the governorship of one of the larger senatorial provinces as proconsul. In the Imperial provinces, senators served as legates of the legions, and governed provinces as *legati Augusti pro praetore.* It is suggested that the Imperial system stifled free speech and debate, and apathy set in, with emperors being obliged to exercise a little coercion to achieve a quorum at meetings. Claudius, for instance, tried and failed to stimulate discussions. If the Senate was subdued and apathetic, this was not true of individual senators, who were the leading protagonists of usurpation whenever the occasion arose.

### Assemblies

During the Republic, the people of Rome had a greater share in government than in the Empire, but only insofar that they could vote for candidates for office and accept or reject proposals that were put to them by the magistrates, without having any right to amend anything contained in the proposals. The main assemblies were the *comitia curiata* and the *comitia centuriata.* The *comitia curiata* was the oldest, based on the thirty *curiae* or divisions of the populace under the kings. During the Republic, the *comitia curiata* confirmed the appointment of the magistrates and conferred *imperium* on them by means of a law (*lex curiata de imperio*). The *comitia centuriata* was not as ancient as the *comitia curiata,* and its functions were much more closely bound up with the army. In the early Republic, the composition of the voting centuries and the military centuries was the same, derived from the so-called Servian reforms. A century denoted literally one hundred men, but with regard to the voting centuries it is perhaps best interpreted as a general term for group, and with regard to the army, a century comprised 80 men. In later years as army organization changed, this close relationship became redundant and was abandoned. The *comitia centuriata* elected the censors, consuls, and praetors and was empowered to enact laws. Its most important function with regard to the army was that this assembly was responsible for the declaration or rejection of war, and in some cases it proved reluctant to advocate war.

The importance of the various *comitia* had already begun to dwindle toward the end of the Republic, but as the Empire was established the electoral process atrophied, and after the reign of Tiberius the magistrates were elected by the Senate. Although the assemblies were not actively abolished, Imperial rule made their traditional functions redundant.

## The Dictator

A Dictator was usually appointed only in times of emergencies for a period of six months, with complete control of the armed forces. The consuls remained in office but were subject to the Dictator, resuming their own supreme powers when he resigned. In the normal course of events, the Dictator laid down his office when the emergency was over, but when Lucius Cornelius Sulla returned to Rome in 83 BC after his eastern campaigns, he used the appointment to force through his own agenda rather than to protect Rome from danger. He finally relinquished his powers toward the end of his life, satisfied that his work was done. This abdication astonished Julius Caesar, who was appointed Dictator more than once during the civil war, culminating in his acceptance of perpetual dictatorial powers shortly before his assassination. Mark Antony abolished the office in 44 BC.

## The Consuls

The derivation of the title "consul" is not known, nor is it clear whether the first consuls were always elected in pairs, but the collegiate principle is firmly entrenched in Republican tradition. If a consul died before the termination of his office, the other consul was obliged to hold elections to replace him, presumably to remove the temptation for the surviving consul to exercise supreme power unchecked. Fear and loathing for the rule of one man was so strong that throughout the Republic, men could be executed for aspiring to *regnum*, or kingship.

The principal duties of the consuls of the Republic were to raise and command the armies, and to attend to all aspects of state. Once the Empire was established, direction of state affairs was no longer their prerogative, but the consulship was still a coveted office. The emperors themselves could hold the consulship, sometimes repeatedly year after year, and since the elections were obliterated, candidates stood little chance of attaining the office unless the emperor recommended them. Since one of the annual posts was often taken up by the emperor or one of his relatives, the number of available consulships declined, and this decline was from time to time accompanied by a corresponding shortage of experienced officials to take up the administrative posts that normally followed a consulship. A useful device was instituted, allowing the *consules ordinarii*, who gave their names to the year, to retire from their office after a short tenure, to make way for extra consuls called *consules suffecti*. These suffect or substitute consuls were appointed whenever the ordinary magistrates died, resigned, or were removed from office. Therefore, this quite normal procedure was adapted to create legally appointed extra consuls who could then go on to further posts having gained a little experience of government at home. The tenure of the suffect consulship was usually at least six months, but in some instances there were multiple suffect consulships. The future Emperor Severus was suffect consul in AD 190, but his experience of office was limited to about two months, since there were no less than twenty-five consuls in that year (Birley, 1988; Southern, 2001).

### The Praetors

The chief magistrates of early Republican Rome may have originally been called praetors, a title that derives from the verb *praeire*, meaning "to go before." The consuls soon took over as chief magistrates, and from then onward the powers of a praetor were slightly inferior to those of the consuls. The post eventually became one of the stages on the path to the consulship. Originally, only one praetor was elected, who could command armies and was left in full charge of the city when the consuls were absent. His duties involved legal functions as well as command of armies.

The number of praetors was continually increased to cope with a growing workload as the Empire expanded. The first provinces were governed by praetors. For a short time under Julius Caesar there were sixteen praetors, but the final total under Augustus was twelve. In the Imperial era the praetors retained some of their judicial functions and acquired the additional function of organizing and financing the all-important games to entertain the people. After holding office, the ex-praetor's subsequent post was usually as legate of a legion or as governor of a senatorial province.

## The Pro-Magistracies

Until the late Republic, the two consuls usually spent their year of office at the head of the armies, campaigning or waging war as circumstances demanded. The consuls were usually recalled when their term of office expired, but on occasion the Senate could vote for an extension of the term if it was deemed necessary. The appointment of the new magistrates would still go ahead as planned for the year, while the existing consul ceased to be one of the eponymous annual magistrates, but was still authorized to act with the powers of a consul. The first recorded instance of this procedure occurred in 326 BC when the Senate voted an extension of command (*prorogatio imperii*) to the consul Quintus Publilius Philo, whose term of office was due to expire at the very moment when he was about to capture the city of Naples. Instead of dispatching a new commander and risking the failure of the enterprise, the Senate granted to Philo the powers of a consul (*imperium pro consule*) without actually reappointing him consul. The powers of a praetor could also be extended in the same way, by the grant of *imperium pro praetore*. It has been pointed out that during the Republic the prolongation of a command often had far less to do with military necessity than with political influence at Rome, but the establishment of the pro-magistracy was a useful device that separated the annual magisterial office on the one hand and its function and power on the other. It also had the advantage of doubling the number of available personnel to carry out administrative tasks at Rome, to govern the provinces, and command the armies. In Caesar's day, it was customary to remain in Rome during the tenure of the consulship or praetorship, and then to proceed to a province as proconsul or propraetor, depending on the nature of the task to be performed. Augustus adapted this administrative procedure to establish the form of provincial government that was maintained for the next 200 years.

## Tribunes of the Plebs

When they seceded from the state in the fifth century BC, the plebs created their own council called the *concilium plebis* with two elected officials called tribunes (distinct from the military tribunes who commanded the legions). The *tribuni plebis* were sacrosanct: anyone who harmed them was subject to terrible curses. This office evolved into one of the most useful organs of the state, and their numbers were eventually increased from two to ten. They entered office in December, slightly earlier than the rest of the magistrates. Although they were not magistrates themselves and were not eligible to command armies, they possessed certain political powers (all embraced under the heading of *tribunicia potestas*) that were designed to protect the plebs from harm, the chief one being the right of *intercessio,* or veto, against proposals emanating from any other tribune or any magistrate except the Dictator. The tribunate gradually acquired more influence as the rights of the plebs were recognized. At first the tribunes were excluded from the Senate and confined to summoning the plebeian assembly, but in the third century BC, they were allowed to listen to senatorial debates and were soon granted the right to convoke meetings of the Senate. Sulla tried to muzzle the power of the tribunes, but his successors undid all his legislation in this respect and the tribunate was restored. Toward the end of the Republic, tribunes were sometimes bought by ambitious politicians to enable them to put their schemes into operation.

From Augustus onward the emperors permanently adopted the power of the tribunes, which had become an important and effective means of legitimate government. Tribunes were still elected during the Empire, and the office was regarded as an entry qualification for membership of the Senate. In reality, however, the emperors included in their titulature the reminder that they held tribunician power, usually in abbreviated form as *trib. pot. III* or *trib. pot. VI* in accordance with however many times it had been annually renewed.

### Alliances, Colonies, and Client States

Some of the political institutions that were employed to treat the peoples inside and on the periphery of the Roman Empire can be traced back to the Republican era, when Rome was slowly emerging as the predominant power in Italy and developing methods of dealing with her neighbors. Military needs were always of prime importance to the Romans when entering into alliances or any agreements with other states.

Occasionally, the Romans forged peaceful alliances whereby mutual benefits were exchanged with the allies under obligation to fight for Rome in the event of a war. In less peaceful circumstances, Rome achieved preeminence by outright conquest of a tribe, a city, or a region, followed by the formation of alliances, leaving the cities and towns relatively free but with the usual obligations to furnish soldiers for Rome. More rarely, territory was annexed and incorporated into the Roman state; it was often a last resort after military and political measures had failed to restore peace. Eventually, annexation became a habit and then an established aim, necessitating the installation of troops to ensure external defense and internal peace.

Before the unification of Italy under Roman rule, the treaties of alliance with the Latins were formulated on a different basis to those with the Italians. The Latins were distributed among several independent states that sometimes fought each other, but after the foundation of the Roman Republic the Latins formed an alliance against Roman domination. The Latin League made two attempts to free themselves from Rome, at the beginning of the fifth century and in the later fourth century BC. Each war ended in Roman victory, and the Latin states were henceforth allied to Rome but forbidden to make alliances with each other. This was an early example of the Roman policy of divide and rule. It worked to Rome's advantage, and during the greatest stresses of the war with Hannibal none of the Latin allies deserted Rome.

Latins and Romans were granted the right to intermarry (*conubium*) and were allowed mutual trading and business rights (*commercium*). A child of a Roman father and a Latin mother was counted a citizen of Rome, and the boys were eligible to serve in the Roman citizen legions. Citizenship was interchangeable. A Roman became a Latin citizen if he resided in a Latin colony, but if he moved back to Rome he resumed his Roman citizenship. A Latin colonist who left a son in his hometown, so that recruitment was not jeopardized, could take up Roman citizenship. The attractions of Rome eventually proved too tempting, creating a shortage of Latin recruits. Accordingly, in 187 and 173 BC, the Romans agreed with the Latin communities to repatriate all those Latins who had migrated to Rome, which implies that proper records had been kept, with full names and dates of entry to the city. The repatriation of the Latins indicates that the allied troops were of great importance to the Republican Roman authorities when drawing up their armies.

Treaties of alliance with the Italian allies (*socii Italici*) usually took into account the various customs of each separate allied city, and there was little or no Roman interference in local government. Local languages, laws, religious practices, and festivals continued as before. No taxes were levied. There was usually a mutual obligation to refrain from giving aid to the enemy. In other words, the allies could not exercise their own foreign policy, but they could appeal for help if they were attacked. The treaties usually stipulated that troops must be levied for Rome. There was a list of allies, the *formula togatorum,* that detailed how many men the individual allied cities and tribes could be called upon to raise, and the recruits were said to be furnished *ex formula.* The allied troops were collectively labeled *Alae Sociorum,* literally "the wings of the allies" because their fighting position was on the wings of the main army of the legions. During the Empire, the name *ala* referred exclusively to auxiliary cavalry units, but in the early Republic the *Alae Sociorum* comprised both infantry and cavalry. Where the allies had special talents or resources, Rome utilized them for her military needs; for instance, the coastal cities of southern Italy, called *socii navales,* provided ships and crews.

Another means of providing protection for Roman territory, and men for the army, was the establishment of colonies, which served a dual purpose as a tried and trusted method of siphoning off surplus population and of guarding strategic points and protecting routes. Livy called the early colonies both barriers and gateways. They were rarely completely new foundations, being established mostly in existing cities, sometimes by dispossessing the original inhabitants. Land allotments went with the foundation of each colony, since no city can survive without its surrounding lands to produce food. The majority of the colonies established in Italy had Latin status rather than full Roman citizenship. They were allowed considerable autonomy, but they were also instruments of voluntary Romanization.

Colonies of Roman citizens with full voting rights (*civitates optimo iure*) were fewer in number than Latin colonies and were largely restricted to the coastal towns, where it was once thought that the prime duty of the citizens was to provide garrison troops, an opinion that has since been revised. Roman citizenship could occasionally be conferred on whole towns, and in the later Republic it could be bestowed on individuals. Full voting rights could be exercised only by personal attendance in Rome. Roman citizenship was a prized asset, and eventually Rome started to ration the grant of full voting rights. Instead, a new kind of grant called *civitas sine suffragio* was instituted, which bestowed the legal rights and privileges that went with citizenship, without the voting powers. This relationship with Rome was extended to some of the towns of Latium, Campania, and Etruria. As with the allied states, the military obligations to fight on behalf of Rome remained in place.

The first permanent colony outside Italy was set up in 118 BC at Narbo in Provence, France (the modern name derives from *provincia,* as the area was once designated as the province before it became known as Gallia Narbonensis). Toward the end of the second century BC, more colonies were established in Africa and Gaul, mostly to accommodate discharged veterans from the armies; then under Julius Caesar, Augustus, and succeeding emperors, the practice spread to the Rhine, Spain, and the eastern provinces. The colonies ranked higher than the other cities of the Empire, and emperors could confer colonial status on settlements.

As the Romans acquired more territory and extended their influence over the peripheral states and tribes, a different kind of relationship with non-Roman peoples was developed (Braund, 1984). Modern historians call this system client kingship, but a better term would be *friendly king,* since the Romans used the phrase *rex sociusque et amicus,* denoting a king who was both an ally and a friend of the Roman people, under an arrangement that was ratified by the Senate. This was a personal agreement between the individual king or queen and the sovereign Roman people, through the medium of Roman magistrates. When the friendly ruler died, the relationship could be terminated, or it could be renewed with the successor. Although the agreement did not involve outright annexation, the ultimate fate of the kingdoms of many friendly kings was exactly that.

Rome supported the client rulers in their own kingdoms, and the clients were expected to provide troops and to use their local knowledge to aid Roman expeditions. Client kingdoms sometimes acted as first-line protection against inroads by the peoples beyond their boundaries and were occasionally expected to monitor unrest among their neighbors. This was a particularly useful method of dealing with the tribesmen beyond the northern frontier of the Empire and with the eastern states between Roman territory and the Parthian Empire. The process was an important feature of Imperial rule, building on the precedents that were developed during the Republic.

## ECONOMY AND FINANCE

For the early period of Rome, there is little evidence that allows us to reconstruct the details of economy and finance. Wealth was probably reckoned in terms of agricultural produce, and exchange of this produce in a regional context supplied basic needs. Of state finances, nothing is known, except that under the kings and the early Republic, it was not considered necessary to use coins. The development of the coinage was probably related to commercial contact with the Greek cities of Italy, especially in neighboring Campania. The need to trade perhaps necessitated the introduction of a monetary system comparable to the Greek model. Throughout Rome's history, there was never a policy of regular minting, so that coins tended to remain in circulation for long periods. When minting did take place, it was most often related to the needs of the army. Response to a financial crisis was usually in the form of debasement of some or all of the coinage, for instance, during the war with Hannibal when there was a great strain on resources, the silver coinage was debased. A new system was introduced when the Romans began to feel that the tide of war was turning in their favor, but in order to provide the funds for it, a tax was levied on property. One of the new coins was the silver *denarius,* which continued in use until the troubles of the third century. The silver content varied with the fortunes of the Empire. Control of the coinage was in the hands of each successive emperor, and management of finances and issue of coins were intimately related. Domitian's coinage was the purest that was ever attained, perhaps reflecting his rigid control of all aspects of Imperial administration, but when war broke out in the Danube provinces in AD 85, he had to debase the coinage, reverting to the levels of Nero's day. The coinage suffered at the beginning of the third century AD, when the silver content of the *denarius* under Severus fell to less than 50 percent.

The use of Roman coins spread throughout Italy after the second Punic War, and then to Sicily and most of the Mediterranean. As the Empire expanded, the coinage spread of necessity because the taxes that were collected were demanded mostly in coin, or in a combination of coin and kind. The need to pay taxes engendered the use of coin all over the Empire, and although in the eastern provinces this was not a new phenomenon, in the west it was revolutionary.

The soldiers stationed in the western provinces constituted one of the few categories of people who received pay, and for most of the Imperial period they were paid in coin. Opportunities to spend it were soon provided for them, as the presence of coinage in the western provinces stimulated the economy. This development did not entirely oust local barter systems, but it readily opened up the possibilities of wider trade.

The military coinage struck by Caesar, Pompey, Mark Antony, and Octavian was produced specifically to pay the troops and provides useful information about the armies of the civil wars. Antony's coins honoring his legions were issued in enormous quantities and remained in circulation for many years. The Augustan reform of the coinage established the norm for the Empire, based on the gold *aureus,* the silver *denarius* and *sestertius* (four *sestertii* equaled one *denarius*), and the bronze *as* (four *asses* equaled one *sestertius*). Modern equivalents for these coins are somewhat meaningless without some indication of purchasing power and how long it took to earn the necessary amounts (Shelton, 1998). In order to qualify for entry to the Senate during the early Empire, an individual had to prove that he was worth at least 1 million sesterces (*sestertii*), while a soldier of the same period earned a paltry 1,200 sesterces. The personal wealth of senators far outstripped the wildest dreams of the soldiers, even when military pay was supplemented by *donativa* or gifts from the emperors, and booty from the wars.

The basis of personal wealth all through the Roman Republic and Empire always rested on agriculture (White, 1970). The dividends accrued from ownership of land were considerable, enabling magnates like Pompey and Crassus to raise, equip, and pay armies of their own. Crassus used to say that no man could call himself wealthy unless he could pay an army. Ownership of land was an ingrained concept in Roman society, and wealth from agriculture was the main yardstick of political worth, never superseded in Roman ethics by any amount of wealth derived from commerce or industrial production.

Nonetheless commercial activity played a large part in the Roman Empire, and money exchanges were established at Ostia and at Rome in the Forum of Trajan. Roman bankers were private individuals using their own systems. The aristocracy did not need the services of bankers, since they had their own staff and managed their own affairs. The individual bankers acted as moneylenders and administered cash deposits, but they never combined to form a corporate banking system. Roman state finances were primitive in comparison to modern equivalents, and tended to destabilize when the central government was weak or under stress. During the Republic, there was no annual budget or long-term planning, and although tax payments (*tributum*) were levied on an irregular basis from Roman citizens, this was a reactive rather than a proactive approach; sometimes new taxes had to be created in order to solve the problems of cash flow (Duncan-Jones, 1982, 1994; Jones, 1974).

Republican revenues were derived from the direct tax of the *tributum* and some indirect taxes, and from payments of rent on state-owned lands, mines, and other enterprises. Precious metals are rare in Italy, so state control of mines did not feature in early Republican government until the late third century BC when Romans and Italians began to work the silver mines of southeastern Spain, after the victory over Carthage in 201 BC. With the expansion of the Empire, gold and silver mines were generally designated the property of the state and leased to contractors, though privately owned mines existed side by side with state-owned ones. The monies accrued from the state revenues were housed in the treasury (*aerarium*), located in the temple of Saturn in the Forum. In the Republic it was administered by officials called quaestors with a clerical staff to help them. The administrators of the *aerarium* were subject to several changes: Caesar placed minor officials called aediles in charge instead of the higher ranking quaestors, then Augustus removed them and appointed prefects. Claudius returned to quaestors and Nero replaced them with prefects. During the Republic, expenditure was controlled by the Senate and covered the maintenance of roads, harbors, and public buildings, and the costs of war. Although the soldiers of the early Republic provided their own equipment, there was an increasing tendency to recruit men who could not afford to do so, especially during emergencies and prolonged campaigns.

Although the expansion of Roman territory involved considerable cost, the booty that was brought back to Rome at the conclusion of the wars and the indemnity payments that were raised from defeated enemies vastly increased Rome's wealth, to the extent that in 167 BC, direct tax on Roman citizens living in Italy was abolished. This privilege was never extended to Roman citizens living in the provinces; they paid whatever rate of tax was levied according to provincial regulations, unless they lived in provinces that had been granted Italian rights (*ius Italicum*), in which case they were exempt from tax. Initially, the Romans took over unaltered the taxation systems that prevailed in the territories that they annexed. For example, the tithe payments levied on agricultural produce in Sicily were probably still operative and farmed by Roman tax gatherers at the beginning of the first century AD. The variations in methods of payment continued into the Empire; the Roman author Hyginus outlined the different tax systems when describing the importance of correctly delineating boundaries on landed estates, so that an accurate picture could be obtained of how much produce was derived from the land.

From the reign of Augustus the rates of taxation and the identification of those liable to pay taxes were gradually established by the provincial census. The information was presumably kept up to date, but apart from information from the province of Egypt, where the census was taken every fourteen years, it is not known whether there was any regularity in collecting data. The census was taken every five years in Republican Rome, but this regular timescale may not

## TAXATION

During the Republic there were two kinds of indirect tax comprising customs dues on goods carried into and out of the ports (*portoria*), where the cash was raised initially to help with the maintenance of the harbors, and the 5 percent tax paid by anyone liberating slaves (*vicesima libertatis*). The profits from indirect taxes were probably always less than the revenues from the direct tax of the *tributum,* but the amounts could be increased and new taxes on any produce or activity could be created relatively easily. In his youth Octavian Augustus created an entirely new tax to raise money to finance the coming war against the assassins of Julius Caesar. Working with Mark Antony and Lepidus as the formally constituted "Triumvirate," he and his colleagues decided to levy a new wealth tax on 1,400 women whose property exceeded a certain amount. They were foiled by protests from a delegation led by Antony's mother Julia, Octavian's sister, and Hortensia, the daughter of the orator Hortensius, who jointly protested that as women they had no political rights and therefore did not see why they should pay for a war in which they had no voice. The Triumvirs conceded the point and had to find money in a variety of other ways, some of which were extremely ruthless and involved mayhem and murder.

The indirect taxes of the Republic were retained by Augustus and his successors. The customs duties (*portoria*) were extended in the Imperial period from simple harbor dues to the internal trade in the provinces, levied on goods transported along the major routes, and on goods crossing the boundaries

of the Empire, though the evidence for this derives mainly from the eastern provinces. Augustus introduced further indirect taxes in order to finance his new projects. Three of these were directly related to the upkeep of the armed forces of the Empire. The first two were introduced in AD 6 to provide funds for the newly established pension scheme for military veterans. The money was provided from a 1 percent tax on sales at auction (*centesima rerum venalium*) and a tax of 5 percent on legacies to people other than the immediate family of the deceased (*vicesima hereditatum*). Romans were notorious legacy hunters, cultivating relationships with wealthy people who had no known heirs, so Augustus exploited this unsavory predilection to help to finance the armies. The third new tax was introduced in AD 7 to pay the *vigiles,* the 700-strong, semimilitary fire brigade of the city of Rome; this was a 4 percent tax levied on the sale of slaves (*quinta et vicesima venalium mancipiorum*).

After the civil war of AD 69 Vespasian reckoned that the shortfall in state finances amounted to 4,000 million sesterces, and he set out to recoup this sum by doubling some taxes and imposing some rather novel extra taxation, such as his notorious tax on urine. The fullers of Rome used urine because of its ammonia content which acts as a cleansing agent, so they thoughtfully provided urinals outside their premises to collect as much of the necessary product as they could. Allegedly Titus protested to his father about this tax, but Vespasian simply gave him a few coins and asked him if he could smell anything.

have applied to all parts of the Empire. The responsibility for carrying out the census resided with the provincial governor, and special staff were engaged to help with the task.

According to the jurist Ulpian, who wrote a compilation of Roman law at the beginning of the third century AD, landed properties were to be registered in the census, giving the name of the estate and the city whose territory it was in, followed by the names of the neighboring estates. The acreage of the arable sown within the previous ten years was to be estimated, followed by the number of vines, the size of the olive groves if appropriate, and the orchards. Pasture-lands and the meadows mown over the last ten years were included in the esti-mates, as was the productivity of woodland for felling purposes. Allowance was made for agricultural disasters such as droughts, and loss of production through landslides, in which case tax relief could be given. The enumeration of the slaves was quite meticulous, taking note of their ages and various abilities (*Digest* 50.5.4; Levick, 2000, no. 66).

The information collected in the census was used to define the amounts that each taxpayer should pay, under the two headings of *tributum soli,* relating to the size of agricultural estates and other types of property, and *tributum capitis,* a poll tax based on the number of slaves working on the estates. In Egypt the poll tax was levied on all Egyptian males from the age of fourteen to the age of sixty. In other provinces, the Romans adhered to the practices already in place, so that the taxes were sometimes levied in cash and sometimes in produce or in goods. The hated *publicani* who bid for the privilege of collecting the direct taxes during the Republic were largely replaced in the Empire, when the indi-vidual cities became responsible for the taxes of their administrative regions. In the eastern provinces, city officials called *decaproti* are attested from the reign of Nero, but in the west, where the establishment of cities was a much later phe-nomenon introduced by the Romans themselves, the methods of collection are not so well known. Contracts were still let out during the Empire to the eques-trian companies of *publicani* for the collection of indirect taxes, except for some evidence that in Illyricum in the second century AD these collectors had been replaced by officials appointed by the state. How far this was followed in other provinces is not known.

Under the emperors, the administration of the taxation system as a whole in each province was the responsibility of officials called procurators, of which there were several categories. Some were governors of smaller provinces with few or no troops, whereas others were limited to specific financial tasks. In the Imperial provinces, procurators were powerful individuals with access to small numbers of troops to aid them in supervising the collection of both direct and indirect taxes, as well as the revenues from the Imperial estates belonging to the emperors. In senatorial provinces governed by proconsuls, the presence of a procurator probably always indicated the existence of Imperial estates.

The emperors derived considerable income from their own lands, which were augmented from time to time when bequests were made and when the es-tates of various people were confiscated. The emperors' own property was termed *patrimonium* and *res privata.* Not enough is known to differentiate clearly between the two types of property or to describe how either of them op-erated. The property of each outgoing emperor was passed down to his successor whether or not there was any family relationship. The residences used by the emperors and their extensive provincial estates were assigned to the category of *patrimonium* or *res privata,* but not much is known about their administration. They probably provided revenues both in cash and in kind. There was an Imperial treasury called the *fiscus* (Brunt, 1966), but it is not known how it worked in relation to the *aerarium* or the *patrimonium.* From the middle of the first century AD, the *fiscus* was an established body, since Nero appointed a praetor to manage the legal side of its affairs, and Hadrian substituted an *advocatus fisci.*

The rationalization and extension of the taxation system under Augustus enabled the emperor and his financial staff, mostly freedmen, to estimate income and expenditure with a little more precision than had been possible during the Republic. At his death, Augustus left a statement accounting for his expenditure (*Res Gestae Divi Augusti* 15; 17; 18; 19–21), listing the sums that he had paid out to the people of Rome (*congiaria*), to the soldiers settled in colonies, and to the state treasury when it was exhausted. He also listed the buildings he had erected or repaired, and in AD 6 he contributed 170 million sesterces from his own funds (*ex meo patrimonium*) to the newly established *aerarium militare* designed to provide pensions for time-served soldiers.

Although the emperor was the sole controller of all revenue and expenditure, the administration of the state finances was too large an undertaking for the head of state working alone. At some time in the first century AD, a new post was created to take charge of the financial administration. This official was called *a rationibus,* usually translated as financial secretary or finance minister. The creation of this post was part of the administrative reorganization that saw the development of the Imperial secretariats, for correspondence (*ab epistulis*), petitions (*a libellis*), and trials (*a cognitionibus*). The post-holders were initially the palace freedmen, but during the second century equestrians took over their responsibilities.

Various attempts have been made to estimate the income of the Empire (Brunt, 1981; Duncan-Jones, 1982; Hopkins, 1980). A figure of 800 million sesterces has been suggested, but it is not certain for how long a period this would be valid. It also has to be admitted that there is not enough reliable information to present a budget sheet for the whole of the Imperial era. Whatever the revenues may have been, wars ate them up at such speed that there was sometimes a need to increase taxes, invent new ones, or resort to extraordinary means of raising cash. Marcus Aurelius, concerned that the treasury had been depleted by prolonged wars, recouped the deficit in part by auctioning off the Palace furniture and valuables, using the proceeds to pay the army. Courageously, he refused the soldiers' demands for a donative after they had won victories against the tribesmen of the Danube area, where the wars were fought for several years. Marcus still managed to control his armies despite not paying them extra on this occasion; other emperors were not so fortunate.

State expenditure during the Empire included first and foremost the payments to the army. Military pay was only rarely increased, and when there was a pay rise, it was usually related to some political need. Julius Caesar doubled the soldiers' pay at the beginning of the civil war with Pompey, but then military pay remained static for about a century, when Domitian increased it by a third. Septimius Severus came to power via the army, and continuing support for his reign derived from military sources. He increased army pay, and when he died he told his sons to make sure that they paid the soldiers and not to worry about anyone else. The historian Dio (75.2) blamed Severus for the decline of the Empire, because he burdened the state with this increased expenditure to finance the army. In an earlier passage (52.6), however, Dio showed that he understood the need to pay the soldiers, when he invented a speech for Agrippa advising Augustus to bring in revenues from all sources to provide the necessary funds.

Apart from regular military pay, the state was expected to finance the irregular donatives to the army, which were once again usually related to a political development. It became the norm to pay fairly substantial sums on the accession of an emperor, but other circumstances warranted a one-off payment, such as the occasion of an Imperial visit when the soldiers would put on military displays (Campbell, 1984).

State expenditure for the upkeep of the army probably accounted for at least half of the revenues. Other expenditure included the upkeep of roads and ports, the salaries of government officials, the purchase of grain for the free distribution to the people of Rome, the maintenance of the Imperial postal system (*cursus publicus*), and the expenses of the Imperial court. In times of peace and financial stability, all these expenses could be met, especially after Trajan's conquest of Dacia, which gave Rome control of the gold mines of the Carpathians. In contrast, the chaos of the third century severely disrupted the administration and organization of the Empire; revenues declined, and the ability to collect those that were still operative was impaired, while expenses rose. Inflation reached unimaginable proportions. The coinage was debased until it was almost worthless, and the state would not accept its own coins as tax payments. For a while, the troops and Imperial officials were paid in food and clothing instead of in cash. Strong central government was reestablished under Diocletian, who set the Empire back on its feet, though in a changed form. Romans from the Augustan age, transported to the beginning of the fourth century, would have found themselves in another world.

## CIVIL-MILITARY RELATIONS

Romans of the early Republic made little or no distinction between civilians and soldiers, since it was the duty of all men of a certain property value to serve in the army and to return to civilian life and their farms after the end of the campaigning season. Even in the later Republic and early Empire when the army was beginning to be distinct from the mass of civilians, the career paths of officers still combined an intermix of military and civilian posts.

The presence of the army had a profound effect on the lives of civilians in the provinces, not only in establishing internal law and order and protection from external dangers, but in changing and boosting the economy and in the gradual Romanization of the provincials. This was never enforced; Romanization was never a proactive mission of the army. The Romans cultivated the local elite wherever they could do so, and they ruled via the aristocrats with whom they associated. If the local elite and the rest of the provincials expressed an interest in Roman customs and values, they were encouraged; if there was no interest, then the ideology of Rome was not enforced. The evidence from Roman Britain serves to illustrate this point. Romanization made most progress in the south, where the military occupation was temporary until Wales and the north were conquered, and thereafter the presence of troops was minimal. In the newly established towns, Roman-style houses were built, complete with courtyards and gardens, mosaic floors, and painted walls and ceilings. Several excavations of Roman villas have revealed an unbroken progression from Iron Age round houses and field systems to well-appointed Roman farmhouses. Although it could be argued that on each and every site the natives were ousted and Romans moved in, this is considered unlikely. It seems that aristocratic Britons of the southern lowlands readily converted to living in Roman towns and villas, whereas in the northern uplands, where the majority of the armed forces were permanently stationed in considerable numbers, Romanization gained little headway and the natives lived as they had always lived, in clusters of round stone huts, albeit using Roman goods inside them (Millett, 1990).

The status of civilians all over the Empire differed according to whether they were Roman citizens with valued rights and privileges at law, or ordinary free provincials who lacked Roman citizenship. These non-Romans were called *peregrini,* meaning foreigners. Their legal rights were inferior, and it is possible that all non-Roman provincials may have been disarmed (Brunt, 1975). Provincials could rise to eminence via service in their town councils, after which they received citizenship (Gardner, 1993; Sherwin-White, 1972, 1973).

No matter what was the predominant lifestyle in any province, Roman and non-Roman civilians could scarcely avoid coming into contact with soldiers in some capacity, even in provinces where there was no permanent garrison. The army was ever present largely because it performed all the functions that modern societies divide into different categories, such as police, customs guards, tax collectors, and juries, as well as road builders, architects, and engineers. Relations between the military forces and civilians sometimes extended to soldiers erecting buildings on behalf of civic communities. Military architects were sometimes seconded to civilian projects. Tacitus (*Agricola* 21) relates how the governor of Britain, his father-in-law Julius Agricola, encouraged and helped the Britons to build temples, marketplaces (*fora*), and private houses, implying that official sanction for these activities involved the loan of military builders. Inscriptions from other provinces attest the presence of military builders in civilian projects. A veteran of *legio III Augusta* called Nonius Datus was sent to help with the reconstruction of a tunnel that had been started badly (*CIL* VIII 2728 = *ILS* 5795). It was part of a scheme to bring water to the town of Saldae in the province of Mauretania Caesariensis in North Africa, and no one except Nonius could advise on what to do after the project failed. Another inscription from the province of Dacia (modern Romania) records that soldiers built the walls of the city of Romula (*ILS* 510). The legionary surveyors sometimes established boundaries on behalf of civilian communities, as at Ardea in Italy in the reign of Antoninus Pius, and there are at least two instances of legionaries marking out the boundaries of new towns that were laid out for veteran settlers in Africa (*ILS* 9375) and in Pannonia (Hyginus, *Categories of Land* in Campbell, 1994).

This cooperation between army and civilians can sometimes lead to the mistaken conclusion that there was a military presence where none was ever established. For instance, finds of bricks and tiles from certain legions may merely represent a building project that had no military purpose, nor do they indicate that any soldiers participated at all in the building work, since bricks and tiles produced by the legions were sometimes sold to private building companies, a procedure that can be traced all through the Imperial period and into the fourth century. Hence, archaeological material that seems to suggest the presence of military buildings must be regarded with caution (MacMullen, 1963).

In provinces where the army moved on from their forts and fortresses as the conquest progressed, the old fort sites were often given over to civilian occupation. Some of these towns had a long and independent civilian life, whereas others retained their military associations because the old fort sites were converted into colonies of veterans. Where the army units settled down as the frontiers were crystallized and forts became permanent, the relationship with civilians developed and expanded. While the Empire was expanding, the prime purpose of the army was fighting battles, but once the Empire ceased to expand, the army only occasionally fought in preemptive strikes or in reaction to attacks (Whittaker, 1994). Whenever army units settle in any place and in any period, civilians feature more in their daily transactions. Soldiers begin to form relationships with local women, to trade with local people, and to cultivate the land. Literary and archaeological sources confirm that fields and meadows were laid out within the immediate vicinity of Roman forts. Roman occupation was not simply a matter of placing forts in isolated territory. Civilians soon moved in to take advantage of the pay that the soldiers received and wanted to spend. Within a short time, towns clustered around forts. The growth of the *canabae* around legionary fortresses and the *vici* around the smaller forts has been demonstrated archaeologically in many provinces. Some of the civil settlements were very close to the forts, and others were situated at some distance. For example, at Lambaesis in North Africa, the *canabae* and the legionary fortress were about a mile apart, while at Carnuntum on the Danube, the civil settlement was wrapped around the fortress on three sides. Eventually, a second civil settlement was established nearby, at the modern town of Petronell.

The archaeological evidence from the *vici* and *canabae* can show the number of buildings, their extent and orientation, and on occasion archaeology can give hints as to their purpose. Although it cannot finally prove who lived in them, where they came from, or how they made their livings, a study by Sommer (1984) tentatively answers these questions. Some of the buildings of the *vici* around Roman forts are so similar to the internal structures of the forts themselves that it has been postulated that it was the army that built them. Extrapolating from this, we can assume that the fort commander had complete jurisdiction over the inhabitants. Tacitus (*Histories* 4.22) relates that when the legionary commanders at the fortress of Vetera in Germany needed to strengthen their ramparts, they demolished buildings that had been put up in close proximity to the fortress, to prevent them from being of use to the enemy.

A few inscriptions show that the people who dwelt in the *vici* developed a sense of corporate identity in that they referred to themselves as *vicani*, or "the *vicus* people," who on occasion acted together to make decisions. The inhabitants of the *canabae* appointed *magistri*, curators, and aediles, and there were public buildings such as baths, temples, marketplaces, and even amphitheaters. The relationship between the people who clustered around the forts and the soldiers who manned them was probably complex. It is assumed that some of the inhabitants of the *vici* and *canabae* were the womenfolk and offspring of the soldiers. By law, soldiers were forbidden to marry, in order to discourage any commitment to civilians, but most soldiers nonetheless formed associations with local women that were tolerated and given tacit recognition by the authorities.

In some cases, the *vicus* was expanded into a small town, and even when the fort was abandoned and the soldiers moved on to another location, the town sometimes remained in occupation. It cannot be demonstrated whether the same inhabitants remained, or whether new people moved in and the occupants of the old *vicus* followed the army unit. In some cases, the legal status of the existing *vicus* or legionary *canabae* was upgraded by the reigning emperor to that of a municipality (*municipium*) or a *colonia* (MacMullen, 1963). Trajan made the civil settlement at Xanten in Germany into a *colonia*; Hadrian made the *canabae* at Carnuntum into a *municipium*; and Severus upgraded it to colonial status.

The protective role of the Roman army is the least documented aspect of the military presence in any province, though the benefits of the Roman peace are extolled by some ancient authors. Pliny (*Letters* 10.77–8) records that a legionary centurion was sent to Byzantium by Trajan to assist the government in protecting the citizens, in a city that was a vast crossroads, with many travelers passing through, but when asked to extend this privilege to another town, Trajan refused because he did not want to set a precedent. There are two famous literary passages that serve to praise the *pax Romana,* one dating from the reign of Antoninus Pius by the Greek rhetorician Aelius Aristides, and another by the Christian author Tertullian, whose works date from the late second and early third centuries AD. Aristides made a speech in the city of Rome (*Romes Encomium,* or *In Praise of Rome*) extolling the virtues of the political institutions and military forces that kept the Empire safe. This speech is often quoted as proof of Imperial peace and efficiency, but it must be remembered that it outlined the view of the ruling classes. Similarly, Tertullian (*De Anima* 30.2–4) praises the universal peace, the productivity of the fields, and the conquest and taming of the wilderness, rounding off his eulogy with the words "Everywhere there are homes, everywhere people, everywhere order, everywhere life." He then goes on to destroy this image of peace and prosperity, insisting that the pressures of population are too great and threaten the survival of the Empire. "Necessities are in short supply," he says, "and among everyone there are complaints." Between the yin and yang of these extremes lies a modicum of truth, that for the most part Roman provincials lived in relative peace that was ensured for them by the soldiers.

The problem is that people do not usually record the good things or kind acts quite so often as they record their grievances. This is why the most common evidence of the relationship between the army and civilians concerns the arrogance and bullying tactics of the soldiers. As a model governor, Julius Agricola spent his first winter in Britain correcting abuses that the soldiers and a coterie of administrative officials perpetrated against the natives. The army drew some of its supplies from civilian sources. One of the schemes that the soldiers employed to make money for themselves was to ask the civilians to transport the requisitioned grain and other produce to a distant objective, and then suggest a money payment to transport it themselves, which the provincials most likely paid out of gratitude for not having to make an unnecessary journey. Another abuse may have concerned false measures when the civilians brought their grain to the appointed depot; the corn-measure from Carvoran fort near Hadrian's Wall in northern England, dating from the reign of Domitian (reigned AD 81–96), actually holds more than the amount stated on the side of the vessel. This may be one of the means of cheating the natives that Agricola tried to eradicate.

Troops were allowed to requisition goods and animals from civilians, but they were supposed to have a permit from the military authorities. Frontinus (*Stratagems* 2.3.23) describes how Domitian, when he set out on his campaign against the Chatti in Germany, insisted that compensation should be paid to the natives for lands taken for building forts. This was not the usual practice of all emperors, and it was certainly not true of individual soldiers. In describing his adventures after being magically transformed into a donkey, Apulieus relates (*The Golden Ass* 9 –10) how he was taken from his new owner in Greece by a legionary, who used violence to gain him, and then sold him because he was going to Rome and had not needed him in the first place. In many cases, soldiers used force to extract goods from civilians, who were powerless at the time of the event and also thereafter if they tried to obtain justice and the return of their goods. Sometimes the abuses of the soldiers extended to demands for *hospitium* or what amounted to billeting. It was not illegal, just as requisitioning goods was not illegal, but though officially sanctioned, it was supposed to be kept within certain reasonable limits. The inhabitants of the village of Skaptopara in Thrace (modern Bulgaria) complained to the Emperor Gordian in AD 238 that the soldiers were abusing their privileges by taking whatever they wanted free of charge and were ruining the village: the population was declining because people could not support the depredations of the soldiers. The emperor replied to them but referred them to the provincial governor.

The duties of the provincial governors were outlined by law and included the prevention of illegal requisitions or billeting. However, the civilians who should have been protected by the law suffered from a grave disadvantage in that the governor to whom they had to make their complaint was also the commander of the army, with a vested interest in fostering the loyalty of the troops. Many civilians would probably not even bother to bring a charge, and even if legal proceedings were started, soldiers could be tried only by the military authorities. Literary sources are unanimous in underlining the difficulties any civilian faced in bringing a charge against a soldier (Shelton, 1998, 264 ff.).

Legal proceedings against other civilians were more likely to find a sympathetic audience with the military authorities. In some provinces, the commander of the nearest fort was the only man whom civilians could approach to seek justice, as revealed by the correspondence of Flavius Abbinaeus, *praefectus alae* at the fort of Dionysias in Egypt (Bell, 1962). Much of the evidence for this civilian and military contact comes from Egypt, because the rate of survival of papyrus documents is higher there than in damp northern European climates. It is likely that the same activities went on in other provinces, but the documentation has not been preserved. In the more remote areas, it is postulated that the fort commanders, usually centurions, were also responsible for the administration of the surrounding areas. This role is indicated by one of the writing tablets from Vindolanda where at the end of the first century AD a centurion at Carlisle in northern England was responsible for the region (Bowman and Thomas, 1983). This is further supported by two inscriptions from Ribchester, also in northern England, where two different legionary centurions are described as commander of the unit and the region (*RIB* 583; 587). Similar evidence of a centurion being in command of a region has been found in Egypt, Noricum, Pannonia, and Gallia Lugdunensis (Campbell, 1994).

It is attested that in several provinces centurions exercised judicial functions in both military and civilian cases, in some instances because the centurion was the highest ranking official in the vicinity and in other cases because he was the officer sent to arrest people who had been accused of crimes and his judgment was accepted by the civilians. In the province of Dalmatia in the early first century AD, a centurion was sent to adjudicate between two neighboring tribes and to establish and mark boundaries between them (*ILS* 5950). In Egypt at around the same period, a civilian sent a letter to a centurion asking for help to stop the depredations of his neighbors on his property (*Oxyrhynchus Papyri* 2234). Sometimes a centurion was appointed as a judge by another higher ranking official, such as a praetor. Civilians may have found that they were handed rough justice by the military men, but they simply had to accept it (Campbell 1984, Appendix I).

## VALUE SYSTEMS

Romans of the upper classes never relinquished their Republican zeal for military glory and political high honors. It was Augustus's task to channel these ideals into the aims of Imperial government without entirely suppressing them. He needed to foster a sense of individual achievement without allowing individualism to grow into an attempt to usurp him. Not all emperors managed to sustain the necessary equilibrium. In the first two centuries AD when usurpers tried to seize the Empire, it was usually in response to incompetence, insanity, or sheer malice on the part of the existing ruler.

Descent from the oldest and noblest families in Rome merited the highest status in Rome, and after that the criteria for acclaim rested upon wealth. The most important attribute of all was freedom, in two senses of the word—being freeborn and not a slave, and having the freedom to speak and to act, within defined parameters of acceptable behavior. The aristocrats viewed themselves as a highly superior and exclusive body, to whom everyone else should look up, including politicians from the new nobility of plebeian ancestry. The gradual but inexorable shrinkage of truly aristocratic families who could trace their family trees back to the old Republic meant that new nobles filled the gap without ever quite being accepted. Cicero, for instance, was the first of his family to make a political name for himself, and as a new man (*novus homo*) in the Senate, however eloquent he was and however many legal cases he won, he was still an outsider.

Words and titles were of great importance in the Roman world. The stern Romans of the old Republic valued above everything else their *dignitas* and *gravitas,* which signified uncompromising honesty, courage, endurance, stead-fastness, and high principles. Strict observance of the law and religious prac-tices, and of obligations to family, friends, and the state, all came under the heading of *pietas,* which translates as piety, but to the Romans the word had more connotations than are attached to the modern meaning of the word. The Romans admired skill in generalship and in political oratory (Goodman, 1997). Those men who had distinguished themselves in these two important areas of Roman life were imbued with *auctoritas,* an intangible but enormously presti-gious attribute that played a large part in assuring the position of Augustus when he became the self-appointed ruler of the Empire. *Auctoritas* was not a political office, nor was it an established legal status, except insofar as it lent per-suasion to the opinions and pronouncements of those invested with it. Usually it was elder statesmen who possessed *auctoritas* by dint of their experience and services to the state, but Augustus managed to assume the mantle of an elder statesman even though he had not reached the supposed statutory age to stand for the consulship. He emphasized his position as leader of the Senate (*prin-ceps*), or first among equals, ruling only because of his acknowledged and ac-cepted precedence.

The *virtus* and *pietas* of the emperors were frequently advertised and cele-brated on the coinage. *Virtus* included many of the Republican ideals, and a rigid translation (virtue) does not do justice to the Roman concept. One of the honors granted by the Senate to deserving emperors was the title *pater patriae,* "father of his country," which denoted his supreme authority over the state, just as a *pater familias* had total jurisdiction over the members of his family, coupled with a moral obligation to protect them. In the late Republic, the title was be-stowed on Cicero after he had unearthed the conspiracy of Catiline, and Augus-tus received it when he was sixty years old. His successor Tiberius did not accept it, and some of the emperors who followed did not survive long enough to war-rant the title, but from the third century onward, emperors adopted it more reg-ularly.

In matters of religion, Rome was tolerant of most cults and local customs. Where religious practice conflicted with the interests of the state, the Romans tried to suppress the perpetrators. For instance, the growth of Christianity whose adherents would not swear the oath of allegiance to the emperor, threat-ened to create a state within a state, and the Christians were therefore perse-cuted. Other cults enjoyed a trouble-free existence side by side with the old Ro-man gods such as Jupiter, Mars, and Apollo. When Augustus came to power there was a revitalization of religion. A new feature was the institution of the Imperial cult, which spread throughout the Empire, binding the provincials to Rome and the emperor. The deification of emperors after their deaths became the norm, and one of the means available to the Senate of obtaining revenge on a particularly bad emperor was to refuse to sanction his deification. This posthumous deification is to be distinguished from worship of the living emperor. In the east, the ruler cult was accepted from earliest times, and Augustus became the object of worship in the eastern provinces, with temples and cult statues dedicated to him. The people of the western provinces and particularly Rome and Italy found this worship of the living person harder to accept, but a useful compromise developed combining the worship of the deity Roma and Augustus, which survived the death of Augustus himself and was successfully transferred to his successors. In the western provinces, worship centered around great altars rather than temples, such as the Altar of the Three Gauls at Lugdunum (modern Lyon) in Gaul, and another center at Colonia Agrippinensis (modern Cologne) in Germany. The Imperial cult was never imposed by force, but it had great political value in providing a cohesive influence and in promoting loyalty to Rome.

### REFERENCES AND FURTHER READING

Alston, Richard. 1995. *Soldier and Society in Roman Egypt: A Social History.* London: Routledge.

Bell, H.I., et al. (eds.). 1962. *The Abbinaeus Archive: Papers of a Roman Officer in the Reign of Constantius II.* Oxford: Clarendon Press.

Birley, Anthony R. 1988. *Septimius Severus: The African Emperor.* London: Batsford. 2nd ed. Reprinted by Routledge, 2000.

Bowman, Alan K., and Thomas, J.D. 1983. *Vindolanda: The Latin Writing Tablets.* London: British Museum Press.

Braund, David C. 1984. *Rome and the Friendly King: The Character of Client Kingship.* London: Croom Helm.

Brunt, P.A. 1966. "The *Fiscus* and its development." *Journal of Roman Studies* 56, 75–91.

———. 1971. *Social Conflicts in the Roman Republic.* New York: W.W. Norton.

———. 1975. "Did Imperial Rome disarm her subjects?" *Phoenix* 29, 260–270.

———. 1981. "The revenues of Rome." *Journal of Roman Studies* 71, 161–172.

Campbell, J. Brian. 1984. *The Emperor and the Roman Army 31 BC–AD 235.* Oxford: Clarendon Press.

———. 1994. *The Roman Army 31 BC–AD 337: A Sourcebook.* London: Routledge.

———. 2002. *War and Society in Imperial Rome 31 BC–AD 284.* London: Routledge.

Chevallier, Raymond. 1976. *Roman Roads.* London: Batsford.

Cornell, Tim, and Matthews, J. 1982. *Atlas of the Roman World.* Oxford: Phaidon.

Duncan-Jones, Richard. 1982. *The Economy of the Roman Empire.* Cambridge: Cambridge University Press. 2nd ed.

———. 1994. *Money and Government in the Roman Empire.* Cambridge: Cambridge University Press.

Frayn, J.M. 1979. *Subsistence Farming in Roman Italy.* Fontwell: Centaur Press.

Gardner, J.F. 1993. *Being a Roman Citizen.* London: Routledge.

Garnsey, Peter, et al. (eds.). 1983. *Trade in the Ancient Economy.* London: Chatto and Windus.

Goldsworthy, Adrian K. 1996. *The Roman Army at War 100 BC–AD 200.* Oxford: Clarendon Press.

———. 2000. *The Punic Wars.* London: Cassell.

Goodman, Martin. 1997. *The Roman World 44 BC–AD 180.* London: Routledge.

Hopkins, Keith. 1980. "Taxes and trade in the Roman Empire, 200 BC–AD 400." *Journal of Roman Studies* 70, 101–125.

Jones, A.H.M. 1974. *The Roman Economy: Studies in Ancient Economic and Administrative History.* Oxford: Oxford University Press.

Le Bohec, Yann. 1994. *The Imperial Roman Army.* London: Routledge.

Levick, Barbara. 2000. *The Government of the Roman Empire: A Sourcebook.* London: Routledge. 2nd ed.

Lintott, Andrew. 1993. *Imperium Romanum: Politics and Administration.* London: Routledge.

———. 1999. *The Constitution of the Roman Republic.* Oxford: Oxford University Press.

MacMullen, Ramsay. 1963. *Soldier and Civilian in the Later Roman Empire.* Cambridge, MA: Harvard University Press.

———. 1974. *Roman Social Relations 50 BC to AD 284.* New Haven, CT: Yale University Press.

———. 1980, "How big was the Roman army?" *Klio* 62, 451–460.

Masson, Georgina. 1973. *A Concise History of Republican Rome.* London: Thames and Hudson.

Millett, Martin. 1990. *The Romanization of Roman Britain: An Essay in Archaeological Interpretation.* Cambridge: Cambridge University Press.

Mitchell, R.E. 1990. *Patricians and Plebeians: The Origins of the Roman State.* Ithaca, NY: Cornell University Press.

Parkin, T.G. 1992. *Demography and Roman Society.* Baltimore, MD: Johns Hopkins University Press.

Potter, Tim. 1987. *Roman Italy.* London: British Museum Press.

Robinson, O.F. 1997. *The Sources of Roman Law: Problems and Methods for Ancient Historians.* London: Routledge.

Rostovtzeff, M.I. 1957. *Social and Economic History of the Roman Empire.* Oxford: Clarendon Press. 2nd ed.

Scheidel, W. 1996. "Measuring sex, age, and death in the Roman Empire: explorations in ancient demography." *Journal of Roman Archaeology* Supplementary Series no.21, Ann Arbor, MI.

Shelton, Jo-Ann. 1998. *As the Romans Did: A Sourcebook in Roman Social History.* Oxford: Oxford University Press. 2nd ed.

Sherwin-White, Adrian N. 1972. "The Roman citizenship: a survey of its development into a world franchise." *Aufsteig und Niedergang der Römischen Welt,* Vol. 1, part 2, 23–58.

———. 1973. *The Roman Citizenship.* Oxford: Clarendon Press. 2nd ed.

Shotter, David. 1994. *The Fall of the Roman Republic.* London: Routledge.

Sommer, C. Sebastian. 1984. *The Military Vici in Roman Britain.* Oxford: BAR 129.

Southern, Pat. 2001. *The Roman Empire from Severus to Constantine.* London: Routledge.

Talbert, Richard J.A. 1984. *The Senate of Imperial Rome.* Princeton, NJ: Princeton University Press.

White, K.D. 1970. *Roman Farming.* London: Thames and Hudson.

Whittaker, C.R. 1994. *Frontiers of the Roman Empire: A Social and Economic Study.* Baltimore, MD: Johns Hopkins University Press.

# CHAPTER 3

# The Roman Army

## ORIGINS

### The Army of the Roman Republic

The Roman army of the pre-Republican regal period comprised 3,000 infantry and 300 cavalry drawn from the wealthiest of the equestrian order, who could afford to provide their own horses and equipment and whose name *equites* denotes their association with the mounted section of the army. The rounded figures reflect an equal contribution of 1,000 infantry and 100 cavalry from the three tribes of Rome, the *Ramnes, Tities,* and *Luceres,* perhaps representing the Latins, the Sabines, and the Etruscans, respectively. As Lawrence Keppie (1984) points out, however, these names are all Etruscan, indicating that Rome was under the influence of her Etruscan neighbors. There is no information about how the army of the kings was organized, or how it was commanded, but one feature was to prove constant throughout the history of Rome: it was called the *legio,* which means "the choosing," and refers to the method of recruitment, or the levy.

### *The So-Called Servian Reforms*

Etruscan influence on the early Roman army was likely considerable, given that Rome itself was ruled by Etruscan kings. The Etruscan armies were modeled on the Greek phalanx, heavy infantry or hoplites armed with the round shield (*hoplon*), and a long spear. The introduction of the phalanx in Rome is linked to the so-called Servian constitution, traditionally dated to the sixth century BC. The penultimate king, Servius Tullius, reorganized the electoral body and the army on the basis of wealth, ensuring that voting rights were related to military service. The cavalry was drawn from the middle classes, as before. The infantry was provided by the rest of the population, divided into five classes. The men of the first class could afford to equip themselves with a round shield, cuirass, greaves, spear, and sword. The second class lacked the cuirass, whereas the third class lacked both cuirass and greaves. The fourth class was equipped with spear and shield, and the fifth class was composed of slingers, armed with stones. Ranking below the five classes was a large number of men with little or no property. These were the *capite censi*, indicating that they were counted by heads and not by wealth. They were not eligible for service in the army, though in emergencies they did fight, usually grouped separately from the main army.

Each of the five classes was subdivided into centuries of *seniores* over the age of forty-six, who defended the city, and *juniores* aged seventeen to forty-five, who went to war. For voting purposes, the centuries of all the classes were brought together in the *comitia curiata*, also called *exercitus*, "the army." The place of assembly was outside the city boundary (*pomerium*), on the Campus Martius, the exercise ground. Votes were cast by century and were weighted in favor of the wealthy classes, since the *equites* and the first class together comprised ninety-eight centuries and the second to the fifth classes comprised ninety. The *capite censi* were all placed in one century and thereby denied any political influence.

The historians Livy and Dionysius of Halicarnassus provide limited information about the early Roman phalanx, perhaps derived from the books of Fabius Pictor, who wrote c. 200 BC. Dionysius says that the shields of the first class were of the Greek Argive style, the round *hoplon*, and Livy uses the Latin term *clipeus*, also denoting the round hoplite shield. The phalanx consisted of 4,000 infantry and 600 cavalry, plus a century of carpenters and smiths attached to the first class, and a century of trumpeters and horn players attached to the fifth.

The phalanx had been used to good effect by the Greeks since the seventh century, and was imported to Italy by way of their colonies. The hoplites lined up close together, usually in units with twelve men in a line and eight ranks deep, with their round shields overlapping, advancing almost as one body, like a roller, the literal meaning of phalanx. Although it generally required the protection of cavalry or lighter armed troops on the wings, the phalanx was a formidable fighting force when deployed in suitable terrain, but on rough ground, the close formation could not be maintained. The Spartans and the Macedonians created a more flexible phalanx by training some of the men to fight in smaller units, for different purposes. The Spartans trained units of about forty men to wheel off at the flanks and turn at right angles to the phalanx, or to turn back to join the rear of the phalanx to increase its depth. The Macedonians combined the phalanx with other units of differently armed fighting men, thus creating a more versatile army.

It is not fully understood how the Roman phalanx-legion operated with the other four lines drawn up behind it, as seems to be indicated by the sources. Some authors suggest that in the early period there may have been only one class (*classis* means "calling"). Another suggestion, taking the five classes at their face value, is that the phalanx comprised the men of the first class, and the other four classes provided light armed troops, deployed on the wings. None of this is corroborated by the ancient evidence.

### The Change from Hoplite Formation to Maniples

At the beginning of the fourth century BC, a fearsome enemy erupted from the north. The Celtic tribes of Cisalpine Gaul (literally translated as Gaul on this side of the Alps), embarked on plundering raids, threatening Etruria. Embassies failed to halt them. The Roman army assembled to meet them on a tributary of the Tiber known as the Allia, a name that would become a synonym for disaster. The Roman survivors fled, and the road to Rome was open. The city was evacuated except for a small garrison that held out on the Capitol for several months until the Gauls melted away, and the citizens returned.

It took forty years to recover from the attacks of the Gauls, not least because the members of the Latin League, together with the Aequi, Volsci, and Etruscans, seized the opportunity to try to shake off the domination of Rome while she was weakened. Fortunately for the Romans, the tribes failed to unite. Thereafter the organization of the army changed, most likely because the Romans had not prevailed over the loose, open-order fighting methods of the Gauls. The phalanx-legion was broken up into more maneuverable sections or maniples (from the Latin *manipuli*, meaning "handfuls"). The round *clipeus* was abandoned in favor of the oval *scutum*, which was already in use by some of the Italian allies. The exact date when the *pilum* (perhaps best translated as javelin) became part of the standard military equipment is very much disputed. It is not attested in the literary sources until the second century BC, but a significant factor is that the tight formation of the phalanx would not allow sufficient space for the soldiers to throw their *pila*, so it is possible that introduction of the looser manipular formation and the introduction of the *pilum* are related, but there is no proof for this hypothesis.

### Livy and the Army of the Mid-Fourth Century BC

By 362 BC, the annual levy had increased from one to two legions. Rome often had to fight simultaneously on more than one front, and eventually the army was doubled again to four legions. Livy implies that this had already happened by 340 BC, but the first reliable evidence for the increase dates from 311 BC.

Writing retrospectively and using unknown sources, Livy described in some detail the organization of the Roman army in 340 BC. Keppie (1984) doubts that

Livy's legion ever existed, but it has also been suggested that the very idiosyncrasies in the account actually support its veracity (Connolly, 1998). According to Livy, each legion was 5,000 strong, drawn up in three main battle lines. At the front were fifteen maniples of *hastati,* heavy infantry composed of the younger men, and attached to each maniple were twenty light-armed soldiers (*leves*), each carrying a spear and light javelins. Their task was presumably to form a screen for the whole army and to operate as skirmishers. Behind the *hastati* were another fifteen maniples of *principes* who were older and more experienced soldiers. The third battle line consisted of three types of troops: first the veterans (*triarii*), then the less experienced men of the *rorarii,* and finally the *accensi.* The term *triarii* is easily translated as the men of the third rank, but scholars have racked their brains about the possible meanings of the other two words. The *accensi* turn up in later Roman armies as servants, but the *rorarii* defy clarification. It is tempting to equate the five types of troops of Livy's battle line with the five classes of the Servian constitution, but it cannot be affirmed that there is any direct descent from one system to the other. On a linguistic basis, the *accensi* were more likely to be attendants and not soldiers, but they did occasionally take part in battles, notably in the war against the Latins under the General Decius Mus. Livy explains that each division of the third line was a *vexillum* (later this was the name of the standard of a detachment or vexillation). Each *vexillum* contained sixty men and two centurions, implying that there were two centuries of thirty men. It is likely that the maniples of the *hastati* and *principes* were similarly organized.

This was probably the type of army that the Romans employed in the Samnite Wars (343–341 BC; c. 324–304 BC; 298–290 BC), which possibly entailed some adaptive techniques on the part of the Romans. The Samnites were hill fighters and were reluctant to come down to the plains, so the Romans had to wage war in hill country, disastrously at first. If it had not already occurred, this was possibly the occasion for the introduction of the *pilum,* because the Romans now needed some way of engaging the enemy without closing. Livy (10.39) mentions the use of *pila* in his account of the third Samnite War, but this may be a retrospective misuse of terminology most familiar to his readers.

Since the Romans were fighting at some distance from Rome against a highly mobile enemy, the practice of building marching camps may have begun during the Samnite Wars. There is no firm evidence, but at some point the Romans learned, and the Samnite Wars provide a valid context for the lessons. Livy refers to camps several times, in one instance relating how the Samnites attacked the camp of the consul Marcus Valerius and saw soldiers "behind the ramparts." The Samnite Wars also taught the Romans about organizing supply lines, and about communications. One of the first projects that was undertaken after the conclusion of the second war was the building of the Via Appia from Rome to the city of Capua. Routes were of obvious importance in military maneuvers but could also provide access for the inroads of the Samnites, so colonies were planted at strategic points to guard against hostile incursions and to provide bases for Roman counterattacks.

### The Roman Army of Polybius

On the eve of the war with Hannibal (221–202 BC), the Roman army emerges in a clearer light in the detailed documentary work of Polybius (*Histories* 6.19–42). He describes the enrollment of the legions and the allied troops, their organization, the layout of the military camp, the hierarchy of command, and the system of military rewards and punishments. The context in his narrative is after the account of the battle of Cannae in 216 BC, a somewhat ironic placement in that this was the most serious military defeat that any Roman army had experienced. As Polybius points out (3.118), however, although Rome's military reputation was in tatters, their national characteristics and constitution enabled the Romans to recover, and within a very short time they not only defeated the Carthaginians but made themselves masters of the world.

Polybius tells us that the consuls presided over the annual levy of four legions and 300 cavalry drawn from Roman citizens, and dispatched messages to

Hannibal fighting a Roman legion in the Alps, by School of Raphael. (Araldo de Luca/Corbis)

each of the allied cities, declaring the number of men that each must raise, as well as the date and location of their assembly. The army officers were selected at each annual levy. Although the same men may have served in the same capacity several times, reentry into the newly enrolled army at the same rank was never guaranteed. Six military tribunes, usually of equestrian rank and with some military experience, were appointed to each legion. These posts were highly prestigious, since the Republican tribunes commanded the legions, and even ex-consuls served their turn. The tribunes were responsible for maintaining discipline among the troops and in the camp, and for supervising the administrative routines such as passing on the orders of the consuls to the cavalry prefects and the centurions, giving the watchword to all troops at night, and receiving reports in the morning.

The men who were eligible to serve were described by the formula *cives qui arma ferre possunt,* meaning "citizens who are capable of bearing arms." This was a reference to each citizen's census qualification, and not proof of physical fitness. The normal service obligation was a maximum of sixteen seasons between the ages of seventeen and forty-six. It was not necessary to serve every year, and there would always be a pool of men to call upon in emergencies. If the necessities of war involved remaining under arms continuously for more than one season, the soldiers who had served for six consecutive years were sent home, but for the remaining ten years they could be called to the levy as *evocati.*

After the appointment of the tribunes, the citizen cavalry was enrolled, 300 for each of the four legions, selected from the wealthiest citizens. The allocation of the infantrymen to each of the four legions was a lengthier procedure. The recruits were divided into their tribes, and men were chosen from each tribe in groups of four, strictly by rota, so that each legion in turn was granted the opportunity to make the first choice. The next task was to administer the oath to all the soldiers. This was carried out by selected tribunes, who paraded their legion; then each tribune chose one man who took the oath to obey his officers and carry out their orders. The rest of the men took the oath in turn, repeating the formula "*idem in me,*" colloquially translated as "the same for me." At the close of the proceedings, the tribunes appointed another day for the next assembly, when the names of all the men in the newly enrolled legions and cavalry were written down. In each legion, 600 of the older men in their thirties and forties were chosen for the rear battle line, or *triarii.* The men in the prime of life were assigned to the *principes,* then the younger ones were assigned to the *hastati,* and the youngest of all made up the *velites.* The *hastati* and *principes* comprised ten maniples of 120 men, and the *triarii* were divided into ten maniples of 60 men. The three-line formation was called the *triplex acies,* ignoring the fourth category of the 1,200 *velites,* who were not formed into maniples but were divided into groups of forty men. Probably one group was attached to each of the maniples in the other three classes. The *triarii* always remained at a total of 600 men, but the numbers of *hastati* and *principes* varied according to circumstances. Polybius acknowledges this variation, especially when describing the layout of the military camp.

The difference in age between the *velites* and the other ranks was matched by a corresponding difference in their armament, the *velites* being the lighter-armed troops. The date when the *velites* were introduced into the army is disputed. They may already have been part of the army during the first Punic War, but some modern scholars consider that they were instituted as late as 211 BC, based on Livy's description (26.4.9) of the siege of Capua, when he says that the custom was established of combining the heavy-armed legions with light-armed troops, or *velites* (Gabba, 1976). Some authors suggest that the introduction of the *velites* is associated with a reduction of the census qualification for army service. According to Livy, the property qualification at the time of the Servian reforms was 11,000 bronze *asses*. This requirement had been lowered by the time of Polybius to 400 Greek *drachmae*, or the equivalent of 4,000 *asses*. These men of limited wealth would not have been able to provide their own equipment, but it is probable that very few of the soldiers armed themselves. Polybius says that in his day only the *hastati* provided their own arms and armor, which implies that there was a state system in place to provide the equipment of the other ranks.

The *hastati*, the *principes,* and the *triarii* elected their own centurions, who were chosen for their steadiness in battle and their dependability, rather than for recklessness and daring, which implies that they were well known to the men. Each of the three battle lines elected ten senior centurions (*priores*), who appointed ten junior centurions (*posteriores*). When he was acting alone, the senior centurion commanded both centuries, but with both centurions present the senior commanded the right half of the maniple and the junior commanded the left. Each centurion appointed an *optio,* who acted as an assistant to his centurion and as a rearguard officer. Other officers in each maniple were the *signifer* or standard bearer, and the *tesserarius,* whose title derived from the clay *tessera* that he passed around each day with the watchword written on it. It was the responsibility of the *tesserarius* to post the sentries each night.

The *hastati, principes,* and *triarii* were supported by the 300 Roman citizen cavalry, divided into ten *turmae.* From each *turma* three decurions were elected, the first being the overall commander of the squadron. Each decurion appointed an *optio,* just as the legionary centurions did.

### The Allied Contingents

Each consul commanded two of the four legions, accompanied by contingents of allied troops, the *Alae Sociorum,* furnished by the Latin and Italian allied states. The number of allied infantry troops usually matched the number of men in the legions, but the allied cavalry was three times the size of the Roman citizen cavalry. The allied troops as described by Polybius were commanded by Roman *praefecti sociorum.*

The allied forces attached to each consular army did not always operate together. Polybius explains that one-fifth of the infantry and one-third of the cavalry were specially picked by the Roman prefects. These men were known as *extraordinarii.* They were at the consul's disposal, being allocated spaces in the camp near to his tent. They accompanied him on the march, and they could be dispatched on special duties. They were usually placed at the head of the column when breaking camp, followed by one wing of the allies, then the two legions, and finally the other wing of the allies. If an attack from the rear was expected, the *extraordinarii* formed the rearguard instead of the advance guard.


## Marius's Mules

The next documented changes to organization of the Republican Roman army were instituted by the General Gaius Marius, who probably assessed the innovations that had already occurred and put the most useful ones together. Marius gained his military experience in Spain at the siege of Numantia (143–133 BC), and in Africa with his patron, the consul Quintus Caecilius Metellus, in the campaign against the Numidian king, Jugurtha. Marius was allowed to return from Africa to Rome for the consular elections for 107 BC. Once he was elected, he maneuvered successfully to gain the African command and began to recruit, not to raise new legions but to fill gaps in the ranks of the army already in North Africa. This was a *supplementum,* not the annual levy, and his required numbers were not very high; Keppie (1984) estimates that he needed about 3,000 men. In order to obtain them, Marius asked for volunteers, specifically targeting the *capite censi,* who were technically not eligible for army service. It was not an unprecedented step, since the *capite censi* had been recruited in the past during emergencies, and Marius may not have intended by this one act to set the pattern for raising armies in the future. He did not abolish the property qualification for military service, but it had been progressively lowered to the point where the state was now supplying most, if not all, of the military equipment. Thus, there was no firm reason to exclude a mass of men who were of the right age and physically fit.

With the help of his quaestor Lucius Cornelius Sulla, Marius ended the war in Africa and returned to Rome. Another war was imminent. The Celtic tribes had inflicted serious defeats on three Roman armies in southern Gaul in 109, 107, and 105 BC and then veered off toward Spain instead of invading Italy, but the Romans were badly shaken and it was expected that the tribesmen would soon reappear. Marius was elected consul for 104 BC. The consul for 105 BC, Rutilius Rufus, had assembled an army and embarked on a training program combining arms drill and a physical fitness regime, derived from the gladiator schools. Frontinus (*Stratagems* 4.2.2) says that Marius was more impressed with these troops than his own. He took them over, raised more men, and stationed them in Gaul, where he spent the waiting time in developing the training regime initiated by Rutilius Rufus. Since the Roman people elected him consul for 103 and 102 BC, he remained in command and kept up the training. When the tribes moved back toward Italy he was ready.

Marius exchanged the manipular formation for a different organization based on the cohort. There were precedents, since cohorts made up of three maniples had been employed in the war with Hannibal, and perhaps also in Spain, but only as a temporary arrangement, and a "cohort" at this period may not have signified a unit of a standard size. The main feature of the cohorts was uniformity in equipment and training, and the command structure was simplified, since there were only ten cohorts in the new structure, which in turn implies that there were ten officers to relay commands to their units. The problem is that no certain legionary cohort commander has ever been attested in any source. The cohorts were large enough to operate independently and also small enough to work in combination with others. The three battle lines of the old-style legions were retained, with four cohorts in the first line and three in the second and third lines, but variations were possible according to the needs of the moment.

The soldiers were nicknamed Marius's Mules, because each soldier carried not only his equipment but also his rations for several days and the means of cooking them. Marius's armies were intended to be mobile and self-sufficient, not bogged down with baggage carts or a mass of camp followers, who were all chased away. While Marius fought the Celtic tribesmen with his new-style army, the other manipular legions stationed in other areas were presumably converted to the cohort formation, but the fine details of the reorganization and how it was carried out are not known. Marius ensured that the legions acquired a strong corporate identity. Each legion previously displayed five different animal standards—an eagle, a wolf, a man with the head of a bull, a boar, and a horse, curiously reminiscent of the five Servian classes—but now Marius chose to emphasize the eagle (*aquila*), familiar to us from the Imperial period as the standard of the whole legion.

### The Social War and Its Military Consequences

After the reorganization of the legions, political changes were effected when the Italian and Latin allies were grudgingly admitted to Roman citizenship after the Social War. The grant of citizenship to the allied communities now qualified the Latins and Italians for service in the legions. The result was the disappearance of the *Alae Sociorum* and the consequent need to find replacements for these troops. Toward the end of the Republic, it was common practice to form temporary units from native communities who lived near the areas where Roman armies were operating. The Romans made good use of the specific talents of their non-Italian allies; for instance, the Numidians, the Gauls, and the Germans were excellent horsemen, so they served for the duration of a campaign as much-needed cavalry. The Romans themselves displayed no particular talent as horsemen, and the citizen cavalry arm gradually died out. For other military purposes, special units of archers were hired from Crete, and slingers were brought in from the Balearic Islands. Various friendly kings provided troops for Pompey's campaigns in the east, and Julius Caesar employed Gallic and German tribesmen. These troops usually fought under their own leaders and were retained only until the wars were concluded. They were not yet the *auxilia* of the Imperial army, which were organized in regular sized units, served for specified lengths of time, received regular pay, and were rewarded with the grant of Roman citizenship upon discharge. The non-Italian allied troops of the late Republic enjoyed none of these benefits.

### The Civil Wars and the End of the Republic

The history of the Republic in its last century is a convoluted mixture of foreign conquest and political upheavals as ambitious men sought power and used the armies to attain it. In the civil war of 48 BC, Julius Caesar defeated Pompey and absorbed many of his troops into his own armies, but after Caesar's assassination civil war broke out again as Mark Antony and Octavian fought the assassins, and then turned on each other. After the fall of Alexandria to Octavian in 30 BC, Antony and Cleopatra conveniently committed suicide, and Octavian was in the happy position of having eliminated all opposition. He took over Egypt intact and kept it as his own preserve, administering it via equestrians and forbidding any senator to enter the province without express permission.

The fabulous wealth of Egypt enabled Octavian to fulfill his promises to the soldiers and to keep a firm hold on supreme power while he effected the changes that transformed the Republic into the Empire and its former citizen militia into a permanent professional army. At the conclusion of the civil wars, there were more than sixty legions and vast numbers of native troops distributed over the Roman world. Many of the soldiers were conscripts with no desire to remain under arms, so some of them were discharged and settled as veterans on land allotments, while others were dismissed to their homes. As far as possible, Antony's promises to his troops were honored, if only to avoid a resurgence of hostility based on grievances.

The foundations of the Imperial Roman army were laid down now, as Au-

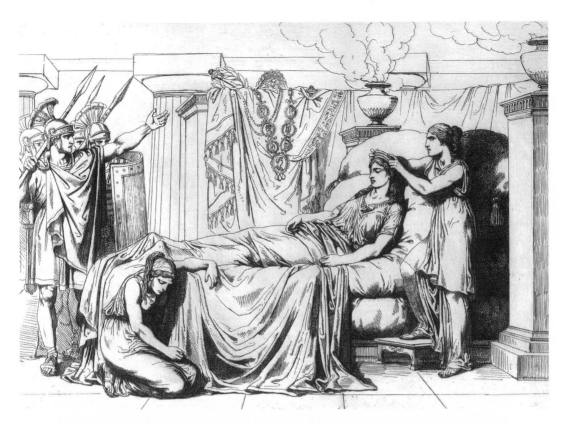

Roman soldiers enter Cleopatra's chamber as she is dying. Once Antony and Cleopatra were gone, Octavian took over Egypt and kept it as his own preserve, administering it via equestrians and forbidding any senator to enter the province without express permission. (Library of Congress)

gustus reduced the number of legions to twenty-eight, gradually settling the discharged veterans in colonies in Italy and in the provinces. This tremendous undertaking satisfied only present needs. In order to eradicate the problems that had beset the last years of the Republic, Octavian needed to take total control of the administration, organization, and deployment of the army. There was no question of returning to the Republican system of raising troops when wars threatened and then disbanding them. The Empire was too large to defend by raising a few legions for the duration of a campaign. Provincial government required resident armed forces to protect the territories and keep internal order, and so the standing army was established, along with the necessary machinery to pay the soldiers, to equip them with clothing, armor, and weapons, to feed and house them, to train them, to doctor them, to discipline them, to reward them for bravery, to instill a sense of duty and loyalty, and to provide for their retirement. At the time of Augustus's death in AD 14, this reorganization had been largely achieved, and the army that he created remained essentially the same for the next two centuries

# ORGANIZATIONAL STRUCTURE

## The Legions

The twenty-eight legions that were kept under arms at the end of the civil wars were not issued with new numbers running from I to XXVIII. The highest legionary numeral in Augustan times was XXII. The existing legions were reconstituted under their own numbers and distinguishing names, such as *V Alaudae*, which started out in Gaul under Julius Caesar. Some legionary numbers were duplicated or triplicated. For instance, there were *III Augusta, III Cyrenaica,* and *III Gallica, IV Macedonica* and *IV Scythica, V Alaudae* and *V Macedonica, VI Ferrata* and *VI Victrix,* and *X Fretensis* and *X Gemina.* The title *Gemina* (twin) usually signified that the remnants of two legions had been combined.

The number of legions did not remain constant throughout the centuries. There were spectacular losses, the most serious being the annihilation of three legions in Germany under the Governor Quinctilius Varus in AD 9. These were *legiones XVII, XVIII,* and *XIX.* They were never reconstituted, and the numbers were never reused in legionary lists. For some years after this disaster, the total number of legions did not exceed twenty-five. The distribution of the legions under Tiberius is described in a famous passage of Tacitus (*Annals* 4.5), in which he enumerates all the armed forces as they were in AD 23. There were eight legions on the Rhine, two each in the Danubian provinces of Pannonia and Moesia, three in the newly pacified provinces of Spain, two in Africa, two in Egypt, four in the eastern provinces, and two in reserve in Dalmatia, within easy reach of Italy in case of emergencies.

New legions were created when necessary, two in AD 39 (*XV Primigenia* and *XXII Primigenia*) and one under Nero in AD 67 (*I Italica*). In the civil wars that brought Vespasian to power in AD 69, two more legions, *I Adiutrix* and *II Adiutrix,* were created from marines from the fleet, but no less than five legions were disbanded for their rebellious actions, even though one of these had only just been created. There is another list of legions, dating from the reign of Antoninus Pius, on an inscription found in Rome and now in the Vatican museum (*CIL* VI 3492=*ILS* 2288). It extends over two columns and lists the legions by their numbers and titles, arranged in their provincial groupings. At some unknown date, the names of the legions that were created after the reign of Pius were added to the list at the end, out of geographical sequence. These are *II Italica* and *III Italica* raised by Marcus Aurelius, and *I, II,* and *III Parthica* by Severus. Significantly, the emperors who created new legions, such as Vespasian, Domitian, Trajan, Marcus Aurelius, and Severus, were involved in protracted civil or foreign wars.

Some legions were awarded extra titles after they had performed well in battles or proved loyal to the emperors in civil wars. For instance, *XX Valeria* may have been awarded its title *Victrix* after the suppression of the Boudiccan revolt in Britain, and *I Flavia Minervia,* raised by Domitian in 83, declared for him in the revolt of Saturninus six years later and was henceforth known as *I Flavia Minervia pia fidelis.* As well as their distinguishing names the legions adopted symbols, usually real or mythical animals. For instance, a Capricorn was adopted by *IV Scythica* in Moesia and *XXI Rapax* in Germany, and a running boar was the symbol of *XX Valeria Victrix.*

### *Length of Service*

The term of service for legionaries was originally six years during the Republic, with an obligation to serve for a further ten years, but these years did not need to be consecutive. Augustus increased the obligatory term to twenty years, but after serving for sixteen years soldiers were designated as veterans, whose duties were much lighter for the remaining four years. This term of service was increased at a later date to twenty years with probably five more as a veteran, though this is not unequivocally stated. There is some evidence that soldiers were retained into old age at the beginning of the Empire, before the systems for discharge had been properly established.

### *Organization of the Legion*

One of the most fundamental questions about the Roman army cannot be answered. No extant source states the number of men in any of the legions. It is possible that in different provinces and at different times legionary strengths varied; there may have been less rigid uniformity than modern authors expect. Most scholars opt for a legionary strength somewhere between 5,000 and 6,000, because there simply is not enough evidence to be more specific.

In theory, all legionaries were Roman citizens, but during the civil wars of the late Republic, when manpower resources were stretched, the distinction between citizens and noncitizens was ignored. As more peaceful conditions were restored, recruitment to the legions was confined as far as possible to citizens. Fortunately, the pool of available men expanded as citizenship was granted to more individuals, to specific communities, and even to whole provinces. The western legions were eventually able to draw on Gaul and Spain for their recruits, but in the eastern provinces, it was sometimes necessary to bestow citizenship upon new recruits when they joined the legions.

The smallest group of men within the legion was the *contubernium,* denoting eight men sharing a tent or quarters in the barracks. These eight men would share the restricted space of the barracks room, cook their food, and eat to-

gether, and more importantly they would fight together in the battle line. Although there would be separation by deaths, transfers, or retirements, this
would be the closest knit community in the legion. The *contubernium* had no
tactical significance, but each soldier would form close bonds with his seven
colleagues (*contubernales*), and such associations would help foster a strong esprit de corps in the legions.

Ten *contubernia* constituted one century, which totaled eighty men rather
than the hundred implied by the title "century." Each century was commanded
by a centurion, whose subordinate officers, called *principales,* included those familiar from the old Republican army; the *optio,* who commanded in the absence
of the centurion; the *signifer,* who carried the standard (*signum*) of the century;
and the *tesserarius,* whose main responsibilities concerned guard duties. The
*tesserarius* earned one and a half times standard pay, and the standard bearers
and *optiones* were on double pay. Some men held all these posts in succession,
whereas others were promoted to the centurionate after holding one of the
posts. It is possible that all the *optiones* were qualified to become centurions
eventually, but some of them felt obliged to point out that they were destined
for promotion by expanding their titles to *optio ad spem ordinis,* or *optio spei,* or
other variations on the theme.

Six centuries constituted one cohort, and ten cohorts made up one legion.
From the late Republic onward the cohort was the tactical unit of the legion. It
was the equivalent of three of the old-style maniples, though with an adjustment to make up the numbers to 480 men per cohort. Although the early Imperial army dispensed with the two-century manipular formation, the centuries
were still paired off in camp. As Keppie (1984) points out, traces of the maniples
remained in the titles still used in the Imperial army for the six centurions of
each cohort, the most junior being *hastatus posterior* and *hastatus prior,* then
*princeps posterior* and *prior,* and the most senior were *pilus posterior* and *pilus
prior* (*pilus* was used instead of *triarius*). It is possible that the most senior centurion of the six centuries, the *pilus prior,* commanded his own century and also
the cohort. Significantly, the term *manipularis* was still used to describe a soldier, but maniples did not feature in tactical formations or on inscriptions,
where soldiers generally described themselves as belonging to a particular century, or working under a particular centurion.

### The First Cohort

From the late first century AD, the first cohort in some legions was almost double strength, comprising five centuries instead of the usual six, and each century
contained 160 men instead of 80. The centurions were senior to all the others in
the legion, and their titles were slightly different, starting with the most junior

as *hastatus posterior,* then *princeps posterior,* rising to *hastatus,* then *princeps,* and finally the most coveted of posts, *primus pilus,* which translates literally as "first spear."

The legionary fortress at Inchtuthill in Scotland, dating to the late first century AD, provides unequivocal evidence that the first cohort of the legion there was divided into five double-strength centuries. Next to the headquarters building, five houses with courtyards stood at the ends of five pairs of barracks. One of the houses was more refined than the other four, with a larger courtyard and under-floor heating in some of the rooms, and it is postulated that this was the residence of the *primus pilus.* No archaeological or epigraphic evidence attests the name of the occupants of the fortress, but Inchtuthill is now ineradicably associated with *legio XX Valeria Victrix,* which for much of its residence in Britain was housed at Chester (*Deva*). Archaeological excavations at Chester are restricted because the modern city overlies the fortress, so it cannot yet be shown whether the layout compares or contrasts with Inchtuthill.

The late Roman author Vegetius provides additional evidence that the first cohort was double the size of the others. Writing of the legionary cavalry (*equites legionis*) of the third century, Vegetius indicates that the cavalry of the first cohort was twice the strength of the horsemen of each of the ordinary cohorts (*Epitoma Rei Militaris* 2.6). Thus, there is some evidence that the first cohort in some of the legions were double strength, but it is still not possible to state categorically that all legions in all provinces and at all times had a double first cohort. It has been suggested that the first cohort was largely composed of veterans, but this does not answer the question whether all legions adopted the same policy. There may have been special circumstances in which the first cohort was strengthened, for instance, for a campaign. Some modern armies recruit extra soldiers in wartime, so it is possible that only a few of the legions had an enlarged first cohort, and it is also possible that this was not intended to be a permanent situation.

### The Legionary Cavalry

Each legion contained 120 mounted men (*equites legionis*). Only one source, Flavius Josephus, attests to this number, and strictly interpreted this simply means that when Josephus wrote his description of the army in Judaea under Vespasian and Titus, the legionary cavalry numbered 120 men. In the absence of any other evidence, it is usually extrapolated from Josephus's statement that the same number applied to all legions of the first two centuries AD.

For administrative purposes, the *equites legionis* were allocated to different legionary centuries, which may signify that they all trained as infantrymen on enlistment, and after being appointed as cavalrymen they remained on the registers of their original centuries. Epigraphic evidence attests that the horsemen were commanded by centurions like the rest of the soldiers, and not by decurions who were the commanders of all other cavalry. One inscription records an *optio equitum* serving in the fifth century of the seventh cohort of *legio III Augusta* (*CIL* VIII 2568, 18), and a tombstone from Lincoln in Britain shows that the horseman Quintus Cornelius served under the centurion Cassius Martialis. It cannot be proved whether the *equites* lived in the barracks of the centuries where they were first enrolled or whether they remained on the century records but were in fact housed all together somewhere in the legionary fortresses.

Apart from the literary evidence of Josephus, there is no further documentation about the numbers of legionary cavalry until the middle of the third century. During the reign of Gallienus when the Empire was under threat of disintegration, the numbers of the *equites legionis* were vastly increased to 726 horsemen. This figure derives from the work of Vegetius, who says that there were 66 cavalry in each cohort and 132 in the first cohort (*Epitoma Rei Militaris* 2.6). The functions of the legionary cavalry are not firmly established at any time in its existence. It has been suggested that the horsemen were mounted messengers, but it seems that they trained together as a unit and performed the same exercises as the ordinary cavalry, using the same weapons. When Hadrian addressed the troops after their military exercises at Lambaesis in Numidia, he praised the *equites legionis* for their javelin throwing, performed while they were wearing the legionary cuirass (*CIL* VIII 18042; *ILS* 2487; 9133–9135).

Although it is known that the legionary cavalry trained as a unit and was grouped together on the march, it is not known if there was an officer in command of the *equites*. Some authors have suggested that if there were such an officer, he would be a centurion, while others favor the *optio*, mainly because this is attested on an inscription (*CIL* VIII 2568). In the third century, when the Emperor Gallienus required an armed force of great mobility and speed to deal with threats on several different fronts, he amalgamated all types of cavalry from the auxiliary units and from the legions and created a mounted army with its own commander, called Aureolus. Vegetius says that the legionary cavalry of the later Empire was divided into *turmae* and commanded by decurions.

### Engineers, Artillerymen, and Other Specialists

In the Imperial Roman army there was no engineer or artillery corps. The engineers and artillerymen, as well as all other specialist workers, were registered as members of individual centuries. The men who performed specialist duties were *immunes*, who were exempt from fatigues, guard duties, laboring jobs, and other tasks such as latrine cleaning. *Immunes* are first attested in the mid-second century, but the concept probably dates from a much earlier period.

There was no extra pay for specialists, and *immunis* was not a rank, but the men were allowed to devote their time to their specific tasks.

The jurist Tarrutienus Paternus compiled a list of the *immunes* of the legions (*Digest* 50.6.7), perhaps when he was appointed Praetorian Prefect in the reign of Marcus Aurelius. The list appears to be in no particular order, but broadly categorized it includes the personnel who performed engineering duties, those who manufactured weapons and armor, the clerical staff who kept the records of the unit, the staff of the hospitals and assistants to the surgeons, and the staff who dealt with the animals belonging to a legion.

Of those who can be included under the modern heading of engineers, Tarrutienus includes surveyors and ditchers, who would be necessary when marking out new camps or fort sites, and those who were most likely involved with building works and the transport of materials, such as roof-makers, stone cutters, woodworkers, metal cutters, glass-workers, plumbers and water-pipe makers, cartwrights, blacksmiths, coppersmiths, lime-burners, and charcoal-burners. Specifically associated with the manufacture and repair of weapons and equipment were the men who made arrows, bows, and swords, and those who made trumpets and horns. The clerical staff included a range of assistants, with responsibility for keeping records of the grain store, and for various financial accounts such as the cash on deposit and the monies left by soldiers who had no designated heirs. Inscriptions attest clerical *immunes librarii*. One was set up by Septimius Licinius, *immunis librarius* of *legio II Parthica* at Albano in Italy (*ILS* 2427), commemorating the death of his daughter, who lived three years, four months, and twenty-four days. The other (*ILS* 3380) was set up by Marcus Ulpius Firminus at Potaissa (modern Torda) in Dacia.

Building work played an enormous part in a legionary's working life. It was the legionaries who built the roads and bridges, the forts and fortresses in any province, and they are also attested to have worked on canals and river-widening projects, and even on sinking mines. Tacitus (*Annals* 11.20) reports that a commander called Curtius Rufus employed soldiers to excavate a silver mine in the territory of the Mattiaci (around Mainz and Wiesbaden in Germany). Curtius received triumphal honors (*ornamenta triumphalia*) for his exploits in Germany, and the soldiers wrote to the emperor, suggesting that he should award an honorary triumph *before* a commander set out, so that if he had already received an award he might not be so keen to earn glory by working them so hard.

Roads were of particular importance to communications and troop movements, and the legions built thousands of miles of roads all over the Empire. Much of the information about who built the roads comes from milestones and other inscriptions. One milestone (*ILS* 5834) from the province of Arabia mentions paving for the road that was built by troops of the provincial governor Gaius Claudius Severus in the reign of Trajan. Paving for roads was a comparatively late development and was not universally adopted in all provinces, and in this instance the fact that it is specifically pointed out indicates that it was a worthy and unusual achievement. Legionaries from *legio IIII Flavia* and *legio VII Claudia* built Trajan's road along the river Danube by cutting back the cliff face, and an inscription found near the river Orontes in Syria attests to road building by four legions, *III Gallica, IV Scythica, VI Ferrata,* and *XVI Flavia.* The inscription also attests to the presence of soldiers from twenty auxiliary units, which are not mentioned in building inscriptions as often as legions (Campbell, 1994).

Each legionary fortress contained a workshop (*fabrica*), where the production and repair of arms and armor was carried out. Some of the workmen attached to the *fabricae* also made bricks and tiles, which was an important section of any legion, but the place of manufacture was sometimes at a depot situated a short distance from the legionary headquarters, as at Holt near the legionary fortress of Chester in England.

The Romans employed various types of artillery, described under several names in the sources, such as *catapultae, scorpiones, ballistae, carroballistae,* and *onagri,* or categorized under the general heading of *tormenta,* as in Caesar's accounts of the Gallic War. The projectiles were arrows or bolts of different sizes, and stones. The heavier engines were employed only in sieges, but some Roman artillery was light enough for use in the field. In his chapter on machines, the architect Vitruvius (*On Architecture* 10.10–13) includes a short section on artillery and siege engines, giving a description of how to construct them and the dimensions of each section, depending on the length of the arrows or the weight of the stone projectiles. Josephus describes the use of artillery in the sieges of the Jewish war under Vespasian, and in the later Empire Ammianus Marcellinus gives an account of the siege of Amida. Vegetius discusses the use of artillery in the legions (*Epitoma Rei Militaris* 2.25). These descriptions combined with archaeological finds of various sections of artillery pieces from different provinces enable modern historians to make reconstructions that work very efficiently. (For more on artillery see Chapter 5.)

Less is known about the soldiers who operated the machinery. Artillerymen (*ballistarii*) are specifically mentioned in Tarrutienus's list of *immunes,* but there is little evidence of their numbers or how they were organized. Vegetius indicates that eleven men from each century were allocated to the operation of the *carroballista,* which fired large arrows. Marsden (1969) points out that on Trajan's Column, only two men are shown working with an arrow-firing machine, but there would be other soldiers who were designated to look after the animals and the carriage used for transport. By the middle of the first century AD, it is probable that each century had one artillery engine, firing arrows or stones. Goldsworthy (1996) estimates that 70 wagons and 160 animals would be needed to carry the artillery of one legion.

The men who manufactured and maintained the artillery pieces would probably be *architecti,* who are mentioned as *immunes* in Tarrutienus's list. The legionary workshops could easily produce and repair artillery pieces, with the help of the *ballistarii,* under the supervision of the camp prefect (*praefectus castrorum*). A tombstone found in Rome records the career of a legionary *architectus* called Gaius Vedennius Moderatus in the first century AD (*ILS* 2034). Vedennius started his service in *legio XVI Gallica* in Lower Germany, but was transferred to the Praetorian Guard, and after discharge was asked to remain in service in the Imperial arsenal, because of his skills as "*arcitect[us]*" (*sic*).

### Headquarters Staff

Soldiers who possessed a high standard of literacy could be appointed to the administrative and clerical staffs of the legionary officers. These men, like the small group of lesser officers attached to each centurion, were called *principales.* The standard bearers, the *aquilifer,* who carried the legionary eagle, and the *imaginiferi,* who carried the lesser standards, ranked as *principales* of the headquarters, which was served by a collection of clerical staff, commonly called *librarii,* who attended to the financial and administrative functions of the legions under the watchful eyes of the *cornicularii.* The equestrian

Bronze figurine of eagle standard bearer, first century AD, from Alba Fucens, Roman (the legionary eagle was a symbol of power of Rome). (The Art Archive/National Archaeological Museum Chieti/Dagli Orti [A])

tribunes, the camp prefect, the *tribunus laticlavius,* and the legionary legate all employed a staff of clerical and other assistants in their *officia.*

### Pay

This section deals primarily with the pay of the legionaries, and the matter of auxiliary pay is discussed below in the section on auxiliaries. The soldiers of the early Republic were not paid, but were expected to serve in the army out of a sense of duty, providing their own equipment. When the army was mustered each year for the duration of the campaigning season, and then sent home in time for harvest, the absence of remuneration was not burdensome, but not all wars could be brought to a conclusion within one season. The war with the Etruscan city of Veii involved a long siege, lasting from 406 BC to 396 BC. The men were kept under arms for the winters as well as the summers, so the soldiers were given no opportunity to return home to gather the harvest. Although there was not normally any state assistance for the soldiers, in this instance military pay (*stipendium*) was introduced, probably calculated on a daily basis, but nothing is known of the amounts paid or whether officers received more than the men. It was possibly at this time that financial assistance for the cavalry was introduced.

There is little evidence to show how much the soldiers were paid in succeeding years until the second century, when Polybius says that the rate was 2 obols per day for the soldiers, 4 obols for the centurions, and 1 drachma for the cavalry. Since Polybius wrote in Greek, he converted the amounts into Greek equivalents, which causes problems for scholars who try to estimate equivalent Roman monetary values. There are only a few pieces of evidence that attest to exact figures for legionary pay, so historians must extrapolate backward and forward from these fixed points to theorize about earlier and later rates of pay. It is known that under Augustus the legionaries received 225 *denarii* per annum, paid to them in three installments (*stipendia*) in January, May, and September (Alston, 1994; Tacitus, *Annals* 1.17). It is not attested that there had been any increase in pay from Julius Caesar's day, so it can be assumed that under Caesar and under Augustus military pay was 225 *denarii* per year. It is known that Caesar doubled pay before the civil wars were fought with Pompey (Suetonius, *Divus Julius* 26.3), so it follows that the previous rate of pay was 112.5 *denarii.*

This does not sit well with the evidence of Polybius, who sets the daily pay of the legionaries at 2 obols, which were worth one-third of a drachma. If the drachma was equivalent to the Roman *denarius,* the pay works out at a fraction over 3 *asses* per day, a figure that some scholars find hard to accept. Watson (1969) suggests that the problem hinges on the retariffing of the bronze *asses* at some unknown date during the Republic. In the early period there were 10 *asses* to the *denarius,* and Watson estimates legionary pay at 5 *asses* per day, a total of 180 *denarii* per annum. When the *as* was retariffed at 16 to the *denarius,* military pay was reduced to 112.5 *denarii.* This implies a reduction in the standard of living of the legionaries, but since Gaius Gracchus passed a law in 123 BC abolishing the deductions for clothing, this probably compensated for the reduction.

From Caesar to Domitian, a period of over a hundred years, there was no increase in military pay. Probably in AD 83, Domitian awarded the soldiers a rise, either by rounding off the three installments of 75 *denarii* to 100 *denarii,* or as

## SUPPLEMENTS TO MILITARY PAY

From time to time soldiers could look forward to extra cash from Imperial donatives, from booty, and from their own financial activities such as money lending and property transactions. On their accession, emperors usually awarded a donative to the Praetorian Guardsmen, but payments to the rest of the army are only rarely attested. At his death Augustus bequeathed certain sums to all the armed forces, including 125 *denarii* to each Praetorian Guardsman and 75 *denarii* to each legionary. Succeeding emperors generally paid out sums to the army whenever an important victory had been won. Marcus Aurelius, however, refused to do so when his finances were strained. Other emperors paid unexpected donatives on special occasions. Hadrian, for example, paid a total of 75 million *denarii* to the soldiers during his reign, on various special occasions, for instance to mark his accession, and sometime later to celebrate the adoption of his intended heir Aelius Caesar. Antoninus Pius paid sums on the marriage of his daughter, but the amounts are not known. There may have been more occasions when extra cash was paid to the army, but unfortunately the sources are lacking. After the reigns of Severus and Caracalla, donatives were paid to the army more regularly (Campbell, 1984; Le Bohec, 1994).

The value of booty taken in wars is harder to assess, but it was always a possible means of increasing income. Tacitus (*Histories* 3.19.6) says that the spoils from a city taken by storm were awarded to the soldiers. In AD 260, during the reign of Gallienus, the whole of Gaul, Spain, and Germany broke away from Rome. For the next fourteen years the western provinces were ruled by provincial governors who styled themselves emperors and their territory the *Imperium Galliarum,* or the Gallic Empire. The rulers of this breakaway state could not always control their armies. The soldiers' lust for booty was too strong for the Gallic Emperor Postumus, who was murdered by his troops because he refused to allow his armies to sack Moguntiacum (modern Mainz, Germany). Some idea of the amount of booty brought home from foreign wars can be ascertained from the monuments in the Forum in Rome, specifically the reliefs on the Arch of Titus celebrating the conquest of Judaea, and on the Arch of Severus showing the spoils from the Parthian capital.

Extortion was another means of supplementing military pay. This is securely attested in the eastern provinces, where records are better preserved, but presumably the soldiers were no better behaved in the western provinces. The number of times that the Prefect of Egypt issued edicts to try to curb the behavior of the soldiers only serves to illustrate that the authorities were powerless to eradicate the problem. A papyrus dating to the second century AD records the accounts of a businessman who regularly entered certain sums paid to soldiers for extortion, for which he uses the Greek word *diaseismos* (Campbell, 1994). This may have been a sort of protection racket, perhaps only one example among many.

Soldiers were exempt from direct tax payments and from the reign of Domitian they did not pay the indirect taxes of *portoria* or *vectigalia*. The exemption extended to veterans and to their wives, children, and parents (Tacitus, *Annals* 13.35.2). Military men could run businesses while they were still serving, and many of them probably did so without hindrance or breaking the law, but most of the evidence for soldiers as businessmen and property owners derives from the law codes, concerning cases where there were disputes. A soldier called Cattianus sought justice because a dealer had illegally sold his slaves (*CJ* 4.51.1) and another soldier complained that his brother had sold his share in a vineyard, without asking his permission, in order to settle a debt (*CJ* 3.37.2). Typical of Roman realism, tax exemptions were declared invalid on the soldiers' illegal transactions (Tacitus, *Annals* 13.51.1).

Marble head of the Emperor Septimius Severus, who openly acknowledged that his power rested on the army. He realized the importance of making military service more attractive, raising soldiers' pay for the first time in a century and legalizing their marriages. When he died he told his sons to look after the soldiers and ignore everyone else. (Photo courtesy of David Brearley)

Suetonius implies (*Domitian* 7), by adding a fourth *stipendium* so that the soldiers were paid on a quarterly basis instead of every four months, either of which methods effectively raised the rate of pay to 300 *denarii* per annum. If Domitian did add a fourth installment, there was a reversion to the old system later on.

The rate of inflation was probably negligible in the first two centuries AD, but a series of price rises has been detected beginning in the reign of Marcus Aurelius. This may explain in part the increase in military pay by Severus, but there is no evidence to show exactly what the rise was worth. Scholars therefore fall back on estimates, which vary from 400 to 500 *denarii* per annum. No one is on sure ground from this point onward, so when the sources attest that Caracalla granted a further increase worth 50 percent of the sums arranged by his father, the estimates vary from an annual rate of 600 to 750 *denarii*. After the death of Caracalla, the Emperor Macrinus could not afford to pay the wages that had been promised to the troops, but at the same time he could not afford to refuse to pay them if he was to remain emperor (Dio 78.36.3). In the third century, it is suggested that the Emperor Maximinus doubled the pay, but some scholars dispute this, insisting that military pay remained the same until the reign of Diocletian (Le Bohec, 1994). With or without an increase in the later third century, inflation drastically reduced the buying power of the soldiers' salaries. For a short time, pay in cash was commuted into pay in kind, until the financial problems of the Empire were solved.

The pay of the junior and senior officers is more difficult to establish. According to Polybius, the centurions of the Republican armies were paid double the rate of the soldiers. This double rate may have continued into the Empire.

Standardization presumably applied, since as Fink (1971) points out, the centurions who took up successive posts in several legions in different provinces would hardly have done so if there were variations in the pay scales. The only evidence for senior officers' pay derives from an inscription from Thorigny in France (*CIL* XIII 3162), which reveals that the annual salary of a tribune in the third century AD was 6,250 *denarii*, but there is no evidence on the inscription whether he was a senatorial *tribunus laticlavius* or one of the less senior equestrian tribunes. Le Bohec (1994) presents a table of likely rates of pay for officers of the legions and their auxiliary equivalents, basing his figures on work by Dobson (1972; 1974).

Junior officers, the *principales,* and some men with specialist functions were paid at one and a half times and twice the rate of basic pay, and were called accordingly *sesquiplicarii* and *duplicarii.* Only one instance is known of a *triplicarius,* a soldier on triple pay (Le Bohec, 1994). There was a distinction between the soldiers called *immunes* who performed special tasks and the higher paid junior officers, in that the *immunes* were only paid at the basic rate and received nothing for their special skills. The standard bearers such as the *signiferi,* the *imaginiferi* who carried the portrait of the emperor, and the *aquiliferi* who carried the legionary eagle, all qualified for extra pay, as did the clerical staff such as the *beneficiarii* and the *commentarienses.*

When pay was due, three times each year, the soldiers were lined up on the parade ground to receive their money. The preparations for pay day probably involved calculating how much surplus was already in the fort's coffers and how much extra would be required, and then requesting cash to be sent from provincial headquarters to cover the necessary amounts. A collection of letters survives, detailing large amounts of money to be transported to military units in Egypt: 73,000 *denarii* for the soldiers of an *ala,* 65,000 *denarii* for the men of a cohort, and 343,000 *denarii* for legionaries (Alston, 1994). Military escorts were sent to transport the pay. There is evidence that a convoy of soldiers from Dura-Europos in Syria performed this task in the third century AD (Le Bohec, 1994). (Unlike Western films, sword-and-sandal Roman epics never make much use of this inviting scenario.)

Josephus describes a Roman pay parade during the war in Judaea (*Jewish War* 5.349–351). This particular pomp and ceremony was arranged to impress the Judaeans, but perhaps it describes the normal procedure at most pay parades, when the money due to each man was counted out. Certain deductions were made—for food, clothes, weapons, armor, personal savings, and the burial club, where money was collected to give the deceased a good send off and a nice tombstone. Tacitus (*Annals* 1.17) lists the grievances of a soldier called Percennius, who complained that out of his salary he had to pay for clothing, weapons, and tents, and also had to find money to bribe the centurions to avoid doing extra fatigues. The latter payment was taken on by the more kindly emperors after Otho started to pay centurions *vacationes munerum* to cover this little unofficial privilege.

Papyrus records show that although some amounts such as those for food were standard, other deductions varied. This discrepancy would probably arise because the first deductions for weapons and armor need not be repeated for some considerable time, unless the soldier had lost or damaged some of his equipment. A famous papyrus from the double fortress of Nicopolis (Egypt) itemizes the deductions from the military pay of two Roman citizen soldiers, Quintus Julius Proculus and Gaius Valerius Germanus. The record covers all three installments (*stipendia*) in January, May, and September of AD 81, but unfortunately no unit is named. Some scholars consider that the two men were legionaries (see Alston, 1994; Fink, 1971; Watson, 1969), whereas others insist that they were auxiliaries (Goldsworthy, 2003; Speidel, 1973). It is known that auxiliary units were present with the legions at Nicopolis, and the fact that the soldiers were Roman citizens does not preclude the possibility that the papyrus concerns auxiliary pay, since citizens could and did serve in the *auxilia.*

The argument will probably never be solved, but taken from a purely administrative point of view, the information reveals how the records were kept and how deductions were taken from each man's pay, which in many eastern provinces was issued in Greek *drachmae* rather than *denarii*. On each of the three pay days the two soldiers were charged 80 *drachmae* for food (*in victum*), 12 *drachmae* for boots and socks (*caligas fascias*), and 10 *drachmae* for hay (*faenaria,* interpreted either as bedding or a share in the feed for a pack mule, if the soldiers were legionaries, or fodder if they were auxiliary cavalrymen). There were deductions from each installment, the first one in January being 20 *drachmae* for the camp Saturnalia; this was possibly a mess bill for the holiday celebrations held in the previous December. From the second installment, both soldiers paid out 4 *drachmae* to the standards (*ad signum*), which may have been a contribution to the burial fund, and on the third pay day the two men were charged 145.5 *drachmae* for clothing. Since there are no comparable records revealing such minute detail, it is impossible to say whether this was typical of all units.

There was a savings bank system where the soldiers could deposit money, though the amounts were probably paper figures rather than actual cash, and the final totals probably had to be calculated and requested when the men were due to retire. No one can say how much money there would be in the strongrooms of a legionary fortress at any one time, but it is known that Domitian set a limit on the amount of savings in cash that any soldier could keep inside the fort. This was after the Governor Saturninus attempted to usurp him in AD 89, gathering together the soldiers from the double legionary fortress of Mogontiacum (Mainz), and presumably with their consent, extracting all their combined savings to finance his venture.

The military records were scrupulously kept by the clerks, showing how much money each soldier had already saved, how much he had deposited from his current installment, and the new total in the regimental savings bank. The Roman clerical assistants would keep at least two sets of financial records, since their accounts were sent to the procurator (Davies, 1967).

## Supplies

The Romans of the Republic learned about supply systems empirically, from their experiences in several wars. During the long struggle with Hannibal, the Carthaginians constantly raided and destroyed crops, so valuable supplies were denied to the Romans. Until they had secured Sicily and Sardinia, the Romans had to buy grain at tremendously inflated prices from Egypt and then had to guarantee its transport, protecting their sea lanes and above all their ports.

The wars with Carthage placed the Romans on a rapid learning curve with regard to all aspects of war and in particular about supplies. After the disaster of Cannae and Hannibal's efforts to seduce or force the Italian cities away from their alliances with Rome, the city of Capua defected and was besieged from 212 to 211 BC. Livy (25.20.1–2) describes how the Romans secured their supply lines for this siege to provide for two consular armies, by establishing a depot for the collection of grain at Casilinum north of Capua and building a new fortification at the mouth of the Volturno River, covering the routes from the west. In the south, General Fabius Maximus fortified the port of Puteoli to ensure the delivery of supplies for the armies in Campania.

When the Romans went abroad to fight, they fared less well. During the first invasion of Sicily, their supply lines were not fully operational, and in Spain, Gnaeus and Publius Scipio complained of the lack of supplies. Special dispatches of clothing and provisions were hastily arranged by the Senate (Livy 23.48.10–23.49.4), but there was a scandal when the Romans experimented with the use of contractors, who failed to deliver what they had promised. The problem of supplies in Spain had not changed much by the time Pompey the Great arrived there, and he wrote in desperation to the Senate complaining that he had used his own money to buy food and other supplies for his armies. It should be noted that it is particularly difficult to maintain an invading army in Spain. As King Henri IV of France (1589–1610) pointed out, it is a country where small armies are defeated and large ones starve, so the Spanish experience is perhaps not wholly representative of the problems of supplying Roman armies campaigning abroad.

Using a variety of means, the Romans were able to obtain all their needs, including food and water for the soldiers and animals, fuel for campfires and cooking, and all the materials that an army needs such as clothing, harness, and other equipment. During peacetime there was a regular supply system using the well-established roads of the Empire to bring in produce and materials from near and far. On campaign the Romans combined foraging, requisitioning (bordering on pillage), and supply lines (Roth, 1999). Caesar's works are particularly illuminating with regard to supplies and how they were obtained, transported, and guarded. Appropriation of other people's crops was common while on campaign. Caesar recounts how he captured the stores at Avaricum (*Gallic War* 7.32) and later how he captured the stores of the Bituriges (*Gallic War* 8.3). Josephus refers to sickles carried by the soldiers (*Jewish War* 2.95), and Tacitus says that during the reign of Nero in the AD 60s Corbulo's troops harvested the crops when they reached cultivated land (*Annals* 14.24).

There is some debate as to how much the soldiers were expected to carry on the march. It was said that Severus Alexander provided supply dumps for his troops, so that they did not have to carry supplies for the usual period of seventeen days (Severus Alexander, *Historia Augusta* 47.1). Ammianus Marcellinus (17.92) also says that it was normal practice for soldiers to carry rations (*annona*) to last seventeen days. Modern scholars have disputed this figure, especially since Josephus (*Jewish War* 3.95) says that the Romans carried food supplies for three days. Much depends upon the type of food that was carried; it has been suggested that some of it may have been in biscuit form, which weighed less than grain (Le Bohec, 1994).

With the growth of the Empire, the supply system had to evolve in order to provide for thousands of soldiers, horses, and pack animals stationed in permanent forts and fortresses in most of the provinces. The tried and tested methods of supplying an army at war were still relevant, since even when the frontiers were established, the Romans did not abandon offensive or defensive campaigns, where foraging and supply lines were necessary. For the troops stationed in the provinces, however, foraging was not suitable, so other methods were necessary, combining the transport of food and other supplies over long distances, requisitioning supplies from the local area, and growing crops and raising animals on military lands.

The Romans were quite capable of long-distance transport of goods. Apart from the shipments of grain to feed the population of Rome, there are documented cases where the produce of one province was shipped or carried to another. Dio records (60.24.5) that the governor of the Spanish province of Baetica was responsible for gathering and transporting grain to Africa across the straits of Gibraltar, and in the third century, grain from Britain was shipped to the Rhine for the army of the German provinces. Conversely, analysis of grain from South Shields in northern England showed that it probably came from the Netherlands. Perhaps over shorter distances, supplies were carried by ships along the Danube, as attested in the duty roster of *cohors I Hispanorum Veterana,* which records that some soldiers had been sent to the grain ships (*ad naves frumentarias*).

Local provision was probably the most widely used method of supplying the armies. The produce to be purchased was estimated by the provincial governor, and a fixed price was set for foodstuffs. Collection was carried out by the military authorities, or by the procurator and his staff where relevant, or by the local townsmen or tribal leaders, depending on the area where the supplies were to be requisitioned. Papyrus records show that men were detailed to collect barley, which was normally used to feed the horses, and the soldiers were given a hay allowance in cash for which they signed receipts (Fink, 1971). It has been suggested that the military presence stimulated provincial agriculture, providing an incentive to grow more crops than were necessary to feed the natives. In northern Britain it has been suggested that the highland zones, more notable today for stock raising than for agriculture, could have produced more grain than hitherto imagined, enabling the army in the hinterland of Hadrian's Wall to provision itself from sources close to home.

It is also possible that the army grew some of its own food. Tacitus refers to fields set aside for the use of the soldiers, and at Newstead in southern Scotland sickles were found inside the fort. They had been well used and repaired. An inscription (*CIL* VIII 4508) mentions a detachment that was sent to make hay, and a soldier from *cohors I Hispanorum Veterana* was sent across the Danube "to defend the crops." The accumulated evidence indicates that the soldiers guarded and harvested crops, but of course there is no proof that these crops were grown on lands that belonged to the army. The possibility should not be rejected since Roman auxiliary forts and legionary fortresses were surrounded by clearly demarcated lands that were owned and administered by the army, usually designated by the terms *prata* and *territorium*. In Spain, two inscribed boundary stones marked the division between the *prata legionis* of *legio IV* and the lands of Juliobriga and Segisama (*ILS* 2354; 2355), and another from Dalmatia attests to a boundary between a private estate and the *prata legionis* at the settlement of Burnum. The legion had moved from Burnum, but it is probable that the military authorities still regarded the land as theirs (Wilkes, 1969). In Britain, an auxiliary cavalry unit claimed the land at Chester-le-Street seemingly after it had been absent for a while (*RIB* 1049; Salway, 1991), but the term used is *territorium*. An inscription from Aquincum records building work on the *territorium legionis* of *legio II Adiutrix* in the reign of Severus Alexander (AD 222–235).

There is considerable debate about the exact meanings of *territorium* and *prata,* and how they related to each other. It is probable that *territorium* refers to all the lands administered by the military authorities, and *prata* refers to only a part of the whole (Le Bohec, 1994). Strictly interpreted, *prata* ought to refer to meadows, perhaps for grazing animals and for producing hay.

The staple diet of legionaries and auxiliaries was wheat. In the papyrus records, barley is mentioned several times. Soldiers were delegated to collect it, usually denoted by an entry saying "to the barley" (*ad hordeum*) or equivalent abbreviations (Fink, 1971). Although its main purpose was feed for the horses, the soldiers did eat it when necessary, and it was used as a punishment ration. According to Vegetius (*Epitoma Rei Militaris* 1.13), recruits who did not perform well were issued barley rations until they could demonstrate their proficiency before their senior officers. It used to be thought that cereals formed the main part of the military diet, but the soldiers ate meat whenever they could. Part of the standard military fare was fresh or salted pork, and sausages, ham, and bacon were also eaten. Other rations would include peas, beans, lentils, cheese, salt, olive oil, and wine (Davies, 1971; Roth, 1999).

Food was stored inside the forts in specially constructed granaries, usually sited next to the *principia* or headquarters building. The stone-built granaries are usually immediately recognizable from their ground plans. The walls were reinforced by evenly spaced buttresses, and the floors were usually raised on pillars, to facilitate the circulation of air, and to prevent rats and mice from entering. It is not known whether the grain and other produce was stored in bins, or in sacks stacked up or laid on shelves. There was probably a particular day when grain rations were given out to each *contubernium*, as both Livy (23.2.2) and Caesar (*Gallic War* 1.16.5; 6.33.4) refer to distribution days for rations, but this may only concern an army on campaign.

In the later Empire, payments to the army were made partly or wholly in rations, under a system that is not fully understood, known as the *annona militaris* (Develin, 1971). Some scholars suggest that this could have begun as early as the reign of Trajan (Le Bohec, 1994). A large part of the food supply of Rome was levied as a tax in kind administered by an equestrian with the title *Praefectus Annonae*, so it is possible that the system was extended or diverted to feed the army, but this remains hypothetical.

Under the heading of supplies, an ever-present need of any army is for water and for fuel. The water supply of several forts has been studied in Britain and Germany, where storage tanks, extensive lead piping, and sophisticated bathing establishments are well known. On campaign, lack of an adequate water supply could shift the balance between success and failure, especially for cavalry operations.

Fuel consumption in a Roman fort or fortress would have been vast. Caesar regarded shortage of wood for campfires as seriously as shortage of food itself. In the case of the Roman Imperial army, huge amounts of timber would have been needed for cooking, for central heating in officers' houses and in some headquarters buildings, and most of all for heating the baths that were attached to all forts. The Romans distinguished between timber for building and wood for fuel (*lignum*), and foraging for fuel was termed *lignari* (Roth, 1999). The papryus records of *cohors XX Palmyrenorum* at Dura-Europos in Syria show that in the early third century Zebidas, son of Barneus, from the century of Nigrinus, had been sent to gather fuel for the baths (*missus lignari balnei*) (Fink, 1971). There is some evidence from Britain that the Romans used coal for fuel.

## ELITE OR SPECIAL UNITS

This section incorporates Roman military units that differed from the legions and the *auxilia,* but were not necessarily "elite" in the sense that they were high-status, hand-picked troops chosen for their prowess, appearance, or proven ability. The Praetorian Guard and the *equites singulares* readily fall into the category of elite units, but the other types of units are described here because they performed specific tasks, and they were stationed in Rome and Italy, rather than in the provinces.

### Guard Troops: The Praetorian Guard

During the Republic, a general at the head of troops was forbidden to cross the city boundaries, and there were no official bodyguards for any of the magistrates. On campaign, military commanders assembled a *cohors praetoria* to guard them, taking the name from the *praetorium* or camp headquarters. Both Mark Antony and Octavian assembled large bodyguards, and at the end of the civil wars Octavian did not disband his praetorian cohort. In 27 or 28 BC he established nine cohorts of the Praetorian Guard to protect him and his family. From the second century AD, the Praetorians accompanied the emperors to various wars but without tactical functions. They trained as legionaries, although their dress, armor, and equipment were much more elaborate, their status was much higher, and they were paid more than the legionaries and auxiliaries.

There were good career prospects for Praetorians. In the early first century, when the legionaries were paid 225 *denarii* per annum, the Praetorians probably received 375 *denarii.* The differential increased under Domitian, who raised legionary pay to 300 *denarii* and that of the Praetorians to 1,000 *denarii.* Whenever the emperors paid a donative to the troops, the Praetorians always received more than the soldiers. The custom was soon established of paying a money gift to the Praetorians on the accession of a new emperor and on any special occasion such as a military victory, or the promotion of a member of the Imperial family. As a result, the Guardsmen and officers could soon accumulate a small fortune, and since they served for only sixteen years they could progress to further military posts while still only in their mid-thirties. A Praetorian Guardsman could be directly promoted to centurion in one of the provincial legions. An ex-centurion of the Guard had even greater advantages and could reach the rank of *primus pilus* in a legion and then perhaps return to Rome and go on to a

Sculptural relief of the second century AD, showing officers and soldiers of the Praetorian Guard. (The Art Archive/Musée du Louvre Paris/Dagli Orti )

succession of commands in the various military forces in the city. Some of them could progress to an administrative career, becoming Imperial procurators in the provinces.

Augustus excluded senators from command of the Praetorians, appointing two equestrian Praetorian Prefects in 2 BC, on the same collegiate principle as the consuls so that one could keep the other in check, the notorious Sejanus being one exception to this rule. The Praetorians did not enjoy direct political power, but they exercised enormous influence, and their acquiescence or otherwise at the accession of new emperors was crucial. During the reign of Augustus, only three cohorts of the Praetorian Guard were intended to be in Rome at one time, while the other six were housed in different Italian cities. However, under Tiberius, when Sejanus's influence was at its zenith, the Praetorians were housed all together in their newly built camp (*castra praetoria*) on the northeastern outskirts of Rome.

There is some debate about the size of the Praetorian cohorts. In Augustus's day they probably comprised 480 men like the legionary and auxiliary quingenary cohorts, though some scholars insist that they were 1,000 strong from the very beginning. More recently, Le Bohec (1994) has suggested that the *castra praetoria* at 16.7 hectares was too small to accommodate cohorts of 1,000 men. At an unknown date before AD 47 three more cohorts were added to the original nine, and in AD 69 during his short reign Vitellius dismissed the Praetorians and created a new guard, allegedly of 16 cohorts, each 1,000 strong. This new force could scarcely have been properly housed and organized before Vespasian came to power, and reduced the Praetorians to the Augustan levels of nine cohorts of 480 men. Domitian created a tenth cohort, but opinion differs as to whether or not he also increased the size of the cohorts.

After the assassination of the Emperors Commodus and Pertinax, the Praetorians sold out to the highest bidder, Didius Julianus, who was emperor for just over two months after paying the Praetorians a large donative. When Severus became emperor in June 193, he disbanded the original Praetorian Guard and reconstituted it with loyal soldiers from his own armies, with a cohort strength of 1,000. The Praetorian Guard finally met its end at the hands of Constantine, who abolished it in AD 312, because the soldiers had fought for his rival Maxentius.

The Praetorian cohorts were numbered I to IX, increasing to X under Domitian, and were commanded by tribunes. Each cohort was divided into ten centuries, commanded as in the legions by centurions. The most senior centurion of the Guard was the *trecenarius,* and his second in command was the *princeps castrorum.* The title of the *trecenarius* is indicative of his command of 300 mounted Imperial guardsmen (*speculatores*), an elite force of horsemen incorporated into the Guard, and forming a special bodyguard for the emperor, distinct from the mounted guards or *equites singulares Augusti* (Le Bohec, 1994, 21; Speidel, 1994, 33–34).

Initially, all the Praetorians were Italians, but in the second century recruitment was opened up to a few men from Pannonia and Dalmatia, and then Severus brought in his Illyrian troops. This difference in origins, and the close association to the emperors who relied on their support may have contributed to the growing arrogance of the Praetorians of the third century, who terrorized the inhabitants of Italy.

## Guard Troops: The Equites Singulares

The forerunners of the *equites singulares Augusti* were the German horsemen that Julius Caesar gathered together as a bodyguard while campaigning in Gaul (Speidel, 1994). The *Germani corporis custodi* were taken over by Augustus, but were disbanded after the Varan disaster of AD 9, when the German tribes wiped out three legions. Under Tiberius the guard units reappeared. The name *Germani* is attested by Josephus and Suetonius, but on gravestones the more usual title is *Caesaris Augusti corporis custodes.* In the first century AD, the bodyguards were not regular army units and could be commanded by anyone whom the emperor thought fit. Caligula appointed a gladiator called Sabinus.

The *equites singulares Augusti* were probably established under the Flavian emperors (Campbell, 1994) or under Trajan (Speidel, 1994). Trajan's 1,000-strong guard unit, largely recruited from the Batavians of Lower Germany, was housed in a camp in Rome on the Caelian hill near the modern Lateran palace, until Severus doubled the size of the *singulares* and built a second camp next to the old one for another 1,000 men. Both camps remained in occupation throughout the history of the guards.

The *singulares Augusti* were commanded by a tribune and divided into *turmae* under decurions like other cavalry units. They accompanied the emperors on campaigns and provided cavalry support for the Praetorians, so the Praetorian Prefects were ultimately responsible for them. Recruitment was predominantly from cavalry units of Germania Superior, Germania Inferior, Raetia, Noricum, and Pannonia, roughly equating to modern Germany, Austria, and Hungary. Thracians enlisted in AD 114 (*ILS* 2182), and a cavalryman called Ulpius Titus was selected from an *ala* in Pannonia in the late second century (*CIL* VI 3308=*ILS* 2210). In the early third century, more Batavians were recruited (*ILS* 2188).

In the provinces, the governors assembled bodyguards called *equites singulares,* together with an infantry equivalent, *pedites singulares,* but these were not permanent units. The men were seconded from the cavalry and infantry units of the provincial garrison on temporary postings. They remained on the registers of their original units and received the same pay as before; the honor of serving in the provincial guard units did not extend to a pay rise. The numbers of *singulares* attached to a governor's entourage may have varied. In a large province there may have been units of 1,000 men, made up of 500 infantry and 500 cavalry, but this is only speculative. The commander of the *singulares* was usually listed as a *praepositus,* which often signifies a temporary or extraordinary command, in keeping with the temporary nature of the governor's bodyguard.

## Troops in Rome: The Urban Cohorts and the Vigiles

The need for a city police force was glaringly apparent at the end of the Republic, but the establishment of such an organization was not really possible under the old system, when there was no tradition of standing army units and the scramble for personal power escalated to the point of civil war. Significantly, Augustus waited until probably 13 BC before creating the Urban Cohorts (*Cohortes Urbanae*), commanded by the city prefect (*Praefectus Urbi*). The date is nowhere attested beyond doubt, but it is thought that when the senator Lucius Calpurnius Piso was appointed as the first permanent city prefect, the troops were most likely established at the same time.

Each of the Urban Cohorts was 500 strong and commanded by a tribune assisted by six centurions. There were three cohorts in Italy, and at a later date two more Urban Cohorts were established—one at Lyons, where there was an important mint, and another at Carthage. Augustus placed some of the Urban Cohorts in other Italian cities so that not all of them were brigaded together in Rome, but when the Praetorian camp was built in the reign of Tiberius the Urban Cohorts were housed there, even though they were answerable to the senatorial prefect of the city and not to the equestrian Praetorian Prefects. Some of the men may have occupied smaller watch-houses within the city, and some may have been outstationed. For instance, there is evidence that single Urban Cohorts were stationed at the ports of Puteoli and Ostia.

Later emperors increased the number of Urban Cohorts to six at some time before AD 47 and to a maximum of seven under Claudius. When Vitellius seized power in AD 69, he reduced the number to four cohorts, and Antoninus Pius returned to three cohorts. Severus retained the three cohorts but increased the numbers of men. Aurelian moved the Urban Cohorts in AD 270 to a new purpose-built camp, called the *castra urbana,* which was situated on the Campus Martius. Constantine spared them the fate of the Praetorians, but they became less and less of a military force.

The *vigiles,* or city fire brigades, were created by Augustus in AD 6. Republican Rome was a closely packed city with many timbered buildings and was therefore always at risk from fires. During the late Republic, Marcus Licinius Crassus had notoriously kept a force of trained slaves to fight fires, not for the good of the city but so that he could buy up burning properties at ridiculously cheap prices, put the fire out, and develop the site. If the owner would not sell, then the property burned and Crassus remained as rich as he was before. Under Augustus, the aedile Egnatius Rufus gathered another slave fire brigade with which he successfully controlled several fires, but political ambition led to his downfall. He was accused of conspiracy by the Senate and executed. In 21 BC Augustus took over the remnants of Rufus's gangs, and placed a force of 600 slaves at the disposal of the aediles to put out fires. These men formed the basis of the units of *vigiles.*

Augustus divided the city of Rome into fourteen administrative regions; the division of the *vigiles* into seven cohorts each 1,000 strong therefore implies that one cohort was responsible for two regions of the city. Each cohort was commanded by a tribune and contained seven centuries, commanded by centurions. The overall commander of the *vigiles* was an equestrian prefect (*Praefectus Vigilum*), ranking below the other equestrian prefectures, of the food supply (*annona*), Egypt, and the Praetorian Guard. Evidence from inscriptions show that a centurion of the *vigiles* often progressed to the post of centurion in the Urban Cohorts, then the Praetorian Guard, and thereafter to varied careers in the legions, sometimes reaching the post of *primus pilus* (Campbell, 1994).

Tacitus did not include the *vigiles* in his list of armed forces in AD 23, indicating that they were not regarded as soldiers. Although the original units were formed from slaves, the status of the *vigiles* steadily rose in importance. The ranks were filled by freedmen under Augustus, and in Tiberius's reign the term of service was set at six years, after which the men received Roman citizenship. Later this was reduced to three years, and citizens began to enrol in the *vigiles.* At the beginning of the third century, they were regarded as soldiers, but they did not fulfill military functions.

## THE AUXILIARY UNITS

The antecedents of the *auxilia* of the Imperial army can be seen in the *Alae Sociorum* of the early Republic and in the temporary troops usually requisitioned from friendly kings in or near to the areas where the Roman army was to operate. For the Gallic campaigns, Caesar raised 4,000 cavalry from the Aedui and their allies (*Gallic War* 1.15), from the Remi, the Lingones, and other states (*Gallic War* 8.11–12). The commanders of the horsemen were usually native chiefs with the title of prefect (*praefectus*). For instance, Caesar calls Vertiscus prefect of the horsemen of the Remi, and Dumnorix commanded (the word used is *praeerat*) the cavalry of the Aedui. Client kings sometimes contributed troops for a campaign under the terms of their agreement with Rome. When the wars were over, they were usually dismissed to their homes. Very little is known about how or if these soldiers were paid, how they were quartered in camp, or how they fought.

As the Roman Empire expanded, the need for permanent, more regularly organized units increased. The early history of the *auxilia* is not clear. Tacitus informs us that the provincials outside Italy contributed recruits for naval crews, cavalry *alae,* and infantry cohorts, but in his enumeration of the troops in AD 23 he excuses himself from listing the auxiliary units because they were constantly moved around, and their numbers varied from time to time, reflecting the fluid situation before permanent forts were established. The stages in the transformation of the temporary auxiliary troops into the regular units have been examined by Saddington (1982), and though Cheesman's book (1914) is nearly a century old, it is still useful.

It may have been Augustus who regularized the number of soldiers in the early auxiliary units, establishing the size of the cohorts at six centuries of eighty men commanded by centurions, making a total of 480 like the legionary cohorts. Cavalry *alae* contained 512 men, made up of 16 *turmae* of 32 horsemen, commanded by decurions. For administrative purposes the numbers were rounded up or down to 500, as reflected in the titles *cohortes* and *alae quingenariae*. Commanders of these quingenary units were equestrian prefects (*praefecti*).

In the first century, perhaps under Vespasian or his sons Titus and Domitian, larger auxiliary units of 1,000 men were established, called *cohortes* and *alae milliariae*. The milliary infantry cohorts contained ten centuries of eighty men, and the milliary *alae* were made up of twenty-four *turmae*, each containing thirty-two men. They were commanded by tribunes, experienced officers of equestrian rank. The tribunes of the milliary *alae* ranked as senior to all other auxiliary commanders, but since there was never more than one of these units in each province, only a few officers would reach this post. *Cohortes equitatae* or mixed units containing infantry and cavalry, both 500 and 1,000 strong, began to appear during the early Empire. Their ancestry is obscure. It is usually considered that the horses and riders of the *cohortes equitatae* were inferior to those of the *alae*. The inference is found in the *Adlocutio* delivered by Hadrian at Lambaesis (*CIL* VIII 18042; *ILS* 2487; 9133–9135), which conveys the impression that the cavalry of the cohorts performed less brilliantly than the cavalry of the *alae*. This should not be interpreted to mean that the horsemen of the *cohortes equitatae* were nothing more than mounted infantry who rode to battle but fought on foot. The cavalry of the mixed units fought alongside the cavalry of the *alae* and not with the infantry centuries of their own cohorts. An unresolved problem concerns the exact number of horsemen in the *cohortes equitatae*. It is assumed that quingenary mixed units contained six centuries of infantry, with perhaps four *turmae* of cavalry totaling 128 horsemen, while milliary units contained ten infantry centuries and perhaps eight *turmae*, totaling 256 horsemen. Some scholars prefer to round these totals down to 120 and 240, respectively, but the rounded figures do not make sense if the horsemen were divided into *turmae* of 32 men. In the end, despite much use of scholarly ink and keyboard skills, no one knows the full complement of men in the *cohortes equitatae*.

Unit titles in the *auxilia* usually reflected the nationality of the original recruits, such as the *ala I Batavorum* raised from Batavian tribesmen, or *cohors V Lingonum* raised from the Lingones of Gaul. The soldiers were eventually replaced by local recruits from the areas where the units were stationed, so that after a few years there would be none of the original tribesmen left in the unit, but the name was retained even though it no longer reflected the ethnicity of the soldiers. As an exception to this practice of drawing replacements from the local area, the special units such as the Syrian or Palmyrene archers continued to recruit form their original homelands. Other units took their titles from the family name of the emperor. For example, several *alae* and cohorts were given the title *Flavia*, often in conjunction with a national name, such as *cohors I Flavia Damascenorum.* The function or armament of some units was occasionally included in the name. For instance, *ala I Hamiorum Syrorum sagittariorum* indicates a unit of mounted Syrian archers (*sagittarii*). Honorary titles were awarded after particularly loyal service, usually expressed as *pia fidelis,* abbreviated in documents and on inscriptions to *p.f.* Another abbreviation in some unit titles is *c.r.* indicating Roman citizens, but only the original soldiers were citizens, raised by Augustus from freed slaves when there was an urgent need for troops during the Pannonian revolt in AD 6, and after the Varan disaster in Germany in AD 9, when the supposedly defeated German tribes wiped out three legions while the Governor Quinctilius Varus was making arrangements for the settlement and Romanization of the conquered territories. Slaves legitimately received citizenship when they were freed, but Augustus insisted that only freeborn Roman citizens should serve in the legions, so he bent the rules a little to form citizen *cohortes* and *alae.* These units recruited their replacements from noncitizens as was the case for all other auxiliary forces, but kept their titles.

Conditions of service for the auxiliaries differed from those of the legionaries. Auxiliary soldiers served for twenty-five years, and at the end of their service they received Roman citizenship for themselves and their children. Serving soldiers were forbidden to marry, but the wording of auxiliary discharge certificates showed that the government recognized the relationships that the men may have formed with local women, and also the children born of the union.

The rate of pay of the auxiliary troops is a perennial problem for modern historians. Some scholars, without the benefit of absolute proof, have long believed that auxiliaries must have been paid less than the legionaries. The suggestion that auxiliary infantrymen were paid five-sixths of legionary pay was revived by M.P. Speidel (1973) and reiterated by M.A. Speidel (1992). Since it is known from Polybius's work and from Hadrian's address to the troops of Numidia that cavalrymen were paid more than the infantry, pay scales have been reconstructed that show three basic rates, with the auxiliary infantry as the lowest paid, then the legionaries equated with the cavalrymen of a *cohors equitata,* and finally the *equites legionis* on the same pay as the cavalry of the *alae* (Campbell, 1994). More recently, Alston (1994) argued for parity between legionary and auxiliary pay, on the premise that when regular pay was instituted for auxiliary troops, only the standard rates for infantry and cavalry would have been applied.

Like the junior officers in the legions, some of the auxiliary officers were paid at double and one and a half times the normal rate, indicated by their respective labels *duplicarii* and *sesquiplicarii*. The lack of precision as to what exactly *was* the normal rate hampers any calculation of the likely figures represented by one and a half times ordinary pay and double pay. The fact that a legionary could be appointed as a *duplicarius* in an *ala* ought to indicate that double pay in the auxiliary cavalry was worth more than the ordinary pay of a legionary, but this still does not help to establish what the ordinary rate was. For various estimates of the relative values of legionary and auxiliary pay for ordinary soldiers and for junior officers, see the tables in Watson (1969), Campbell (1994), and Le Bohec (1994).

## Camel Riders (*Dromedarii*)

In the eastern provinces, Roman army units often contained a few camel riders, who were usually attached to a *cohors equitata*. Between thirty-two and thirty-six *dromedarii* are listed in the rosters of *cohors XX Palmyrenorum equitata* at Dura-Europos in the early third century, and one or two were sent on missions with the cavalry and infantry. An entire 1,000-strong camel unit, the *ala I Ulpia dromedariorum milliaria*, was raised by Trajan and stationed in Syria. There was no consistency in the organization of the *dromedarii* as either infantry or cavalry. This probably depended on the systems in place in each province. The 1,000-strong unit just described was categorized as an *ala*, whereas the camel riders in *cohors XX Palmyrenorum* in Syria were attached to the infantry centuries. Their names were commonly listed at the end of each entry after all the other infantry soldiers, but in Egypt a *dromedarius* called Cronius Barbasatis was assigned to the cavalry *turma* of the decurion Salvianus. He was a volunteer and had not been transferred from another unit, so his skills were presumably recognized immediately on enlistment. However, it is generally considered that a *dromedarius* would usually enlist as an infantryman and serve for a few years in that capacity before becoming a camel rider.

## The National *Numeri*

Under the Emperor Trajan or possibly under Hadrian, a different type of military formation was established on the frontiers—the so-called national *numeri*, found principally in Germany, Dacia, and Africa. The title *numerus* simply means "unit," and unlike *ala* or *cohors* it does not denote a specific troop of a standard size or organization (Southern, 1989). Authors such as Caesar (*Gallic War* 1.18; 7.31) and Livy (33.22.7) use the term to describe "a number of soldiers," and Tacitus (*Agricola* 18.2) uses it to describe the military units of all types in Britain.

There is archaeological and epigraphic evidence that from the second century onward ethnic units of varying sizes were established in frontier forts, in particular in the Odenwald region of Germany, where small forts of 0.6 hectare were garrisoned principally by *numeri Brittonum*—British tribesmen perhaps withdrawn from northern England and southern Scotland by Trajan, or possibly by Hadrian. These units are described on inscriptions either as *numeri Brittonum*, or simply as *Brittones*. It seems that the title was not as important as the ethnic name, and often this name was followed by another distinguishing name derived from the place where the unit was stationed, for example *Brittones Triputienses*, or *Brittones Elantienses*. Similarly, *numeri* composed of soldiers from the eastern provinces were designated by an ethnic name and a place name, such as the *numerus Syrorum Malvensium*, a unit of Syrians in Africa, and the *numerus Palmyrenorum Porolissensium*, Palmyrenes stationed at Porolissum in Dacia.

The origins of the *numeri* can probably be traced to the occasional employment of irregular troops on campaigns, such as the Palmyrene archers who were attached to the Roman army in Judaea under Vespasian and Titus in AD 70–71. Similarly, groups of Moorish tribesmen (*Mauri*) were attached to the troops of the governor of Mauretania Caesariensis in AD 68 and may have been the forerunners of the *numeri Maurorum* in Dacia. Although these troops probably took part in campaigns, the functions of the *numeri* stationed on the frontiers may have been to patrol the less populated regions and to protect convoys, particularly in Dacia where they may have patrolled the routes to and from the mining areas. They may have acted as scouts beyond the frontiers, if the titles of the *numeri exploratorum* from the British and German frontiers are indicative of their purpose. One of these units, the *numerus exploratorum Germanicianorum Divitiensium*, occupied the large fort of Niederbieber from the early third century AD and may have been at least 1,000 strong. There was no uniformity of unit size in the *numeri*, which were perhaps organized on a tailor-made basis for different purposes. The *numeri* were frequently commanded by legionary centurions, who were sometimes given the title *praepositus*. This did not denote a specific rank such as prefect or tribune, but was a title often given to an officer in a temporary command. Sometimes the centurion in command of a *numerus* was also called *curator*, or the unit was described as "in charge of" (*sub cura*) a centurion. In the third century, commanders of *numeri* were more often prefects and tribunes.

## OFFICERS

During the Republic, the officers next in line to the consuls were the six tribunes of the legion and the prefects commanding the *Alae Sociorum*. Subordinate to these were the legionary centurions and the centurions and decurions of the allied troops. During the early and middle Republic, these Roman officers would serve for one season and then the troops would be disbanded, but during the war with Hannibal when the troops were in the field for many seasons, a body of experienced officers grew up, whose expertise would be useful in further campaigns. Without the institution of a standing army, expertise and experience could not be preserved, but there was already a class of semiprofessional soldiers who enrolled in one army after another, campaigning in Spain, Greece, and the east. Only a few decades after the second Punic War, the career of Spurius Ligustinus, narrated by Livy (42.34), demonstrates how soldiers could reenlist again and again in different armies and pursue what amounted to a military career. Ligustinus served in Macedonia, Greece, and Spain, mostly as a volunteer, and several times he was promoted to centurion after exemplary service. He did not resume the same rank when he reenlisted, but he always earned his promotion, along with his many rewards for bravery.

In the Imperial Roman army promotion was always a possibility, depending on ability, personal connections, and opportunities. There was a division between senatorial and equestrian posts, but it was not a boundary that could never be crossed. Social mobility for equestrians and for military men increased from Augustus's reign onward. Equestrian families could assemble sufficient resources for their descendants to qualify for entry to the Senate, and some military men could rise from the ranks to become centurions and eventually achieve equestrian status. Promotion was more rapid in wartime, so if an officer performed well and came to the notice of the emperor, he could be entrusted with special commands and be elevated to the Senate as a reward. A few soldiers rose through various appointments to become consul, as the several career inscriptions of Valerius Maximianus demonstrate. In the third century, when military men dominated the Roman world, an ordinary soldier could rise from the ranks to become emperor.

## Senatorial Officers

A senator would begin his military career in his twenties as a *tribunus laticlavius* in a legion, possibly in a province where a relative or other patron was governor. Appointments were sought by the young men themselves or by their relatives and friends on their behalf, and no shame attached to the procedure. Patronage at all levels was dispensed and accepted as a matter of course, as demonstrated by the surviving letters of recommendation that were addressed to officials and military commanders. Pliny recommended his friends to a provincial governor, perhaps Javolenus Priscus, with the comment that since the governor had no doubt found places for all his own friends, now it was the turn of Pliny's circle (*Letters* 2.13).

## EMPERORS WHO ROSE FROM HUMBLE BEGINNINGS

Roman emperors of the first two centuries were born into the senatorial class, but toward the end of the second century AD men who had started out from humbler origins rose to the position by dint of their political merit or their position in the armies. Publius Helvius Pertinax was one of the protégés of Marcus Aurelius, an emperor who noted the energies and talents of equestrians and army officers and promoted them to senatorial status. Pertinax was the son of a freedman whose business interests were in timber supplies. When Pertinax entered the army he quickly became an officer, commanding military units in several provinces, then went on to administrative posts. The Danubian Wars of Marcus Aurelius saw several officers rise in status, and Pertinax commanded various combined detachments called vexillations in Pannonia, a legion in Raetia, and rose to the consulship in AD 174 or 175. He governed Upper and Lower Moesia, Dacia, and Syria, and in 185 was sent to Britain to quell a military revolt, which he did with efficiency and ruthlessness. When Commodus was assassinated in AD 193, the Praetorian Prefect, Laetus, was instrumental in the acclamation of Pertinax as emperor. Despite giving the Praetorians a respectable donative, the guardsmen tired of him, allegedly because he was too strict for their tastes, and he was assassinated after only a few months.

The origins of the Emperor Macrinus were said to have been very lowly, but although he may have been born into a poor family in Mauretania in North Africa, he presumably acquired an education, since he served under Severus in Rome as legal adviser to the Praetorian Prefect, Plautianus. Macrinus was appointed by Caracalla as one of the Praetorian Prefects, the other candidate being Oclatinius Adventus, who had started out as a common soldier.

Accompanying the emperor into Parthia on the ill-fated expedition, Macrinus let it be known that there was an Imperial plot to remove him, and on this basis he arranged for the assassination of Caracalla in AD 217. Two days later the troops declared Macrinus emperor, and the Senate confirmed the appointment, glossing over the fact that he was not a senator. He survived until AD 218, only to meet his end at the hands of Severus's sister-in-law, Julia Maesa, who established her family members Elagabalus and Severus Alexander as emperors.

The first emperor to rise from the ranks of the army was Maximinus Thrax (the Thracian). He possessed enormous strength, but other qualities were presumably in evidence to allow him to reach officer status and go on to the command of a legion in Egypt. When Severus Alexander mounted his expedition to the Rhine in AD 235, Maximinus was in command of recruits from Pannonia. His military record ensured that when the young emperor was assassinated, the troops declared for him, but not unanimously. Some of the eastern soldiers were loyal to Severus Alexander, and some of the senatorial officers did not wish him well, but after eradicating all his immediate opponents, Maximinus remained emperor for another three years, campaigning successfully in Germany beyond the Rhine, finishing off what his predecessor had started. Preoccupied with these military necessities, Maximinus did not find time to go to Rome to strengthen his position. The Senate had confirmed him as emperor, but not with good grace, and a series of revolts and attempts at usurpation broke out. Fighting for his position, Maximinus treated his troops with great severity, turning some of them against him. He was killed by his own soldiers in AD 238.

The normal tour of duty as *tribunus laticlavius* was perhaps a year or longer, and after this a senator usually took up a succession of civil administrative posts before seeking appointment as legate of a legion. In the late Republic and particularly in Caesar's army, legates were selected by the general himself, to command legions or to carry out specific tasks. Republican legates were responsible to their general, not the Senate, a policy that Augustus could not afford to condone. He adopted the policy of personally appointing legionary legates, whose title *legati Augusti legionis* left no doubt about who had bestowed the command on them and to whom they were ultimately answerable, even if they were also subordinate to the authority of the provincial governor. These legates remained in command of the same legion for three or four years before moving on to other posts. In the early Empire, a senator was usually appointed as legionary legate after he had served as quaestor and aedile in Rome. By the end of the first century, however, the legionary legates were ex-praetors, in their early thirties and more experienced.

From the middle of the second century, if a senator was more interested in civil administration, he could excuse himself from taking up the post of legionary legate. This is demonstrated by the career inscription of Gaius Popilius Carus Pedo (*ILS* 1071), who served the Emperor Hadrian in a wide variety of administrative posts, but his military experience was limited to one tour of duty as tribune of *legio III Cyrenaica*. Perhaps this turned him against a military career, leading him to refuse a post as legionary legate. On the other hand, some men served as legate several times. Gaius Julius Quadratus Bassus, for example, was legate of eight different legions in the mid-second century (Campbell, 1994). It is generally considered that under Hadrian civil and military careers began to diverge, and the two inscriptions outlining the almost contemporary activities of Pedo and Bassus support the theory that senators began to specialize in either administrative or military matters in the second century.

Legionary command in Egypt did not follow the above pattern. Augustus installed an equestrian governor as soon as he took control of the country, and forbade any senator from visiting the province without special Imperial permission. This rule was never relaxed by his successors. The governors of Egypt were always equestrian prefects (*Praefecti Aegypti*), and the legionary commanders were not senatorial *legati,* as was normal in other provinces, but equestrian *praefecti legionis.* There was no senatorial *tribunus laticlavius* in the Egyptian legions.

Most senatorial officers spent only a short time in the armies and quickly went on to more prestigious and lucrative appointments as provincial governors. The ultimate aim was the consulship and then a senior post as governor of one of the larger provinces, where they commanded all the armed forces. They had no formal training except by experience. They may have read military manuals, studied the theory of warfare, and learned from other generals, but there was no officer training school and no necessity for recognized qualifications. As Goldsworthy (2003) points out, Roman army officers were by no means comparable to the professional officers of the armies of the eighteenth and nineteenth centuries. The first desirable attribute of a senatorial officer was the approval of the emperor, without which no one could hope to advance his career. Other desirable attributes included high social status, wealth, and intelligence.

## Equestrian Officers

It was only in times of prolonged wars that more professional officers emerged with extensive military experience, and in the later second century, Marcus Aurelius began to choose men who had shown great aptitude in preference to men whose only recommendation was birth and status. He found several of his officers among the equestrians with long service records, and he promoted them accordingly, usually by making them senators so that technically they qualified for the positions to which he promoted them. From then onward, the equestrians rose in importance in the army. The Emperor Septimius Severus created three new legions and placed equestrian prefects in command of each of them in place of senatorial legates, and in the mid-third century, the Emperor Gallienus divorced nearly all senators from command of the army, employing equestrians more frequently as legionary commanders and as provincial governors.

As in the Republican army, there were six tribunes in each Imperial legion; one of them was the senatorial *tribunus laticlavius,* and

Marcus Aurelius, emperor of Rome, 121–180. Marcus Aurelius found several of his officers among the equestrians and promoted them accordingly. (Library of Congress)

the other five were equestrian *tribuni angusticlavii.* Pliny obtained a post as military tribune for the author Suetonius (*Letters* 7.22), but Suetonius declined and recommended his relative Silvanus instead (Campbell, 1994; Watson, 1969). The *tribuni angusticlavii* were responsible for administrative duties, for overseeing the security of the camp gates, and for some judicial functions.

The career path of the equestrian officers differed from that of the senators (Devijver, 1989, 1992). Some equestrians were directly appointed as legionary centurions, but more often they chose appointments as commanders of the auxiliary units. During the first century AD, a standardized succession of three appointments began to evolve (*tres militiae*). An equestrian usually took up a first post as prefect of a 500-strong auxiliary infantry unit before becoming tribune of a legion, or possibly tribune of a 1,000-strong infantry cohort. The third post was usually as prefect of a cavalry *ala.* These successive appointments were commonly held for about three to four years and usually took the officers to different provinces. There was no compulsion to serve in all three posts. A few equestrian officers served in a fourth post (*militia quarta*) as commanders of milliary *alae.* Alternatively, there were other career prospects for equestrians. For instance, some of the smaller provinces with no legions were governed by equestrians, originally with the title prefect, but after the later first century AD the title changed to procurator.

The troops in Rome offered an alternative career to equestrians. The cohorts of the Praetorian Guard, the Urban Cohorts, and the *vigiles* were commanded by equestrian tribunes, and the pinnacle of the equestrian military career was the appointment to one or more of the four prefectures, of the food supply (*Praefectus Annonae*), of the *vigiles* (*Praefectus Vigilum*), of Egypt (*Praefectus Aegypti*), and of the Praetorian Guard (*Praefectus Praetorio*).

## Camp Prefect

One of the most senior officers of an Imperial legion, third in command after the legate and the *tribunus laticlavius,* was the camp prefect (*praefectus castrorum*). He was senior in rank to the five *tribuni angusticlavii.* The first attested camp prefect dates to the end of Augustus's reign, significantly when more permanent forts were being established. The duties of the camp prefect were concerned with maintenance of the fortress, ensuring that everything was in working order and, where relevant, cleaned. The post required extensive experience of military administration and functions, and was usually filled by men with long service records who had just served as *primus pilus,* the chief centurion of the legion.

## Primus Pilus

There was only one *primus pilus* post per legion, and it was usually only held for one year. The remaining fifty-eight centurions in each legion had only a limited chance of obtaining this prestigious post. After their year of service, the *primipilares* were eligible for equestrian rank. Some men served for a second term in another legion (*primus pilus bis*). Most commonly, a chief centurion moved on to become camp prefect in his own or another legion, and then perhaps could obtain promotion to tribune in one or more of the Rome cohorts, or to an appointment as provincial governor of the less militarized provinces.

## Centurions

There were several routes to a post as centurion, including promotion from the ranks, though this was the slowest and rarest of all, requiring about fifteen years of service and a progression through the clerical or junior officer posts, as the career of the centurion Petronius Fortunatus demonstrates (*ILS* 2658). He served successively as *librarius, tesserarius, optio,* and *signifer* before being appointed centurion "by vote of the legion" (*ex suffragio leg[ionum]*). Thereafter he served as centurion in over a dozen legions in Britain, Lower Germany, on the Danube, and in the eastern provinces (Campbell, 1994).

Another means of obtaining an appointment as centurion was by direct entry as an equestrian. Tiberius Claudius Vitalis entered the legion in this way in the second century AD (*ILS* 2656). Some centurions joined the legions after serving in the Praetorian Guard. Marcus Vettius Valens started as a Guardsman, then became clerk to one of the Praetorian Prefects, next as centurion of the *vigiles,* the Urban Cohorts, and the Praetorians, to become a legionary centurion. From there he was promoted to *primus pilus,* returned to the troops in Rome in a succession of posts as tribune, was admitted to the equestrian order, and became procurator of the province of Lusitania.

Some men tried and failed to obtain an appointment as legionary centurion. Suetonius (*On Grammarians* 24) quotes the case of Marcus Valerius Probus who gave up after waiting for some time, and in the third century the future Emperor Pertinax failed to become a centurion in a legion and instead obtained a post in an auxiliary unit. Service in auxiliary units did not exclude soldiers from reaching the rank of centurion in a legion. An inscription (*CIL* VIII 2354) shows that one soldier started out as a legionary in *legio III Augusta,* then became *duplicarius* (soldier on double pay) in the *ala Pannoniorum,* rose to the rank of decurion, and then returned to *legio III Augusta* as centurion.

## OTHER RANKS

### Recruitment

During the Republic, the Romans were able to recruit enough citizens to raise several armies in times of war, provided that the crisis did not last many years. The second Punic War stretched resources almost to breaking point, and recruitment reached unprecedented levels as the Senate committed more and more troops to foreign campaigns even while Italy was threatened. There were about twelve or fourteen legions on active service in 215 BC, rising to eighteen in 214 and about twenty-five in 212–211 BC, each accompanied by an equally high number of allied troops. Roman and allied manpower was not inexhaustible, as demonstrated by the refusal of some of the Latin colonies to provide any recruits for the *Alae Sociorum* in 209 BC, and there were no levies at all in the following year. The Romans were forced to enroll younger and older men than normal, and more of the poorer element as needs pressed; manpower remained problematical, since Gaius Gracchus introduced a bill in 123 BC, making it illegal to recruit men younger than seventeen.

With the growth of Empire, recruitment patterns inevitably changed. The enfranchisement of the allies after the Social War made more men available for service as legionaries but reduced the number of allied troops, which from then onward were recruited from the noncitizen provincials. The anarchy of the civil wars at the end of the Republic interrupted the pattern, when more or less anyone who could use a weapon was recruited into the legions regardless of status. Augustus reestablished Roman citizenship as a requirement for legionary service. Recruits had to state on oath that they were freeborn Roman citizens, but it seems that there was no readily available documentary proof that canceled all doubt as to whether a man was freeborn and a Roman citizen, or not. Goldsworthy (2003) quotes the case of an *optio* who was denounced as a noncitizen and had to produce witnesses to vouch for him. Slaves and criminals were excluded from the armies, and suspicions about the legal standing of recruits were closely examined. Pliny wrote to Trajan asking what to do about two recruits who were thought to be slaves (*Letters* 10.29–30) and received the answer that it was important to find out whether they were conscripts or volunteers. Trajan explained that if the recruiting officer had not noticed that the men were slaves, then he was at fault. If the slaves had volunteered and lied about their status, then they should be executed, but if they were substitutes (*vicarii*), then the men who sent them to the recruiting officer in their place were to blame.

In the legions, Italians predominated until the second century when citizens from the western provinces such as Gallia Narbonensis (southern France), Baetica (southern Spain), Africa, and Macedonia began to serve as legionaries.

Citizenship gradually spread over much of the Empire during the first two centuries AD, producing more eligible candidates for the legions, with the result that provincial recruitment broadened and Italian recruitment declined. New legions were normally raised in Italy, but replacements for the existing legions were increasingly found in the provinces, especially after expansion slowed and legionary fortresses became more permanent establishments. Le Bohec (1994) envisages a progressive recruitment pattern, first from a wide area covering more than one province, then in the surrounding region, and eventually in the immediate locality of the legionary fortress, when men from the *canabae* were brought into the legions. These may have been sons of soldiers, who were listed in the records *origo castris,* indicating that they came from the camp. It has been suggested that this phrase was also applied to soldiers from the vicinity who were not strictly eligible, but the fictional description satisfied the regulations.

There is some debate as to whether there were always enough volunteers to preempt the need to fill up the ranks by conscription (*dilectus*). Some authors suggest that conscription was only used in emergencies, when preparations were being made for wars (Goldsworthy, 2003; Watson, 1969). Other authors, however, consider that sometimes volunteers were in short supply and that compulsory service, or at least Rome's right to enforce it, remained the norm throughout the Empire (Brunt, 1974). High-ranking officers were put in charge of conscription; they were called *dilectatores* in the Imperial provinces and *legati ad dilectum* in senatorial provinces (Le Bohec, 1994). As demonstrated by Trajan's response to Pliny about the slaves, conscription and voluntary entry were both feasible, and the fact that men who did not want to serve in the armies were entitled to produce willing replacements presupposes that conscription was in force in some provinces at certain times, since eager volunteers were not likely to send substitutes. An inscription from Africa, dated to the first century AD, refers to a soldier of *legio III Augusta,* Lucius Flaminius, who was "chosen in a levy by Marcus Silanus" (Campbell, 1994).

It is estimated that about 18,000 replacements were needed over the whole Empire in peacetime during the first two centuries, but although this is not an impossibly high number for such a vast expanse of territory, the Romans were scrupulous about the standard of their legionary recruits, and therefore many men would probably have been rejected. Vegetius (*Epitoma Rei Militaris* 1.4–5) outlines the qualities that were sought in recruits. Candidates for the legions had to be of regulation height, between 5' 10" and 6' Roman measure (5'8" and 5'10" modern measure). The recruits were expected to be in good health, with good eyesight, and ideally able to understand Latin, and in some cases recruiting officers looked for men who could read and write so that they could fulfill the several clerical roles. The Roman army was a bureaucratic organization, and some men may have spent their entire military careers in offices keeping records up to date, the ancient equivalent of pen-pushing or more recently, keyboard-bashing. For the majority of recruits, physical strength was the most important criterion. Vegetius dismisses certain occupations, such as weavers, as not worthy of consideration, but young farm laborers were prized because they were used to working hard in the open air for long hours. The ideal age for joining the legions was about eighteen to twenty-one, but from gravestones and other inscriptions it is known that men joined up anywhere between the ages of seventeen and their late twenties. In emergencies, men up to the age of about thirty or thirty-five could be recruited (Dio 55.23.1; Livy 22.11).

After the recruit had undergone his initial examination (*probatio*), he took an oath of loyalty (*sacramentum*) to the emperor, and was issued with his identification tags (*signaculum*), a leather pouch to hang around his neck, containing an inscribed lead tablet. He was assigned to his unit and sent on his way with a travel allowance (*viaticum*), usually 75 *denarii*, or 3 gold pieces (*aurei*). Depending on how far he had to travel, most of this money was probably spent by the time he arrived at the relevant headquarters. Then he would be entered on the registers of the unit; for instance, between January and May in AD 156 *cohors I Augusta Praetoria Lusitanorum equitata* received nine recruits, all volunteers, approved by the Prefect of Egypt, Sempronius Liberalis. Seven of them were assigned to infantry centuries, one cavalryman was placed in the *turma* of the decurion Artemidorus, and one *dromedarius* (camel rider) was assigned to the *turma* of Salvianus.

Recruitment of the auxiliary soldiers from among noncitizens followed roughly the same pattern as the legionaries in that initially most of them were levied from the tribes on the periphery of the Empire, and then more and more often replacements would be recruited from the noncitizen provincials closer to where the units were stationed. Epigraphic evidence from the first century AD attests to the presence of ethnic tribesmen in auxiliary units. For example, at Colchester, Longinus, a trooper in the *ala I Thracum,* was described on his tombstone as the son of Sdapezematygus. It has been disputed whether Sdapezematygus is truly a Thracian name in a Romanized form, but Longinus came from the district of Serdica (modern Sofia), which strongly suggests a Thracian origin (*RIB* 201). A unit with this title was still in Britain under the Emperor Trajan, named on a diploma found at Malpas in Cheshire, England (*ILS* 2001). Ethnic unit names were retained, even though they no longer reflected the nationality of the original soldiers (see above under Auxiliaries).

## Training and Indoctrination

When the army was recruited annually and disbanded at the end of each season, there was little or no chance to train the soldiers over long periods. As Polybius comments (3.89), the troops were therefore inexperienced in comparison with

## THE MILITARY OATH

On the accession of a new emperor, everyone in the Empire, including soldiers and civilians, swore allegiance to him. Soldiers were obliged to renew their oath every year. The text of exactly what was pledged has not survived, and it is disputed whether this oath is linked to the oath to which Augustus refers in the memoir of his achievements that he left at his death (*Res Gestae* 25.2). When he was about to embark on the civil war with Antony and Cleopatra, Octavian, the heir of Julius Caesar, was careful to demonstrate to the whole world that this civil war was a just one, and moreover one that was demanded of him by the people of Rome and Italy. In his laconic style in the *Res Gestae* he says that the people of the whole of Italy swore an oath of allegiance to him, "*sponte sua*" of its own free will, and chose him as the leader in the coming war. The senators who had not fled to join Antony were with him, but that was not enough. Octavian needed a sort of referendum, and doubt has been cast, by both ancient and modern authors, on the short and telling phrase "*sponte sua.*" In his biography of Augustus even Suetonius was of the opinion that the whole event must have been carefully engineered. Dio's chronology implies that Octavian declared war first and then sought the approval of the people in the form of the oath, but this would have been unlike Octavian who moved slowly but surely and exercised caution in all his projects, the more so at this stage when he was not yet undisputed head of state. Syme (1939), followed by other authors, preferred to place the oath before the declaration of war.

The oath of allegiance to each succeeding emperor may have been modelled on this successful version arranged by Octavian, but since no one knows the words that were spoken, this is disputed. It is also disputed whether Octavian had in mind the precedent, already in use for centuries, of the military oath sworn by the soldiers when they enlisted. This, too, is problematic because no source preserves the exact words. Writing of Republican practice, Polybius (6.21.1–3) relates how one of the soldiers was selected to speak the whole of the oath, and the others simply said "*idem in me*," meaning "the same for me." It is not known if this simplified ceremony was adopted during the Empire when recruits were sworn in, either when there were relatively few in the batch who were to be sent on to their units, or on those occasions when recruitment of tribesmen was carried out en masse, usually as part of the terms of a treaty after a war.

Watson (1969) summarizes the evidence from the ancient sources about the military oath. According to Livy, the Republican soldiers took the oath voluntarily, but when he deals with the period just before the battle of Cannae, he says that the tribunes formalized the taking of the oath and made it compulsory. Dionysius of Halicarnassus (10.18.2) describes the army of the early Republic, when the soldiers swore to follow the consuls wherever they commanded, not to desert, and not to break the law. In another passage (11.43) he says that the generals were granted the power to execute deserters. According to Vegetius, who wrote his military manual in the fourth century, the military oath had been heavily Christianized, so the recruits swore by God, Christ, and the Holy Spirit, and by the majesty of the emperor to perform what the emperor commanded, to brave death in the service of the state, and not to desert. The military oath seems to have remained remarkably similar throughout the centuries from the Republic to the late Empire, but of course the purpose behind it was the same, since obedience to the generals and the embargo on desertion would be of paramount importance. The oath was renewed each year, originally on 1 January, but under the Flavians the date changed to 3 January. It is not known whether the ceremony or the words differed from the original oath.

Hannibal's army, since the Carthaginians were born and bred for war and trained continually from childhood. The Romans performed their personal exercises on the Campus Martius outside the city, but there was no formal training scheme or military college. Professionalism grew only with continued, corporately organized practice, and the lack of it showed to Rome's disadvantage. During the war with Hannibal, the legions and the *Alae Sociorum* were kept under arms for long periods and learned how to cooperate with each other from sheer necessity. So a kind of surrogate training took place, but it was not centrally organized or coordinated.

Theoretically, the Romans knew the importance of proper training, and the commanders who devoted some time to a training program were admired. Probably several generals spent time training their men, and the input from the tribunes and the centurions must not be discounted, but owing to the considerable bias in Polybius's account, his readers could be excused for imagining that whenever the Roman army was trained it was only the Scipios who were doing it. Publius Cornelius Scipio was wounded in the early stages of the war with Hannibal at the skirmish near the river Ticinus, and rather than commit his men to battle again, Polybius says that he advocated spending the winter in training the troops. Some decades later in Spain, Scipio Aemilianus resorted to rigorous training sessions to bring the troops to a peak of fitness. Livy (26.51.4) describes Scipio's program of marching in full armor, maintaining and cleaning weapons, and mock battles with wooden swords.

The gladiatorial training instigated by Rutilius Rufus in 105 BC was much admired by Marius, who presumably continued to employ the arms drill, the route marches, running, jumping, and swimming that became the standard training regime. The most detailed source for training and physical fitness is Vegetius, who compiled his books in the late Empire at a time when much of the old Roman discipline was failing, but he admitted that he had used the works of earlier authors, so most modern scholars accept what he says as authentic. According to Vegetius (*Epitoma Rei Militaris* 1.8), all recruits were made to do basic training for a period of four months in order to weed out the unsuitable men who had to be rejected. He mentions route marches of twenty Roman miles in five hours in summer and twenty-four miles at quick pace. The Roman mile was shorter than the modern measure, and the days were divided into an equal number of hours, so that in summer the hours were longer. With this in mind, Watson (1969) says that Vegetius's marches are probably commensurate with the three miles an hour of more recent armies.

Initial weapons training was carried out using wooden swords and wicker shields that were the same size but much heavier than standard service weapons. Recruits practiced their sword strokes against a post, just as gladiators did, until they were proficient. Then they were regularly paired off with an opponent for mock battles. In order to strengthen their arms, soldiers used heavy *pila* in practice sessions, and they were also taught swimming, archery, how to use a sling, and vaulting onto horseback, even if they were destined for the infantry. Eventually, the recruits practiced with their real weapons, though in mock combats the points were tipped with leather buttons to avoid unnecessary accidents. The arms drill was called *armatura* and was wholeheartedly recommended by Vegetius, who deplored the demise of the procedure. This sort of training had lapsed in Vegetius's day, but he says that soldiers with only limited experience of *armatura* were clearly better at fighting than those who had none at all.

It is usually suggested that cavalrymen were initially taken on as infantry and perhaps even served in the ranks for a while before being assigned to the mounted units. There they would start by improving their riding skills. They were taught to mount from both the right and the left side of the horse, in full armor and carrying their weapons, essential if they were brought down in battle. Wooden horses were provided for the practice sessions, and once they were proficient they would also practice on their live mounts. Arrian (*Ars Tactica* 43) says that cavalrymen were trained to mount when the horse was running, a regular feature in their displays. When the soldiers were thoroughly experienced in handling their horses, using only one hand on the reins and controlling the mount with the knees and legs, they could begin weapons training. One of the more important ways of training the riders to work together was the cavalry displays (*hippika gymnasia*), such as the performance witnessed by Hadrian at Lambaesis and the maneuvers described in detail in Arrian's account (*Ars Tactica*).

The officers who were responsible for training were known by different titles, such as *campidoctor,* or *magister campi,* and sometimes as *exercitator.* It is not known whether there was a subtle difference in these titles. Nor can it be shown that there was any attempt at standardization, or whether the titles were used exclusively of each other at different periods or in different parts of the Empire. Many of the trainers were legionary centurions. Titus Aurelius Decimus, centurion of *legio VII Gemina* in Spain was *praepositus* and *campidoctor* (*ILS* 2416) in the reign of Commodus. His titles suggest that he perhaps undertook a special mission combined with training, since *praepositus* was a title bestowed regardless of the recipient's permanent rank and often denoted an officer in a temporary command. Several of the *campidoctores* and *exercitatores* who are known from inscriptions were associated with the *equites singulares Augusti* or with the Praetorians. Four *centuriones exercitatores*—Ingenuus, Julius Certus, Ulpius Agrippa, and Valerius Bassus—are mentioned in an inscription on a monument erected in AD 139 when forty-nine Thracian *equites singulares* retired after twenty-five years' service (*ILS* 2182). Three more *centuriones exercitatores*—Aelius Flavianus, Aurelius Lupus, and Ulpius Paetus—are named on an inscription dating to AD 205 (*ILS* 2187). A legionary centurion from *legio II Adiutrix* from Aquincum calls himself *exercitator* (*ILS* 2453), and may have been assigned to training legionaries. It is not known how the centurions were chosen, or whether they had to apply for the posts, or even if they received a little extra pay.

One of the unsolved problems connected with training is the existence or otherwise of the indoor exercise halls mentioned by Vegetius (*Epitoma Rei Militaris* 2.23). He records that horsemen could continue to practice in winter and in bad weather in riding schools covered with tiles or shingles, or with thatch. An inscription from the fort at Netherby in Britain (*RIB* 978) attests to a *basilica equestris exercitatoria,* built in AD 222. The location of the *basilica* is not known, and the find spot of the inscription does not help since it was reused as a drain cover and need not have been anywhere near the building that it commemorates.

Some archaeologists have suggested that the so-called forehalls, usually built of timber, that have been discovered in front of the *principiae* or headquarters buildings of several forts, may have served as the cavalry exercise halls. It is perhaps more likely, however, that the riding schools stood outside the forts, not least because of the potentially chaotic scenario of batches of horsemen trotting up and down in front of the entrance to the headquarters and the mingling of human and equestrian traffic all trying to go about their business (Dixon and Southern, 1992).

Indoctrination of recruits and serving soldiers was expressed in the military oath that all soldiers swore when they enlisted and in the Romanization of native names, or the substitution of Roman names for native ones. Latin was the language of command and for recordkeeping, except for some of the eastern provinces, where Greek was sometimes used in military records and correspondence. Altars were dedicated to Jupiter Optimus Maximus (Jupiter Best and Greatest) with the text in Latin, and sometimes soldiers hedged their bets by setting up inscriptions in two languages. For instance, the Palmyrene units in Africa used Latin as well as their own script. Although the men were allowed to worship their own gods, they were absorbed into purely Roman rituals in the calendar of celebrations and festivals that the army observed as a corporate body. The festivals of the most important Roman gods were regularly observed. The anniversary of the founding of Rome was venerated by a parade and sacrifices, and the emperor's birthday was similarly celebrated. Dead and deified emperors were honored, and great ceremonial attached to the decoration of the standards, which took place in May. This fostered unit cohesion and esprit de corps.

## Promotion

Even though a great deal is known about the career paths of several serving soldiers who were promoted from the ranks, there is not enough accumulated evidence pointing to a structured approach to promotion or to discernment of whether it was a purely arbitrary process. It may be that soldiers were deliberately given an all-round training to broaden their experience, but this does not seem to be the case if the surviving evidence is taken as representative of normal practice. Quite often, promotion depended on the recommendation of powerful individuals, so patronage, effort, and self-help were at least as important as ability. In Egypt in the second century AD, a soldier called Terentianus, who wanted to transfer from the fleet to a legion (and was ultimately successful), complained that letters of recommendation were of no use unless a man helped himself. He also said that money was the only thing that really helped. Self-advertisement was essential for promotion. Writing home to his father to tell of his progress, the new recruit Julius Apollinaris congratulated himself on avoiding hard physical labor by going straight to the top, asking the governor of Egypt, Claudius Severus, for a clerical post on his staff. Instead, he was offered a clerical post in a legion, with a more or less firm promise of promotion (Campbell, 1994). Timid and reticent recruits who could not read and write probably never escaped from back-breaking labors.

It has been estimated that it would probably take about twelve to fifteen years for an ordinary legionary to rise to the rank of centurion, often by means of transferring to another unit, as in the case already quoted above (*CIL* VIII 2354). In this case, a legionary in *legio III Augusta* reached the rank of centurion in the same legion by way of a transfer to an auxiliary cavalry unit as *duplicarius* and then as decurion. Such a transfer did not always automatically lead to the post of centurion, as the career of Tiberius Claudius Maximus shows. This soldier performed well in Trajan's Dacian Wars, even claiming that he had captured the Dacian king Decebalus. He served in the legionary cavalry and the commander's guard, became a standard bearer, and then served as *duplicarius* in an *ala,* but he never reached the rank of legionary centurion (Campbell, 1994; Speidel, 1970).

### REFERENCES AND FURTHER READING

Alston, Richard. 1994. "Roman military pay from Caesar to Diocletian." *Journal of Roman Studies* 84, 113–123.

Breeze, David J. 1971. "Pay grades and ranks below the centurionate." *Journal of Roman Studies* 61, 130–135.

Brunt, P.A. 1950. "Pay and superannuation in the Roman army." *Papers of the British School at Rome* 18, 50–75.

———. 1974. "Conscription and volunteering in the Roman Imperial army." *Scripta Classica Israelica* 1, 90–115.

Campbell, J. Brian. 1984. *The Emperor and the Roman Army 31 BC–AD 337.* Oxford: Clarendon Press.

———. 1994. *The Roman Army 31 BC–AD 337: A Sourcebook.* London: Routledge.

Cheesman, G.L. 1914. *The Auxilia of the Roman Imperial Army.* Oxford: Clarendon Press.

Connolly, Peter. 1998. *Greece and Rome at War.* London: Greenhill Books. Rev. ed.

Davies, Roy W. 1971. "The Roman military diet." *Britannia* 2, 122–132.

Develin, R. 1971. "The army pay rises under Severus and Caracalla and the question of the *annona militaris.*" *Latomus* 30, 687–695.

Devijver, H. 1989. *The Equestrian Officers of the Roman Army.* Vol. 1. Amsterdam: J. Gieben.

———. 1992. *The Equestrian Officers of the Roman Army.* Vol. 2. Stuttgart: F. Steiner.

Dixon, Karen R., and Southern, Pat. 1992. *The Roman Cavalry.* London: Batsford.

Dobson, Brian. 1972. "Legionary soldier or equestrian officer? A comparison of pay and prospects." *Ancient Society* 3, 193–208.

———. 1974. "The significance of the centurion and 'primipilaris' in the Roman army and administration." *Aufstieg und Niedergang der Römischen Welt* II.1, 392–434.

Fink, Robert O. 1971. *Roman Military Records on Papyrus.* Cleveland, OH: Case Western Reserve University for the American Philological Society.

Gabba, Emilio. 1976. *Republican Rome, the Army and the Allies.* Oxford: Blackwell.

Goldsworthy, Adrian K. 1996. *The Roman Army at War 100 BC–AD 200.* Oxford: Clarendon Press.

———. 2000. *The Punic Wars.* London: Cassell.

———. 2003. *The Complete Roman Army.* London: Thames and Hudson.

Keppie, Lawrence. 1984. *The Making of the Roman Army: From Republic to Empire.* London: Batsford. Reprinted by Routledge, 1998.

Le Bohec, Yann. 1994. *The Imperial Roman Army.* London: Batsford. Reprinted by Routledge, 2000.

Marsden, E.W. 1969. *Greek and Roman Artillery: Historical Development.* Oxford: Clarendon Press.

Roth, Jonathan P. 1999. *Logistics of the Roman Army at War (246 BC–AD 235).* Leiden: Brill (Columbia Studies in the Classical Tradition Vol. XXIII).

Saddington, Dennis B. 1982. *The Development of the Roman Auxiliary Forces from Caesar to Vespasian, 49 BC–AD 79.* Harare: University of Zimbabwe Press.

Salway, Peter. 1965. *Frontier People of Roman Britain.* Cambridge: Cambridge University Press.

———. 1991. *Roman Britain.* Oxford: Clarendon Press.

Southern, P. 1989. "The *Numeri* of the Roman Imperial army." *Britannia* 20, 81–140.

Speidel, M.A. 1992. "Roman army pay scales." *Journal of Roman Studies* 82, 87–106.

Speidel, Michael P. 1970. "The captor of Decebalus." *Journal of Roman Studies* 60, 142–153.

———. 1973. "The pay of the *auxilia.*" *Journal of Roman Studies* 63, 141–147.

———. 1994. *Riding for Caesar.* London: Batsford.

Syme, Ronald. 1939. *The Roman Revolution.* Oxford: Clarendon Press.

Watson, George R. 1969. *The Roman Soldier.* London: Thames and Hudson.

Wilkes, John. 1969. *Dalmatia.* London: Routledge.

# CHAPTER 4

# Culture of the Roman Army

## PHYSIOGNOMY

### Ethnic and Racial Composition

The two elements of the early Republican Roman army were first, the legions and the citizen cavalry, made up of homogeneous Romans from the city of Rome, and second, the non-Roman troops comprising the Latin and Italian allies. The latter were perhaps allowed to fight with their own weapons and equipment at first, but eventually their organization was brought into line with the Roman legions. Their fighting position was on the wings (*alae*) of the main Roman army, which earned them the title *Alae Sociorum,* literally meaning "the wings of the allies."

The individual contributions from each of the allies consisted of infantry, eventually labeled cohorts, and cavalry, grouped into small units called *turmae*. The cavalry all fought together in battle, separated from the infantry. There seems to have been no rigid standardization of unit size, but the infantry was eventually organized into cohorts each 500 strong. The individual allied troops were commanded by one of their own local magistrates with the title of *praefectus*. The overall command of the combined allied armies was entrusted to Roman citizens appointed by the consuls, the cavalry commanders being men of senatorial rank with the title *praefecti equitum* and the allied infantry commanders being of equestrian rank and called *praefecti sociorum*.

For a long time Rome resisted granting full citizenship to the Latins and Italians, but after the Social War of 91 to 87 BC, all the inhabitants of Italy became Roman citizens and therefore eligible for service in the legions. This meant that although there was a much broader base for legionary recruitment, it was necessary to find replacements to fulfill the functions of the allied troops. The gradual evolution of the permanent auxiliary units of the Empire can be traced in part to the temporary use of native troops in various campaigns of the late Republic and early Empire. When campaigns were fought outside Italy, the commanders usually recruited local tribesmen from the environs of the theater of war. Many Gauls and Germans were recruited by various generals for wars in Gaul and Spain, and during his eastern campaigns Pompey called upon local rulers and petty kings to furnish his additional troops. These contingents were often allowed to fight in their own way under their own commanders, and were usually sent home when peace was concluded.

As the Empire expanded, absorbing western tribesmen and eastern cites and kingdoms, ethnic origins receded in importance, overtaken by the more important distinction between Roman citizens and noncitizens. The grant of citizenship could be bestowed on individuals or whole communities, and with the grant were included political and legal privileges and obligations, divorced from any connotation of Roman nationality, so that it was no longer a requirement for citizens to be born in, or to be domiciled in Rome itself. In the later second century there were Roman citizens who had probably never set foot in Italy, let alone the city of Rome, and in the reign of Caracalla, Roman citizenship was extended to all freeborn inhabitants of the Empire in AD 212, thus changing the face of military recruitment, and also broadening the base of taxpayers liable to contribute to the emperor's coffers.

## Legionaries

The legions were theoretically recruited from Roman citizens, with a predominance of Italians in the early Imperial legions, superseded by a rising number of provincial Roman citizens toward the end of the first century. Apparently, the Gallic provinces of Narbonensis and Lugdunensis provided many legionaries, followed by the Rhine and Danube provinces of Lower Germany, Noricum, and Pannonia (Le Bohec, 1994). The western provinces generally supplied more recruits than the eastern areas. In Egypt, easterners formed the basis of the early legions, until regular recruitment of Africans began in the mid-first century. By the second century, there were more Africans than easterners, and by the third century, Egyptians had superseded the native Africans (Alston, 1995). This demonstrates the theory that, in general, legionary recruitment originally spread over a wide area covering more than one province, then narrowed to the territory of the province or its neighbors, and finally became more and more localized as the armies settled in permanent forts, and citizenship and Romanization spread, becoming embedded in the local culture.

Exceptions to this generalization arose in times of emergencies when men who would normally be excluded, such as slaves, freedmen, and non-Roman provincials, could be recruited with the aid of a legal fiction whereby freedom and perhaps even Roman citizenship were conferred on the soldiers (though in some if not all cases, the recruits possibly retained their non-Roman status).

Citizenship could be bestowed on certain individuals, especially in the eastern legions, where some men who were not strictly qualified to join were nonetheless enlisted. The records describe some legionaries as originating from the camp (*origo castris*), and there is some dispute as to whether this really means that the men were born in the legionary *canabae*, or whether the phrase is used as a euphemistic term for the recruitment of non-Roman citizens.

## Auxiliaries

Noncitizens in any province were termed *peregrini*, which means "foreigners," or more specifically people who were not Romans. The *peregrini* were less privileged than citizens, but full citizenship was not impossible of attainment. The men who served on their town or city councils were rewarded with Roman citizenship, and for the less wealthy another method of obtaining citizenship was through the army. Although the citizen legions were theoretically closed to them, the auxiliary units were recruited from the provincial *peregrini* and various tribesmen, who served for twenty-five years and received citizenship for themselves and their descendants on honorable discharge.

The names of many auxiliary units reveal that they were raised from the various tribes inside and sometimes outside the Empire. The several *cohortes* and *alae Gallorum* attested on diplomas and inscriptions reveal the large number of Gauls who were recruited; similarly, there are several units of Thracians. Some units were recruited from single Gallic or German tribes, such as the Batavi, the Bituriges, the Lingones, and the Tungri. Although all provinces contributed soldiers, the western provinces supplied the majority of the auxiliaries, with the Celtic regions providing most of the cavalry. The eastern auxiliaries such as the Syrian and Palmyrene archers were regarded as specialists, and replacements were usually recruited from the original homelands, but the other auxiliary units would choose their replacements from the areas where they were stationed. The units retained their ethnic titles, but after two or three decades these names would be meaningless as a guide to the nationality of the soldiers.

As time went on, the military authorities did not always rigidly adhere to the distinctions between citizens and noncitizens when they were recruiting replacements for existing units or raising new units. Greater social and physical mobility facilitated the movement of individuals all over the Empire, and while the legions relaxed their rules and regulations, the auxiliary units took on more Roman citizens, so that the distinctions between them blurred.

In the mid- to late first century, new auxiliary units called *numeri* began to appear in the frontier provinces. The best known of these units are the Mauri and Palmyreni stationed in Dacia and Africa, and the Brittones stationed on the Odenwald frontier in Germany. Little is known about the circumstances of their original recruitment, but the tribesmen were likely recruited with the main purpose of guarding routes and policing the frontiers where the population was sparse and large-scale warfare was not a perceived threat, relieving the ordinary auxiliary units of these more mundane tasks. Occasionally, the Romans resorted to recruitment en masse of barbarian tribesmen from beyond the frontiers, usually in accordance with a treaty after a war. These men were often dispersed by allocating them to several auxiliary units, but sometimes they were kept together and sent to a distant province. For example, Marcus Aurelius sent 5,500 Sarmatians from the Danube region to Britain. The settlement of displaced tribesmen within the Empire became quite common from the second century AD, in large numbers if the ancient historians are to be believed, and some of these settled tribes were obliged by the terms of their treaties to provide soldiers for the army. In the later Empire, these recruits were sometimes formed into units of *foederati* or *laeti*. Very little is known about the internal structure or the command systems of these units.

## Women

The Roman army was an all-male institution; women did not feature as combatants, and the soldiers were forbidden to marry. Nonetheless, they formed unofficial liaisons with local women. The original marriage ban may have been instituted by Augustus in the aftermath of the civil wars. Just as Marius removed camp followers from the army that faced the Celtic tribes at the end of the second century BC, so Augustus avoided the encumbrance of families, which adversely affected the mobility of the troops. If a soldier was married when he enlisted, the marriage was broken off.

By the second century AD, most units were settled in permanent forts and were only moved to another post in times of expansion or emergencies. In these cases, the unofficial associations with local women could hardly be stamped out, and since a discontented army perhaps posed more of a threat to the Imperial rule than an army with families, no emperor chose to enforce the ban on marriages. All that could be achieved was to refuse to recognize the union during the soldiers' service lives, but when time-served men were discharged, the right to marry (*conubium*) was granted, and the existing and future children of the union were enfranchised. As evidence we have the diplomas that were issued to the auxiliaries, the sailors of the fleets, the Praetorians, and the men of the Urban Cohorts. It is generally agreed that the legionaries did not receive diplomas, but they were granted the same privileges with regard to their marriages and their children. The ban on marriages concerned all ranks up to that of centurion, but equestrian officers who served for only a short time with the army were exempted. The writing tablets from Vindolanda in northern England reveal that officers' wives resided at the forts where their husbands commanded. Senatorial governors and some commanders regularly took their wives to their provinces.

Many soldiers honored their associations with their chosen women, who were much more than mistresses to them. The majority of the women were non-Romans (*peregrinae*), but on inscriptions there is no distinction between citizens and noncitizens. Nor is there any mention of legal or illegal unions. Funerary inscriptions set up by serving soldiers mention "wives" despite the lack of legal sanction for their marriage; conversely, there are epitaphs for soldiers set up by their wives (Le Bohec, 1994). Septimius Severus made the break with tradition and legalized soldiers' marriages, condoning what was already a fact of military life and giving it Imperial sanction.

## MORALE AND DISCIPLINE

### Military Justice System

Roman military law was formulated in the first century BC and the first century AD, and after receiving special attention under Hadrian, its development continued in the second and third centuries AD. Apart from Polybius's description of Roman military discipline and punishments during the Republic, the sources for military law all date from the late Empire. These sources incorporate pronouncements and opinions from the second century onward, but looking back from a fifth- or sixth-century viewpoint means that it is not possible for modern scholars to reconstruct the corpus of military law for any one period of the Empire. The *Codex Theodosianus* of the fifth century is a compilation of civil and military laws and legal decisions, whereas the sixth-century *Digest of Justinian* lists a wider range of legal opinions, usefully attributing them to their original authors. Another compilation concerned purely with military law is found in the work of Ruffus, or Rufius, who may be Sextus Rufius Festus, a provincial governor under Valentinian II. Other scholars believe he was an officer on the staff of the Emperor Maurice (Brand, 1968).

Soldiers enjoyed a privileged legal position. They were exempt from torture and condemnation to the mines, and in the civil courts, the satirist Juvenal complained that military men were favored and not subject to the delays and frustrations that ordinary people suffered (Campbell, 1984). They were still subject to military discipline, in which the Romans took great pride. Anything that jeopardized military discipline or threatened the security of the unit, the camp, the fort, or the army in general was usually classified as a crime. The list of crimes includes committing treason, conspiring with other soldiers against the commanders, inciting violence, insubordination, striking an officer, fleeing from battle, leaving the ramparts, entering the camp over the walls, feigning ill-ness to avoid battle, betraying the camp, and giving information to the enemy. Trials of soldiers guilty of these and other crimes were conducted in the camp or fort, and an officer, usually a tribune, was given the task of investigating the matter, while another officer passed judgment.

## Punishments

The Romans of the Republic devised rewards and punishments that kept their soldiers under strict discipline and eager to win the recognition of their officers and comrades. Polybius stresses the great importance that Republican Romans attached to military honors and obedience, and in the early Roman army pun-ishments were brutal. Those found guilty of certain offenses were clubbed to death, a process called *fustuarium*. Anyone who failed to keep the night watch properly endangered the whole army, so the death penalty was deserved. It was also applied to those who stole from other soldiers, to those who gave false evi-dence, to men who engaged in homosexual acts, and to anyone who had already been punished three times for lesser offenses. A deeply ingrained sense of honor ensured that most of the soldiers stayed at their posts, preferring death to dis-grace; if they lost weapons or their shields, Polybius recounts that most men fought savagely to get them back or die in the process, rather than suffer the shame that attached to throwing weapons away or running from the battle. If whole units turned and ran, about one-tenth of the men concerned were cho-sen by lot and clubbed to death (decimation) and the rest were put on barley ra-tions instead of wheat.

The Imperial army retained many of these Republican procedures, but it seems that the regulations were enforced more rigorously in wartime than in peacetime, and there was always a case for mitigating circumstances. Ruffus rec-ommended that soldiers who committed offenses while under the influence of drink should not be subject to capital punishment, but should be transferred to a different unit (Brand, 1968). Tacitus (*Annals* 13.35) implies that first offenders and new recruits were treated with leniency by most commanders, depending on the seriousness of their crimes. Much depended on a soldier's rank, his char-acter, and his previous service record, which were well known to the officers. For instance, according to Appian (*Civil Wars* 3.7), when Mark Antony wanted to identify the troublesome elements among his troops, the officers were able to produce a list from their records.

Occasionally, whole cohorts or entire units were punished. The legions that survived the battle of Cannae, for example, were sent to Sicily, where they lived under canvas for several years, until Scipio Africanus took them to Africa, where they redeemed themselves. Some units or parts of units were made to camp outside their forts and were often given barley rations instead of wheat. This is psychological punishment with an in-built element of public humiliation, a procedure that Augustus adopted when he made a soldier stand outside his tent clad in only a tunic and holding a clod of earth. Commanders were at liberty to dream up variations on this theme, and soldiers had few means of making a protest.

The main forms of punishment included execution, beating, payment of fines, extra fatigues, demotion or loss of rank, and dishonorable discharge (Campbell, 1984; Watson, 1969). Although certain punishments were prescribed for certain offences, they were not rigidly applied by commanders, who usually used their discretion. The death penalty was reserved for serious crimes such as inciting mutiny or rebellion, insubordination, going over to the enemy, or striking an officer. On some occasions emperors and commanders could order executions quite arbitrarily, usually when it was necessary to set an example or to restore discipline that had become lax (see Tacitus, *Annals* 11.18; 13.35). The stern Domitius Corbulo treated his eastern troops very severely, going so far as to execute a man who put his sword down while digging a trench.

Loss of armor and weapons could incur the death penalty, but more often flogging was the punishment. Ruffus states that the theft of pack animals was treated even more severely because while the theft of weapons affected only one or two men, the theft of pack animals endangered the whole troop, so the penalty was to cut off the hands of the offender (Brand, 1968).

Punishments such as loss of rank could mean that a soldier remained in his own unit without his previous rank (*gradus deiectio*), or he could be moved to another less prestigious unit (*militiae mutatio*). A cavalryman could be sent to a part-mounted cohort (*cohors equitata*), and legionaries could be transferred to an auxiliary unit. There is a record of just such a circumstance in the strength report of *cohors I Augusta Lusitanorum,* where a legionary was transferred to an auxiliary unit, but it is not specifically stated that this is a demotion as punishment for some misdemeanor (Fink, 1971; Watson, 1969). Fines and loss of pay, with or without the imposition of extra fatigues, were probably the most common forms of punishment, but there is less information about it for the Imperial period. During the Republic, legions could be deprived of pay or put on half- pay, but the small-scale activities of officers exacting penalties from individuals tend to go unrecorded.

A more hard-hitting punishment was dismissal from the service, which was approximate to cashiering (*missio ignominiosa*), since this stripped the soldiers of all the privileges that would have been their due if they had served their full term and been honorably discharged (*honesta missio*). In the Jewish War, Titus dismissed a soldier who had been captured by the enemy, even though he had managed to escape, because soldiers should not be captured alive. The threat of the loss of pension and privileges, and the prohibition on joining any other unit probably served to keep many soldiers on the side of the law and military discipline.

## Desertion

The Romans recognized various types of desertion and dealt with them accordingly. The first duty of captured soldiers was to escape, and if they failed to do so they could be classified as deserters. The laws did, however, recommend that inquiries should be made into the circumstances of desertion, distinguishing between running away on the spur of the moment, being absent without leave, or more seriously, going over to the enemy, which was not unknown. In the *Digest* (49.16.4.5), mitigating circumstances are listed for a man being absent without leave, including illness, family problems, or pursuing a fleeing slave, which were considered legitimate reasons for the soldier's actions. Once again, the man's character and previous record were taken into account.

Ammianus Marcellinus says that the most common cause of desertion was fear of punishment (Goldsworthy, 2003a), implying that the soldier or soldiers concerned had already committed some crime or minor offense. If men returned voluntarily to their units, they were treated more leniently than if they had to be traced and brought back by force, and if a whole group deserted but returned within a specified time, they could avoid corporal punishment, but were often split up and distributed among other units. There would probably be an enquiry into any crimes committed before and during their period of absence, and this could influence the judgment.

Deserting in the face of the enemy, or going over to the enemy, usually incurred the death penalty, to maintain discipline and discourage emulation of these acts. Domitius Corbulo, the general who fought wars in the eastern provinces in the reign of Nero (54–68), executed deserters who had been brought back (Goldsworthy, 1996; Tacitus, *Annals* 13.35), probably without inquiring into the circumstances. Harsh treatment failed to eradicate the problem in Corbulo's army or in any other, especially during the major wars. Roman soldiers went over to enemy leaders and rendered them valuable service, and from the second century onward when treaties were arranged at the conclusion of the wars, there were usually clauses demanding the return of deserters (Dio 68.9.5; Goldsworthy, 1996). At the conclusion of the Marcommanic Wars, Commodus arranged a treaty demanding among other things the return of deserters and captives (Dio 73.2.2), but it is not recorded whether he punished them. Deserters who had gone over to the enemy were considered to be enemies themselves.

Execution or corporal punishment was not always strictly applied in all cases. Soldiers were valuable commodities, and in the mid-fourth century when they were in shorter supply and desertion was rife, the Emperors Valentinian and Valens passed laws to flush out deserters and return them to the ranks, punishing the people who protected and hid them (*Cod. Th.* 7.18.1).

## Leaves and Furloughs

Soldiers of the Roman army had no statutory right to a specified number of days' leave of absence during the year, but they could arrange with their officers, usually in the form of cash payments, to be released from fatigues and normal duties. Tacitus indicates that up to a quarter of the men of a military unit could be outside the fort on leave at any one time or in camp but would be excused fatigues, having bribed their officers and in some cases having resorted to robbery to obtain the money (*Annals* 1.17; *Histories* 1.46).

The writing tablets from Vindolanda contain a batch of letters requesting leave (*commeatus*), six of the letters being addressed to the same commander, Cerialis (Birley, 2002). The majority adopt the same formula, expressing the hope that the commander holds the soldier worthy to be granted leave. These are not simply requests to be relieved of duties, but to go away to another place, which in three cases is actually named in the letter. At the beginning of the second century, a soldier called Julius Apollinaris serving in Egypt wrote to his relatives to say that he would try to come home for a visit as soon as his commander started to grant periods of leave (Campbell, 1994). Another letter dated to the third century records a family problem in that a young man who had enlisted in a legion wanted to become a cavalryman in an *ala,* but his relatives could not visit because they were restricted by the leave granted to the boy (Campbell, 1994).

# TRADITIONS

## Unit *Esprit de Corps*

Before the Imperial standing army was established, the soldiers of the Republican legions and allied troops developed a short-lived pride in their unit's achievements and the awards for bravery to individual men. Even in protracted wars, however, when the units remained together for some considerable time, there was always an impermanence about them that prevented the development of a strong sense of corporate identity. When Marius reorganized his troops to fight the invading Celtic tribes at the end of the second century BC, he gave each legion its eagle standard that survived into and through the Empire, as an object of veneration and a symbol of unit cohesion. Toward the end of the Republic, if not earlier, distinguishing names were given to the legions, such as Caesar's *V*

*Alaudae* (the larks), but even among those legions that did not immediately acquire names, there was a growing sense of unity. The soldiers of Caesar's Tenth legion, for example, identified very strongly with their unit.

The Imperial legions and auxiliary cohorts and *alae* were distinguished by unit numbers and names, and sometimes with the additional titles earned from battle honors or significant loyalty to the emperor. Thus, *VII Claudia pia fidelis* and *XI Claudia pia fidelis* (meaning loyal and true, usually abbreviated to *p.f.*), which were probably raised in the late Republic, earned their titles for loyalty to Claudius in AD 42, and *I Flavia Minervia p.f.* raised by Domitian achieved its extra titles by remaining loyal to him in the revolt of Saturninus in AD 89. Auxiliary units were also awarded titles that reflected their battle honors or significant achievements. For example, *cohors I Flavia Ulpia Hispanorum milliaria civium Romanorum equitata,* a 1,000-strong equitate cohort raised by Vespasian and given his family name Flavia, at some point in its career earned the title Ulpia from the Emperor Trajan and also won a block grant of Roman citizenship for all the soldiers. This may indicate that the unit saw distinguished service in the Dacian Wars of Trajan, fought in the early second century AD in what is now Romania. After all the citizen soldiers had been discharged, the cohort retained its title *c.R.,* though the replacement soldiers would be noncitizens.

Distinguishing titles, battle honors, and corporate unit history all contributed to esprit de corps, which was reinforced by the unifying influence of religious ceremonial. Soldiers worshiped a variety of gods, some of them abstract concepts such as *Disciplina, Honos,* and *Virtus,* representing much more than is conveyed by the simple respective translations discipline, honor, and virtue, and indicating much more than an individual's sense of duty. Officers and soldiers set up altars to the *Genius,* or spirit of the legion or auxiliary unit. The eagle standard of the legions was honored on its anniversary (*natalis aquilae*), and in May the standards of each unit were decorated (see Holidays and Observances later in this chapter).

## Decorations and Medals

Conspicuous bravery on the part of officers and men was always rewarded. The decorations (*dona*) of the Imperial army were rooted in the Republican past, continuing the traditions that had been laid down when Rome had no Empire and no standing army. The ethics behind the awards and the physical evidence for them have been intensively studied by Maxfield (1981). For saving the life of a Roman citizen or an allied soldier, the reward was the civic crown (*corona civica*). The consuls usually presented the hero with gifts, and the soldier who had been rescued often gave his savior an oak-leaf crown. The first man to climb over the walls of an enemy city received the *corona muralis,* and likewise the first man across the ramparts of an enemy camp received the *corona vallaris.* Both of these crowns were made of gold. For relieving a besieged garrison, the reward was traditionally a grass crown (*corona obsidionalis*). Polybius describes how soldiers who had seized an opportunity or used their initiative in a skirmish to wound an enemy or take his weapons were praised and presented with rewards in front of the whole army, which encouraged young soldiers to face danger with bravery. These ceremonials were carried over into the Imperial period, when emperors or victorious generals on campaigns would parade the whole army and present the decorations to named individuals. The honors were always given in the emperor's name to encourage loyalty to him rather than to the general who recommended the soldiers and officers.

In the Imperial army, the crowns mentioned above remained the most prestigious of the decorations awarded to individuals, usually to officers rather than serving soldiers, but the latter were by no means excluded from receiving these awards. Different emperors adopted different approaches to the award of decorations; for instance, Trajan was considered to be generous with his rewards while other emperors were less so.

The award to the *primus pilus* was usually a silver spear (*hasta pura*), while centurions usually received only crowns. Below the centurionate, the decorations consisted of *phalerae,* torques, and *armillae.* Several sculptures are known; the majority of them are tombstones showing these decorations on the soldier's chest, and the accompanying inscriptions specifically mention the awards and sometimes the circumstances in which they were won. The *phalerae* were shaped like discs and were normally displayed on a leather harness over the soldier's armor. The torques were of two kinds, one to be worn round the neck, Celtic warrior fashion, and others smaller and usually hung on the leather harness with the *phalerae,* near the shoulders. *Armillae* were like bracelets, worn on the wrists. Although the decorations were made of precious metal, they were not worth much in terms of cash, but the value to the soldiers was very great. Goldsworthy (2003a) quotes the case of a cavalryman of the late Republic who was initially refused the award of *armillae* because he had started his career as an ex-slave. He was offered money instead but refused the offer, clinging firmly to the ideal of military awards, which he eventually received.

Auxiliary soldiers were not usually personally rewarded for individual exploits, but their contributions were recognized by means of granting honorary titles to the entire unit, such as *torquata* or *armillata.* If there was more than one occasion when awards were granted, the unit titles would reflect this; for instance, some units were known as *bis torquata.* For exceptional valor, the soldiers of an auxiliary unit could be granted citizenship en bloc, before they had completed their service, and the unit titles again reflected this honor, usually abbreviated *c.R.,* The titles were retained throughout the life of the unit, but that does not imply that all the soldiers were Roman citizens, since recruitment of replacements would continue from among non-Romans.

## Uniforms

The literature of Republican Rome contains references to "putting on military dress," so it is clear that soldiers and civilians were distinguishable from each other just by looking at their clothing. Judging solely from popular modern literature and from historical documentaries and feature films, casual observers could be forgiven for assuming that the type of arms and armor of the legionaries and auxiliaries of the first to the third century AD easily reveal a soldier's unit, but the reality is much more complicated. The Roman army did not wear uniforms in the same way that more modern armies identify different sections of their armed forces by clothing and hats of different colors and styles, adorned with appropriate insignia.

A great deal is known about what Roman soldiers looked like as a result of finds by archeologists and art historians. Archaeologists have discovered significant amounts of military equipment, weapons, and armor from several provinces and from several periods, and art historians have studied the various monuments that depict soldiers. Yet, it is still not possible to present a concise or complete portrait of the army at any period over the whole Empire. No doubt regional and temporal variations have escaped the record. Some authors consider that, on occasions, Roman soldiers would wear whatever they could lay their hands on, but this probably applies to most armies, especially when soldiers have fought protracted campaigns. It is perhaps significant that in several museums the erstwhile pristine, unsullied portrayals and models of Roman soldiers have been replaced by scruffier versions showing men with two weeks stubble and wearing patched cloaks. This new attempt at realism reflects the difference between soldiers doing their daily work and soldiers on parade, or soldiers looking noble and nearly perfect on Roman monuments. The Roman army engaged in several parades and ceremonies throughout the year, and the soldiers were probably no strangers to the "spit and polish" regimes familiar to their modern counterparts. Decorative parade armor certainly was worn on ceremonial occasions, though it is not certain how much of this equipment was also used in battle.

The main sources of information about Roman clothing and armor include sculptural evidence, archaeological finds, and literary descriptions. Bishop and Coulston (1993) warn against too ready an acceptance of what is found on funerary reliefs, particularly on propaganda sculptures such as Trajan's Column, which were designed to present Roman achievement in the best possible light and espoused idealism and artistic merit rather than reality. In addition, the

## MILITARY DRESS

Greek and Roman authors do not refer to military uniforms in the modern sense, but they do describe the act of "putting on military dress" in times of crisis. If there was a military dress code as opposed to civilian dress, it must be asked what it was that distinguished soldiers from civilians, apart from the rather obvious items such as armor and weapons. Soldiers of the Roman Republic provided their own clothing and armor, so it was perhaps only a fortuitous accident if there was ever a discernible standardization in their appearance. Later, when the state began to provide these items, it is perhaps a little more admissible to speak of Roman military uniforms but definitely not in the modern interpretation of the term. Goldsworthy (2003a) quotes a document from Egypt in which the military authorities stipulated that clothing ordered from a civilian contractor should be of a standard design and quality, but how far this extended to other provinces at other times cannot be determined, so it is not known whether there was ever an attempt to create anything approaching a military uniform across the Empire.

Many funeral reliefs show soldiers without armor, but instead simply dressed in tunics and cloaks. It was thus presumably some other attribute of dress that marked an individual as a military man. Most authors agree that it was the leather belt more than anything else that proclaimed the wearer as a soldier. The belt was known as the *cingulum,* a term that is not attested before the third century. Variations include *cingulum militare* or *cingulum militiae* (Bishop and Coulston, 1993). The belt was both functional and decorative. Metal plates were attached to it, both for decoration and to strengthen the belt. Also attached were various hooks and loops called "frogs" to which the dagger and initially the sword would be attached, though later the sword was worn on a baldric over one shoulder. An important feature was that mail armor was usually hitched up over the belt, thus relieving the wearer's shoulders of the full weight of the armor. In the early Empire, soldiers are generally depicted on their tombstones wearing two belts crossed at an angle over the hips like cowboy belts, but later the fashion was for only one belt, perhaps because this was more practical and comfortable when segmented armor was introduced (Bishop and Coulston, 1993). The military belt also served to attach the leather thongs or apron, like a sporran, that afforded some protection but probably hindered running (Goldsworthy, 2003a). There were most commonly four to six straps in the apron, with metal studs and terminals for decoration and perhaps to weight them.

sculptural evidence does not present the whole picture; on many reliefs such as funerary monuments, much of the detail would have been added to the stone work with plaster and paint, some traces of which still remain on a select few sculptured figures. If they could be viewed with their original antique trappings, the plain and austere grave monuments that we know from museums all over the world would probably seem unacceptably brash and gaudy to modern eyes. It would be invaluable to be able to check the finer details that are now lost on the surviving plain stone carvings.

Archaeological finds present problems of their own in that there are never enough of them to be able to reconstruct an Empirewide scenario, or a developmental chronology of armor and weapon types, but archaeologists and historians must work with what they have in hand, and make the necessary additions and subtractions when new finds are discovered. Literary references often assume a great deal of reader knowledge and tend to concentrate on the spectacular, so that the more mundane questions cannot be answered from these sources. Ancient authors were generally unconcerned with the details that modern scholars would like to have elucidated for them, such as how did particular sections of the armor fasten together and what color were the tunics and cloaks.

Tunics may have been dyed in various colors, but there is hardly any evidence for the use of color. White tunics are found on the famous Egyptian funerary portraits, which may represent veteran soldiers (Goldsworthy, 2003a), and Tacitus reports a triumphal entry into Rome after the death of Nero, in which the officers were dressed in sparkling white. These examples may not be representative of the rest of the Roman world. Goldsworthy suggests that perhaps white tunics were worn by ordinary soldiers and red ones by centurions. He suggests further that there may have been different colors and patterns for different occasions, perhaps even for different units. These suggestions cannot be verified, but they are not impossible. Indeed, Vegetius (*Epitoma Rei Militaris* 4.37) describes the blue/green tunics of the marines, together with the blue/green sails that helped to camouflage the operations of the Roman fleets.

It is generally agreed that military tunics differed from civilian versions in that they were actually longer but were worn hitched up over the belt and therefore appeared shorter. Augustus punished soldiers for misdemeanors by making them stand outside headquarters clad only in their tunics and without their belts, so they looked rather ridiculous in long tunics and deprived of the one item that marked them as soldiers (Suetonius, *Augustus* 24.2). Some relief sculptures show the tunics hitched up at both sides, forming a curved skirt at the front and presumably the back. This arrangement perhaps eased the problems of marching or running, freeing the legs just as modern sports shorts are often cut away at the sides. The tunic was made of wool or linen, formed from two squares or rectangles of cloth sewn together with holes left for the head and arms. Sleeves were mostly worn short, but evidence from some cavalry tombs shows that at least some of the cavalrymen wore long-sleeved tunics. In any case, long sleeves became more common for all soldiers from the third century onward. Some tunics were worn off one shoulder, with a split down the back and perhaps with the loose material knotted. Since this would not be comfortable with armor on top, it was perhaps just an arrangement that freed up the arms when working—for instance, felling trees and chopping wood.

Cloaks of different types are shown on several reliefs and fall into three main categories. The *sagum* was a simple square draped around the wearer and fastened with a brooch on the right shoulder, leaving the sword arm free. It was probably made of wool and could be decorated with a fringe. Another type of cloak was the *paenula,* which was more like a poncho, perhaps oval in shape and put on over the head, with a split down the front joined by toggles or buttons, and sometimes equipped with a hood. This would not be a specifically military garment since its practicality would appeal to everyone who had to work in the open air in inclement weather. Similarly, the *byrrus* or *birrus* was not necessarily a purely military item, but at least one soldier is on record asking his relatives to send one (Bishop and Coulston, 1993). In the later third century, the *birrus britannicus* was a valued British export, specifically assigned a maximum price in Diocletian's Edict on Prices in AD 301. Its waterproof qualities perhaps appealed to the soldiers as well as the civilians of the northern provinces, and judging from the fact that soldiers could ask for such items to be sent to them, they were probably allowed to wear clothes that kept them warm and dry even if they were not regulation issue. Military officers wore a more decorative cloak called the *paludamentum,* reminiscent of the toga in that it was draped over the left shoulder and wound round the left arm. The portrait of Marcus Favonius Facilis, centurion of *legio XX,* shows this type of cloak quite clearly. The *paludamentum* was associated more and more with the emperors after the first century AD (Bishop and Coulston, 1993). Cloaks will have been dyed in various colors, but the available evidence is too scanty to be certain. Generals often wore red cloaks, and in the late Republic Crassus was censured for wearing an ill-omened black cloak (Goldsworthy, 2003a).

Soldiers' boots (*caligae*) are almost as distinctive as military belts, as attested by the terminology of the military records, where the number of soldiers present is often listed as *caligati.* The Emperor Caligula derived his name from *caliga* because his father had a miniature suit of armor made for him, complete with military boots, so the soldiers of the legions on the Rhine gave him his nickname Little Boots (*Caligula* is the diminutive form of *caliga*). There are fortunately enough extant examples to elucidate all the details of how the boots were made. The uppers looked more like modern sandals, being cut away to form the equivalent of straps that could be laced together at the front to fit most foot sizes. The uppers, the insoles, and the outer soles were nailed together with studs arranged in patterns that prefigure modern training shoes (Bishop and Coulston, 1993). An army marching along a stone-paved road must have created a considerable clatter, and the studs would have helped to maintain grip in turf and rough terrain, but they did not serve the centurion Julianus very well in Judaea in AD 70: he slipped on a paved surface, fell heavily, and was killed before he could get up (Goldsworthy, 2003a). In order to keep warm, the soldiers wore socks (*udones*), which probably had no toes or heels, as shown on a sculpture depicting Praetorians. One of the Vindolanda letters contains a request for *udones,* and from the same source material it is known that underpants (*subligares*) were worn under the tunic. Cavalrymen on some sculptures, especially on Trajan's Column, are shown wearing leggings that come down to the bend of the knee, but it is likely that legionaries and auxiliary infantry wore them as well, as shown on the sculptures from Adamklissi, in the Dobrudja plain of southern Romania.

Body armor for all categories of Roman soldiers from the first to the third century AD consisted of mail, scale, and the segmented armor made up of separate bands hinged at the shoulders and joined together by leather straps and hooks. These three types are respectively known to modern scholars as *lorica hamata, lorica squamata,* and *lorica segmentata,* but it should be noted that *lorica segmentata* is not a term that the Romans themselves used. Mail armor was made of iron rings about 7 millimeters in diameter, stitched onto a backing. It was worn by both auxiliaries and legionaries, and probably continued in use among the legions even after the introduction of segmented armor, which is exclusively associated in the popular imagination with legionaries. A tombstone from the Flavian period shows a legionary wearing mail, and the Adamklissi reliefs also reveal that legionaries still wore mail armor in the Trajanic Wars (Bishop and Coulston, 1993). The shoulders were protected by doubling, as shown on various monuments; as mentioned above, the mail shirts were usually hitched up over the belt so that the whole weight was not carried on the shoulders.

Scale armor was worn by some legionaries and by auxiliary infantry and cavalry. The scales varied in size, being wired together and sewn onto a cloth backing in overlapping rows. Smaller scales were introduced in the Antonine period (AD 138–193). Scale armor was prone to damage, and it was not so easy to repair as mail, where individual rings could be replaced. Fortunately for archaeologists, finds of scale armor are relatively frequent compared to the other types.

The study of segmented armor was vastly illuminated in 1964 when parts of three sets were found in a box at Corbridge, a fort and town just to the south of Hadrian's Wall in northern England. Previously, the most common finds were the bronze fasteners and fittings from this type of armor because the bronze survives and the iron sections do not. The only clues as to how it all fitted together derived mostly from sculptures. Using the material from Corbridge, H. Russell Robinson reconstructed the cuirass, with its hinged shoulder plates and the main body plates on their leather harness (Bishop and Coulston, 1993; Goldsworthy, 2003a). Segmented armor is not found exclusively on legionary sites, so it is not yet possible to affirm that it was worn only by legionaries (Connolly, 1998).

Body armor would not be worn directly on top of the tunic, but not much is known about the kind of protective jackets, probably padded, that may have been worn underneath the armor. Additional protection is sometimes shown on sculptures, such as the arm guards worn by the soldiers in the Dacian campaigns, but it is important to note that these segmented arm guards were not invented solely to counter the fearsome Dacian *falx.* They are found in other

Cavalry helmet, Roman Britain, third century. It can be difficult to determine whether a helmet was intended for full combat use or for parades and cavalry sports events. This helmet, originally fitted with a pair of protective cheek pieces, may have served both roles. (The British Museum /Topham-HIP/The Image Works)

provinces, dating to different periods, and gladiators were familiar with them (Goldsworthy, 2003a).

Senior officers wore a more elaborate type of cuirass, usually molded to enhance the muscled appearance of the wearer, with fringed leather strips (*pteryiges* or *pteruges*) at the waist and the shoulders. The relief sculptures of the Ahenobarbus monument and Trajan's Column show officers in this type of armor, which was also worn by the emperors. Apart from the sculptures, there is little other evidence for the muscled cuirass, which may have been made of metal, or perhaps of leather, or possibly both (Connolly, 1998; Goldsworthy, 2003a).

The several designs of Roman military helmets have been well documented, but an attempt to produce a strict chronology to illustrate their evolution is always problematic. The links have not necessarily been found, and it may be a mistake to assume that there was a linear development covering the whole Empire. A whole range of modern terminology has been invented to illustrate types, but none of the labels would be meaningful to the men who wore the helmets.

In simplistic terms, helmets developed to provide protection from blows, downward via the forehead, across the back of the neck, to the cheeks, and primarily to the top of the head. Early Roman helmets were little more than an inverted bowl made of one piece of metal, with a rudimentary neck guard at ninety degrees to the body of the helmet. Hinged cheek pieces could be attached to the sides. This is typified by the developed Montefortino type, which had been used in a simplified form since the third century BC. In the first century AD, the Coolus type superseded this helmet, with a similar neck guard and an additional brow guard. The Imperial Gallic and Imperial Italic helmets improved on these designs in that the neck guard was provided with ribs and angled down to reduce the space between the old-type neck guard and the shoulders. Protective ear pieces were added to some helmets, and the cheek pieces became more elaborate with the rear section angled outward, to deflect blows from connecting with the side of the neck. Some helmets were very elaborate, made of iron with decorative bronze fittings and studs. On Trajan's Column, some legionaries are depicted with reinforcing cross pieces on the tops of their helmets, but no actual examples were known until comparatively recently (Connolly, 1998). A significant feature of Roman helmets is the so-called drawer handle that was attached to the neck guard for ease of carrying it; these pieces survive in greater numbers than the helmets themselves.

Most of the helmets had a knob or some other attachments at the top for fitting a crest, and the Coolus type was equipped with a slot at the side for plumes. Polybius says that the Republican soldiers sported black or purple feathers in their helmets, to make themselves seem taller and more imposing. According to Vegetius, centurions were distinguished by a wide crest running transversely over the helmet, rather than the more usual form running from front to back, but no fittings have yet been discovered to verify this statement. It is not certain whether the Romans went into battle wearing their crests and plumes. On Trajan's Column it seems that these were fitted only for parades and ceremonies, but Julius Caesar describes an occasion when fighting broke out unexpectedly, giving the soldiers no time to take off their shield covers, or to fit their plumes to their helmets. It may have been a case of fashionable practice at certain times, or perhaps it was left to the discretion of the general in command.

## Military Music

Musical instruments are known from Roman military contexts, attested by archaeological finds, from sculptural representations, and from literary references. These sources have enabled modern craftsmen to reconstruct the instruments, and so the probable range and type of sounds that they made can be ascertained. It is not known for certain, however, what combinations of notes were played on them in Roman times—despite the efforts of the epic film industry to produce likely compositions. In the military context, it is likely that there were standard musical compositions for parades and festivals, but the majority of the meager information that has come down to us concerns musical instruments used for tactical signals.

The three main instruments commonly used in the Roman army are the *tuba,* the *cornu,* and the *bucina,* played respectively by the *tubicen,* the *cornicen,* and the *bucinator.* The *tuba* was a straight trumpet, while the *cornu* was an almost circular instrument that wrapped right around the player's arm, with a bar across the middle for grip. Very little is known about the *bucina,* but it was probably used to give signals in camp (Frontinus, *Stratagems* 5.17; Tacitus, *Annals* 15.30; Vegetius, *Epitoma Rei Militaris* 2.22; 3.5).

Literary sources reveal that the Romans used these instruments to sound reveille (cock-crow) and for the changing of the guard when in camps or forts (Frontinus, *Stratagems* 1.1.9; Josephus, *Jewish War* 3.5.3). Tacitus (*Annals* 1.28) records an occasion when the light of the moon seemed to wane, and to ward off the evil omens, soldiers blew on every kind of trumpet and clattered brass instruments, whereupon the moon obligingly brightened for a short time. The main responsibilities of the *tubicen* were to sound the advance and the retreat, and the signal to leave camp. In Caesar's army at the battle of Thapsus, before the Caesarians engaged, the overenthusiastic *tubicen* on the right wing sounded the charge without orders from Caesar himself, and from then on it was impossible to hold the soldiers back.

According to Vegetius (*Epitoma Rei Militaris* 2.22), each legion had thirty-six horn blowers (*cornicines*), and Arrian (14.4) says that there were thirty-eight trumpeters (*tubicines*)—three for the officers, three in the legionary cavalry, five in the First Cohort, and the rest assigned to the remaining cohorts (Le Bohec, 1994). Certain *tubicines* or trumpet players are recorded on inscriptions. Two gravestones from different parts of the Empire record *tubicines* and include a carved "portrait" of each soldier carrying his *tuba.* One was found at Cologne, commemorating Caius Vettienus, *tubicen ex[s] (sic) leg[ione],* but unfortunately the legion is not named (*ILS* 2351). The other was found in the Chersonese, near Sebastopol, recording Aurelius Salvianus, *tubicen* of *legio XI Claudia,* who served for thirteen years and died aged thirty-six (*ILS* 2352). The *tubicines* of *legio III Augusta* are recorded on an inscription (*ILS* 9096), and from the fort of Brigetio on the Danube, the *tubicines* of an unnamed legion, probably *I Adiutrix,* set up a corporate dedication to Minerva (*ILS* 2353). Significantly, they called themselves a society or college of trumpet players (*scola tubicinum*), indicating a sense of corporate identity, if not an actual college. This sense of cohesion was enhanced by a ceremony called the *tubilustrium,* which was carried out probably every year, to purify the instruments. This was not a purely military observance, since the *tubilustrium* was celebrated in Rome to purify the trumpets used in religious ceremonies.

## Holidays and Observances

The Romans did not have weekends and statutory periods of annual holiday or leave, but they celebrated a large number of festivals throughout the year. The army celebrated the most important Roman state festivals and ceremonies, probably all over the Empire and at all times, but the most detailed evidence that has come down to us derives from the *Feriale Duranum,* the calendar of events concerning one unit, *cohors XX Palmyrenorum* at Dura-Europos in Syria in the early third century AD. The ceremonials and holidays celebrated at Dura likely applied to all units in the Empire, but for lack of firm evidence, no one can state categorically that they did. It is noteworthy, as Watson pointed out (1969), that the tenor of the Dura calendar is overwhelmingly Roman, in a unit formed predominantly from easterners serving in an eastern province, with a variety of local and regional gods and observances to choose from. While worship of local gods was not generally banned, the *Feriale Duranum* makes it clear that as far as the military authorities were concerned the official state festivals were what counted, and the local ones could be left to personal discretion.

The official Roman state festivals observed by the army included the annual sacrifices and ceremonies in honor of the chief gods, Jupiter, Juno, and Minerva, on 3 January. It was customary to sacrifice an ox to Jupiter, a cow to Juno, and another cow to Minerva. A series of altars from the parade ground of the fort at Maryport in the northwest of Britain may be related to this ceremony (Goldsworthy, 2003a). Of the several altars found there, seventeen were dedicated "to Jupiter Best and Greatest" (in Latin, *Iovi Optimo Maximo,* abbreviated to I.O.M.). Two auxiliary units feature on the altars, *cohors I Baetasiorum c.R.* and *cohors I Hispanorum equitata,* so it cannot be said that the practice was limited to only one occupying unit. The dedicators were usually the commanding officers, acting on behalf of their cohorts and signifying that this was a corporate ceremony. It was probably an annual event, since such a high proportion of altars of this type have been found.

Other Roman gods besides Jupiter were honored by the army. On 19 March there was the Qinquatria in honor of Minerva, and on 9 June there was a festival dedicated to Vesta. The anniversary of the foundation of Rome, an important festival that stressed the uniformity of the Empire and focused everyone on the emperor and the central ruling city, was celebrated on 21 April. The reigning emperor's birthday was always celebrated, and certain deified emperors were honored each year, which meant that as time went on the number of observances increased. Among others, Julius Caesar was honored on 12 July, and Marcus Aurelius on 26 April; there were also celebrations in honor of Germanicus, the son of Tiberius's brother Drusus, adopted by Tiberius in AD 4. He was in line for the succession but never became emperor. He was much loved by the soldiers in his own day and his popularity with the army never waned.

The official Roman state festivals observed by the army included the annual sacrifices and ceremonies in honor of the chief gods, Jupiter, Juno, and Minerva, who is pictured here. (Library of Congress)

The purely military observances included elaborate ceremonies on 7 January, the day of *honesta missio,* when the time-served veterans were honorably discharged. If this major event in a soldier's life went unmarked, the incentive to serve what was essentially a hard taskmaster would be considerably diminished, so it was in the army's own interest to make much of this festival. On 10 and 31 May, the military standards were decorated in a ceremony called *rosaliae signorum,* and in the legions the anniversary of the eagle standard was observed (*natalis aquilae*), tantamount to the birthday of the legion, which implies that different legions would celebrate this on a different day. All these ceremonies would serve to enhance unit esprit de corps, as well as emphasizing *Romanitas* and the sense of belonging to a larger society than the immediate military environment.

It cannot be stated precisely what kind of activities accompanied these various religious and military ceremonies, but it is likely that parades in fine armor and military maneuvers played a significant part. Feasting probably ensued, especially after the ritual sacrifices had taken place.

## VETERANS

The term *veteranus* was first used at the end of the Republican period to describe a discharged soldier who had served for a specified term. At this stage the *veterani* had usually served for a theoretical maximum of six campaigns and had then returned to civilian life, but many of them reenlisted when fresh Roman armies were raised. There were always foreign wars in which to serve, and with their experience of the army they were prime candidates for the recruitment drives of the various magnates of the later Republic, as they assembled their own private armies to fight not the foreign enemy but their personal rivals. When Octavian was in need of soldiers after the assassination of Julius Caesar, men who had served with Caesar flocked to his standards. There were always ex-soldiers in Italy in need of employment because the Republican government did not feel itself obliged to cater for the welfare of time-served veterans. The requests for land grants that habitually followed upon a victorious general's return to Rome were not a normal part of the military system, a situation that led to a mutually dependent relationship between generals and troops. The generals could achieve nothing without loyal soldiers, and the men could not hope for any rewards, apart from booty, unless they relied on their generals rather than the state. In the early Republic, the farmer soldiers took part in short campaigns and went home to their farms, but as time went on the campaigns lengthened and veterans returned to find themselves landless and without employment. The generals who managed to force through the necessary legislation to award plots of land to their soldiers had to find money to buy the plots, or provide the political and military force to dispossess existing landholders and install the new ones. This was clearly not a viable system for the standing army that developed under Augustus and his successors.

At the end of the civil wars when there were thousands of soldiers ready for discharge, the most common method was to place large numbers of them in colonies, usually created in existing towns or cities, or more rarely new foundations specially built for the purpose. Julius Caesar, Mark Antony, and Octavian-Augustus settled many of their veterans in colonies, in Italy, and the provinces. Those established in Italy up to 14 BC have been studied by Keppie (1983). In his account of the achievements of his long reign (*Res Gestae*), Augustus stated that he had settled 120,000 soldiers in twenty colonies in Italy in 31 BC, then 100,000 men in colonies in Spain and southern Gaul in 14 BC, followed by another 96,000 in 2 BC. These are vast numbers; spread over nearly three decades, the impact was perhaps less disruptive than it seems at first sight, but it is hardly representative of a properly organized and regular military system. There was a lot of ground to cover before the fully fledged Imperial procedures for discharge of veterans could be instituted. The first stage was to regulate and standardize the term of service for soldiers of the legions and of the nascent auxiliary units, and then institute a program of regular discharge and the concomitant recruitment of replacements. Toward the end of Augustus's reign, discharge of veterans and their return to civilian life was gradually regularized.

Under Augustus, veterans were semiretired but still attached to their units, undertaking lighter duties, for the last four years of their service. They were formed as a *vexillum*, under a *curator* (Le Bohec, 1994). The *curatores veteranorum* attested on inscriptions may be officers in charge of these semiretired men. A tombstone from Milan names Publius Tutilius as *curator veteranorum* of *legio V* (probably *Gallica*). Tutilius was born as Octavian was coming to power, and he died in the reign of Tiberius (*ILS* 2338). Another tombstone, from Verona, attests Lucius Sertorius Firmus as *curator* of *legio XI Claudia* (*ILS* 2339). These men were both standard bearers (*signiferi*) who had become eagle bearers (*aquiliferi*), so they may have been chosen as *curatores* because they were officers, and they would be literate, experienced in keeping records, and trustworthy, since part of their duties involved accounting and issuing the soldiers' pay. At least one *quaestor veteranorum* is known from *legio VIII Augusta*, with a service record of twenty-eight years (*ILS* 2466).

Most of the soldiers served for their full term and were honorably discharged, but there were two further kinds of dismissal from the army besides *honesta missio*. These alternatives are outlined in the *Digest* (49.16.13.3). Soldiers could be dishonorably dismissed from the service (*ignominiosa missio*) if they had committed a crime or signally failed to meet army standards. Another reason for dismissal from the army, before the expiry of the statutory length of service, was on medical grounds, which included both physical and mental problems (*causaria missio*). Dishonorable discharge carried severe penalties, since the usual rewards and privileges were denied the soldier who had disgraced himself. For an auxiliary this meant that he was not entitled to Roman citizenship, and for all soldiers it meant that their pensions and the tax exemptions enjoyed by veterans were annulled. Those who were dismissed in this way were specifically forbidden to live in Rome or to join the entourage of the emperor.

Dismissal on medical grounds probably incorporated the grant of *honesta missio*. On a discharge diploma issued to a soldier who started out as a marine but later transferred to *legio II Adiutrix* in AD 70, it is stated that he was a *causarius*, but had also been granted *honesta missio*. An inscription records a legionary of *II Parthica*, who was *ex causa missus,* but it is also emphasized that he had been honorably discharged (*CIL* VI 3373). The law codes state that if a man were discharged on medical grounds after having served with an untarnished reputation for twenty years, then he was entitled to the normal rewards and privileges granted to other veterans. If he had not served for this length of time, he received a reduced pension, calculated pro rata from the term he had completed (Campbell, 1994).

The importance of having been honorably discharged is illustrated by the fact that several ex-soldiers felt it necessary to mention it on career inscriptions, or to instruct their heirs or the executors of their wills to include it on their tombstones. In some cases, the information is reduced to a formula, *M.H.M.*, standing for *missus honesta missione* on an inscription naming Gaius Gentilius Victor as a veteran of *legio XXII Primigenia* (*ILS* 2472). Another legionary from *XXII Primigenia,* and two men from *I Minervia,* also felt the need to prove that they had been honorably discharged (*ILS* 2312; 2463 *bis*).

When the standing army was established, the discharge of veterans was carried out on a regular basis, instead of en masse, as, for example, after the battle of Actium. After the initial mass discharges undertaken by Augustus, in the early Empire there was less need to establish dozens of veteran colonies all at once. In Flavian times, the practice of founding veterans colonies in Italy died out, and under Hadrian it ceased in the rest of the Empire. The Caesarian and Augustan colonies were usually formed by evicting the existing occupants from various towns, but in the provinces the colonies were usually new foundations on the edge of newly conquered territory, or they were sometimes laid out on lands that the army had just vacated.

Colonies were still established during the early Empire for veteran soldiers, though not exclusively for ex-soldiers. At Colchester in southern England, veterans of the Twentieth legion settled among the civilians, and a colony was established at Lincoln when *IX Hispana* moved on to the new fortress at York. In North Africa the veteran colony of Timgad was founded in AD 100 for soldiers of *III Augusta* stationed at Lambaesis. The core of the town resembles a military camp with straight streets outlining square blocks, but the buildings on the out-

# DIPLOMAS

There is far more information about veterans from the auxiliary units than from the legions, because, from the reign of Claudius onward, if not earlier, the auxiliaries received diplomas upon honorable discharge (*honesta missio*). "Diploma" is a modern term describing the hinged, two-leaved bronze tablet that was issued to auxiliaries; it is not the name by which the soldiers would have known them. The diplomas that have been found from all over the Empire are listed with their full texts and commentaries by Margaret Roxan (1978, 1985, 1994) and Roxan and Holder (2003). A copy of each diploma was made and hung on the wall at the rear of the temple of the divine Augustus in Rome.

It was usual practice to wait until several soldiers from different units of a province were ready for discharge. Diplomas were then issued to each individual, giving his name and origin, and the unit from which he was being discharged. He may have served in other units before he joined the one named on the diploma, but these are not listed. It is fortunate for archaeologists and historians that the wording on the diplomas usually follows a formula, first naming the reigning emperor with all his titles, then listing all the units within the province from which soldiers were being discharged. These lists do not represent the full compliment of units in the province, since it is unlikely that all of them would be discharging time-served men at the same moment, but comparison of diplomas from different periods helps to build a picture of which units remained in a province for any length of time. The governor of the province is also named, and a precise date is given. For instance a diploma was issued to Liccaius of *cohors VII Breucorum* on 17 June in the consulship of Aulus Licinius Nerva Silianus and Publius Pasidienus (AD 65). On occasion, the men were still serving in their units when the diplomas were issued or citizenship was granted, perhaps as a reward for distinguished service. A diploma from Dacia (modern Romania) records that the Emperor Trajan granted Roman citizenship to soldiers of a *cohors equitata* of Britons before they had completed their military service (Campbell, 1994, no. 326). The man named on this particular example is an infantryman, a British tribesman called Novantico, originally from Ratae (modern Leicester).

It is stated on each diploma that the right of marriage is granted to each soldier, and Roman citizenship is awarded both to the discharged soldiers and to his children and descendants. After AD 140 there was a change to the grant of citizenship in that only the children born after the soldier's discharge were included in the grant, thus excluding the offspring who were born while their father was still serving in the army (Roxan, 1986; Campbell, 1994). This system may have been adopted in order to reduce the number of citizens around the military camps who were then eligible to join the legions rather than the auxiliary forces, but this theory is disputed.

Diplomas were also issued to marines from the fleets; the first known diploma (*ILS* 1986) was issued to a marine in AD 52. The Praetorians and the soldiers of the Urban Cohorts received diplomas, but seemingly these documents were not issued to legionaries, a fact that begs many unanswered questions about the discharge of legionaries. Legionaries were awarded *honesta missio* in the same way as the marines, the Praetorians, the Urban Cohorts, and the auxiliaries. Since legionaries were already Roman citizens, they perhaps did not require the same documentary proof of their civilian status as the auxiliaries, but then the Praetorians and men of the Urban Cohorts were also citizens, and yet they received diplomas. It has been suggested (Campbell, 1994) that it was not necessarily the case that diplomas were routinely issued to all discharged soldiers and marines; it is possible that the Praetorians, the men of the Urban Cohorts, and the auxiliaries, had to request their diplomas, and perhaps even had to pay for them.

skirts are laid out with much less rigidity of plan, suggesting a gradual accretion of civilian settlers.

Although the foundation of colonies continued into the Empire, and land grants were still made to veterans, the Imperial government largely washed its hands of its veterans once they left the service, neither providing for their welfare nor directing where they should live. The choice of place of settlement was left to the individual. Veterans could go home to their original homelands, choose to live in a city, or settle near to the camp where they had served and probably had families, even though marriage was forbidden to soldiers. Tacitus (*Annals* 14.27) records an early Imperial attempt to establish veterans in colonies at Tarentum and Antium in Italy, but instead of settling whole units with their officers as had been done in the past, the authorities tried to mix soldiers from different units. As a result, the men did not form a homogeneous community and started to pack up to return to the places where they had served. Many of the men did remain near their forts in the *vici* and *canabae*, where they integrated into civilian society. Veterans and civilians cooperated with each other in the settlements around the forts. For instance, at Aquincum on the Danube, an inscription records the veterans and Roman citizens together (*veterani et cives Romani consistentes ad legionum II Adiutricem*). Similarly at Troesmis, an inscription (*ILS* 2474) records the veterans and Roman citizens of the *canabae* of *legio V Macedonica*.

There is not enough information to document what most of the veterans did with their lives after discharge, but a few inscriptions suggest that many of them went on to other careers, setting themselves up in business or taking an interest in their local communities. A veteran of *I Minervia* was described as a seller of pottery at Lugdunum (modern Lyon). He died at the age of fifty-nine, so depending on his age at enlistment he could have worked at his new career for ten to fifteen years (*ILS* 7531). Another legionary veteran, this time of *legio XXII Primigenia*, described himself as *negotiator gladiarius* (*ILS* 2472), indicating that his business was concerned with swords. Other veterans became town councillors of their local communities. Quintus Annaeus Balbus served as *duumvir* at Thuburnica in North Africa, and in Italy an inscription was set up at Capua in the first century AD in honor of the veteran Lucius Antistius Campanus, who had "completed his military service in dangerous campaigns," and who had benefited his community by gifts of money, perhaps serving on the local council as well, though this is not mentioned on the inscription (Campbell, 1994).

## Pensions

In the late Republic and early Empire, the normal means of rewarding veterans was by providing plots of land (*missio agraria*), either by granting them individual farms or by settling them in veteran colonies. The settlement process did not die out altogether until the reign of Hadrian, but from the later years of Augustus's reign a cash payment became the more usual form of gratuity to time-served soldiers (*missio nummaria*). In order to provide cash pensions to discharged soldiers, a great deal of money was required, and it had to be available on a regular basis. The generals of the later Republic often promised monetary rewards to their soldiers when they had concluded the war for which they enlisted, or completed their term of service, whichever came first. The generals then had to assemble the cash, often by dubious means if they were not as wealthy as Pompey or Crassus, who could afford to raise and pay armies of their own, but this was only in the short term. Such *ad hoc* and sometimes desperate measures were not reliable and not sufficient to cater for the payment of a standing army and the provision of pensions for veterans.

In AD 6, Augustus founded the *aerarium militare*, or military treasury, with the specific purpose of providing a pension fund for the soldiers. He started it off with a huge cash injection of 170 million sesterces from his own funds, and he set up taxes to sustain the treasury, namely, a 1 percent tax on sales by auction (*centesima rerum venalium*) and a 5 percent tax on inheritances (*vicesima hereditatum*). There were particular treasurers of the *aerarium militare* who would deal with payments to the veterans when each batch of soldiers was discharged. Records of each soldier were kept in unit headquarters and probably also at provincial headquarters, so in any province it would be possible to enumerate how many men were due for discharge in any year and to calculate how much money would be necessary to pay out the pensions. In the early Empire from Augustus to Claudius, a retiring legionary received 3,800 *denarii* on discharge, and Praetorians received 5,000; by Caligula's reign, legionary pensions had increased to 5,000 *denarii,* and by the early third century, they had risen to 8,500 *denarii* (Le Bohec, 1994).

In addition to their cash pensions, veterans from all the armed services would also draw their savings that they had accrued during their service, so they could start out on their new lives as civilians with considerable sums. Financially, veterans were better off than ordinary civilians in that they were exempt from certain taxes. These exemptions applied in whichever community they chose to settle, though it seems that on occasion veterans had to prove their status and even go to law to fight for their privileges. Documents from Egypt reveal that exemption from the poll tax was perhaps not as automatic as might be expected (Alston, 1995; Campbell, 1994). Veterans were still eligible to pay contributions toward the repair of the roads, and had to pay the usual taxes on their property. If elected to their local councils, they had to fulfill their obligations, but according to an edict of the Emperor Domitian issued in AD 88–89, veterans were not subject to other public taxes and tolls. This privilege extended to their wives, children, and parents.

As noted above, some veterans chose to invest in businesses and others were able to benefit their chosen communities. So even though the state showed little interest in them after their service and did not set up military hospitals for them or attend to their welfare, Roman army veterans were far from poor and ragged ex-soldiers who needed to beg a crust on street corners. It was in the interests of safe government to ensure that Italy and the provinces were not full of discontented, poverty-stricken men who could join together under a strong leader and make trouble, particularly as they were still relatively young and fit when they retired, and thoroughly trained in the fighting methods of the troops who would have to be sent against them.

### REFERENCES AND FURTHER READING

Alston, Richard. 1995. *Soldier and Society in Roman Egypt: A Social History*. London: Routledge.

Birley, Anthony R. 2002. *Garrison Life at Vindolanda: A Band of Brothers*. Stroud, Gloucestershire: Tempus.

Bishop, Michael C., and Coulston, Jon C.N. 1993. *Roman Military Equipment*. London: Batsford.

Brand, C.E. 1968. *Roman Military Law*. Austin: University of Texas Press.

Campbell, J. Brian. 1984. *The Emperor and the Roman Army 31 BC–AD 337*. Oxford: Clarendon Press.

———. 1994. *The Roman Army 31 BC–AD 337: A Sourcebook*. London: Routledge.

Connolly, Peter. 1998. *Greece and Rome at War*. London: Greenhill Books. Rev. ed.

Fink, Robert O. 1971. *Roman Military Records on Papyrus*. Cleveland, OH: Case Western Reserve University.

Goldsworthy, Adrian K. 1996. *The Roman Army at War 100 BC–AD 200*. Oxford: Clarendon Press.

———. 2003a. *The Complete Roman Army*. London: Thames and Hudson.

———. 2003b. *In the Name of Rome: The Men Who Won the Roman Empire*. London: Weidenfeld and Nicolson.

Keppie, Lawrence. 1983. *Colonisation and Veteran Settlement in Italy 47–14 BC*. British School at Rome.

———. 1984. *The Making of the Roman Army: From Republic to Empire*. London: Batsford. Reprinted by Routledge, 1998.

Le Bohec, Yann. 1994. *The Imperial Roman Army*. London: Batsford. Reprinted by Routledge, 2000.

Maxfield, Valerie A. 1981. *The Military Decorations of the Roman Army*. London: Batsford.

Roxan, Margaret. 1978. *Roman Military Diplomas 1954–1977*. University of London, Institute of Archaeology Occasional Publication no. 2.

———. 1985. *Roman Military Diplomas 1978–1984.* University of London, Institute of Archaeology Occasional Publication no. 9.

———. 1986. "Observations on the reasons for changes in formula in diplomas circa AD 140." In W. Eck and H. Wolff (eds.), *Heer und Integrationspoltik: die Romischen Militardiplome als Historische Quelle.* Cologne and Vienna.

———. 1994. *Roman Military Diplomas 1985–1993.* University of London, Institute of Archaeology Occasional Publication, no. 14.

Roxan, Margaret, and Holder, Paul. 2003. "Roman military diplomas." *Bulletin of the Institute of Classical Studies Supplement* 82.

Watson, George R. 1969. *The Roman Soldier.* London: Thames and Hudson.

# CHAPTER 5

# The Roman Army at War

## DOCTRINE AND STRATEGY

From their earliest beginnings to the late Empire, the Romans consistently adopted a warlike disposition. This attitude was inbred into the majority of the senatorial class of the Republic, who regarded war as part of life, the primary means of achieving lasting fame and glory for Rome and for their descendants. The absolute stubbornness of the Romans ensured that even though they were sometimes thoroughly beaten in a battle or a series of battles, in the end they won through sheer staying power. Their advantages in the Republic included their organization and administration, their discipline, and not least the fact that their manpower was potentially unlimited, at least in the short term, since they could call upon their own citizens and their allies in Italy. The wars of the early Republic could be described, with a little imagination, as mostly defensive, but once the theater of war extended into other territories and Rome discovered the Mediterranean world, then wars of aggression, sometimes but not always leading to conquest and annexation, also entered into the Roman ethic. After the early years of the second century AD, expansion via annexation was rare, but the emperors were no less aggressive than the Republican Senate. The wars with Parthia were most often begun by Rome, as preemptive strikes or reactions to perceived threats, but these expeditions did not result in a steady eastward progression of Roman dominion. Elsewhere, wars were more often reactions to internal rebellions or to attacks or incursions by Rome's neighbors.

Each war fought by the Romans was portrayed as a justified action, or *bellum justum*. Whether it was a defensive action, a punitive expedition, a war of conquest, or a war of pure aggression, the politicians of the Republic, and later the Imperial equivalent of modern "spin doctors" cleverly placed all the blame on the enemy, whatever the circumstances. An example of the tortuous political prelude to wars is provided by Octavian's elimination of Mark Antony. It was Antony who was the rival who stood in Octavian's way, but since Antony was a Roman and there had been enough civil wars to last for several lifetimes, Octavian exploited Antony's unfortunate if not unwise association with Queen Cleopatra VII of Egypt. Antony's name was besmirched, it is true, but that was normal in the Roman political arena—a number of Romans who were cast as villains managed to cleanse themselves and emerge as heroes—but careful propaganda ensured that Cleopatra and Egypt were seen as the enemy. It was rumored that Cleopatra wished to take over the Roman state, and it was said that she often began her musings with "When I dispense justice from the Capitol." Whipped up by Octavian, the people were clamoring for him to mobilize against Cleopatra, and he revived an ancient ritual whereby he designated a little plot of land as enemy territory, threw a spear into this symbolic Egypt, and so declared war.

On occasion, Rome fought wars on behalf of another state, kingdom, or tribe, after appeals for assistance from a threatened monarch or chieftain. The result was not always annexation of the chieftain's territory, although certain stipulations may be made, such as raising troops for the Roman army, and an understanding that the chief who enjoyed Roman support should keep his own warriors under control and watch his borders to guard against the people who might one day threaten Roman interests. Significantly, when the Romans decided upon annexation, it tended to occur where there was a profit to be made, a concept that embraced both political advantages and/or economic gains. Pompey the Great showed how immensely profitable foreign wars could be, though the eastern territories offered more economic potential than the west, where certain generals like Julius Caesar and Germanicus won great political kudos but not quite as much wealth.

During the Republic, the Senate made corporate decisions about whether or not to go war, whom to place in command, how many troops to raise, and the resources that should be voted to the generals. This applied especially when the Romans were operating in Italy, but as the number of provinces increased, governors acted more independently, a situation imposed by the distances involved and the speed of communications. Governors were not given an entirely free hand, but their remit seems to have been broad enough to allow them to make decisions to wage war on a tribe or people, always provided that the relevant reasons could be produced to label the action a "just war." In the early years of the Principate, senators continued to act as their predecessors had done, but Augustus rapidly made it clear that the degree of independent action for provincial governors was severely curtailed. Marcus Licinius Crassus, grandson of the more famous Crassus who met his end in Parthia, successfully conducted a war in Moesia in 29–28 BC, and claimed a triumph, which he was granted. His demands did not end there, however, since he also claimed the title *Imperator*, which was normally voted to a successful general by his troops, and the rare honor of *spolia opima*. This was awarded to a Roman general who had personally killed an enemy leader in battle, and it bestowed the right to dedicate the spoils of war in the temple of Jupiter on the Capitol. These last two honors were refused. Henceforth the title *Imperator* belonged exclusively to the emperors, and generals who claimed signal honors were dissuaded from making too much spectacle. The emperors made decisions about going to war, where to wage it and through whom, and the chosen generals were designated appointees or legates of the emperor, subordinate to him in all matters. The award of the triumph, the pinnacle of the Republican military career, ceased for anyone except the immediate family of the emperor, and to demonstrate the point, Augustus's right-hand man, the faithful Marcus Vipsanius Agrippa, was awarded the honor twice but refused it, along with other honors voted to him by the Senate. During the Empire, successful generals had to be content with the lesser award of *ornamenta triumphalia,* the insignia of a triumphant commander, but they did not have the honor of parading in the triumphal chariot through the streets of Rome, displaying the booty and captives that they had won, ending the procession on the Capitol Hill where the trophies were dedicated to the gods.

Emperors sometimes curtailed the exploits of a successful commander in case they ventured too far and embroiled Rome in wars that she did not want, or in case the generals got above themselves and started to think in terms of running the whole Empire. Claudius prevented Domitius Corbulo, legate of Lower Germany, from following up his victory against the Chauci. Corbulo was operating across the Rhine, but the army was brought back to the Roman side of the river. The lessons learned from the disaster of Varus were perhaps still too vivid, but it is also possible that Claudius did not want his generals to eclipse him.

Augustus quickly made it clear that supreme power and all honors were in his gift and his alone, and his successors saw no reason to relax this unwritten rule. Significantly, lesser powers and honors were granted to the military commanders, whose achievements had to be acknowledged in some way, without allowing them more power and influence than the emperors, all of which highlights the continual dilemma of the Imperial regime. The Empire had to be defended, so armies had to be stationed at convenient points with commanders in charge of them. The commanders had to have enough ability and power to be able to organize this defense if circumstances demanded it, but at the same time they must not be encouraged to imagine that they could run the Empire rather better than the reigning emperor. Given the long time span of Imperial rule, it is perhaps surprising that there were not more attempts at usurpation and a change of ruler in the first two centuries. If defense was to be effective, a warlike spirit had to be instilled into the provincial armies, but the troops in the frontier forts were no longer all Romans or Italians from the core of the Empire, so their ideology of Rome would be based on the concept of a central ruling power but not of a homeland where they could find repose after their service. They had other loyalties besides their duty to Rome. If the right leader emerged making all the right promises, the provincial armies showed themselves ready to make war on whoever was marked out as the enemy, whether they were Roman, non-Roman, or otherwise. The Roman war ethic could just as easily be turned inward as outward. The armies were instrumental in creating emperors such as Vespasian and Severus, and if the provincial armies did not create the emperor, other troops such as the Imperial German bodyguard or the Praetorians were just as persuasive.

It is unlikely that there was a strategic plan for the whole Empire at any time in its history, from Gaius Julius Caesar to Justinian, and it is not possible to disentangle the reasons for going to war from literary rhetoric and the personal justification of each emperor who waged war (Campbell, 2002). Neither forward planning nor a holistic view of the Empire seems to have applied consistently to Imperial rule. The Roman Empire was after all very large, and it was culturally as well as geographically diverse. The senators of the Republic conceptualized Rome at the center of the universe with a god-given right to extend Roman rule over everyone else, but they did not look at the entire Empire and then clutter up their lives with corporate goals, targets, time scales, mission statements, and business plans in order to achieve this vaguely perceived ambition of world rule in logical stages. The emperors perhaps conceptualized the Empire as a collection of regions with different profit potentials, different problems, and different internal and external threats. They did not have a uniform strategy for dealing with the Empire, inherited from their predecessors, and finely honed by themselves and their successors. Their political and military policies tended to be reactive rather than proactive, piecemeal and tailored to the area concerned. This was not simply a concomitant factor of physical geography and the constraints imposed by terrain. Goldsworthy (1996, 2003) claims that political geography more than anything else determined how Rome dealt with their Empire and its neighbors. Military and political procedure was generally dictated by the way in which a population or a tribe was organized, whether they were urbanized and centrally governed, or scattered and answerable to a chieftain whose power was always precarious and rapidly became ineffective as soon as he began to lose influence. Physical geography affected the way in which the army operated tactically, but what Rome wished to achieve and how she went about obtaining it depended on the enemy's internal politics. Strategy to the Romans was basically a matter of going to war if they thought they could win and that there would be some advantage to doing so. This done, strategy consisted of staying in control, either by means of moral domination or by annexation. The fine details could be worked out empirically on the spot, utilizing a combination of military activity and political diplomacy, not to mention cunning and guile. None of the literary sources makes any mention of either short-term or long-term strategy, and even the works such as Frontinus's *Stratagems* simply retail anecdotal evidence in roughly classified groupings, without outlining an overall strategy for the Empire (Millar, 1982).

Romans of the Republic, or at least the senatorial class, thought of the supremacy of Rome in terms of power without end (*imperium sine fine*), a con-

Soldiers building a fort on the northern bank of the river Danube during the Dacian Wars. Drawn by Paolo Fumagalli, G. Bramati, and others, from the reliefs on Trajan's Column. (Stapleton Collection/Corbis)

cept that never entirely disappeared from the Roman mindset all through the Empire. At the end of his long reign, Augustus exhorted Tiberius not to try to conquer and annex any more territory. The disaster of Varus in AD 9 and the consequent loss of three legions in Germany had shaken Augustus, and the Romans had pulled back from whatever their goals were beyond the Lower Rhine. Modern scholars have argued that originally Augustus intended to push Roman rule as far as the river Elbe and then join this new boundary to the Danube, which looks so strategically sensible on modern maps, but it is by no means proven that Augustus had any such notion or that he and his contemporaries conceived of the geographical features of the Empire in this way. The suggestion that the Elbe was the ultimate goal distorts the modern view of Roman strategy, since plans that seem eminently logical to modern strategists, with the benefit of atlases and nearly 2,000 years of hindsight, may not have appealed to the Romans, whose own planning was perhaps not motivated by logic, but by opportunism, flexibility, and feasibility.

Tiberius may have agreed wholeheartedly with Augustus's advice not to extend the Empire, but other emperors added new provinces, usually after a war of retribution. Perhaps the most notable exception is Claudius's conquest of Britain, which was not a response to any serious threat to Rome, but equally it may not have been entirely due to Claudius's lust for personal military honors that had been hitherto denied to him. Whittaker (1994) doubts that Augustus intended to place a complete embargo on further expansion, and suggests that Augustus simply meant that conquest just for the sake of it should be avoided. This type of aggressive warfare in fact became less common from the early second century onward when the Empire reached its greatest territorial extent under Trajan, but there were many other reasons for the Romans to go to war, apart from territorial acquisition, usually as reactive responses to attack or to perceived threats. Domitian's Danubian Wars resulted from a Dacian incursion across the river into Moesia, where the provincial governor lost much of his army and also his life. The army sent to restore the balance also failed, at which point Domitian spent a year in raising and equipping another army before he risked going to war again. After Domitian was assassinated, his short-lived successor Nerva did not attempt to continue the war, but Trajan eventually picked up the tab, and even he had to go to war twice before the problem was solved and the province of Dacia was created. Thereafter, the major shifts in Roman boundaries were often centered on the eastern provinces, where Severus tried to solve the always delicate balance of power by annexing Mesopotamia.

In Republican times, the Senate voted on whether or not to go to war, but in the Imperial era the decision for war or peace rested with the emperor. Usually, there was also a consultation with the senators to gain their approval, paying lip service to the old Republican traditions and attempting to eliminate potential trouble at home while the armies fought in distant provinces and sometimes beyond them. The emperors went to war for a variety of reasons—to defend their provinces from outside attack, occasionally to preempt attacks, or more often to punish the offenders after raids. Sometimes wars resulted from internal rebellions, which tended to break out while a new province was still being pacified. This is the context for the German rising against Varus and for the rebellion of Boudicca in Britain. The enemies of the emperors were not always foreigners, threatening the Empire from beyond its boundaries; increasingly, as the Empire progressed into the third and fourth centuries, Roman generals at the head of Roman armies fought each other in civil wars.

The emperors who extended the Empire were usually very popular. Demonstrations of support for their expansionist policies may have been assisted by a little manipulation here and there, by the use of propagandist images in art and architecture, on the coinage, and in the descriptive phrases included in the string of titles adopted by the emperors, illustrating their conquests in the name of Rome. One of the prime examples is Severus, who advertised his conquests in his titles Adiabenicus, Arabicus, Parthicus, and Britannicus, later Parthicus Maximus and Britannicus Maximus. He was also declared to be *fortissimus* and *felicissimus*, emphasizing his great prowess and his good fortune—everything that the Romans could desire their emperor to be, one who could protect them against all evils, whether military or political, and extend Roman authority, bringing wealth to the city and opportunities for the businessmen to expand their trade.

Undated etching depicting a scene of Romans and Dacians in battle, from the continuous narrative circling the column of Trajan (AD 106–113) in Rome, Italy. Italian caption reads: (left) A Dacian gives himself up to a Roman soldier, grasping the Roman's right hand with his own right hand as a sign of trust: (right) Dacians laying conquered in this fourth battle, while others have been made prisoners, or, dead, pile up on top of one another. (Bettmann/Corbis)

Emperors who called a halt to continual expansion were conversely unpopular. It is probably true to say that men like Nero and Domitian would have achieved unpopularity entirely unaided, without the suggestion that they were not entirely devoted to constant conquest, but their lack of commitment to expansion damaged their reputations. Nero was said to have considered giving up Britain at some unknown point in the history of the province, perhaps just after his accession when the Governor Didius Gallus was struggling to pacify the province, or perhaps more likely after the losses incurred by the suppression of the rebellion of Boudicca. Whatever the context, the idea was received with alarm, not least by the upper-class moneylenders who had several eminent Britons firmly in their pockets. There was no military withdrawal, but after the revolt of Boudicca there was a marked change of policy in Britain, where less warlike governors were sent out whose expertise was in the political or legal spheres. In Germany, although Domitian had waged a successful war against the Chatti, he seems to have drawn a line and halted. This line consisted of a road skirting the Taunus and Wetterau regions, with watch towers spaced out along the route. It is attributed to the Flavian period, if not to Domitian himself, but in reality neither the road nor the towers can be dated with absolute accuracy. Some authorities believe it constitutes the first Roman frontier in Germany, an assumption that is fraught with enough controversy to fill several volumes, the first of which would be devoted to defining exactly what frontier means (Elton, 1996; Schönberger, 1985). Tacitus, who hated Domitian passionately, clearly thought that the halt was a temporary measure and that it was always part of the plan to conquer Germany, but it was taking an awfully long time: *tam diu Germania vincitur* (*Germania* 37). In fact, it was never completed.


## Forts and Frontiers

Any discussion of Roman strategy must take into account the establishment of the various military installations and the frontiers of the Empire. The establishment of legionary fortresses and auxiliary forts was a result of early Imperial military policy, as the standing army gradually evolved from the temporary armies of the Republic. Troops of the Republican era had often been kept together for the duration of campaigns, sometimes for years at a time, but even though they may have constructed forts to house them through the winters, these installations do not classify as forts in the strict Imperial sense. Only when the army became permanent did the need arise to house the troops, and so the typical Roman forts and fortresses came into existence in the provinces. Although there was much standardization in fortress and fort design, there were variations between the provinces and even within one province, as archaeological research constantly demonstrates. The ideology behind Roman forts consisted primarily of dominance and control. Forts did not cling to hillsides for protection and should not be confused with the large and very dominant fortified castles of the medieval period. Roman forts were placed in areas with access to water and food, and on major routes providing for rapid communications and troop movements. Quite often, in many areas of Europe occupied by the Romans, a map of the railway networks and the major stations can be a guide to where the Roman forts were placed, thus emphasizing that one of the most important priorities for the Romans concerned communications. Legionary headquarters were established at communication centers, where it was quite usual for medieval cities to grow up on top of them, not simply because there were already some buildings in existence there, but because in the distribution of their forts the Romans had an unerring eye for topographical advantage. This distribution pattern changed in the early Empire as circumstances worsened, but the principles remained the same: forts were planted as bases from which to mount small or large expeditions, in places where the army could control territory and guard routes, where ease of communications and supply was assured. Forts housed the headquarters and administrative centers of the individual units, but the soldiers themselves were not permanently cooped up inside these forts. Many, if not most, of them would be engaged in tasks outside their bases, sometimes quite far distant from them.

When the frontiers were established, the forts and fortresses became part of the overall scheme. Usually, the legions were based at some point in the hinterland of the frontier areas, and the auxiliary forts were either brought right up to

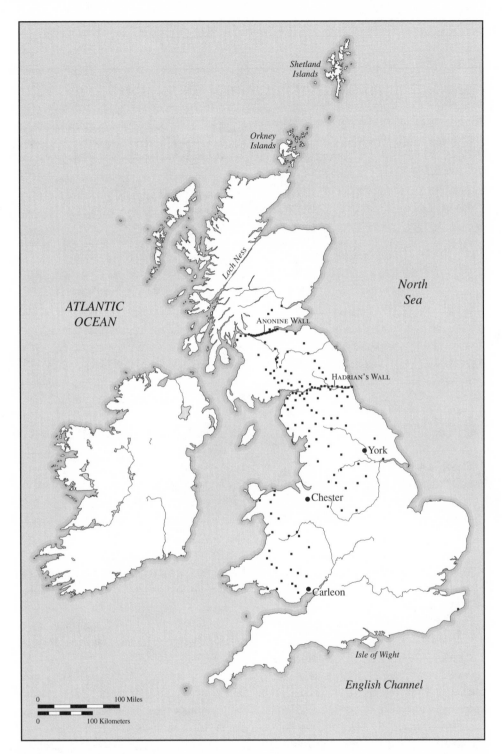

Map showing the locations of the frontiers of Roman Britain. Hadrian's Wall was built after the Emperor Hadrian visited the province in AD 122. It was built of stone, originally with the forts in the rear, but shortly after construction began the forts were moved to the frontier line itself. Under Antoninus Pius another frontier was built of turf, but it was manned for only a short time, and Hadrian's Wall was put back into commission as the permanent frontier of Britain despite the fact that several campaigns were mounted beyond the frontier in succeeding years.

## ROMAN FORTRESSES, FORTS, AND FORTLETS

A typical Roman fort of the Imperial period was shaped like a modern playing card, with two short sides and two long sides, and rounded corners. This is the evolved version of a Roman fort, since the earlier fortified camps of the early Empire were not so regularly shaped and were not generally designed as permanent bases for troops. The fort and supply depot at Rödgen in Germany was ovoid in shape, and while the fortress of Haltern was more regular in plan, it does not compare with the later permanent forts of the Empire.

Typically, early Roman forts were built of earth and turf ramparts (called *murus caespiticus*), topped by a timber breastwork, with access by timber gateways with towers on either side. There were usually interval towers ranged along the walls and at each corner. Forts were usually surrounded by one or more ditches, shaped like a letter V but with an aptly labelled "ankle-breaker" drainage channel at the bottom. The Romans usually took this drainage feature seriously, judging by the number of excavations that show that the ditch had been cleaned out and squared off. In the second century AD from the reign of Trajan onward, when the majority of forts had become permanent bases rather than semipermanent ones while the provinces were pacified and Romanized, forts and fortresses were generally, but not universally, built of stone. In some cases this meant refronting existing forts by cutting back the turf rampart, and in others building in stone from the outset.

Depending on the type of unit stationed in them, forts varied in size from 0.6 hectares for the small *numerus* forts in Germany and Dacia, to 20 hectares for a legion. There were a few double legionary fortresses such as Vetera (modern Xanten, Germany) and Mogontiacum (modern Mainz, Germany) until the failed revolt of Saturninus, who gathered the combined savings of his legionaries to attempt a coup against the Emperor Domitian. After this, Domitian decreed that no two legions were to be housed together.

Plan of a legionary barrack block. The centurion lived in a well-appointed house at the end of the block, while eight men of each contubernia or tent group shared two rooms between them. Theoretically there should be ten double rooms, as shown in this plan, to accommodate the 80 men of the century, but in practice there were often eleven or twelve sets of rooms, for reasons which no one can satisfactorily explain. (Redrawn by John Clark)

The internal arrangements of fortresses and forts was on the whole standardized, but with regional or local variations. The center range usually housed the headquarters building (*principia*), flanked by the commander's house (*praetorium*) and the granaries (*horreae*). There were four main streets within the fort, and the orientation of the fort was taken from the direction that headquarters faced. The road running across the fort in front of the headquarters was the *via principalis*, with its two gates labeled for the right and left sides (*porta principalis dextra* and *porta principalis sinistra*). The road that connected the *principia* to the front gate (*porta praetoria*) was the *via praetoria*, and behind the headquarters another road, the *via decumana*, ran to the rear gate (*porta decumana*).

In several forts archaeological evidence shows that there were other communal buildings, for example the workshop (*fabrica*) where metalworking, woodworking, and repair of equipment and weapons would take place. There was also a hospital (*valetudinarium*). It should be acknowledged that from the ground plans alone, the workshops and the hospitals might have been confused, each consisting of small rooms off a central courtyard, but in a few cases medical instruments have been found, which strongly supports the label "hospital." The forts on Hadrian's Wall at Wallsend and Housesteads, and the fortresses at Vetera (modern Xanten, Germany) and Novaesium (modern Neuss,

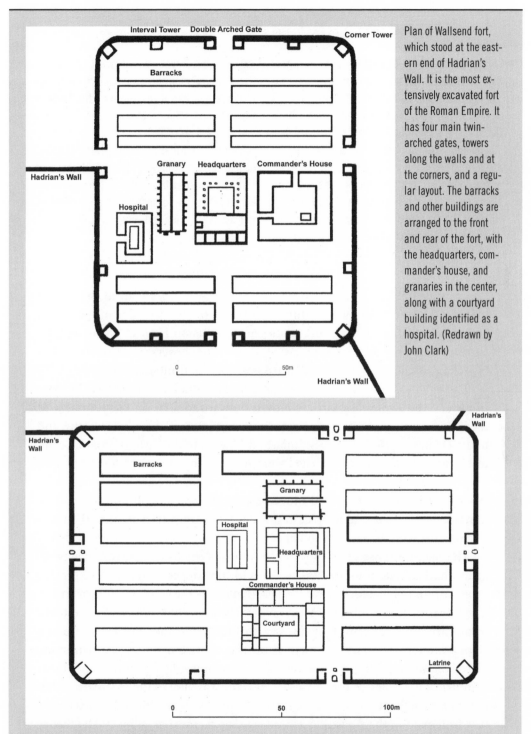

Plan of Wallsend fort, which stood at the eastern end of Hadrian's Wall. It is the most extensively excavated fort of the Roman Empire. It has four main twin-arched gates, towers along the walls and at the corners, and a regular layout. The barracks and other buildings are arranged to the front and rear of the fort, with the headquarters, commander's house, and granaries in the center, along with a courtyard building identified as a hospital. (Redrawn by John Clark)

Simplified plan of Housesteads fort on Hadrian's Wall, arranged in similar fashion to Wallsend except that here the layout was altered to fit the long narrow site on the crest of the hill, so that the barracks were parallel to the long axis rather than lying across the fort. (Redrawn by John Clark)

## ROMAN FORTRESSES, FORTS, AND FORTLETS (continued)

Germany) are among examples where hospitals have been found. The majority of the buildings inside the fort would be the barrack blocks. For the infantry in legionary fortresses and auxiliary forts, barracks were normally laid out with ten rooms subdivided into two parts, one for sleeping and eating and one for storage, each room accommodating eight men, and therefore housing one complete century of eighty men. A verandah ran the full length of the ten rooms, and at the end of the barrack block there was usually a suite of rooms for the centurion. Cavalry barracks were different, reflecting the organization of the *turma*. From the evidence at the fort at Dormagen on the Rhine, and Wallsend on Hadrian's Wall, it seems that the men and their horses were housed together. In at least three of the Dormagen stable blocks, there were double cubicles, with soakaway pits in those along one side, and hearths in those on the other, indicating that men and mounts shared the blocks (Müller, 1979; Dixon and Southern, 1992).

the frontier line, as on Hadrian's Wall and the Antonine Wall in Britain, or placed a kilometer or two behind the line, as on the frontier in Germany. Smaller installations like the milecastles and turrets on Hadrian's Wall and the corresponding small forts (Kleinkastelle) and watch towers in Germany probably served as patrolling bases and guard posts on the frontiers.

The emperor who is indelibly associated with Roman frontiers is Hadrian. In his day, the armies had already moved outward to forts on the periphery of the Empire, toward the northern parts of Britain, to the Rhine in Germany, and to the Danube in Noricum, Pannonia, and Moesia. In the eastern provinces and in North Africa, running barriers were not employed, except for an area of North Africa where lines of stone walls of Hadrianic date are considered to be less of a military frontier and more of a means of controlling the seasonal movements of a pastoral people, to prevent them from straying into the more settled areas with their flocks and herds.

The main purpose of establishing frontiers is ostensibly to avoid having to go to war. The system allowed the Romans to control people outside the Empire by more tranquil means. The whole package besides the erection of the frontiers sometimes included subsidies to the natives beyond the frontiers, the bestowal of privileges in the form of alliances with Rome, and the granting of trading rights. Modern scholars are divided on the importance that the tribesmen placed on trading with Rome, some arguing that it was by no means fundamental to tribal life, whereas others posit that trade was vital to the chieftains, if not the tribesmen themselves, because it afforded them the wealth and kudos necessary to remain in their position as leaders. One factor that supports the theory of the importance of trade is the ancient writers' suggestion that abolition of markets caused genuine hardship to the tribes (Tacitus, *Germania* 41.1; *Histories* 4.64; Dio 71.11.3; 71.11.15–16; Ammianus 27.5.7).

Arch of Hadrian at Athens.  Hadrian traveled all over the Empire and many buildings are associated with him, but he is chiefly associated with the establishment of the frontiers.  (Library of Congress)

These less bellicose means of control should not imply timidity on the part of the Romans. The ascendancy still rested with them, but Hadrian and his successors chose to demonstrate their ascendancy without constantly dashing about at the head of armies. The only serious fighting under Hadrian was in the Jewish revolt of Bar Kochba (AD 132–135); otherwise, Hadrian's reign was notable for his rationalization of the Empire and total lack of wars of conquest. He had fought in several wars under Trajan, so his negative attitude to expansion of the Empire cannot be attributed to an absence of military experience. He had other ideas about how to control the Empire and about how much of it the Romans could administer. He abandoned some of the territories just conquered by Trajan, and then he gradually enclosed most of the Empire within firm boundaries, creating solid barriers in some of the provinces and in others marking the boundaries by roads lined with forts and towers, on the same pattern as the Flavian emperors.

The study of Roman frontiers is understandably vast, not least because of the territorial extent of the Empire, and the equally large extent of the various physical remains of the frontiers themselves and the installations associated with them. The majority of the modern archaeological and historical literature on frontiers is devoted to the actual walls or earth and timber barricades, and the towers, forts, and fortresses of the frontier zones. From these remains alone it is not easy to illuminate the ideology of the Roman emperors. It has to be admitted that we do not know what the Romans wanted to achieve by maintaining their frontiers; there may have been different aims at different times, achieved by adapting the administration, personnel, and functioning of the frontiers. The lack of certainty allows for much modern debate. For Luttwak (1976) it was all downhill for the Romans after the establishment of rigid frontiers, because their aggressive, energetic expansion up to this point had been successful and the momentum ought to have been maintained. According to Professor John Mann (1974), the frontiers marked the places where the Romans simply ran out of energy, and thereafter the retention of the solid barriers and the frontier lines was due to simple inertia.

If it was indeed lack of energy that influenced the Romans, an explanation needs to be found for the fact that various emperors from Hadrian onward nurtured, repaired, and reconstituted the frontiers, sometimes on slightly different alignments but not generally on a completely different pattern or principle. As soon as Hadrian was dead, his successor Antoninus Pius advanced Roman occupation further northward in Britain, and he also advanced a few miles further eastward in Germany. Having achieved this forward movement, he built exactly the same kind of frontiers that Hadrian had established. In Scotland he built the structure labeled the Antonine Wall, an earthen barrier with forts along it, and in Germany he replicated the palisade frontier, accompanied by watch towers with forts a short distance away in the hinterland.

Modern portrayal of Antonius Pius, emperor of Rome, AD 86–161. After Hadrian's death, Antoninus Pius advanced Roman occupation further northward in Britain and a few miles further eastward in Germany.
(Library of Congress)

Since it is not known what the Romans wanted from their frontiers, it cannot really be said that the static lines were failures from their point of view. If the frontiers were not working properly, or if circumstances had changed so much in later periods that they were outmoded, it is likely that energetic emperors who repaired frontier works would have devoted their time and energies to developing some alternative. Severus visited Britain and campaigned in the north of the province for some time at the beginning of the third century, and he repaired Hadrian's Wall so thoroughly that early scholars were convinced that he had in fact built the Wall. For some time it was thought that Hadrian's only contribution was to mark the frontier with the ditch to the south, known to modern archaeologists as the Vallum. Building inscriptions naming the governor as Aulus Platorius Nepos (*RIB* 1637; 1638), who is confirmed from military diplomas as governor from AD 122 until at least AD 124, established the original work as Hadrianic. Severus also repaired and renewed the frontiers of Germany, and in the fourth century Count Theodosius rebuilt and repaired frontier works in Britain after the destruction of AD 367.

Several strong-minded emperors followed in Hadrian's footsteps and did not tear apart the work that he did in favor of some other radically different plan. Therefore, it is just as safe to assume that the frontiers provided whatever the Romans wanted from them as it is to assume that all the emperors from Antoninus Pius to Honorius suffered from a crippling inertia that prevented them from taking stock and applying some thought to the matter. Modern historians and archaeologists can offer some generalizations about how Roman frontiers worked. It used to be thought that the frontiers were sharply defined barriers where language, culture, and lifestyle were markedly different on each side, but more recently this opinion has been revised. It is clear that frontiers did not mark the limit of civilized *Romanitas* and the beginning of barbarism, nor were they dividing lines between two completely different or inimical cultures. They were not laid out with any regard for tribal boundaries or for the territorial limits of more developed states. In some instances, the frontiers divided communities, embracing some of the inhabitants and leaving others outside the boundary. In Britain, for example, it is suggested that while the large majority of the Brigantes dwelt to the south of Hadrian's Wall, some part of the federation also dwelt to the northwest, cut off from their compatriots (Salway, 1991).

It is highly unlikely that any of the frontiers of the Empire were ever meant to serve as exclusive, impermeable barriers. None of them, however they were constructed or manned, was designed to withstand a concerted and determined attack. Indeed, this level of threat was probably not even envisaged, since the Romans were in the ascendancy and simply by a display of overt power they could, for the most part, discourage unified action. The frontiers represented reactions to perceived threat, and the potential enemies that faced Rome on the other side of the barriers could be controlled by various means and prevented from uniting without the necessity for constant military action. River frontiers were just as effective as physical barriers, provided that the territory on the opposite bank was also under Roman control just as the territory beyond the running barriers was watched, not just by means of bridgehead forts and patrols in a narrow area near to the banks, but by political, diplomatic, and military control extending much deeper into the lands beyond the rivers.

The frontiers were zones rather than lines, where peoples and cultures were already remarkably similar or gradually melded. Behind the frontier zones lay fully administered Roman territory, and beyond them were states and tribes that though nominally free were still controlled by Rome in her own interests. The Roman emperors dealt with peoples beyond their frontiers in different ways, usually fostering the elite groups among city-states or tribes, bestowing honors and gifts on them in return for their cooperation in keeping their compatriots under control. Subsidies were sometimes paid to tribal leaders, in the form of prestige gifts, plain and simple cash, and sometimes foodstuffs. On occasion, the Romans discovered that they had backed the wrong group, and then they had to mount an expedition to restore order and control, and choose to cultivate another group. Sometimes they had to go beyond the frontiers to prevent a tribe or a confederation of tribes from obliterating the more peaceful and tractable ones. Marcus Aurelius fought for years to bring stability to the areas beyond the Danube, and there is some suggestion that he intended to annex the lands and create new provinces called Sarmatia and Marcomannia, but if this is so it never happened, and after the death of Marcus, his son Commodus brought the wars to a speedy end with a treaty that demanded soldiers for the Roman army. This combination of diplomacy and war, or the threat of war, served to extend Roman influence far beyond the frontiers.

The forts and fortresses in the vicinity of the frontiers provided bases where troops could be assembled if all other means of control had failed and it was decided that a war was the only solution.

The barriers themselves restricted unauthorized small-scale movement, channeling it through points where supervision was possible and customs dues could be paid. The Knag Burn gateway east of Housesteads fort on Hadrian's Wall, and the elaborate gateway through the German Raetian frontier at Dalkingen may have served these purposes.

## TACTICS AND OPERATIONAL CONCEPTS

On the subject of tactical operations of the Roman army, historians are reliant almost wholly on literary evidence, which includes the military manuals that have survived (it is known that several manuals have been lost), the eyewitness descriptions of the army in action, and the accounts of various battles. There is a respectable body of information about the order of march at different periods and in different circumstances, and accounts of various battles, including some that the Romans lost. In addition, considerable literary information exists on the layout of the military camp, accompanied by a wealth of archaeological detail, chiefly from Britain and to some extent from Germany, where camps have been identified. Unfortunately, the marriage between these two sources is not one of wedded bliss, and it is often difficult to reconcile the words of the ancient authors with the archaeological evidence that emerges from marching camps.

## Order of March

The main sources for the order of march are Polybius for the Republican army, Caesar for the late Republic, Josephus for the first century AD in Judaea under Vespasian and Titus, Arrian for the second century AD in Cappadocia in the reign of Hadrian, and Vegetius, whose account does not concern a specific time or place. While the finer details of the order of march will have depended on the terrain and the perceived threat from the Roman point of view, these accounts are sufficiently similar to allow some general conclusions, mostly related to common sense and good practice (Campbell, 1994; Gilliver, 2000; Goldsworthy, 1996, 2003). Scouts would head the column, perhaps on all occasions, even when the purely historical accounts neglect to mention them. During the Republic, the allied troops were placed just behind the scouts, with their cavalry contingents preceding the infantry. Auxiliary troops fulfilled this function in the Imperial period, often with the horsemen of the *cohortes equitatae* mixed with those of one or more *alae*. Next came the auxiliary infantry, then the legions, and in the center the general and his *singulares,* or the emperor and the Praetorians. The baggage could be carried all together, after the legions and commanders, or split up into different sections following the relevant troops. Caesar most often placed the baggage to the rear. In many cases, the rearguard mirrored the arrangements at the head of the column, with auxiliary infantry and then cavalry to ward off attacks. Cavalry could be used to guard the flanks, patrolling on either side of the marching column, and if attacks occurred while on the march, cavalry could screen the column while the soldiers formed up into battle lines.

An army is in its most disadvantaged and vulnerable position when it moves from place to place, and it is likely that the order of march varied according to circumstances. Polybius indicates that during the Republic in times of great danger, the normal marching order that he has just described was changed, and provided that the ground was open enough, the Romans marched in three columns composed of the *hastati,* the *principes,* and the *triarii,* with the baggage in the spaces between them. With this arrangement, if the army was attacked while moving, the soldiers could turn to the left or the right to face the attack, and form up in advance of the baggage. Polybius admits that on some occasions the *hastati* had to wheel round to get to the front, because if they marched on the left and the attack came from the right, then the troops would turn to the right and the *hastati* would find themselves in the rear. Although it is not specifically mentioned in Polybius's account, the allies would presumably precede and

## ORDER OF MARCH

### Order of march according to Polybius (6.40–41)

At this period an army usually consisted of one of the consuls in command of two legions and the allied contingents

- The *extraordinarii* at the head of the column
- The right wing of the allied troops, cavalry, then infantry
- Their pack animals with their baggage
- The first of the Roman legions
- The pack animals with their baggage
- The second of the Roman legions
- The pack animals with their baggage
- The baggage of the remaining allied troops forming the rearguard
- The left wing of the allied troops, infantry, then cavalry

### Polybius adds some further points:

- The cavalry sometimes ride behind their sections, or sometimes alongside the baggage animals as guards and to keep them together.
- If an attack is expected from the rear, the *extraordinarii* (specially picked soldiers from the allied troops) take up position in the rearguard instead of in the van.

- On alternate days the allies and the legions reverse this order, so that the left wing of the allies leads off with the second legion behind, and the right wing forms the rearguard. This ensures that all the troops have an equal opportunity to find fresh water and forage for the animals.

### Order of March According to Josephus, *Jewish War* (3.115–126)

In AD 67, the General Flavius Vespasianus, who was not yet emperor, marched into Galilee in the following order:

- Light-armed auxiliary troops and archers, to check the terrain ahead to discover ambushes
- Heavy-armed Roman infantry and cavalry
- Ten men from each legionary century, carrying tools for layout of the camp
- Engineers to attend to the roads, to clear obstacles and flatten rough ground
- Baggage of the General Vespasian and of his senior officers, with a cavalry guard
- Vespasian himself with infantry and cavalry guards, as well as his own personal bodyguard
- Legionary cavalry

follow the legions, and when the column turned into line, they would be on the wings, as usual.

Besides Polybius's account, there are other references to marching in areas of low- or high-intensity threat. Although details are not always included in the ancient sources, if the threat was considered to be low, the position of the various units, the baggage, and the flank guards may have differed from the pattern adopted in areas of high-intensity threat. Some scholars have classified marches into different categories, starting with simply moving the army from one place to another, followed by the arrangements for marching through enemy territory, and concluding with marching purposefully into battle. Others have tried

- Mules carrying the sections of the siege towers and the siege engines
- The officers: the legionary commanders, prefects, and tribunes, with guards
- The eagles and the standards
- Trumpeters
- Legionaries, 6 abreast with centurion to supervise
- Servants and baggage
- Auxiliary troops and/or specially raised allied troops
- Rearguard comprising both light-armed and heavy-armed infantry and cavalry

**Order of March in Cappadocia, c. AD 135, from Arrian's *Order of March Against the Alans* (1–11)**

The Alans were a horse people, a branch of the Sarmatians, using heavily armored cavalry but mobile and fearsome to the Romans. Most of the units mentioned by Arrian are attested in the archaeological record, except for the unit called Aplanoi, for which Campbell (1994) suggests Apulians, a unit attested in other sources. Though the list of cohorts, alae, and legions seems quite explicit, there are still several problems of interpretation when trying to decide upon the fine details of this passage.

- Two contingents of mounted scouts, with their own commander

- The Petraean horse archers (*cohors III Petraeorum sagittariorum milliaria equitata*), commanded by decurions
- *Ala Auriana*
- Cavalry of *cohors IV Raetorum*, commanded by Daphne the Corinthian
- *Ala I Aug. Gemina Colon.*
- Cavalry from three-part mounted cohorts (*cohors I Ituraeorum equitata, cohors III Aug. Cyrenaicorum equitata*, and *cohors I Raetorum*) commanded by Demetrius
- German cavalry (*cohors I Germanorum equitata*) commanded by a centurion, the prefect of the camp
- Auxiliary infantry (*cohors I Italicorum* and "those present" of *cohors III Aug. Cyrenaicorum*) commanded overall by Pulcher, the commander of *coh. I Italicorum*
- Bosporan footsoldiers (*cohors I Bosp. milliaria*) commanded by their leader Lamprocles
- Numidians (*cohors I Flavia Numidorum*) under the leader Verus
- Guard cavalry (*Equites singulares*)
- Legionary cavalry (*equites legionis*)
- Artillery
- Eagle of *legio XV Apollinaris* with the commander Valens, the tribunes, and the centurions of the First Cohort

to relate styles of marching order to local conditions and physical geography. All these elements of purpose, threat, and terrain would play a contributory part in a general's decision on his line of march, but not to the exclusion of everything else. There would certainly be greater need for vigilance and keeping close together in enemy territory, and as Polybius demonstrates for the Republican period, it would be important for the order of march to reflect the order of battle so as to reduce the potential chaos if the troops had to turn from column into battle line at short notice. Caesar had this in mind when he wanted to take the Germans by surprise while they were still in their camp. He divided his army into three columns which he describes as the *triplex acies*, and after a rapid eight-mile march he succeeded in taking the enemy unawares and giving battle straightaway (*Gallic War* 4.14). When under tremendous threat and the enemy was closing in, the army would adopt the square formation (*agmen quadratum*), where the baggage was placed in the center and troops marched on all sides. Livy refers several times to this formation, and Onasander also describes a compact formation with the baggage and the medical equipment in the center and the bravest soldiers placed to the front or rear according to the direction of the greatest threat. Marching down the Euphrates in the mid-fourth century, the Emperor Julian protected the head of the column and the flanks with 1,500 *excursatores,* whose purpose was to ward off unexpected attacks (Ammianus 24.1.2; Austin and Rankov, 1995).

The practicalities of marching the Roman armies from one place to another under any circumstances have occupied many scholars, who are at pains to work out how wide and how long any particular column would be. According to Josephus, Vespasian's legions marched six abreast, while Arrian ordered his men to march four abreast. This should not be interpreted too rigidly as the standard practice of the period when each author described the army, nor should it be taken as evidence that a change of policy took place at some time between the Flavian emperors and the reign of Hadrian (Goldsworthy, 2003). It seems that there was never any standard formation for the width of the column, which would be decided by the general, after deliberation about the state of the terrain, the needs of the moment, and his plans for the formation of the battle line.

The length of the marching column would be quite arbitrary, and it would require vigilance to regulate it. There was great danger in allowing the various units to stretch out too far, since a very long line of march is more vulnerable than a compact one. There are references in the literature to centurions going up and down the line to keep everyone together, to round up stragglers and generally sort out any problems.

## Marching Camps and Temporary Camps

At the end of each march, the Romans traditionally enclosed their troops in an entrenched camp. This practice was instituted at some unknown point during the Republic but was fully established by the time Polybius described the Roman army, and it was standard routine during the Empire. Writing of the order of march employed by Vespasian in the first century AD, Josephus says that ten men were drawn from each legionary century, carrying their own kit and tools for marking out the camp, which may be the flags and spears that Polybius says were planted on the site chosen for the commander's tent, at the central point of the lines where the tribunes were to camp, and to mark out the streets.

## THE ROMAN MILITARY TENT

On the march, the eight men of a *contubernium* shared one tent, just as they shared a barrack room in their forts. Different styles of Roman tents are depicted on Trajan's Column, one of them with very low walls, others with higher walls and looking a little more elaborate. The differences may simply be a result of artistic licence, or it could be that it was intended to show tents for soldiers and officers, perhaps the general or the emperor, a question to which no one can provide a definitive answer. Hyginus gives the dimensions of military tents, but since the date is not established for his work, there can be no certainty as to whether these facts applied to the army at all periods of its existence.

Tents were usually made of leather, and various pieces of leather panels have been discovered from different parts of the Empire; however, it was not possible to make anything other than an informed estimate of the structure and size of tents, until the discoveries of full-sized goatskin panels, with evidence of stitching along the edges, at Vindolanda in northern Britain. Carol van Driel Murray, an expert on ancient leather, concluded that at least in Britain if not in other provinces, the Romans used standard panels of different sizes, the largest 76 centimeters by 52 centimeters, smaller ones 52 centimeters by 38 centimeters. Miscellaneous narrow strips, pieces used as reinforcements, and attachments for the guy ropes were also identified. It was possible, from a study of the stitching and stretching of the leather panels, to reconstruct the tent, working out previously unknown factors such as the height of the walls and the pitch of the roof. One of the problems concerned the use of guy ropes to support the tent. Hyginus says that these extended only one Roman foot (slightly less than the modern foot) from the tent walls, implying that they were pegged in at an extremely sharp angle that would not give as much support as ropes pegged much further apart at a more oblique angle. This led to the conclusion that if Hyginus's figures are correct, the tents were probably framed as well, though it has to be admitted that there is no proof for this. Details such as the arrangements for ventilation of the tent, and how the door flaps were arranged and fastened, remain unclear.

The only other source besides Polybius that gives any detail about the location of each section of the army in the marching camp is a work called *De Munitionibus Castrorum,* or *De Metatione Castrorum,* by Hyginus, or as purists prefer, Pseudo-Hyginus, since the authorship as well as the title of this manual is disputed. Its date is also disputed, with several alternatives offered. The scenario depicted by Hyginus concerns a Roman army on the Danube together with the emperor and his retinue, but this could be Domitian, Trajan, Marcus Aurelius, or one of the later emperors who campaigned in the Danube regions. With reference to the study of marching camps and the operations of the Roman army, the date is perhaps not so important as the information contained in the outline of military practice.

Vegetius (*Epitoma Rei Militaris*) and Hyginus describe the most suitable locations for a camp, including the common-sense advice that higher ground with a good view, near to supplies of water, timber, and food is best. Marshy ground and areas liable to flood are to be avoided. Other considerations concerning the location of camps would be dependent on the purpose; some camps were true marching camps, occupied for only one night, whereas others may have been intended to shelter the army for a few days while the men rested, repaired weapons and harness, or foraged for supplies. Yet others were occupied for a much longer period and are better described as temporary camps rather than marching camps. In some places, two or three camps have been discovered superimposed one on top of another, implying the movement of an army on campaign making more than one visit as the army passed through in one direction and then returned. Where several camps are found in the vicinity of a later permanent fort, such as those outside the fortresses at Haltern and Neuss in Germany, some of them may be temporary camps reflecting the comings and goings of the army, and others may be semipermanent installations that housed the builders of the fort. Another type of temporary camp is the siege camp, which by its very nature, was generally occupied for a considerable time. The best known examples are those at Numantia in Spain and at Masada in Judaea, and the extended siege lines enclosing the various camps of Pompey and Caesar at Dyrrachium. It was normal in the Republic for opposing armies to entrench themselves close to each other and to sit there for some time until battle was offered or the food ran out, but this was not a regular part of the military practice of the Empire (Goldsworthy, 2003).

Before the establishment of the standing army, housed in permanent forts and backed up by a regular supply system, a large army was forced to disperse in winter to live, especially in northern climates. Winter quarters (*hiberna*) for a campaign army were often located in towns, where negotiations could be made with the inhabitants of the region and supplies could be stockpiled, but in hostile territory sometimes the Romans spent the winter in camps, on occasion *sub pellibus,* in tents. Quintus Cicero, younger brother of the orator, was famously besieged in his winter camp (*Gallic War* 5.40–49). This camp was an earthwork structure with timber towers, 120 of which were put up in one night, using the timber that had been collected "for the fortification" (*munitionis causa*).

Several of the temporary camps of the later Republic and the early Empire were irregularly shaped, perhaps taking advantage of the natural terrain, but wherever these camps have been partly or fully excavated, the interior layout is more or less regular with blocks allocated for rows of tents and delineated by straight streets. At Numantia and at Masada, the soldiers provided more shelter for themselves by piling up stones around their tents, creating a hybrid hut-cum-tent (Goldsworthy, 2003). This fortunate habit, coupled with the hot dry climates in Spain and Judaea where archaeological remains stand the test of time, enables archaeologists to trace the layout of the camp with more precision. In Britain, the province where by far the greatest numbers of temporary camps have come to light, it is not usually possible to trace the interior design, but there is useful evidence about other features of camps, such as the ditches and gateways.

Temporary camps of the Imperial period were usually more rectangular, with rounded corners like permanent forts. A ditch surrounded the perimeter, and the soil from the ditch was thrown inward to create the rampart. There may have been a palisade on top of the rampart formed from the stakes that the soldiers carried, called *valli* in some sources and/or *pila muralia*. According to Livy, the soldiers of Scipio Aemilianus's army at Numantia each carried seven *valli*. Both Vegetius (*Epitoma Rei Militaris* 1.24; 3.8) and Hyginus (*De Metatione Castrorum* 48) refer to stakes as part of the defenses. The function of the sharpened stakes with an indented hand grip, labeled *pila muralia,* is debated. If these stakes were placed individually into the earth of the rampart, they would not create much of an obstacle, even if they were bound together. If they were combined in groups of three or more, however, they could be used to make large caltrops, somewhat like the antitank beach defenses of World War II (Gilliver, 2000).

Inside the temporary camp, the road that ran around the perimeter was usually wide enough to keep the rows of tents out of range of projectiles thrown over the walls. This road also provided a space in which to form up the army if it had to march out to engage in battle immediately. It has been estimated that it would take two to three hours to erect the camp, but there are many imponderables, such as the available manpower and the type of earth that the soldiers were expected to dig. The British army field manuals for World War I give different estimates for trench digging and the construction of earthwork defenses, depending on the nature of the soils. Another factor that might affect the time taken to erect a camp is whether or not the army was under attack at the time of digging in. Examples are known where this did happen, and part of the army drew up in battle formation and shielded the workers. It is suggested that the first two lines of the *triplex acies* battle formation protected the men of the third line, who did all the digging (Gilliver, 2000), but in reality this was probably not a prescribed formation to be adopted at all times, and the method of defense was probably much more haphazard and flexible. Vegetius (*Epitoma Rei Militaris* 1.25; 3.8) says that all the cavalry and part of the infantry should be drawn up in battle lines to protect those building the camp.

Protection of the gateways would always be a problem without solid wooden doors, and apart from mounting a guard the Romans usually dug a straight ditch and bank (*titulum*) opposite the opening but unconnected to the rampart. Alternatively, they placed a curved ditch and bank (*clavicula*) running directly from the camp wall outward and around the gateway like a protective arm, positioned so that any attackers had to turn and expose their unshielded side to those on the rampart. Some camps had a double *clavicula*, consisting of the outward projecting arm just described, and also an internal one, curving inward. Full-scale attack was never really envisaged in Roman ideology. Camps were not designed to be defended like castles from the tops of the walls, but they were intended to stop unauthorized personnel from entering them. It has also been suggested that one of their purposes was to keep Roman soldiers inside. The laws of Ruffus laid out a severe penalty for crossing the camp or fort wall instead of using the gates, and it probably applied in whichever direction the soldiers crossed the wall.

The Romans attached great importance to training the soldiers to erect temporary camps, as is illustrated by the presence in Britain of what can only be termed practice camps, because they are generally too small to be of use. It seems that emphasis was placed on digging perfect curved corners with accompanying ditches, and the various forms of gateways, with only short stretches of straight wall. Practice camps have been identified in Wales at Llandrindod Common, Castell Collen, and Tomen-y-Mur, and by aerial photography around the fortress at Chester. Such camps leave little trace on the ground, and they are often hard to find without a large-scale map and a guide book. They likely existed in other provinces of the Empire, but have probably been obliterated by agricultural work or by the spread of roads and buildings.

## Battle

The classic arrangement of Roman troops ready for battle was to place the legions in the center, enclosed on each side by the auxiliary infantry, with the auxiliary cavalry on the wings, but this is by no means a fixed organization to be rigidly followed in all circumstances. At the battle of Zama, Scipio Africanus reversed this order, placing the legions on the wings. On occasion, the main battle was fought by the auxiliary troops, with the legions brought in later if necessary. At the unknown location of Mons Graupius in Scotland, Julius Agricola fought the main battle employing only the auxiliary troops in the front line, with the legions in the rear (Tacitus, *Agricola* 35). In this instance, Agricola did not adopt a hastily formed battle plan on the spur of the moment, but he made these arrangements deliberately, with due consideration to the ground where he brought about the battle and the type of enemy he was fighting. Some decades before Mons Graupius, in AD 29, Lucius Apronius, governor of Lower Germany, was faced with a rebellion of the Frisii and had to gather troops rapidly to combat the threat. He sent in his auxiliary forces against the Frisians, at first not very successfully, but just as the enemy were about to overwhelm the infantry and cavalry units, he placed Cethegus Labeo in command of all the remaining auxiliaries, who rushed forward and saved the day (Tacitus, *Annals* 4.73). During another revolt in AD 71 Petillius Cerialis fought the Batavians using mostly his auxiliaries (Tacitus, *Histories* 5.17). Although the exact circumstances of these battles were very different, the enemy shared certain characteristics. Tribal warriors often relied on the psychological impact of their intimidating war cries and the initial shock of their massed charge to break the ranks of their enemies.

The Romans were flexible when it came to drawing up their armies, adapting to the situation in hand. For the legions, the typical *triplex acies* of three ranks was the formation most commonly found in the literary descriptions, usually with four cohorts in the first line and three each in the second and third (Goldsworthy, 1996), but this was not a formula to be rigidly adopted in all circumstances. Some generals employed only two lines, which is how Vegetius describes legionary formation of the "ancient legion," with six cohorts in each line, both of them drawn up with three cohorts at the front and two just behind them, covering the gaps (*Epitoma Rei Militaris* 2.4–14). Four lines were not unknown. For instance, at Pharsalus Caesar noticed that Pompey had stationed himself in command of his left wing, with the First and Third legions, together with all his cavalry and his slingers and archers. In response, Caesar moved individual cohorts from the third line to create a fourth line, to prevent his right wing from being encircled by the Pompeian horsemen.

Protection of the flanks was always of concern to generals of ancient armies, hence the usual position of the mounted troops on each wing. The Romans, like many other peoples, generally utilized natural features if they were available, such as rivers or streams, hills or woods, which presupposes that these areas had been scouted and found to be free of enemy forces or the potential for ambush. The way in which Pompey rested his right wing on a river and strengthened his left has been described above. Arrian, too, had thought about how to protect his flanks by resting them on natural features, to try to prevent the mounted Alani from outflanking or encircling him (*Order of March Against the Alans*).

Arrian clearly knew where he wished to bring the Alani to battle, which was the optimum circumstance for any general: to pick his own ground and bring about the desired battle on it. Second best was to know the ground well, if forced to fight. During his campaign against the Nervii in Gaul, Caesar was attacked while entrenching the campsite. He hastily gathered his men together and drew up the army "according to the character of the ground, the slope of the hill, and the exigency of the moment" rather than in a regular tactical formation (*Gallic War* 2.23). Both Onasander and Vegetius stress the importance of the terrain, where use of the advantages of the ground could make the difference between defeat and victory. Thorough reconnoitring of the battle ground, or an understanding of the hazards of the potential of a campaign area, were important attributes for all generals. Refusing battle could be just as effective as engaging, if the ground was favorable or unfavorable to the enemy. Fighting the numerically superior Belgae in Gaul, Caesar decided to avoid an engagement if he could, but chose a campsite where he could draw up on a slope, and protect his flanks. Instead of attacking from this direction, the Belgae tried to storm the rear of the camp, across the river Aisne. The Romans received the attacks, but that was all, and the Belgae withdrew since they saw that the soldiers did not advance to unfavorable ground for the sake of a battle (*Gallic War* 2.10). Conversely, in a situation that was unfavorable to the enemy, Caesar was able to use his knowledge of the Spanish terrain to his advantage by forcing the Pompeians to encamp on a hill, where they could certainly protect themselves, but not for very long because there was no accessible water supply. They offered battle, but Caesar did not fight them; all he had to do was wait for the inevitable thirsty surrender.

In the protracted civil wars of the first century BC, Republican armies frequently chased each other over whole territories, getting to know it well in the process, and then camped near each other, offering battle on a regular basis, but the opposing side did not always commit their troops. Recognizing and seizing the right moment to commit to battle, or to mount an attack, offered potential for victory—for instance when an opposing army was in the process of drawing up for battle, or breaking camp to move on when the food supplies were exhausted.

Knowledge of the enemy was just as important as knowledge of the ground and was stressed in the military handbooks. Agricola's true merit in Scotland is the fact that he managed to bring his loosely organized tribal adversaries to battle in the first place, since in utilizing their terrain all they had to do was decamp into the mountains and wait, a technique that their descendants used to good effect against other invaders over the succeeding centuries. When he did bring the Britons to battle, Agricola knew what to expect and dealt with it effectively in his dispositions of his troops. Quintus Junius Blaesus did not try to use pitched battle methods when fighting in Africa against Tacfarinas, a mobile enemy whose speciality was hit-and-run raids, frequently classified under the heading of guerrilla warfare. Blaesus divided his forces into smaller groups combining legionaries and auxiliaries, and he constantly chased the enemy, summer and winter, attacking whenever it was feasible, much like General Crook's campaigns against the Native Americans in the nineteenth century. Tacitus says that wherever Tacfarinas's men moved they were confronted by sections of the Roman army, in front of them, on each side, and quite often in the rear (*Annals* 3. 72–73). Keeping the enemy on the move was also employed successfully in the Danubian Wars of Marcus Aurelius, who combined pitched battles with continual harassment. He planted forts in the territory of the Quadi and Marcommani to watch them and keep them moving, never allowing them to settle in one place, so that they could not pasture their animals or plant crops. When they decided to migrate to another land, he hemmed them in and continued the harassment. In this way he finally exhausted them (Dio 72.20).

Some common principles are discernible from the literary accounts that illustrate the way in which the Romans used their troops during battle. Cavalry was used to protect flanks, to prevent encirclement by the enemy, or at the right moment to perform an encircling movement themselves. Horsemen were obviously swifter during the pursuit, and the use of cavalry for chasing the enemy could tip the balance and bring about near annihilation instead of a mere defeat. Caesar's troops gained a foothold in Britain after a desperate battle on the shores in 55 BC, but he had no mounted troops with him. The Britons withdrew, but they were not defeated, and Caesar acknowledged that he would have been able to inflict a more serious defeat on the Britons if his cavalry transports had arrived in time (*Gallic War* 4.26).

There are examples of cavalrymen dismounting to fight on foot. For example, in Spain, Caesar's cavalrymen without mounts fought and won an infantry action (*Spanish War* 15). Agricola ordered his horsemen to dismount after Mons Graupius (Tacitus, *Agricola* 37) and Frontinus reports that Domitian did the same in Germany (*Stratagems* 2.3.23). Normally, cavalry would be placed to fight other cavalry and was not considered to be any match for infantry. Goldsworthy (1996) documents actions where infantry prevailed over cavalry attacks, where the footsoldiers remained in position in a solid mass; once they had broken up, infantrymen could be picked off by horsemen. During the Danubian Wars under Marcus Aurelius, Dio (72.12) records how the Roman infantry chased the Iazyges onto the frozen river, where the enemy turned on them and their horsemen charged, trying to encircle the Romans to attack them in front, flanks, and rear. The Romans formed up all facing outward, each soldier placing a foot on the bottom of his shield to give him purchase on the ice. The troops then not only received the charge without breaking formation, but pulled the horses and riders into the fight by seizing the bridles or the riders' shields. The horsemen could not stop on the ice because of the momentum of their charge.

A typical pitched battle would probably start with a shower of javelins from the Roman infantry and then progress to close combat with the sword, the legionary's main fighting weapon. The auxiliaries on the wings would try to close the enemy in and attack the flanks, or even get round the rear. This aim was not always met, of course, depending on the nature of the enemy and the skill of the opposing leaders. The tribal massed charge depended a great deal on noise, confusion, and sheer terror for its effect, but if it did not carry all before it there was scope for the Romans to rally. Other enemies such as the Parthians and Persians were formidable because of their armored mounted warriors and their archers, whose rapid arrow fire and the famous backward shot as they rode away accounted for several Roman failures. To counteract this menace, Mark Antony took slingers and archers with him when he invaded Parthia via Armenia, but he failed in the end to make any lasting effect and had to withdraw, minus many men and most of his equipment and siege train. Arrian's methods of combating a mounted enemy was to draw up his formations, with a great number of archers and javelin throwers in the fifth to the eighth ranks firing over the heads of the four front ranks. If his battle was successful, Arrian designated his light-armed cavalry for the pursuit of the mounted enemy.

## PLANNING AND STAFF WORK

The Romans appreciated the value of good planning, at least in theory, and the literary references extol the virtues of those generals who were renowned for laying careful plans before engaging in active operations. Tacitus attributed Corbulo's successes to thorough preparation and planning (*Annals* 13). Much of the initial planning took the form of intelligence gathering and reconnaissance work. For example, the Republican general Scipio Aemilianus thoroughly surveyed the ground in the vicinity of Carthago Nova (New Carthage, modern Cartagena) before he laid siege to the city. Geographical considerations were vitally important to the planning process, but so was an understanding of the enemy's characteristics and their daily routines. Vegetius recommends that generals should always get to know their enemies well (*Epitoma Rei Militaris* 3.6; 4.27), and Caesar gathered as much information as he could about the inhabitants of southern Britain as well as the terrain before he invaded in 55 and 54 BC (*Gallic War* 4.20.2–4; Suetonius, *Divus Julius* 58.1).

One of the Romans' desirable aims of good planning was to enable the generals to choose their own battle sites, where they could make maximum use of the terrain to protect their flanks, or to keep reserves hidden from the enemy, and then direct the proceedings with enough flexibility to deal with unexpected crises. The supreme example of detailed planning of this sort is Arrian's *Order of March Against the Alans,* where he not only laid down exactly which troops would march under which commanders, but also outlined how he proposed to fight the battle once he had engaged the enemy. His work is designed for a specific set of circumstances in a specific place against a highly mobile enemy. The danger is, as Goldsworthy points out (1996, 2003), that historians interpret Arrian's arrangements as the universal Roman fighting method for the second century all over the Empire, no matter what kind of enemy the Romans were fighting. While certain broad theoretical concepts may be gleaned from the few close descriptions that we have of the Roman army in action, it is not advisable to extrapolate from them to build up a crystallized static picture of the Romans at war.

In planning how to fight a battle or lay a siege, it was important to form some idea of how to extricate the troops if everything went wrong and it was necessary to retreat. According to Polybius (10.6.11–10.9.1), Scipio planned how to retreat from Carthago Nova (modern Cartagena) in Spain. In this respect, detailed local knowledge would help commanders if they were taken by surprise, so they might have a chance to extricate their armies without too much bloodshed. Since nothing is completely predictable in war, and it is not always possible to preempt a crisis, at times the Romans had no opportunity to make leisurely plans but had to react to unexpected events very quickly, in which case they had to rely on the experience and training of the soldiers. Onasander (32 and 39) lays more emphasis on planning how to fight a battle once the enemy is in sight, so that his dispositions can be observed and arrangements made on the spot to deal with them. A good example of this is at Pharsalus when Caesar saw that Pompey's right wing was very strong, so he strengthened his own left wing to meet the threat. Onasander also indicates that the planning process does not stop even when a battle has started, and generals have to think on their feet.

As part of the planning process, generals usually held a meeting of various chosen officers, corporately termed the *consilium*. This term could also refer to a meeting of a private nature in order to arrange household matters, and each senator was accustomed to conferring with his own personal *consilium* at home. So it is even possible that some of the general's trusted civilian retainers would accompany him to command an army and take part in his planning meetings. Because there was no fixed membership of the *consilium*, Roman commanders could ask whoever they liked to attend and so there could be a mixture of the generals' personal entourage and army officers. The most senior officers certainly attended, and some generals invited centurions to the meetings. The *consilium* was really more like a modern briefing than an actual planning session. Each general would listen to the opinions of his various officers and may have been influenced by their ideas and their knowledge, especially if he had little experience of his own. But total responsibility for the planning procedure lay with him alone, and he could override the decisions of his colleagues if he wished. The order of battle would be given at the *consilium*, and afterward the officers would then brief their own sections, each in a smaller *consilium* of their own. Theoretically, then, even if the troops were not aware of the overall plan, they would know what part they were expected to play once the campaign or the individual battles had started.

A Roman provincial governor was at one and the same time commander of the armed forces and responsible for all civilian matters. His administrative staff included several army officers, often on temporary appointments from another unit, to deal with the paperwork and the transmission of orders in peacetime not only to the army of the province, but also to the judicial staff, the civilian officials, contractors, and businessmen. The *beneficiarii* attached to headquarters played an important part in administration, but it is unfortunately not known if they continued their duties in wartime, or whether the general routinely appointed these officers to his *consilium*. Since there seems to have been no standard system of official posts on the staff of a general, such as those that evolved in, for instance, Berthier's staff in the army of Napoleon, no one can say much about Roman staff work, except by extrapolation from the literature, which is not always very helpful.

## COMMAND AND CONTROL

How the army was controlled in battle or on campaign is one of the least illuminated aspects of Roman military history. The main source of information derives from the various literary accounts, which tend to document the extremes but perhaps not the typical or mundane aspects of warfare. The end result is that modern historians have at their disposal accounts of notable successes and notorious failures, in which heroics and disasters feature significantly but not the mechanics of command and control. One of the problems is that many ancient historians elaborated upon events, often utilizing their largely fabricated prebattle speeches to put across to their audiences a political point of view.

Besides the historical literature, there are the military manuals. Although the manuals offer examples of best practice and outline what *should* happen, they do not help elucidate what really *did* happen in Roman warfare. Some authors, notably Campbell (1987) and Gilliver (2000), have investigated the utility and effectiveness of the manuals, and have concluded that they were in fact an important resource in the training of a Roman commander. This in turn implies that the modern historian can place some cautious reliance on using the manuals as sources of evidence for the Roman army in the field.

During the Empire, the overall commander of the armies was of course the emperor himself, who controlled all operations, either from Rome through his subordinates or directly by his presence in the field. In the first century the emperors were, on the whole, content to leave the conduct of military operations in the hands of their chosen governors. Domitian and Trajan accompanied their armies to the Danube, but after Trajan's victories, the succeeding decades of the second century were more peaceful and emperors reverted to directing operations at a distance. In the later second century, and certainly in the third century, the presence of the emperor in the field was vital.

Whether or not the emperor was with them, provincial governors and army commanders were his legates and subject to his dictates. Generals who operated at a distance from the emperor, such as Aulus Plautius in Britain, Corbulo on the Rhine, and Agricola in Scotland, all had considerable authority within their allotted zones but were still subject to the emperor's wishes. Corbulo was recalled when he seemed ready to progress beyond the Rhine, and Agricola stopped to consolidate and perhaps to sound out the emperor's opinions on what should be done next. Generals would work within the broad general framework of the emperor's instructions but would make their own decisions on the spot as to how to achieve their objectives. As always it was a question of balance; too little power and freedom of action would stultify the generals and risk failure, but too much power and too many troops posed a problem if they should turn into usurpers.

There is a corpus of evidence as to the identity of Roman commanders, and their social and military backgrounds, derived from literary sources and from their career inscriptions. These sources help to document the various tasks that generals could be asked to perform, but they do not inform us how well or how badly they performed them. It is only from this historical record that information can be gleaned as to whether the commanders were ideally suitable for their posts. For the most part commanders of armies were senators, men of education and social standing, and as Campbell (1984, 1994) points out, scarcely any of them would ever question their military or political abilities. During the Republic, generals were appointed by the assembly and were expected to defend Rome or Roman interests and then return to political life, without becoming professional military specialists. Young men such as Scipio Africanus and Pompey the Great rose to power when dangers threatened, and they gained commands without too much public disbelief in their aptitude for war. The Impe–rial system was no longer conducive to the emergence of youthful heroes. While there was never a rigidly prescribed career pattern, aspiring generals followed a broadly similar path. They would gain experience of the legions from their appointments as *tribuni laticlavii* and later as legionary legates, and this, combined with their political experience, formed their training for warfare. There were no staff colleges or training schools, but there were the military manuals and the accounts of the battles of the past, and there were men of experience to talk to and question, all of which Polybius (11.8.1–2) recommends as a means of becoming a general. Cicero says that this was how Lucullus acquired his expertise while traveling to the east to take up the command that was eventually wrested from him by Pompey the Great (Campbell, 1984). None of the sources mentions an Imperial archive or an official corpus of military theory and recorded practice.

It has been stated that Roman commanders were amateurs and that the victories they gained came about almost by accident as a result of the expertise and training of the soldiers and the officers. While the contribution of the centurions and their ability to influence the outcome of a battle should never be doubted, the suggestion that generals were more or less superfluous ignores the fact that responsibility for the conduct of campaigns and individual battles rested with the general. The subordinate officers did not formulate the overall plan for a campaign or a battle, and ultimately they had to obey their commanders even if they did not agree with the planning process.

The quality of these subordinate officers was of some concern to conscientious emperors and Roman generals. Vespasian paid off a centurion who had joined the army merely for the pay, so it could be assumed that aptitude for military service played its part in the appointment of officers and commanders. Not all senators pursued their military careers with great vigor up to the rank of provincial governor of an armed province. Indeed, there would not be enough appointments to satisfy them all, so it was perhaps only those men who did have some ability, either self-professed or observed, for command. Catching the eye of men who could advance one's career was an important route to military appointments, and although the emperors did not take a personal interest in the promotion of all the individual centurions, they certainly did take an interest in the appointments and subsequent performances of their higher officers. In the later second century, social rank alone was not always enough to satisfy the emperors when they sought military commanders. Marcus Aurelius chose some of his officers from among the equestrians whose abilities he had noted, admittedly elevating them to senatorial status so that the proper forms were observed.

Roman officers commanding individual units were not necessarily limited to those single units when it came to battle. Before the establishment of a standing army, Caesar chose his legionary commanders from among his associates, without permanently attaching them to these legions, and his officers were expected to take control of collections of troops for specific operations. During the Empire legionary legates kept their posts for longer, but there was still scope for commanders to take charge of detachments called vexillations. These were temporary units comprising soldiers drawn from several units, sometimes simply to bring them safely to the war zone, or in other circumstances to undertake specific tasks during a campaign. They fought together under their own standard called a *vexillum,* hence the name vexillations. Arrian chose to place commanders of other units in charge of a collection of troops. For instance, he put the camp prefect of a legion in charge of the German cavalry (*cohors I Germanorum equitata*) and grouped all the mounted elements of three *cohortes equitatae* under one officer called Demetrius. The cohort commander called Pulcher took charge of his own unit as well as the men of another auxiliary infantry unit.

Once the command structure had been decided upon for a particular campaign or a specific battle, and the *consilium* had been held, it remained for a general to commit his troops to battle and then control the outcome. The various command positions have been enumerated and discussed in great depth by Goldsworthy (1996), who recounts instances where individual generals led from the front, from among the troops, and from the rear. A general who fought at the front of the army presumably had already outlined what was to happen and then had to leave the soldiers to their own devices, since as Goldsworthy points out it was impossible to observe what was happening on the battlefield. Even if the commander could see what was developing, he could not stop to issue orders. Leading from the front could be said to be a last resort, where maybe the soldiers needed the example of personal bravery and the outcome was uncertain. Mingling with the troops is not much better, though in Caesar's accounts of various wars he describes instances where he dashed into the midst of the troops to try to stop them from running away or to encourage them to fight harder when threatened with disaster. Once the impending disaster was averted, the general would usually take up another position. One of the *topoi* or commonplace remarks in literary accounts of battles, indeed not confined to the Roman period, is that the general "seemed to be everywhere at once," but this may not always be a fabrication when it concerns a general who observed closely what was going on and dashed about to the points where he was needed most. The success of these actions would depend largely on the personality of the general, whether he was a charismatic leader in whom the men believed and would follow anywhere, or a routine commander without the necessary spark that fired the exploits of the great generals of history.

Commanding from the rear allowed the general to observe the whole battle, or however much of it he could see from his chosen position. Thus he was enabled to decide how to deal with specific situations and to issue orders to the troops, perhaps sending in each section when it was called for, bringing in the reserves to threatened points, attempting an enveloping maneuver, or ordering the pursuit. As Goldsworthy (1996) remarks, if the general remained in one place at the rear, messengers could find him more easily to inform him of developments that he may not have been able to see, and he could then make his dispositions accordingly.

There is very little evidence as to how Roman generals transmitted their orders during a battle. Even those writers who had seen the Roman army in action do not always elucidate the specific details that modern historians would like to know, such as how orders were given, how and in what form messages were sent during a battle, who carried them, and what happened when they were received. Caesar's literary works are invaluable for historians trying to document the Roman army in action, but he would never have considered it necessary to give anything more than the barest summary of how he commanded the troops. He simply says laconically "a message was sent," or "the signal was given," assuming that his audience would either know how it was done or would not care about it—much as there is no need in the twenty-first century to elaborate on how we mail a letter by long-windedly explaining that we fold a piece of paper with a message written on it, put it into another piece of prefolded paper called an envelope, and then we gum down the open flap, turn the envelope over to write the address and stick a small colored paper square in the top-right corner, and then place it into a receptacle for collection and distribution. Would that Caesar or any other Roman author had entered into such minute detail. Goldsworthy (1996) enumerates the only known instance when a written message was sent during a battle. This occurred at the first battle of Cremona in the civil wars of AD 69, when a Numidian courier delivered the message and it was left to the officer receiving it to decide what to do (Plutarch, *Otho* 9). This presupposes that the commander had at his disposal at least one officer or perhaps a scribe with writing implements, and possibly a few riders standing by to deliver instructions to various units, but it is impossible to say whether this was normal procedure.

During the Gallic War, Caesar records that he sent a message to Titus Sextius, who was in command of the cohorts guarding the camp, to bring them out and post them at the bottom of the hill in case the Romans were driven back down it, so that the cohorts might be able to stop the enemy who might be in pursuit. Caesar does not say whether this was a written or an oral message. Much of Caesar's narrative concerns signals, but these are not usually fully described. Signaling by various means was common in the Roman army, but it is a subject fraught with controversy among scholars. The emphasis of modern studies has been on long-distance signaling along routes or frontier lines, using fires and torches, for which the evidence has been collected by Woolliscroft (2001). Smoke signals could be given by day and fires could be lit at night to give warning of an attack, or to recall foragers and troops working outside the camp. During battle, signals were given by horn or trumpet. Presumably then, there were a few combinations of notes that translated into specific maneuvers, but if so, we do not know what they were. The literary sources detail instances of these types of signal. The overeager *tubicen* who sounded the signal to join battle without orders from Caesar has already been mentioned, and in another battle, during the Gallic War, Caesar ordered the retreat to be sounded, but the legions on the opposite side of the valley did not hear it (*Gallic War* 7.47). A more complicated example of orders given during battle comes from the African War, when Caesar was surrounded by Labienus's troops and ordered every other cohort to turn round so that the Caesarians could fight on two fronts (*African War* 12). While it cannot be ruled out that this order was transmitted by word of mouth, it does imply that there was a standard signal for a standard maneuver, very simply conveyed, especially in the circumstances that Caesar describes because any confusion or hesitation would have been disastrous.

## COMBINED ARMS OPERATIONS

Roman legions and auxiliary forces united heavy- and light-armed troops, skirmishers, scouts, artillery, and cavalry. The only other military force, separate from the army, was the navy, whose history has been documented by Starr (1960, 1989). The Roman navy began life out of sheer necessity during the Republican period, when Rome went to war, perhaps a little unwisely, against the supreme naval power in the Mediterranean, Carthage. The Carthaginians had a long tradition of seaborne operations, both for trading purposes and for war, and at first the Romans were inexperienced in either of these spheres. After initial disasters they learned quickly, drawing on the expertise and manpower of their coastal allies (*socii navales*) who provided ships. Polybius (*Histories* 10.9–16) documents one of the early operations combining naval and land forces, when Scipio attacked Carthago Nova (modern Cartagena) by land and sea, ordering Gaius Laelius to take command of the fleet to bombard the city with different kinds of missiles, while he brought up 25,000 infantry and 2,500 cavalry to attack from the land. First he defeated the Carthaginians sent out from the city to charge his men, and then he ordered parties to assault and take the walls by means of sheer manpower and scaling ladders. The battle was hard fought, but Scipio had thoroughly investigated the city and knew that the tide would soon start to ebb, leaving the protective lagoon on the seaward side of the city dry enough for another assault party to gain access to the walls. Soon after this successful attack the city fell.

During the later Republic and early Empire, the pirates of the Mediterranean threatened Roman merchant shipping to the extent that food supplies to the city became of chronic concern. Various efforts were made to eradicate the problem by using naval forces as well as land forces, including expeditions like that of Marcus Antonius in 102 and later that of his son in 74, the latter ending in complete disaster (these men were, respectively, the grandfather and the father of the more famous Mark Antony). In 67 BC, pirates sailed into the mouth of the Tiber and threatened the port of Ostia; the Romans were outraged. The greatest general of the day, Pompey the Great, angled for the command and was finally granted it, charged with clearing the Mediterranean of pirates. The Senate, realizing at last that this task required tremendous resources and a commander of wide-ranging powers, voted Pompey 500 ships and 24 legates (some sources say 25) of his own choosing. These legates were responsible to him in the first instance and not directly to the Senate; though a dangerous precedent, it was necessary if Pompey was to coordinate the operation without hindrance. Pompey and his legates were given leave to recruit soldiers, sailors, and rowers, thus providing significant land forces as well as naval forces for the campaign. Another controversial precedent concerned the extent of Pompey's powers, which were to extend up to 50 miles inland from the entire Mediterranean coast. This gave him temporary command of almost the whole Roman world, but again this dangerous precedent was necessary if he was to eradicate the problem, since the pirates were known to occupy land bases, and if flushed out of them would simply move to other places anywhere around the Mediterranean, either by sea or by retreating further inland.

Pompey divided the Mediterranean into thirteen regions and placed a legate with a squadron of ships over each. The names of the thirteen legates who commanded the coastal and maritime areas have been preserved, which leaves eleven or twelve other commanders who presumably directed the land forces, but this must remain an informed guess, since concrete evidence is lacking. The plan was to sweep the seas and the land immediately behind the coasts, except for the rugged inlets of Cilicia, where the main pirate strongholds lay, so that with an open exit they could all be flushed eastward and be bottled up there. In a mere forty days, Pompey had cleared the seas. The price of grain fell as soon as his appointment was announced, and after his success he was the hero and savior of the whole Roman world. After some further wrangling by his friends in Rome, he went straight on to his next command, against the troublesome King Mithradates in the east.

Combined military and naval operations such as this are only rarely documented. Caesar recounts how he used ships and his legions against the Veneti who had detained some Roman envoys who had been sent to gather food supplies for the winter. The Veneti inhabited the Atlantic seaboard of Gaul, and were excellent seamen and navigators, sailing the turbulent seas to Britain and back as a matter of routine (*Gallic War* 3.7–16). Caesar had to have warships built on the river Loire and also gather ships from his Gallic allies before he could deal with the rebellious tribesmen, to curb them before the revolt spread to the rest of Gaul. At the beginning of the campaigning season, Caesar placed Decimus Brutus in command of the fleet, while he himself took command of the land forces. The strongholds of the Veneti could not easily be attacked from the seaward side for fear of grounding the Roman ships, and there were few harbors. As a result, at first the Veneti with their flat-bottomed vessels had the advantage, even though the Roman ships were faster. When the strongholds of the Veneti were attacked from the landward side by the legions, the inhabitants simply brought up their ships, loaded their possessions, and moved off to another stronghold. The Romans finally won the war in a naval engagement watched by the land forces from the cliffs. They resorted to a new tactic against the ships of the Veneti, using hooks on long poles to snag the halyards that held the yard arms to the mast, then rowing at full speed ahead until the yards were brought down. Then the Romans boarded the disabled vessels, greatly assisted by a sudden calm that stopped the Veneti from sailing away. According to Caesar, the Veneti had committed the bulk of their manpower to this battle and from then on could not defend their homes, having lost so many warriors and ships.

In his account of the invasion of Britain, Caesar describes different types of vessels, including transports, warships, and scout ships (*speculatoria navigia*), all of which he used to support the legions as they fought the Britons on the coast, at first in the sea itself and then on land they struggled to gain a foothold. He ordered the warships to come up on the enemy flanks and use their artillery against them, and later he used the scout ships to support the land troops in the same way (*Gallic War* 4.25–26). Naval power as well as land forces were vitally important in the civil wars between the Caesarians and Pompeians, not just as troop transports, but for securing the food supply and for patrolling and guarding the coasts. When he crossed to Greece to follow Pompey, Caesar had only enough ships to transport half his army, and the rest were left behind with Mark Antony as commander, but they were bottled up in Italy by a squadron of the Pompeian fleet under Libo. Watching where Libo came to shore for fresh water, Antony guarded each point until Libo had to withdraw, and then he seized the chance to set sail himself to join Caesar.

As the Empire was steadily growing out of the Republican civil wars, significant naval battles were staged that decided the outcome, such as Naulochus in

36 BC, where Octavian's forces finally defeated Sextus Pompey, the son of Pompey the Great. In this instance there was a sea battle and a land battle, but they were not coordinated, and there was such a lack of communication between the two forces that at first Octavian thought the whole affair had been a defeat. When he came to full power, Octavian instituted permanent fleets, one based at Misenum and one at Ravenna, on either side of Italy. The crews of the war galleys were organized like the legions, in centuries under centurions, and were called soldiers (*milites*), not sailors (*nautae*). War galleys were quite small compared to transports and could store enough fresh water to travel for up to 200 miles (Starr, 1989). In the German campaigns of Drusus and Tiberius, ships were used for naval operations on the Rhine; Tacitus describes the different ships used by Germanicus in AD 16 (*Annals* 2.6). These naval vessels formed the nucleus of the later German fleet (*Classis Germanica*), which patrolled the river and the coasts while the army operated inland. The same functions were carried out by the Danube fleets (*Classis Pannonica* and *Classis Moesica*), especially in supporting Trajan's Dacian Wars. Ships of different types are shown on Trajan's Column, where transports, freight ships, and warships are clearly distinguished, if not correct in every detail.

The Roman expeditions to the north of Britain under the Flavian governor Julius Agricola and later the Emperor Severus were supported by naval power. When Agricola was ready to invade Scotland, he used the fleet for transport of supplies and for reconnoitring, but also for military purposes. Tacitus (*Agricola* 29) describes how the fleet was sent ahead to spread terror and to raid the coastal areas, and he refers to the legions and auxiliaries meeting with the fleet and camping together. Severus followed the same pattern during his Scottish campaigns, using the fleet to supply his troops and to raid the coastal settlements. An inscription from Rome refers to the British war as an amphibious expedition (*CIL* VI 1643). The coinage supports this description, with coins of Severus displaying a bridge with towers and coins of Caracalla showing a bridge of boats and the legend *Traiectus*—a crossing. The most likely locations for these bridges and crossings are the estuaries of the river Forth, where there is a Severan military base at Cramond on the southern shore, and the river Tay, where there is another base at Carpow.

The later third century saw a gradual decline of the fleets. Under Diocletian, only three of the former ten squadrons of the Italian fleets remained, though the British usurper Carausius made effective use of his naval power (*Classis Britannica*) to defend his territories, issuing coinage that showed off his galleys. He was defeated only when Diocletian's deputy, Constantius Chlorus, built a rival fleet. A few years later in 323, Chlorus's son Constantine gathered 200 warships to fight off his rival Licinius, in what Chester G. Starr (1989, 112) calls "the only real sea battle in the history of the Roman Empire." Thereafter, Byzantium, not Rome, claimed mastery of the sea.

## REFERENCES AND FURTHER READING

Austin, Norman J.E., and Rankov, N.Boris. 1995. *Exploratio: Military and Political Intelligence in the Roman World from the Second Punic War to the Battle of Adrianople.* London: Routledge.

Campbell, J. Brian. 1984. *The Emperor and the Roman Army 31 BC to AD 325.* Oxford: Clarendon Press.

———. 1987. "Teach yourself how to be a general." *Journal of Roman Studies* 77, 13–29.

———. 1994. *The Roman Army 31 BC to AD 337.* London: Routledge.

———. 2002. *War and Society in Imperial Rome 31 BC to AD 284.* London: Routledge.

Dixon, Karen R., and Southern, Pat. 1992. *The Roman Cavalry.* London: Batsford.

Elton, Hugh. 1996. *Frontiers of the Roman Empire.* London: Batsford.

Gilliver, Catherine M. 2000. *The Roman Art of War.* Stroud, Gloucestershire: Tempus Publishing.

Goldsworthy, Adrian K. 1996. *The Roman Army at War 100 BC to AD 200.* Oxford: Clarendon Press.

———. 2003a. *The Complete Roman Army.* London: Thames and Hudson.

———. 2003b. *In the Name of Rome: The Men Who Won the Roman Empire.* London: Weidenfeld and Nicolson.

Luttwak, Edward N. 1976. *The Grand Strategy of the Roman Empire.* Baltimore, MD: Johns Hopkins University Press.

Mann, John C. 1974. "The frontiers of the Principate." *Aufstieg und Niedergang der Römischen Welt* II.1, 508–53.

Millar, Fergus. 1982. "Emperors, frontiers and foreign relations." *Britannia* 13, 1–23.

Müller, G. 1979. *Durnomagus: das Römische Dormagen.* Cologne: Rheinlandverlag GMBH.

Salway, Peter. 1991. *Roman Britain.* Oxford: Clarendon Press.

Schönberger, Hans von. 1985. "Die römische Truppenlager der frühen und mittleren Kaiserzeit zwischen Nordsee und Inn." *Bericht der Römisch-Germanisch Kommission* 66, 321–497.

Starr, Chester G. 1960. *The Roman Imperial Navy 31 BC–AD 324.* Cambridge, MA: Harvard University Press. 2nd ed.

———. 1989. *The Influence of Sea Power on Ancient History.* Oxford: Oxford University Press.

Whittaker, C.R. 1994. *Frontiers of the Roman Empire: A Social and Economic Study.* Baltimore, MD: Johns Hopkins University Press.

Woolliscroft, David I. 2001. *Roman Military Signalling.* Stroud, Gloucestershire: Tempus Publishing.

# CHAPTER 6

# Tools of War

## WEAPONRY

The Romans lacked all the technological developments that allow modern armies to kill each other at extremely long range, and so they were reliant upon different types of spears for throwing or thrusting, bows and arrows, swords for thrusting or slashing, and finally their artillery, which gave them the maximum range of ancient weapons.

### The *Pilum*

The *pilum,* a deadly missile weapon, was adopted by the legions at an unknown date and remained in use for centuries. Describing the armaments of the Republican army, Polybius says that the *hastati* carried two *pila,* one heavier than the other—one with a thick shaft, either rounded or squared, and the other with a thinner shaft. Polybius compares both types to medium-sized hunting spears, and the evidence from archaeological finds supports his description, especially those from the Republican siege works at Numantia in Spain, specifically the camp at Renieblas. The archaeological record shows several different designs of *pila,* varying not only in size but in the shape of the head and the method by which the metal shank was attached to the wooden shaft. In some earlier examples, the shank was quite short, and the business end was shaped like a large arrow head, whereas the later versions had a longer shank and the tip was shaped like a small pyramid (Feugère, 2002; Goldsworthy, 2003a).

Some *pila* were attached to the shaft by means of a flat tang riveted to the wood, held by two rivets in the late Republican and early Imperial examples, but this style apparently died out since *pila* of this type are not represented among the finds from the Rhine and Danube frontiers ( Feugère, 2002). The most common type of *pila* are like those from Oberaden in Germany, where the metal shank is set inside a wooden block shaped like a flat-topped pyramid and held

Two soldiers, one with helmet and shield, the other showing weapons and armor. Roman relief from a column. (Erich Lessing/Art Resource, NY)

by three rivets. Other examples of *pila* were equipped with a socket at the base of the iron shank, and the wood was seated inside the socket and held with an iron collar. Only very rarely have there been any complete finds of the metal parts and nothing of the wooden shaft, so it is difficult to discern exactly how long the *pila* may have been. However, it is commonly suggested that the iron shank measured about 2 feet (60 cm) and the wooden shaft was about 4 feet long (1.2 m). On average, then, the whole weapon measured approximately 6 feet or nearly 2 meters (Goldsworthy, 2003).

The *pilum* was designed for throwing and had great penetrative power. Effectively used, it could pass through a shield and injure the man holding it, and since it was difficult to remove it quickly, at the very least it would render the shield unwieldy and therefore useless. A battle would start with the discharge of *pila* before the legions closed in using their swords An additional feature of the *pilum* appears on some sculptural reliefs, in that a spherical object is shown, sometimes more than one, at the top of the shaft. This has not yet been attested in the archaeological record, so it is not possible to say what the ball-shaped object was made of, but it is probable that its purpose was to add extra weight to the weapon.

### The *Lancea*

These weapons were used by the auxiliaries and are attested on many auxiliary tombstones, but so many different kinds have been found on military sites that it is not possible to classify them into groups or to assign specific types of *lanceae* to different kinds of troops. The head was generally leaf shaped, sometimes with very elongated points, which presumably enhanced penetration. The auxiliaries among Arrian's troops in Cappadocia were ordered to throw their *lanceae* over the head of the ranks in front of them.

### Bows and Arrows

The Romans employed several auxiliary units of archers (*sagittarii*), both infantry and mounted; they were usually recruited from easterners whose expertise was highly valued, and unlike other units where new recruits were found from the local population, the ranks of the archer units were refilled from the east. Archery equipment of the Roman period has been extensively studied by Coulston (1985). Usually, the only surviving evidence in the archaeological record for bows consists of the antler tips, since the wooden parts have disappeared. A distribution map of the find spots of antler tips virtually marks the Rhine and Danube frontiers in Europe, and several have been found in Britain.

Bows were quite elaborate in construction. They were known as composite bows because they were made of different types of materials glued together and held with bindings. When not in use the bow was unstrung, and to restring it the archer used his leg to bend it until the string could be attached. Bows and bowstrings were particularly susceptible to damp weather, and archers could be put out of action in rainstorms (Dixon and Southern, 1992; Frontinus, *Stratagems* 4.7.30; Dio 56.21.3).

Arrowheads were usually made of iron and were often triangular in cross section, though some are squared. Bone arrowheads have been found near Porolissum in Dacia and were used by the Germans, Scythians, Sarmatians, and Huns. Arrowheads were either socketed or tanged, and the shafts were most commonly of reeds, pine, or hazel. Shafts and fletchings have been preserved only in the eastern provinces where the climate is dry, but some examples of arrowheads with wood still attached have been found at Housesteads and Corbridge in northern England and at Caerleon (Coulston, 1985). In the west, barbed arrows were often used, which would have been very effective against tribesmen who wore no armor. The arrows were kept in a cylindrical quiver, examples of which are shown on Roman sculptures, and there would have been a reserve of arrows for archers to use when their quivers were empty (Coulston, 1985). Horse archers probably used lighter and shorter bows than infantry and lighter arrows, so the infantry archers would have had a longer range than the mounted *sagittarii.*

## The *Gladius*

Commonly termed the *gladius Hispaniensis,* this type of sword was adopted by the Romans either when they met mercenaries from Spain in Carthaginian employ or when they first campaigned in Spain. The Republican *gladii* tend to be longer than the Imperial examples, but there are so few known examples that it is impossible to be dogmatic on this score. The early Imperial *gladii* were shaped like an elongated leaf with a long tapered point, like the examples found at Mainz in Germany, from which they take their name in modern terminology. These Mainz-type swords are common on Augustan sites and probably survived until the Claudian period, when they were eventually replaced by the so-called Pompeian types, straight sided with a shorter point. The handgrips of wood, bone, or ivory usually had four grooves for the fingers and ensured a good hold; pommels were of wood, possibly covered with sheet metal, or of ivory, and the scabbards were usually made of wood with sheet metal covers, often very highly decorated.

The *gladius* was effective either for cutting or for thrusting and was used by legionaries and auxiliaries. The sword was worn on a belt, suspended from the four rings on the two circlips around the top of the scabbard, but no one knows precisely how or whether in fact all four rings were used (Bishop and Coulston, 1993). This weapon was used by legionaries and auxiliaries, and tombstones from the Rhine frontier show auxiliaries wearing the *gladius,* like the legionaries, on the right side, which enabled the soldiers to withdraw it easily without hindering their shield arm ( Feugère, 2002). Sculptural evidence shows that centurions and officers wore their *gladii* on the left.

## The *Spatha*

This long slashing sword is traditionally associated with the Roman cavalry, but it was used by infantry as well from the late second century, so the presence of a *spatha* in an archaeological dig does not always signify a cavalry unit. This type of sword could vary in length from 26 to 36 inches (65 cm to 90 cm), and in width from 1.5 inches to 3 inches (4 cm to 8 cm). The ends were usually rounded, or only slightly tapered, and the handgrips were of wood, sometimes reinforced with metal. Two cavalrymen of the second century AD were buried at Canterbury in England, each with a *spatha,* with some traces of wood still adhering to the top of the blade (Dixon and Southern, 1992; Feugère, 2002). The *spatha* was suspended from a baldric over the shoulder, usually on the right side during the first century AD. Modern experiments have shown that it is possible to withdraw the sword quite easily from the right side while on horseback, but there was a change in the second century when according to sculptural evidence the *spatha* began to be worn on the left side. A funeral monument from Augsburg shows a soldier called Tertiolus and his servant handing him a baldric and *spatha* (Feugère, 2002).

## The *Pugio*

Legionaries and auxiliaries are shown on sculptures wearing their daggers on the opposite side to their swords. These may not have been used for combat, and they are not mentioned at all by Polybius, even though examples have been found in Spain dating from the second century BC, so they were used by the soldiers whom Polybius described. The daggers and particularly their scabbards were very often more highly decorated than the *gladii* and were clearly of importance to the soldiers. They had a leaf-shaped blade and were shorter than the sword, generally about 35 cm, or just over 1 foot long.

## Artillery

The crews of the field artillery were specialists but were never formed into specific separate units. Instead they were drawn from the legionary centuries to man the machines and presumably to look after them and repair them. The artillerymen were *immunes* and did not have to perform routine fatigues.

Roman artillery was of two kinds, single or double-armed, although the single-armed stone thrower did not come into use until the fourth century (Goldsworthy, 2003). Caesar uses the general description *tormenta* when writing of artillery, without distinguishing between the different types of machines. There is some confusion among ancient and modern works about the terminology applied to Roman artillery, in that *catapulta* as mentioned by Vitruvius (*De Architectura* 10.10) appears less frequently in modern works than the term *ballista,* which is often employed for all types of machines whether they shot

## CATAPHRACTARII AND CLIBANARII

The Parthians used armored cavalry (*cataphractarii*) to good effect against the invading Roman army of Marcus Licinius Crassus in 53 BC. The defeat was decisive and the balance was not redressed until Augustus negotiated for peace thirty-three years later and arranged for the return of the captured standards. The Romans themselves adopted *cataphractarii* perhaps in the late first or early second century AD, but there is no firm evidence of cataphract units until the reign of Hadrian (AD 117–138), when the *ala Cataphractariorum* is attested. The armor extended to both the rider and the horse. Plutarch (*Crassus* 24) describes the horses clad in plates of bronze and steel, and Ammianus (16.10.8) says that the men wore armor of iron plates that fitted the curves of their bodies completely covering their limbs, so that they looked like polished statues, not men. A graffito from Dura-Europos in Syria shows an armored cavalryman wearing this kind of armor, and what appear to be thigh guards or cuisses, perhaps of the type found at Dura, made of rawhide. The graffito also depicts the barding or scale armor of the cavalryman's mount, like a blanket covering the horse's body and reaching halfway down its legs. A complete scale barding was found at Dura-Europos with a hole where the saddle would be placed.

Heavily armored cavalry were not as mobile as the lighter armed mounted units and were soon exhausted by too much exertion, as happened at the battle of Strasbourg in AD 357 (Ammianus 16.12.37–38), but they served their purpose as shock troops, when armed with the *contus* or lance. Some of the *cataphractarii* used bows and arrows as well as the lance. There is some dispute as to whether the *cataphractarii* were synonymous with heavy armored cavalry known as the *clibanarii*, literally meaning "ovens," graphically describing how it felt to wear the scale armor in a hot climate. Some authorities suggest that the *clibanarii* were purely eastern troops from Parthia and Palmyra, still qualifying as cataphracts. Other scholars have suggested that the distinction in terminology reflects the respective armament styles, the *cataphractarii* being armed with the lance and shield in the western tradition, while the *clibanarii* adopted the eastern tradition of bow and lance.

arrows or stones. Strictly, the *catapulta* fired arrows or bolts, and the *ballista* fired stone projectiles (Bishop and Coulston, 1993), but since they operated in the same manner by torsion, like a large crossbow, perhaps the distinction is not so important. Marsden (1969) says that *catapulta* was the main term in use until the fourth century AD, and then *ballista* superseded it. A further complication concerns the names of the one-armed machines. The slang term *scorpio*, or scorpion, is used in the first century AD by Vitruvius to describe the two-armed *catapulta*, but in the later Roman period Ammianus (23.4.4–7) says that it was used of the single-armed stone thrower, because of its upraised sting. This type of machine was also nicknamed *onager* or wild ass, descriptive of its violent kick.

The ancient Greeks had already worked out most of the problems of bolt-shooting and stone-throwing artillery, such as how to draw the bowstring back, how to hold it in place until ready for firing, and how to release it with sufficient

Engraving after *The Catapult* by Edward Poynter. (Bettmann/Corbis)

force to shoot the projectile (Landels, 2000). The material used in bundles for the torsion springs must be fairly elastic but not so much that it stretches too easily, and it must be capable of being woven into a rope to hold the ends together. The ancient engineers used sinew or hair, perhaps horsehair, but especially favored was human hair, especially women's hair. The bundles were gathered together at the ends, and a rod or lever was inserted into them at right angles, then twisted to create the torsion effect, and housed in a wooden casing strengthened by a metal frame. The springs were placed on washers. The two arms of the machine were inserted into the springs and joined together at their opposite ends by the bowstring, which Vitruvius says could be drawn back by several means, by windlass, block and pulley, or capstan (*De Architectura* 10.11). It was especially important to ensure that the two arms were pulled back equally to give them equal thrust; otherwise the missile would go off course (Landels, 2000). Vitruvius explains that the remedy for this was to tune the strings, which he says should respond with the same sound on both sides when struck by the hand (*De Architectura* 10.11.2).

The practical Romans had only to make one or two refinements to Greek models and then put the machines to use. Artillery machines came in several different sizes, the determining factor being the size of the bolt to be shot or the weight of the stone to be projected. Vitruvius explains how this affects the proportions in manufacturing *catapultae* and *ballistae,* including a ready-reckoner relating weight of the stones to the proportions of the machine "so that those who are not skilled in geometry may be prepared beforehand and not be delayed in thinking the matter through at a time of danger" (*De Architectura* 10. 10.–11). The bolts or stones were placed in the central channel, and the bowstring was pulled back onto the trigger, the only difference being that the bowstrings for stone-throwing machines were broader, approximating to a sling that encompassed the stone ball, with a loop at the back for the trigger.

The fragments of artillery engines that have been found on archaeological sites are useful for the reconstruction of the machines, the study of which began with German artillery officers such as Schramm whose work (1918) has been updated by Baatz (1980). Fully functional modern versions of artillery pieces are now operated by several reenactment societies, with frighteningly dangerous results. The metal fittings of a stone-throwing *ballista* were found at Hatra in Mesopotamia, which fell to the Persians in the third century AD, and a fourth-century bolt-shooting machine was found at Orsova in Romania, marking a transition from wooden casing to metal construction (Baatz, 1978). This was an improvement on timber, which does not perform well in hot climates and is subject to warping (Landels, 2000). Bolts from Roman artillery are more commonly found than the parts of the machines that fired them. They varied little throughout the Roman Empire, nor did they change with the passage of time. They had pyramid-shaped iron heads and timber shafts, with fletchings made not from feathers but from thin pieces of wood (Ammianus 24.4.16). The vanes were placed so that one-half of the shaft was smooth, allowing it to slot into the groove of the machine. These bolts could pass straight through armor. During a siege in the later Roman Empire, a Goth was pinned to a tree by a bolt that had passed through his cuirass and his body and had then embedded itself for half its length in the tree trunk (Southern and Dixon, 1996).

The portable artillery machines called *carroballistae,* drawn by mule cart, are attested on Trajan's Column and by Vegetius (*Epitoma Rei Militaris* 2.25). The Romans had batteries of them, and they were used like modern machine guns to pin down the enemy (Landels, 2000), just as the larger machines were used in sieges to keep defenders off the walls. Tacitus relates how with one machine Vitellius's troops were massacring those of Galba at the battle of Cremona in the civil war of AD 69, and some of Galba's men crept up to put the machine out of action by cutting the cords of the springs. Trajan's troops in the Danube Wars took replaceable springs so that the machines would not be out of action for lack of them (Landels, 2000).

In the later Empire artillery was used to defend as well as besiege cities, and special platforms were built for machines on the battlements. In AD 225 the *cohors I Fida Vardullorum* constructed a *ballistarium* at the fort of High Rochester in Northumberland in northern England (*RIB* 1280). Marsden (1969) thought that, despite the name *ballistarium,* the actual machine would have been an *onager,* since the platform was strong enough to support such a heavy piece, but these machines were more useful in besieging a city or fort, or defending a place that had been invested, and the stones fired from them had the power to damage walls and shatter siege towers. At High Rochester it may not have been necessary to shoot down siege towers, but to aim at humans, and the inscription may mean what it says.

### Slingshots and Stones

In the Republican period and the early Empire, the Roman army employed slingers, whose bullets were of stone, baked clay, or lead. At Perusia when Octavian was besieging Mark Antony's brother Lucius, the slingers of both sides inscribed obscene messages on their lead shot, and at other places and periods the name of the commander appears on the bullets. Over fifty lead sling bullets were found at Burnswark, a native hill fort in Scotland that may have served as a practice site for the army, since the defenses of the hill fort had long since fallen out of use before the Romans arrived, but as new generations of scholars take the field, opinion varies.

Finally, the stones that are found on military sites may not always have been fired by artillery. The rounded stones found at South Shields fort in northern England fit snugly into the hand and may simply have been thrown by the soldiers rather than propelled from artillery machines. As Feugère (2002) points out, stones serve as very effective weapons. The English armies in medieval Ireland found this out the hard way, and in the nineteenth century the natives of Afghanistan and northern India acquitted themselves well with simple stones.

## LOGISTICS AND TRANSPORT

The military leaders of Imperial Rome could draw on two or three centuries of experience of moving armies from place to place with all their equipment, tools, artillery, food, fodder, and clothing. Logistical systems developed empirically from Republican times, with a sharp boost during the Punic Wars. Early Roman campaigns were mostly annual affairs and took place not too far from home.

Soldiers supplied their own equipment and probably carried most of it. Since they had only to provide food for the summer months and then went home for the harvest, the problems of supplying the army were not as complicated as they later became, when the army had to remain under arms for the winter.

With the growth of Roman influence over a wider and wider extent of territory, wars lengthened in duration and were fought further away from the city and the homes of the allies, eventually extending to Roman armies operating outside Italy. The Romans were forced to develop a more sophisticated supply system in the protracted wars with Hannibal because their crops and those of their allies were commandeered or destroyed, necessitating the import of food from abroad, for instance, from Sardinia. In turn, this meant creating fortified harbors, such as Puteoli and Ostia, where grain could be landed safely and then transported under guard into fortified bases.

By the early Empire, Roman generals were accustomed to moving armies across seas and establishing themselves in other countries, operating in different types of terrain and keeping themselves supplied with food, fuel, equipment, weapons, clothing, and tools. Despite their experience in the Punic Wars, the later Republican commanders still experienced problems in supplying their armies, not necessarily from lack of expertise but in faulty administration and application of funds. Fighting in Spain against Sertorius, Pompey had to stamp his foot and write stiff letters to the Senate to put his supplies on a proper footing, provisioning himself by sea once he had captured towns and bases on the coast.

Roman armies had at their disposal a variety of means of obtaining and transporting food and materiel, using supply lines overland, or by sea from other provinces, and in the war zone itself by foraging, requisition, and pillage, all of the last three shading off almost seamlessly into one another. The Romans did not use sutlers or merchants as a general means of provision, except perhaps in immediate emergencies. The army looked after itself with regard to supply and transport of all its needs. Whenever practical, the Romans made agreements with their allied princes and chieftains to provide food. For instance, in Sicily, the natives brought provisions to the Romans in 262 BC when the Carthaginians prevented them from foraging (Polybius, *Histories* 1.16–18), and Caesar allied with Gallic tribes such as the Aedui and the Remi, who provided his troops with grain and foodstuffs.

The details of the Empire's logistical systems are not fully elucidated in any source, but Caesar's works furnish one of the best sources, since he took care over his supplies and transport, and mentions the subject frequently (*Gallic War* 1.54; 2.35; 3.28; 4.38; 5.53; 6.44; 7.90). Because Caesar stands on the cusp of the late Republican and early Imperial armies, some of the information can be used to reconstruct the logistics of the Imperial period. In Caesar's day, while the army was on the move, opportunities arose to find food supplies for men and animals by foraging and requisition. Food and equipment was carried with the army either by the men themselves, by pack animals, or in carts and wagons. During the winters, a large campaign army had to disperse to live, so a great deal of the Republican general's time was taken up in finding winter quarters (*hibernae*) and bringing in supplies to see the army through till spring. Sometimes the winter quarters were in towns where stores were already built up, and at other times the army wintered in purpose-built camps. Both of these situations could be used to observe and guard the enemy, or as operational bases. Caesar left Publius Crassus in command at Samarobriva (modern Amiens) with one legion, where he also left the baggage of the army (*impedimenta exercitus*), the hostages from various tribes, some of his documents, and the winter supplies (*frumenta*).

With regard to logistics and transport, the main difference between the Republican and Imperial armies is that until the development of the standing army under Augustus and his successors, there were no permanent bases for the troops. As the Empire expanded, the forts and fortresses gradually percolated to the periphery, and finally in the second century the running barriers and frontier roads were established. Military operations thereafter were conducted within the provinces to squash rebellions or to repulse invasions, or expeditions were mounted beyond the frontiers in preemptive strikes or punitive campaigns. Only in the latter case did the wars resemble those of Caesar in Gaul or the civil wars of the late Republic, creating the need for temporary bases to house some of the troops through the winter while the bulk of the army probably returned to their frontier forts.

Most of the information about logistics in the Roman army is derived from the supply systems of the peacetime army based in the provinces or on the frontiers. In satisfying their vast requirements for food, fodder, fuel, building timber, stone, leather, metals, pottery, clothing, and much more besides, the Romans utilized local resources, and perhaps grew some of their own food in the immediate vicinity of the forts, but long-distance transport did not worry the administrators. Some scholars consider that the supply of the armies actively promoted and stimulated trade (Middleton, 1983). It has been shown that wine was exported from Italy to the troops in Germany and that pottery from Gaul was transported to the army in Britain. The granaries at South Shields in northern Britain contained grain that had come from the Netherlands (Anderson, 1992; Roth, 1999), and in AD 359 in the reign of Julian, British grain was transported to the Rhine (Salway, 1991).

The supply and transport systems of the provincial armies worked well but would not be able to support major campaigns mounted by the emperors. Although the soldiers of each unit would have been provided with carts and wagons, and pack animals (*iumenta*) such as mules, donkeys, and (in the eastern provinces) camels, complete with their harness and saddles, many more animals and vehicles would be needed for a campaign. Carts and wagons could be manufactured, requisitioned, or bought, and pack animals could be assembled from private owners, paid or unpaid. In some cases, private shipowners (*navicularii*) were necessary if transport overseas or along navigable rivers was envisaged. How this vast assembly of supplies and the means of transporting them was achieved is not known. There may have been a central administration, perhaps under the *Praefectus Annonae,* whereby an established but dormant system for requisition and purchase swung into action, but this is speculation. Some scholars think that each emperor intent on campaigning beyond the frontiers had to assemble their needs from scratch (Roth, 1999). Once the army was assembled, there is slightly more information as to what it required and what it carried, but the evidence is uncoordinated inasmuch as it is derived from a variety of different sources from different periods.

A primary requirement in the study of logistics is to try to establish how much of each commodity would be carried and what it would weigh, but there are divergent estimates of how much food and equipment was required on campaign, and how all these items were obtained and transported. Like other campaigning armies, the Romans carried with them not only their food, fodder, and drink, but also the means of harvesting crops, hunting animals, processing and eating food, and vessels for drinking water, wine, and beer. They also carried weapons and clothing, personal effects, tools for entrenching, timber felling, and mending wagons and carts, medical and veterinary equipment, one tent for each *contubernium* of eight men, field artillery for each century, and the siege train consisting of larger artillery if cities and citadels were to be stormed. This list is by no means complete.

The terms that the ancient authors used most frequently for food supply are *frumentum,* commonly found in Caesar's accounts—meaning the grain supply but occasionally applying to food in general—and less commonly *cibaria,* which strictly speaking refers to nongrain food but can stand in for all food stocks. In working out how much food the soldiers would consume, some facts and figures are available, but they only succeed in confusing the issue because exact equivalents of ancient weights and quantities depend on interpretation.

Several modern scholars have investigated the amounts of wheat that were necessary to sustain an entire legion or an individual soldier for a specified period of time. Using Greek measures, Polybius says that the Roman and allied infantrymen received about one-third of a *medimnus* of wheat per month, while the Roman cavalry received two *medimni* of wheat plus seven *medimni* of barley. The allied cavalry were supplied with slightly less, receiving only one and a half measures of wheat and five of barley. Translating Polybius's figures of one-third of an Attic *medimnus* per month into Roman measure, Roth (1999) estimates that one legion required 600 *modii* of wheat every day. Estimating not by measure but by acreage, Goldsworthy (1996) suggests that a legion, rounded down to 5,000 men, would require the produce of 70 acres in one week, or putting it another way, 10 acres a day.

Roth (1999) assumes that the same ration scales for grain or bread apply equally to legionaries and auxiliaries, and points out that the amount of bread allowed for soldiers did not vary over seven centuries: Polybius (6.39) sets the figure at 3 pounds per day during the Republic, and the ration for the sixth-century Roman army was the same. Apart from grain, the archaeological and literary sources reveal that the Roman soldiers ate meat, mostly pork. During the Republic, salt pork was exported from Italy to campaign armies overseas (Polybius 2.15.2–3). Like other soldiers of all periods, the Romans ate any other meat that they could find by requisition or by hunting. Bones from military sites show that beef and mutton formed part of the diet, and Lucullus's army in the campaign against Mithradates ate venison and hare. Lentils and beans are also attested, along with cheese (*caseus*), salt, vinegar, and sour wine (*acetum*), which was mixed with water to form a drink known as *posca*. Vintage wine was not unknown but was usually watered down, and in the Celtic provinces of the west, soldiers also drank beer (*cervesa*). The search for water for soldiers and animals would be a constant need, and in some cases water had to be carried in skins (*utres*). When he was besieging a desert town in Africa in 107 BC Marius transported skins of water by pack trains, and Pompey resorted to the same technique in the Mithradatic War, using pack animals to carry 10,000 skins of water (Roth, 1999). Where it was possible, liquids were probably transported in barrels. One of the scenes at the base of Trajan's Column shows barrels being unloaded from a ship, but it is not possible to discern what they contained.

Horses and pack animals required different amounts of dry fodder such as barley and oats, and green fodder such as grass, clover, and vetch. Horses required the most food and were fussier eaters than mules and donkeys, which can survive on smaller quantities and worse quality foods; oxen were easier still to feed since their digestive systems allow them to extract more sustenance from the foods they eat. However, many authors have wrestled with the conundrum that the more pack animals the army takes on campaign, the more food the pack animals need. Therefore, the more food has to be carried or found on the march. When they are working hard, horses strictly need increased rations, but on campaign they would not necessarily receive the recommended amounts or even the correct kinds of food. Caesar's troops fed their horses on seaweed in the African campaign (*African War* 24), but this was not such an outlandish idea since seaweed supplements are given to horses in modern times.

There are scant references to fodder in the ancient sources. According to Polybius (6.39.12–14), a Roman cavalry soldier of the Republic received 7 *medimni* of barley per month for his horse, while an allied cavalryman received only 5 *medimni* (Dixon and Southern, 1992). It has been estimated that since the cavalrymen were expected to maintain three horses, the rations must have been divided. By translating the Greek measures first into Latin equivalents and then into English, Walker (1973) decided that each horse was allowed 1.5 kg or 3.5 lb of barley per day. This exactly coincides with Hyland's estimate (1990). The only evidence that shows how much barley was actually delivered to a cavalry unit (*ala*) is found in a papyrus from Egypt, dating to AD 187, when a *duplicarius* (a soldier on double pay) from the *ala Heracliana* received 20,000 *artabai* for the horses of his unit. Walker (1973) linked this with a sixth-century papyrus showing that each horse was allowed one-tenth of an *artaba* per day, so the rations received by the *ala Heracliana* would feed 548 horses for a year. Horses and pack animals would also need hay. Hyland (1990) estimates that each horse would require 4.5 kg or 10 lb of hay per day. In Egypt a receipt has been preserved on papyrus for hay for the *turma* of Donacianus in the *ala Veterana Gallica* in AD 130, and other papyri show that the cavalrymen received hay money to the tune of 25 *denarii* for the year. This money was perhaps paid to the men when their horses were put out to pasture, just as the eighteenth-century British army allowed 365 days forage ration but paid the men the surplus when the horses were at grass (Rogers, 1977). During campaigns, foragers would have to find hay, and at Batnae in AD 363 this proved a fatal enterprise, when soldiers started to remove hay from a stack, which fell down and killed about fifty men (Ammianus 23.2.8).

Transportation of all the requirements of a campaign army was a major consideration for Roman generals, who were reliant upon the carrying power of the soldiers and pack animals, and the capacity of vehicles drawn by oxen or mules. The difficulties of transporting the food supplies worried Caesar in the winter of 52 BC, but he was forced to move and take some of the troops out of winter quarters sooner than he would have wished because he had to protect his allies from attack by other Gauls, in case revolt spread. He asked his allies from the Aedui to take care of the transport of food, but he does not say how they accomplished their task (*Gallic War* 7.10). Even if supplies were delivered in ships, the goods had to be carried from the coast or the river banks by the same means using men, animals, carts, and wagons. On campaign, most of the food for men and animals would have to be stored in magazines and transported along supply lines, or alternatively the army carried lesser amounts and when it ran out they foraged and requisitioned supplies at regular intervals. Roth (1999), assembling an impressive array of evidence, considers the use of supply lines as routine for the Romans. The general model was to establish an operational base, often in a port, and then to gather stores of all kinds, not just food supplies but equipment and clothing. From this base, the supplies would be brought to a distribution point in the war zone, usually a fortified camp, and as the army moved forward so would the fortified camps and stores. In some cases, the old bases could still serve as stores and food dumps to relay supplies to the war zone. The forts along the river Lippe in Germany at Holsterhausen, Haltern, Oberaden, and Anreppen have been identified as bases used to supply the armies of Drusus and Tiberius as they advanced into Germany (Keppie, 1984; Roth, 1999). The use of operational and forward bases was adopted in the Republic and is demonstrated in Caesar's operations, particularly in the Gallic War, and the system was retained without much alteration in the campaigns of the Empire. While campaigning in Britain in the early third century, Severus created supply bases at South Shields on the river Tyne, and other bases on the river Forth and the river Tay, so that provisions could be brought in by sea.

How much the soldiers carried has been variously estimated. Vegetius (*Epitoma Rei Militaris* 1.19) says that the soldier's pack (*sarcina*) weighed 60 Roman pounds, but it is not known precisely what the average soldier carried in the pack. Josephus (*Jewish War* 3.95) refers to three days' rations carried by each man, but this reference concerns Vespasian's campaigns and is not to be taken as a standard procedure applicable to other armies at other times. It is not known how much clothing and personal equipment each soldier would carry himself, but the men probably accrued a surplus and the officers perhaps accrued even more. Generals such as Marius who wanted to move fast stripped the army of its camp followers and unnecessary baggage, and probably reduced the amount each man could carry. Scipio Aemilianus decreed that his men should take with them only the barest essentials for cooking and drinking (Frontinus, *Stratagems* 4.1.1; Roth, 1999). This probably did not apply to all campaigns. The finds from the Agricolan base at Elginhaugh in Scotland show that soldiers and especially officers on campaign did not lead a Spartan existence when it came to personal possessions and equipment.

In addition to food and personal baggage, the soldiers also carried tools, in particular entrenching tools for making camp. Josephus (*Jewish War* 3.55) enumerates the items carried by the men: an axe, a saw, a sickle, a basket, a spade, a rope, and a chain. At least some of the men presumably carried these on the march, since Caesar recounts an instance where the soldiers were already entrenching the camp when the baggage train arrived, which implies that the tools were not carried on carts with the baggage but by the men themselves, at least those who were assigned to camp building. It is possible that the tools were issued to the *contubernium* and only certain men were picked for entrenching duty by rota, rather than that the entire force carried their tools at all times.

Some of the items needed by the whole *contubernium* would be included with the baggage train. Surplus tools, the cooking pots, the hand mill for grinding grain, and especially the eight-man tent, would have been carried on a mule or perhaps two mules, but no source states how many mules were allowed per *contubernium*. Most likely it varied according to the supply of pack animals and the personal enterprise of the soldiers. These beasts were highly valued in civilian as well as military life, but in the army the theft of a pack animal, which affected all the soldiers, was regarded as more severe than the theft of personal belongings, which affected only one man.

The number of pack animals and vehicles required to carry the baggage of an army on campaign was staggering. The animals not only carried goods on their backs but draft animals were needed to pull the carts and wagons of the baggage trains and the siege trains. The baggage train was aptly named by the Romans as *impedimenta* and would include the food stores over and above the amounts that each soldier carried, as well as the equipment that was not needed on the march, such as the bridge-building materials described by Vegetius, who says that an expeditionary army carried with it hollowed logs, planks, cables, and iron nails (*Epitoma Rei Militaris* 3.7). Goldsworthy (1996) estimates that at least 640 animals would be required for the baggage of one legion, as well as 59 carts and 10 wagons for the artillery of each century. Vegetius (*Epitoma Rei Militaris* 2.25) adds that each cohort had a larger *ballista*. The siege train would demand even more animals. For example, Plutarch (*Life of Sulla* 12) says that 10,000 pairs of mules were needed for Sulla's siege train alone. The size of the siege train obviously depended on the nature of the war, and siege equipment would not necessarily be taken on every campaign. It is also possible that not all the field artillery pieces would be carried as a matter of routine, but Roman military planners would sometimes have to cope with the maximum load in the baggage train. Josephus counted 160 artillery engines among Vespasian's three legions in Judaea.

The speed of transport by oxen and mules would have been extremely slow, at an average of 2 miles or 3 kilometers an hour for ox carts, and a maximum of 4 miles or 6 kilometers per hour for pack animals (Rickman, 1980). The men themselves would not be able to march very much faster unless they divested themselves of much of their equipment, and they would not be able to keep up a rapid march day after day. Movement of a campaign army would be tortuous in the extreme, and the troops and baggage would cover several miles of road, with the last men reaching the camp long after the entrenching party and the advance guard had established it.

Examples of the transport ships, carts, wagons, and pack animals can be seen on Trajan's Column. The ships carrying barrels have already been mentioned, and others are shown with items that look like large sacks. In two scenes (Lepper and Frere, 1988, plate XXXI, XLVI), mules are shown pulling the artillery pieces (*carroballistae*) on two-wheeled carts. Wagons drawn by mules and oxen are shown delivering supplies in a busy section where the soldiers are building a fort and Dacian envoys are being received by Trajan (Lepper and Frere, 1988, plate XLIII).

The baggage trains required staff to attend to them, and the Roman army appears to have employed slaves, most commonly referred to as *calones,* but other terms are sometimes found in the sources such as *servi, mancipia,* or *pueri* in Latin, and in Greek *therapontes* and *oiketai* (Roth, 1999). The major problem is that no one can yet answer the question as to whether the slaves belonged to individual soldiers or were corporately employed by the army. Officers certainly brought their own slaves with them on campaign, and in some cases ordinary soldiers possessed slaves, too. Roth (1999) suggests that soldiers were discouraged from bringing their slaves on campaigns, but he also says that the ruling did nothing to prevent the occurrence. He quotes passages from the ancient authors in which separate figures are given for the numbers of soldiers and the numbers of servants captured or killed in battle. The main purpose of the *calones* was to guard the baggage. In carrying out these duties, it is clear that they were not always seen as noncombatants, since Caesar records an incident where the *calones* joined in the battle against the Belgae in Gaul (*Gallic War* 2.27). This presupposes that they carried arms of some kind and could be distinguished from another category of unarmed servants, who were sometimes labeled *lixae*. Since the terminology is not precisely defined, it is hazardous to state categorically that the *calones* were light armed and that the *lixae* were not armed at all, but it is probably safe to argue that they were all the property of the army, subject to military discipline, and were necessary adjuncts to the soldiers in logistics and transportation when an army went on campaign.

## INTELLIGENCE

Republican armies were woefully lacking in intelligence gathering and frequently paid for their neglect with disastrous defeats and the loss of many lives. Painful experiences with Hannibal did very little to foster the art of scouting, reconnoitring, and gathering intelligence, but certain generals such as Scipio Africanus and Caesar managed to remain one step ahead of their adversaries by careful observation and then drawing the right conclusions. Austin and Rankov (1995) point out that the interpretation of the knowledge gained by whatever means, and the decisions made thereafter, rested with the general, and some were better than others.

The theory of good intelligence was known to Polybius, who praised Hannibal for reconnoitring not just routes into enemy territory, but the wealth of the lands he was about to enter, the ways of the natives, their political allegiances, and the degree of their affection or disaffection for Rome (*Histories* 3.48). Much later, when the Romans had learned a lot, Vegetius stressed the importance of knowing the habits of the enemy, and castigated those generals who entered territory that had not been thoroughly explored (*Epitoma Rei Militaris* 3.6; 4.27).

Caesar kept his finger on the pulse of affairs in Gaul as far as possible, and though it could be argued that he presented himself to his public as he wished to be seen, in fairness he also documented occasions when he was taken by surprise. When he invaded Britain, Caesar left Labienus behind with three legions and 2,000 cavalry, with instructions to guard the ports and the grain supply, to monitor the situation in Gaul, and to make plans to deal with whatever situation arose in the best way he thought fitting (*Gallic War* 5.8.1). In order to monitor what was happening among the tribesmen, Labienus presumably operated a system of spies and intelligence gatherers, but this is not elucidated. Caesar tells us that he sent out or received news from *exploratores* or less commonly from *speculatores*, though there seems to be no definite distinction between the two. In one passage, Caesar says that he received a report from his *speculatores* that was confirmed the next day by *exploratores*. Actually, there is probably no need to try to attribute radically different functions to the two groups, except insofar as *exploratores* translates best as scouts and *speculatores* as spies, with the same connotations as to how they operated as in more recent times. The *exploratores* were not yet formed into specific units, and it seems that they could be formed from parties of soldiers sent off on missions to find out what lay ahead or what was the general mood of the tribes or civilians who reported to Caesar about other tribes. He learned from the Ubii (*per Ubios exploratores*) that the Suebi were massing and gathering in their warriors (*Gallic War* 6.10; 6.29).

In several instances, the Romans actively gathered information while on campaign or in peacetime. For the most part these were short-range expeditions, before or after battles. Caesar sent out *exploratores* to observe the tribesmen and in this way found out that the Gauls were crossing the Loire near Cenabum (modern Orleans), so he attacked them (*Gallic War* 7.11.8). He also dispatched *exploratores* to keep an eye on Afranius and Petreius at Ilerda in the Spanish campaign. After the battle of Mons Graupius in Scotland, Agricola dispatched *exploratores* to look for the Britons in case they should be forming up again (Tacitus, *Agricola* 38.2).

Information could reach the ears of the Roman high command in various ways. Embassies provided useful opportunities for information gathering, and traders could provide a great deal of information about what they had seen on their travels. Soldiers were often designated to supervise meetings and markets, and could listen carefully to what was being said. All these methods could provide useful information and were among the means that Caesar used to find out all he could about Britain and its inhabitants before he invaded. Pliny (*Natural History* 6.160–161) recounts how Aelius Gallus noted useful facts in Arabia about the people, their tribal structure, and their agriculture. When Cicero was maneuvered into going out to govern Cilicia, his correspondence shows how he was aware of what was going on beyond the borders of his province (Austin and Rankov, 1995).

The use of spies was well known to the Romans and to their adversaries. During the civil wars between the Caesarians and Pompeians, there were two occasions when the Pompeians sent men pretending to be deserters into Caesar's camp so that they could report back on the state of affairs, but they were discovered and unmasked as *speculatores* (*Spanish War* 13.3; *African War*

35.2–4). Genuine deserters could provide more meaningful information than civilian observers because they knew what to look for and what were the most salient points in military operations. In Gaul, while he was besieging Gergovia, Caesar learned from deserters what he already knew from his scouts, that there was a weak spot in the defenses of the town (*Gallic War* 7.44).

Although the *exploratores* mentioned in the earlier sources were not necessarily permanently appointed to their tasks, by the middle or later second century, whole units called *exploratores* or *numeri exploratorum* had begun to appear on the frontiers, and individual *speculatores* became more common, though not all of these were dedicated to intelligence gathering. The several inscriptions commemorating various *speculatores legionis* do not denote spies but specific ranks in the army, but there were some *speculatores* whose function was to collect and sift information. It is probable that the Marcommanic Wars triggered a marked change in intelligence work. Austin and Rankov (1995) link the formation of specific *exploratores* units with the appearance on the frontiers of officials on the staffs of the provincial governors called *beneficiarii consularis*, who were probably responsible for intelligence networks both within the provinces and across the frontiers. Although the emperors were at the hub of the Empire, they could not be instantly aware of everything that was happening since the speed of communications prevented them from receiving immediate knowledge of events, and their decisions as to how to respond could not reach the generals on the spot until it was too late. Intelligence therefore became primarily a provincial or regional affair, and the officials reacted on their own initiative, only secondarily reporting to the emperor, and maybe performing a holding action until reinforcements arrived.

Although there was never any central bureau for intelligence, it is possible that the Imperial secretary *ab epistulis* was responsible for monitoring the reports from the provincial *beneficiarii* and other sources. There is no written evidence that states this unequivocally, but a poem dating from the reign of Domitian addressed to the *ab epistulis* Flavius Abascantus indicates that the post was concerned with correspondence flowing into and out of the capital, to and from the provinces. It has been noted that, although the men who filled this post were usually civilians, from the reign of Marcus Aurelius military men were appointed, T. Varius Clemens being the first, followed by P. Tarrutienus Paternus, who was a lawyer and also a soldier, and who accompanied Marcus to the wars on the Danube. Austin and Rankov (1995) conclude from this that intelligence had become a priority by about AD 160, when the aggressive movements of the northern tribesmen had become a real threat to Rome.

The *stationes* or bases of the *beneficiarii consularis* were not limited to the northern frontiers. They were set up in Egypt in the administrative districts, and in some provinces they were often attached to mining areas. The *beneficiarii* had routinely started out as legionaries and were usually men of long experience; some of them had operated as *frumentarii,* the equivalent of an Imperial secret police, who had first appeared in the early second century AD. Exactly how the *beneficiarii* gathered their information is not known. There will have been several sources, including not just military men, but traders and civilians, undercover agents such as the *frumentarii,* and embassies to and from the tribes and states beyond the frontiers. It is likely that the Romans knew much more about the eastern states than they did about the northern tribes, especially since commercial and ambassadorial traffic was more frequent and better established, and the social and political geography of the east was more in tune with Roman ideals, with roads, towns, and cities all facilitating an urban way of life. The northern areas, on the other hand, were regarded as trackless wastes without proper roads and cities, and the inhabitants were not urbanized (Lee, 1993). The Romans relied on itineraries, or lists of places in their proper order along the route, and their distances from each other, sometimes accompanied by illustrations showing the roads in long strips, naming the major towns and cities. These worked well in the provinces and in the east, but in the northern regions, where settlements could be uprooted and moved on, the natives combined and recombined in different federations, and permanent towns were lacking, the itineraries were not so useful, since a list of tribes, geographical features, and topographical landmarks is so much more vague.

The relative paucity of knowledge about the northern regions beyond the Rhine and Danube may have been one of the motivating forces behind the institution of military interpreters, who are first attested in the late second and early third centuries, especially in the Danube provinces (Austin and Rankov, 1995). One soldier called himself *interpres Germanorum officii consularis* (*CIL* III 10505), and another was labeled *interprex Sarmatarum(?) ex officio consularis* (*CIL* III 14349.5). Both of these men were on the staff of the governor, as were three more interpreters attested on inscriptions, and significantly, all were based at or near provincial capitals. The Romans presumably adopted a policy of speaking with the tribesmen in their own languages and monitoring their opinions (Austin and Rankov, 1995).

The third century was one of the most troublesome and dangerous periods that Rome had ever faced, with large-scale movements of the northern peoples and the advent of a much stronger and aggressive dynasty among the Parthians, henceforth usually labeled Persians. The Empire temporarily fell apart in AD 260, but when it was reunified, starting with the efforts of Aurelian and culminating in the reforms of Diocletian, changes were put in place that affected intelligence gathering. With the development of a centralized and highly bureaucratic administration, the appointment of an overall official called the *magister officiorum* under Constantine enabled the Roman government to coordinate the information coming in from civil and military sources in the provinces and especially from the frontiers. While this all-powerful individual monitored correspondence, dealt with embassies, and inspected the frontiers, Austin and Rankov (1995) suggest that he did not become the head of a military intelligence bureau. Rather, the emperors themselves with the aid of their advisers took control of this important function in the regions where they foresaw the need for military operations. There were several likely operators who could have formed an intelligence group, such as the *agentes in rebus*, or spies and secret police who replaced the *frumentarii*, and the *protectores domestici* whose function was primarily to guard the emperor, but who were also officers in training who usually went on to military command. However, it seems that whenever these men were involved in intelligence work, it was only as a by-product of their situations and circumstances, and not their prime purpose. It seems that intelligence gathering in the late Empire rested with the *magister militum* (literally, master of the soldiers). The first *magistri* were probably appointed under Constantine, but no actual names are known until a later period. They were assisted by a large staff of secretaries and specialists, and were the most likely candidates for centralizing and coordinating intelligence. As Austin and Rankov (1995) point out, there was a gradual improvement in the quantity and quality of intelligence from Caesar's day to the late Empire, corresponding perhaps to the need for it, and by the fourth century the Roman intelligence systems were extremely good.

## COMMUNICATIONS

One of the most enduring aspects of Roman civilization is the elaborate road network that still forms the basis of European communications today. These roads facilitated the movement of troops within a province and greatly assisted the operation of the Imperial postal service, the *cursus publicus*. In areas where there were no roads, the Roman army cleared the way by sending soldiers with tools to remove obstacles and smooth the paths (Josephus, *Jewish War* 3.115) and eventually if they were to maintain a presence in the areas they had fought over, the Romans built roads.

Military communications utilized only a few of the methods familiar to modern armies, being limited to couriers with oral messages, written instructions, or prearranged signals by trumpet, flag, torch, fire, or smoke. Without wireless communication, adequate lighting, or visual aids, the Romans must seem greatly hampered to modern observers, but their so-called primitive systems were what they were accustomed to and they worked well within their limitations.

Communications over a short distance normally consisted of raising the alarm according to a prearranged signal. When Roman generals of the Republic wished to call the men to arms, they usually raised the standard (*vexillum*) outside the commander's tent. Caesar recounts how this was done when he was at-tacked while still making camp (*Gallic War* 2.20). There are several literary de-scriptions of raising the alarm or recalling troops by various means, among the most famous examples concerning the siege of Numantia, where Scipio's lines were very extensive and too long to supervise at all times. The Romans were in-structed to raise a red flag if an attack took place in the daytime, or to light a warning fire if they were attacked at night (Appian, *Spanish Wars* 6.15.90–92). While investing the stronghold of the Aduatuci, Caesar describes how the tribesmen sallied out and the Roman troops were summoned by fire signals, ac-cording to his previous orders (*Gallic War* 2.33), though it is not certain whether these orders applied to the whole army at all times or simply to these specific circumstances. During the civil war when Caesar blockaded Pompey's army at Dyrrachium, Caesar was warned by smoke signals passed from fort to fort that Pompey had attacked the camp of Marcellinus (*Civil War* 3.65). Smoke and fire signals were often used to recall foragers in times of danger. All these types of signals can only pass on a simple prearranged message, over a relatively short distance.

Long-distance signaling by whatever means, including smoke, beacon fires, torches, or flags, requires many relays with all the errors of transmission and re-ception, compounded by the number of relays involved. Modern researchers have devoted some considerable time and effort to investigating the feasibility of passing messages along frontier lines, using the series of watch towers that are known to exist on most frontiers, including those without any physical running barrier. This theory has polarized scholars, setting its advocates and its adver-saries at odds with each other. It could be argued that passing information along the frontier line from tower to tower would have been far less effective than passing it to the forts, so that soldiers could be dispatched to deal with the problem. In some cases, these forts lay behind the frontier itself but could re-ceive warning signals from the towers with only one relay (Southern, 1990). This is just the situation that was revealed on the borders of Roman Jordan, where an experiment was conducted by lighting fires at night at each of the watch towers, in the expectation that most of the signals would be visible along the various sectors of the line, to pass messages up and down the frontier. In fact, the signals were not visible in a sensible linear sequence, but every one of the fires from all sectors were seen at Khirbet el-Fityan, a signal tower on the high ground behind the legionary fortress at el-Lejjun, significantly named after the legion. It is likely that with only one relay to the fortress from this signal tower, legionaries could be turned out to the sector where the trouble arose (Parker, 1987).

There is considerable ancient evidence that beacon fires were used to trans-mit messages over many miles (Woolliscroft, 2001), but the ancient Greeks and Romans were well aware of the limitations as to what types of message could be sent. As Polybius states, beacons work well in warning of attack and summoning help, and can even operate over a distance of two to three days' journey, but they cannot be used to pass on anything more sophisticated, such as a message to say that the occupants of a city have changed sides, or to describe what the enemy is doing at the moment (*Histories* 10.43.1–10). In these passages, Polybius is preparing the ground for an in-depth account of his signaling system using torches to represent each letter of the alphabet, invented by the Greeks Cleoxenus and Democleitus, and improved by Polybius himself. The system requires two sets of torches, one on the left side and another on the right, to indicate the letters of the alphabet, which are divided into five groups, each containing five letters, except for the last group which contains only four letters. The torches of the left side are raised to indicate which of the five groups of letters are required, one torch for the first group, two for the second group, and so on; then the torches of the right side are raised to indicate which of the five letters are indicated. Polybius gives an example of a message, which starts with the letter K, whose position in the Greek alphabet is the fifth letter in the second group, so the signaler would raise two torches to signify the group and five torches to signify the letter. With practice it would be perfectly possible to use this system quite quickly, but without telescopic aids its range would be limited. Nevertheless, complicated messages could be transmitted, provided that the sender converted it into the fewest possible letters (Polybius, *Histories* 45.6–47.4).

A Roman variant on Polybius's scheme was documented by Julius Africanus in the third century AD (Woolliscroft, 2001). There were only three torches in total, arranged on the left, in the center, and on the right, so that there would be more letters in each of these three groups than in the Polybian five-group system, but there would be only one torch, raised once for the first letter in the relevant group, twice for the second letter, three times for the third letter, and so on. The comparison with modern text phones will be immediately apparent, and if the speed that small children achieve in using their mobile phones is any guide, then the Romans would have been able to transmit and receive equally well. The major problem is that there is no further evidence of this system in use in the Roman army, and there is no evidence that any soldiers or officers were put in charge of signal communications, except for the battlefield trumpeters and horn blowers.

In Julius Frontinus's *Stratagems* the section on sending and receiving messages (3.12) is devoted to those delivered orally or via written dispatches. Caesar's commentaries contain several instances of sending messages by both of these methods. Quintus Cicero was besieged in his winter quarters by the tribesmen under Ambiorix and sent dispatches (*litterae*) to Caesar, with the promise of great rewards if the men carried them safely, but the roads were guarded and they were all cut off (*Gallic War* 5. 40). On another occasion Cicero sent letters and also messengers (*litterae nuntiisque*) to Caesar, but some of the messengers and those carrying the written dispatches were captured and tortured (*Gallic War* 5. 45). Caesar always refers to *litterae* in the plural, which may mean that he hedged his bets by sending more than one soldier with the same message to ensure that at least one got through, but in some instances only one man carried a message. A Gallic slave in Cicero's camp was persuaded to carry a letter to Caesar inside the shaft of a javelin or spear (*Gallic War* 5.45), and Caesar replied to Cicero by means of a message tied to a spear that was thrown into the besieged fort but remained stuck in the side of a tower for two days before it was noticed. This letter was written in Greek in case it was intercepted (*Gallic War* 5.48), which implies that this was a possibility and that Ambiorix and his warriors could read as well as speak Latin. At a later period, campaigning in Germany in the sensitive period after the loss of three legions under Quinctilius Varus in AD 9, Tiberius was aware that the disaster had been caused by lack of caution combined with bad communications. He was particularly anxious that all his orders should be clear, so according to Suetonius (*Tiberius* 18) he gave all his instructions for the following day in writing, including warning of sudden emergencies, and he insisted that anyone in doubt about an order should consult him, no matter what time of day or night.

Communications by letter or oral delivery were restricted by the state of the roads, the presence of the enemy, and the speed of the average man, horse, carriage, or ship. The long-distance dispatches (*relationes*) to the Senate or to the emperor from the war zone could take several days to reach Rome. The Imperial post set up by Augustus with relays of fresh horses and posting stations was supposed to be capable of covering 75 kilometers per day, depending on terrain. The famous example of Tiberius's journey from Rome to see his injured brother Drusus in Germany is often quoted as the maximum that Roman transport could achieve, at an average of 300 kilometers each day (Pliny, *Natural History* 7.84). Tacitus records how the *aquilifer* of *legio IV Macedonica* traveled from Mainz to Cologne, a distance of 185 kilometers, in twelve hours with the news that the legions of Upper Germany had joined Galba in his bid to take over the Empire from Nero (*Annals* 1.56). Other dispatches were not so rapid. Austin and Rankov (1995) document the number of days that it took for Cicero's correspondence to travel to and from Rome—about a month for letters from his brother Quintus to reach him from Gaul, forty-seven days for a letter from Atticus in Rome to reach Cicero in Cilicia (*Letters to Atticus* 5.19.1), and seventy-four days for Cicero's dispatches from his province to reach the Senate (*Letters to His Friends* 15.1.2; 15.2.3). It is estimated that the optimum speed of communication from the province of Raetia to Rome would be about three days, five to six days for dispatches from Germany, nine to ten days from Britain, and fourteen days from the eastern provinces (Austin and Rankov, 1995). This emphasizes the problems of governing the Roman Empire and overseeing its military operations. The provincial governors and military commanders had to make their own decisions about how to react to a particular set of circumstances, being unable to rely upon receiving instructions from the emperor in time to avert a crisis. For this reason, from the late first century onward, the emperor ceased to wait at the hub of the Roman world for news of the frontiers and war zones, and took charge himself.

## MILITARY MEDICINE

Medicine in the Roman world was derived almost wholly from the Greeks, but in the area of military medicine the Romans developed and improved upon Greek theory and practice. In particular, they learned how to treat wounds but did not neglect the cure of diseases, and they established hospitals in their forts, particularly in the legionary fortresses. The hospitals were staffed by specialist personnel, and medical staff went on campaign with their units. Hyginus mentions a hospital tent in his work on laying out the camp (*De Metatione Castrorum* 4.35), recommending that it should be placed where convalescent soldiers could find peace and quiet.

The most common staff were the *medici*, attested in all types of units, including legions, auxiliary cohorts, and *alae*, the Urban Cohorts, the Praetorian Guard, the *vigiles*, and the *equites singulares*. The title *medicus* likely covered a range of different ranks and functions (Davies, 1969). Some of the *medici* were probably ordinary soldiers, included with the *immunes* who were excused fatigues, but others were officers, perhaps of considerable status. On some inscriptions, *medici ordinarii* are named, such as Caius Papirius Aelianus at Lambaesis in North Africa, who incidentally lived for eighty-five years, seven months, and fifteen days, in itself a good recommendation for a doctor (*ILS* 2432). In the later Empire at the fort of Niederbieber in Germany, a certain Processus set up a dedication to the household of the emperor, calling himself *medicus hordinarius* (*ILS* 9182), perhaps a guide to the way in which he pronounced the word. It is possible that the *medici ordinarii* held the rank of centurion, but no source confirms this, so it must remain a contested theory. Some scholars suggest that *ordinarius* simply means that the doctor served in the ranks. On a monumental inscription in Rome, listing the officers and men of the fifth cohort of the *vigiles*, there are four *medici*: Caius Runnius Hilaris, Caius Julius Hermes, Quintus Fabius Pollux, and Sextus Lutatius Ecarpus. These men are listed after an enumeration of the centurions and other officers such as the *cornicularii*, but before the soldiers of each century with the centurion's name at the head. The position of their names with the officers lends some support to the theory that the medical men ranked with them. Some or perhaps all of the *medici* in the fleets ranked as *duplicarii* on double pay, as attested on an inscription from Puteoli (*RIB* 2315; see also *CIL* X 3441 from Misenum).

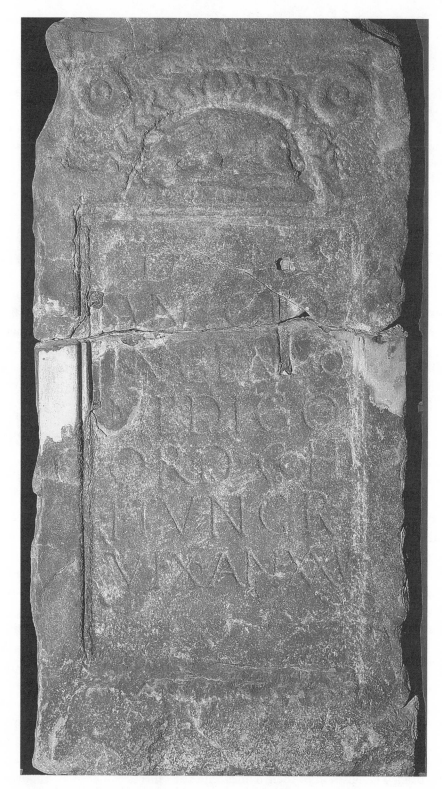

The gravestone of Anicius Ingenuus—a *medicus ordinarius*—is notable for the portrayal of a hare in the arch at the top. (Museum of Antiquities of the University and Society of Antiquaries of Newcastle upon Tyne)

Several of the attested *medici* have Romanized Greek or eastern names, such as Quintus Marcius Artemidorus of the *equites singulares Augusti* in Rome (*ILS* 2193a), Marcus Mucius Hegetor of *cohors XXXII Voluntariorum* (*ILS* 2601), and Marcus Rubrius Zosimus from *cohors IIII Aquitanorum* (*ILS* 2602). Another possible easterner is Marcus Ulpius Telesphorus, *medicus* of the *ala Indiana,* but his name has been reconstructed from only a few surviving legible letters on the inscription (*ILS* 2542). These men may have started out as civilian doctors and then joined the army, but how and where they trained is not known. Teachers or trainers (*discentes*) are known in medical contexts (Le Bohec, 1994), so in some cases perhaps the army trained its own medical staff, choosing likely candidates from among those who had recently joined or showed some aptitude for the work.

Other medical staff include the *optiones valetudinarii* and the *capsarii,* also attested on inscriptions. The *optiones valetudinarii* were *immunes* according to Tarrutienus's list (*Digest* 50.6.7), and their function, if their titles are taken literally, was to assist in the hospital, but in what way is not made clear. They may have been clerical assistants rather than surgical or medical staff. Two inscriptions from Lambaesis mention the *optiones* of *legio III Augusta,* naming one of them as Lucius Caecilius Urbanus (*ILS* 2437; 2438). The gravestone of Caius Luccius Sabinus from Beneventum in Italy shows that in his varied career he started out as an *optio valetudinarii* and then went on to take up a string of other posts, so either he was not, or did not want to remain, a medical specialist (*ILS* 2117).

The *capsarii* who appear on inscriptions along with *medici* and *optiones valetudinarii* may have been responsible for dressing wounds, since the title *capsarius* is derived from the box (*capsa*) that contained bandages, but some authorities say that the box was for scrolls and the *capsarii* may have been clerical assistants. The soldier shown on Trajan's Column bandaging the leg of a wounded man is usually interpreted as a *capsarius.* An inscription from Carnuntum on the Danube (*ILS* 9095) mentions the *capsarii* of *legio XIIII Gemina,* and Aelius Munatius is named as *capsarius* of *cohors milliaria Hemesenorum* (*ILS* 9169). Another inscription from the large late Roman fort at Niederbieber in Germany associates the *capsarii* of the *numerus Divitiensium Gordianorum* with the *medicus hordinarius* called Processus (*ILS* 9182).

Hospitals (*valetudinaria*) are archaeologically attested at the legionary fortresses on the Rhine at Vetera (modern Xanten) and Novaesium (modern Neuss), at Inchtuthil in Scotland. From inscriptions it is clear that a hospital existed at Lambaesis in North Africa. An inscription found at Stojnik in Yugoslavia, dating from AD 179, specifically mentions the *valetudinarium* of *cohors II Aurelia nova milliaria equitata civium Romanorum.* On Hadrian's Wall in Britain, at the forts of Housesteads and Wallsend, the hospitals of auxiliary units have been excavated. A *medicus ordinarius* called Anicius Ingenuus is attested at Housesteads. He died young, aged only twenty-five, and his gravestone is notable for the portrayal of a hare in the arch at the top (*RIB* 1618). The hospital at Wallsend was added to the fort in about AD 180, and it is not known if the timber building that preceded was dedicated to the same purpose. The hospitals were usually courtyard buildings with small light and airy cubicles opening off the open central area, sometimes with a verandah running all round the interior, though the verandah at Housesteads was removed when the courtyard was flagged. It should be noted that not all the buildings of this type of plan were necessarily hospitals. In some cases, buildings inside forts that look like hospitals may actually have been workshops (*fabricae*), which adopted the courtyard plan and small rooms arranged all around it to provide light and air for the metalsmiths and woodworkers who used them.

On campaign, the work of the *medici* would include treating those who had fallen sick, but the treatment of wounds is much better documented. One of the best known manuals is that of Aulus Cornelius Celsus who wrote his *De Medicina* in the early first century AD, relying heavily on Greek works. He writes about diseases, pharmacology, therapy, and surgery. Some of his cures for diseases could only have increased the mortality rate, and it is not certain whether the Romans fully understood contagion and the efficacy of isolating patients. In dealing with wounds, however, Celsus either had valid experience of his own or had gained knowledge from someone who had seen medical service in the wars. He was more of an encyclopaedist than a serving medical officer, but nothing is known of his life. Writing under the Emperor Tiberius, he could just possibly have witnessed the many battles in Germany and Pannonia during Augustus's reign.

Celsus writes in detail about how to remove various types of missile weapons, recommending that if the weapon has not penetrated very far and has not crossed large blood vessels, it should be pulled out through the hole where it had entered. However, if the distance that the weapon has to be withdrawn is greater than the distance that remains, then the best way to extract it is to force it right through, cutting the flesh at the opposite side with a scalpel. This is not recommended for broad weapons because it would create two huge wounds instead of only one, so Celsus describes how to use the Dioclean *cyathiscus*, named after its inventor Diocles. This instrument had a curved end with a hole in it, and it had to be inserted next to the weapon lodged in the flesh, until the hole could connect with the point of the weapon, and then the two could be drawn out together (*De Medicina* 7.5.3–4). Celsus adds notes about how to stop excessive bleeding of wounds and what to do to prevent inflammation; if all else fails he explains how to amputate limbs (*De Medicina* 7.26.21–24; 7.33.1–2). Celsus was aware of the damage that lead sling bullets could cause. If they are simply lodged in the flesh, then they can be extracted with forceps, but there are problems if they have embedded themselves in bones or joints. He explains that sometimes it is necessary to cut around the bullet lodged in a bone by making a

V-shaped cut, and if the bullet is stuck between joints, then the only means of extraction is to pull the joints slightly apart. Roman medical and surgical instruments, looking startlingly like modern versions, have been found at several sites, especially in the legionary fortresses. From Neuss there are needles, scalpels, probes, and spatulas, and from the fortress at Aquincum in Hungary there are scissors and forceps, leg splints, and a lancing fork.

Pharmacology consisted mainly of the use of herbs. Medicinal plants have been found on military sites, especially at Neuss where five varieties were discovered (Davies, 1969). It has been suggested that the courtyards of the military hospitals may have been laid out as gardens where specific herbs could be grown (Liversidge, 1968). One of the best ways of securing good health in the army derived from cleanliness. Elaborate bathing establishments were attached to each fort and fortress, and time was clearly allowed for taking a bath, which probably became a prolonged leisurely affair involving dice games and gambling. Altars to Fortuna are often found in bath houses. Sick and wounded soldiers in the hospitals may have had their own baths, since it is thought that the hospital at Inchtuthil contained a bathroom. There were also kitchens in the hospitals where perhaps special foods were prepared. Celsus stresses the importance of diet in the treatment of the sick, enumerating those foods thought to be the most easily digested (*De Medicina* 2.24.1–3). In one of the rooms in the hospital at Neuss, excavators found the remains of eggs, peas, lentils, and shellfish, all of which are on Celsus's list (Davies, 1969). Sufficient time for convalescence was known to be important in the recovery process, and a papyrus from Egypt shows that some legionaries of *legio XXII Deiotariana* were sent to the seaside for a period of convalescence.

The title *medicus* was also applied to veterinarians who looked after the horses and mules of the army, sometimes appearing in the sources as *medicus veterinarius,* such as the tombstone of Quartianus, *medicus veterinarius* of the first Praetorian cohort in Rome (*ILS* 9071). Another designation is *mulomedicus,* which appears most commonly in Vegetius's *Ars Mulomedicinae.* A tombstone from Gaul shows a *mulomedicus* from Gaul, carrying a *hipposandal,* which may have been used to hold medicines in place like a modern poultice boot (Dixon and Southern, 1992).

## TECHNOLOGY

Roman technology was primitive by modern standards but far in advance of the achievements of most of their enemies. The Romans absorbed most of their scientific and technical knowledge from the Greeks and adapted it to their own needs. In the military sphere, Roman technology is probably better classified as engineering. As builders, the Romans were unsurpassed, whether it be tempo-

## THE ANONYMOUS, *DE REBUS BELLICIS*

Probably in the mid-fourth century, an unknown author, conventionally labelled in modern works as "The Anonymous," wrote a treatise advocating reforms to the financial system, the law, and the administration of the provinces and the army. The text has been preserved along with the *Notitia Dignitatum,* a list of Imperial officials, governors, and army commanders of the later Roman Empire.

With regard to the army, The Anonymous recommends that various types of machinery should be used, some of which are illustrated in the surviving manuscript. They range from the common sense to the fantastic, including a protective screen mounted on wheels to allow soldiers to move in close to the walls of a besieged city or stronghold and engines to hurl projectiles from the walls at a besieging army. He was very appreciative of the effects of artillery and strongly recommended its use in battle. He also advocated the use of scythed chariots which would slice through barbarian hordes when used in battle on the plains. His machinery is regarded by many modern scholars as highly impracticable if not eccentric, but there may have been some value in his temporary bridge made from inflated hides or his ship powered by oxen walking around a central shaft connected to paddle wheels on either side. There is no evidence that any of his technological improvements were ever adopted by the emperors to whom he addressed his work.

rary camps for the army to halt overnight or for a few days, stone fortresses to house a legion, or bridges across rivers and gorges. They were excellent water engineers; their aqueducts are legendary, and the study of the water supply of Roman forts reveals much about their expertise. Lead pipes have been found at the legionary fortress of Chester in England and at several German forts. Roman engineers could drain water-logged marshes and mines, build efficient water pumps, and operate huge overshot and undershot water wheels. They could build cranes and hoists, as illustrated by the tread wheel crane depicted in great detail on the Haterii relief of the second century AD, now in the Vatican, which shows remarkably modern-looking block-and-tackle and pulley systems.

For the army, Roman technological progress was not restricted by the economic constraints that affected other manufactures (White, 1984). With regard to weaponry and defensive equipment, the army could not afford to remain in stasis, as their enemies developed, however slowly, and however much they copied the Romans themselves. The army itself probably produced most of its own needs in their workshops (*fabricae*) in the fortresses and the smaller forts, though not many of these buildings have been identified and fewer still have been studied in depth (Bishop and Coulston, 1993). The Romans were capable metal workers and collected scrap for reworking in their forts. The legions had the trained manpower to manufacture everything, including shields, body armor, and weapons, and as Bishop and Coulston point out, papyrological evidence makes it clear that the *fabricae* could accommodate a large workforce, involving legionaries, probably auxiliaries, camp servants, and civilians, with the majority being the legionaries themselves. In working metal for weapons, the Romans knew how to weld different metals together and how to harden the metal. A sword from Vindonissa was made up of three different metals, with the harder variety on the outside, but though the Romans knew how to harden off, they perhaps chose not to do so for the plates of segmented armor, perhaps deliberately choosing to create softer armor to absorb blows (Bishop and Coulston, 1993). As self-sufficient as they were, Roman military engineers and technicians probably did not manufacture the entire materiel of the army. In different regions, civilian workshops may have been used; there was probably no set pattern across the Empire.

One technological achievement that still baffles modern reconstruction attempts is Caesar's bridge across the Rhine (*Gallic War* 4.17). In part, the difficulty lies with the description, but a bridge completed in ten days across a river that is as powerful and as wide as the Rhine remains an impressive feat. Caesar was chasing the German tribes and considered it undignified to cross the river in boats, so he constructed a timber bridge. The balks were 18 inches thick and sharpened at the ends, floated out on rafts, and then rammed down into the river bed. They were kept apart by two-foot timbers laid between them but clamped together with bracing timbers (*fibulae*, literally, brooches) on the outer sides, but this is where the difficulty lies in understanding what Caesar wished to convey. One set of balks was placed at an angle facing upstream, and the second set was at an angle facing downstream, 40 feet apart at the base, which means that the roadway, consisting of long poles and wattlework, would be somewhat less wide than this. To give the bridge stability against the current, timbers were placed like buttresses on the side facing downstream, and in case the Germans threw in heavy objects to bring the bridge down, more free-standing timbers, perhaps arranged like cutwaters, were placed in the river upstream to take the main shock. The Germans packed up their belongings and fled to the forests as soon as they saw the bridge under construction. Caesar entered free Germany in force, burned the villages and crops, and after three days retired to the left bank of the Rhine, content with the demonstration of Roman power.

## CARTOGRAPHY

How the Romans controlled and administered their vast Empire without the aid of accurate maps can be baffling to modern historians. The evidence for Roman mapping has been studied by Dilke (1985), but he has been criticized for assuming that Roman cartographers drew up their maps in the same way and for the same purposes as modern map makers (Lee, 1993). The Romans possessed fairly sophisticated geographical knowledge, but it was practical rather than documentary, and it found expression in itineraries or lists of places and their distances from their neighbors. Roman surveyors were perfectly capable of marking out large tracts of land when making military camps or founding colonies and new towns with their attendant territories, but they perhaps thought in terms of regions and provinces rather than the whole of the known world. When laying out plots of land, their divisions were straight and regular, and the *agrimensores* were capable of making plans (*formae*) to represent the allotments. Some sections of a cadastral plan of the Flavian period survives at Orange (ancient Arausio) in France. In the reign of Severus, the famous marble plan of Rome was produced (*Forma Urbis Romae*), of which fragments survive showing instantly recognizable buildings and monuments in great detail.

Although the Greeks used maps, the Romans do not seem to have produced any of their own until the reign of Augustus, when Marcus Vipsanius Agrippa drew up a world map with a commentary attached giving measurements (Austin and Rankov, 1995). Although it was placed on the walls of the Portico Vipsania named after Agrippa, it is not known what this map looked like. Presumably there were many other maps that have not survived and have not been documented as Agrippa's was by Pliny (*Natural History* 3.16–17). In the second century AD Claudius Ptolemaeus, better known as Ptolemy, wrote his *Geography* in eight books. His interests were wide, extending from geography to astronomy, and he also wrote several astronomical works, the most famous of which is the *Almagest,* containing the theory of astronomy and his own meticulous observations. Ptolemy was probably the first geographer to use longitudinal and latitudinal coordinates to pinpoint the places he mentions in his lists, which are contained in books two to seven of his geographical work. It is not known whether he produced maps to accompany the text, but it is clear that he expected his readers to draw their own maps from his instructions. His coordinates for Britain produce a notoriously skewed map of Scotland with the northern areas turned through 90 degrees so that they point east to west instead of north to south, and his Mediterranean is too long from east to west. Yet, considering the date of his work, it is an extremely worthy contribution to map making.

Some of Ptolemy's information, especially about Britain, was derived from an earlier work by Marinus of Tyre, who is not otherwise known but who in turn probably derived much of his knowledge from the military expeditions in Scotland under Agricola, when reconnaissance was carried out on land and by sea. At least one civilian took part in this reconnaissance work, as attested by Plutarch, who met a Greek scholar called Demetrius at Tarsus, who had just returned from an expedition to Britain in AD 82, when Agricola was preparing for what would eventually be the final battle in Scotland. It is not known whether Agricola had any maps with him, or created new ones, but some of the information that accrued from his military expeditions survives in Ptolemy's *Geography*.

The known Roman maps and geographical lists date from the later Roman Empire, the only two pictorial examples being the Peutinger Table, a road map

Title page of a medieval edition of Ptolemy's *Geography*. Claudius Ptolemy was probably the first geographer to use longitudinal and latitudinal coordinates to pinpoint the places he mentions in his lists, which are contained in books II to VII of his geographical work. (Library of Congress)

of the lands around the Mediterranean, and a representation of the Black Sea coast on a shield cover from Dura-Europos. Neither is accurate, but presumably both served their intended purpose. The Peutinger Table shows the Mediterranean much as Ptolemy's coordinates would show it, elongated from east to west and much too narrow from north to south. Since much of the surviving geographical information from the Roman word takes the form of itineraries, the Peutinger Table is most likely a graphic representation of a list of places and was never meant to achieve cartographic precision. Apart from itineraries, the Romans documented routes pictorially by means of long strips showing the roads and main places and the distances between them, without regard to orientation, in the same way that John Ogilby documented roads in Britain in the seventeenth century. As well as towns and prominent geographical features, the itineraries listed halting places (Austin and Rankov, 1995). Vegetius (*Epitoma Rei Militaris* 3.6) describes route maps (*itineraria picta*) and recommends that generals should use them, implying that they were common enough in his day. These were presumably devoted to short-range expeditions, but with greater detail, and much more practical to the army commanders than an attempt to compile and use a map of the entire province or a group of provinces.

Despite the evidence for Roman expertise in surveying and for the existence of maps and itineraries, the questions about how the military authorities used them cannot be answered. Within a province, the road systems and the frequency of towns and villages might preclude the use of maps for troop movements, and on the frontiers navigating from one fort to another would have been simple enough, but beyond the frontiers men of expertise would be required who knew the routes. Ammianus (17.10.2; 17.10.5; 27.10.7; 29.4.5) emphasizes the need for native guides beyond the frontiers of the Rhine and Danube. On the other hand, Lee (1993) points out that in the east, the Romans seemed to know their way about, to the extent that the Emperor Julian could use his knowledge to deceive the Persians about which particular route he intended to take, and also had a withdrawal strategy should he need to retreat. It is possible that at provincial headquarters and also in the archives in Rome there were reports of previous commanders who had campaigned in the regions across the frontiers. For instance, the information gained on Agricola's campaigns in Scotland was most likely recorded in some form, perhaps even mapped and used to good effect by the Antonine generals who invaded half a century later and again by Severus in 208, but at 2,000 years distance it is impossible to be sure.

### REFERENCES AND FURTHER READING

Anderson, J.D. 1992. *Roman Military Supply in North East England.* Oxford: British Archaeological Reports, British Series 224.

Austin, Norman J.E., and Rankov, N. Boris. 1995. *Exploratio: Military and Political Intelligence in the Roman World from the Second Punic War to the Battle of Adrianople.* London: Routledge.

Bishop. Michael C. (ed.). 1985. *The Production and Distribution of Roman Military Equipment: Proceedings of the Second Roman Military Equipment Seminar.* Oxford: British Archaeological Reports S275.

Bishop, Michael C., and Coulston, Jon C. 1993. *Roman Military Equipment from the Punic Wars to the Fall of Rome.* London: Batsford.

Coulston, Jon C. 1985. "Roman archery equipment." In Bishop, 1985, 220–366.

Davies, Roy W. 1969. "The *medici* of the Roman armed forces." *Epigraphische Studien* 8, 83–99.

Dilke, Oswald A.W. 1985. *Greek and Roman Maps.* London: Thames and Hudson.

Dixon, Karen R., and Southern, Pat. 1992. *The Roman Cavalry from the First to the Third Century AD*. London: Batsford.

Feugère, Michel. 2002. *Weapons of the Romans*. Stroud, Gloucestershire: Tempus.

Garnsey, Peter., and Whittaker, C.R. 1983. *Trade and Famine in Classical Antiquity*. London: Cambridge University Press.

Goldsworthy, Adrian K. 1996. *The Roman Army at War 100 BC to AD 200*. Oxford: Clarendon Press.

———. 2003a. *The Complete Roman Army*. London: Thames and Hudson.

———. 2003b. *In the Name of Rome: The Men Who Won the Roman Empire*. London: Weidenfeld and Nicolson.

Hyland, Ann. 1990. *Equus: The Horse in the Roman World*. London: Batsford.

Keppie, Lawrence. 1984. *The Making of the Romman Army*. London: Batsford. Republished by Routledge, 2000.

Landels, J.G. 2000. *Enginering in the Ancient World*. London: Constable. Rev. ed. of first edition published by Chatto and Windus, 1978.

Le Bohec, Yann. 1994. *The Imperial Roman Army*. London: Routledge.

Lee, A.D. 1993. *Information and Frontiers: Roman Foreign Relations in Late Antiquity*. Cambridge: Cambridge University Press.

Lepper, Frank, and Frere, Sheppard. 1988. *Trajan's Column*. Gloucestershire: Alan Sutton.

Liversidge, Joan. 1968. *Britain in the Roman Empire*. London: Routledge.

Marsden, E.W. 1969. *Greek and Roman Artillery: Historical Development*. Oxford: Clarendon Press.

Middleton, P. 1983. "The Roman army and long-distance trade." In Garnsey and Whittaker, 1983, 75–83.

Parker, S. Tom. 1987. *The Roman Frontier in Jordan*. Oxford B.A.R. S340, 2 Vols.

Rogers, H.C.B. 1977. *The British Army of the Eighteenth Century*. London: George Allen and Unwin.

Roth, Jonathan P. 1999. *Logistics of the Roman Army at War (264 BC to AD 235)*. Leiden: Brill.

Salway, Peter. 1991. *Roman Britain*. Oxford: Clarendon Press.

Schramm, F. 1918. *Die Antiken Geshütze der Saalburg*. Berlin; new rev. ed. by D.Baatz, Saalburg, 1980.

Southern, Pat. 1990. "Signals versus illumination on Roman frontiers." *Britannia* 21, 233–242.

Toynbee, Jocelyn M.C. 1973. *Animals in Roman Life and Art*. London: Thames and Hudson.

Walker, R.E. 1973. "Roman veterinary medicine." In Toynbee, 1973, 303–343.

Woolliscroft, David I. 2001. *Roman Military Signalling*. Stroud, Gloucestershire: Tempus Publishing.

CHAPTER 7

# The Late Roman Army

From the first to the third century the Roman Imperial army was a successful machine, subject to occasional reorganizations and subtractions and additions of detail, but not needing sweeping reforms. Certain changes came about in response to military pressures, such as the strain on resources caused by the wars in the Danube regions under Marcus Aurelius. This emperor employed commanders with reference to their abilities, rather than their social origins, and thus he opened up more military careers to equestrians. Severus was more aggressive in his reforming zeal, preferring equites to senators in legionary and provincial commands, increasing the size of the army, giving the soldiers a pay rise, and reconstituting the Praetorian Guard. With Severus, the winds of change began to blow across the Roman Empire, and by the end of Diocletian's reign a new world had dawned. A brief overview of what happened to the army in its later life serves to round off the foregoing chapters, but it is important to note that while there is documentation for the fourth-century army in the pages of Ammianus Marcellinus and for the sixth-century army in the works of Procopius, the major changes to the military organization of the Empire took place in the fifth century, precisely the era for which there is hardly any information. The result is that scarcely any conclusion about the late Roman army can be made without debate.

## POLITICAL DEVELOPMENTS

The evolution of the Roman army was a reactive rather than a proactive process, since emperors and commanders could not predict exactly what was to happen and did not have a blueprint for a steady progress toward the ideal military machine. This evolution was accelerated during the third century, which opened with the civil wars that brought Severus to power and closed with those that created Diocletian and the Tetrarchy. Between these two events, the Empire almost fell apart in 260 when all the frontiers collapsed, unable to withstand the

The hard-pressed Emperor Gallienus had to rely upon the remnants of the army that were still available to him after the splitting of the Empire in AD 260. This coin proclaims the loyalty of all the soldiers (FIDES MILITUM). (Drawing courtesy of Trish Boyle)

new pressures from the movement of the northern tribes toward the Empire and the accession of a much more aggressive regime in the east, where Ardashir and his successors set about reconstituting the former empire of the Persians. The reign of Gallienus was regarded as the nadir of the Empire, through no fault of his own, but he was nonetheless reviled for his inability to restore order instantly. In AD 259–260, Gallienus's father Valerian mounted a disastrous expedition to the east, ending in defeat and his capture. He ended his days a prisoner of the Persians, and Gallienus was in no position to rescue him.

In AD 260, the whole of the Gallic provinces broke away in rebellion under their own self-appointed emperors, and much of the east was under the control of the Persians, but Roman interests were temporarily looked after by a Palmyrene noble called Odenathus. In the Alps, the new tribal federation of the Alamanni stood poised to attack Italy. Gallienus could do little but maintain the status quo. When he was assassinated his successors built on his work and started the long haul back to unity, achieved under Aurelian. The century closed with the accession of Diocletian and the institution of the short-lived Tetrarchy, and the accession of Constantine, the architect of the late Roman Empire.

With Constantine, everything changed. He spent some time eliminating his rivals, so once again there was prolonged civil war affecting many parts of the Empire, until AD 324 when the last contender, Licinius, was defeated, leaving Constantine as sole ruler. Rome ceased to be the hub of the Empire, but it was not an abrupt transition, since Rome had not been the main focus for some time. Emperors had taken the field with their armies since the second century, and provincial bases had been established for the Imperial households. The new center of the Empire had to be within reach of the Danube and the east, where the trouble spots were, hence Constantine's choice of Byzantium, which he renamed Constantinople in his typical self-advertising manner. The city was a sound choice, more or less central to both the threatened areas, supplied from the sea if necessary, and eminently defensible. The split into eastern and western Empires came about some time later, but the pattern was created at the beginning of the fourth century.

The Empire was now on the defensive, and territorial expansion was abandoned, but transfrontier expeditions had not died out altogether. The Emperor Valens campaigned across the Danube against the Goths, and Valentinian crossed the Rhine to fight the Alamanni. Peace was restored for a time, the frontiers were shored up, the Goths were held at bay, and negotiations were made with the Persians. In 378, the disastrous battle of Adrianople between Goths and Romans resulted in the near destruction of the eastern army, and in 394 the western army was very badly mauled. The final split into two halves came in AD 395, when the two sons of the Emperor Theodosius the Great, Honorius and Arcadius, took charge, respectively, of the western and eastern Empires. The east was wealthier than the west and eventually recovered, purging the army of the Goths and reducing the number of soldiers to a dangerous all-time low, until they could recruit local Isaurian tribesmen and build up another strong army. The western Emperor Honorius made the mistake of executing Stilicho, the only general who could successfully command the troops and win battles against the tribesmen. Two years later, in AD 410, all the troops were withdrawn from Britain, or at least those who obeyed the call, to help defend Gaul and Italy. The west fought numerous battles against the Huns and the Goths, until the last Roman Emperor Romulus Augustulus was deposed by Odoacer in AD 476, traditionally the date when the western Empire fell. In reality, 476 is only one of several potential dates for the fall of Rome, but it is a convenient marker for ancient and modern scholars to divide history into manageable narrative chunks. There was no reverberating crash. The Goths in Italy tried to be more Roman than the Romans, and life in the west went on in hybridized Roman-Gothic or Roman-Frankish form, as the nascent medieval kingdoms emerged in what would become Germany, France, Italy, and Spain. Meanwhile, the eastern Roman Empire only really came to an end when the Ottoman Turks sacked Constantinople in 1453.

## FIELD ARMIES AND FRONTIER ARMIES

The major change to the army was the ultimate division into mobile field armies and static frontier troops. This did not happen overnight, and the stages in the development are obscure. When Diocletian restored order after the chaos of the late third century, he reorganized the whole state, which was henceforth totally oriented to war. He reconstituted the frontiers, divided up the provinces into smaller units, revised the command structure of the provincial armies, and progressively divided civil and military careers. The Greek author Zosimus was full of admiration for Diocletian and praised him for strengthening the frontiers and protecting the Empire (2.34).

There are two major problems about Diocletian's reforms of the army. One unanswered question concerns the overall size of the army and the strength of individual units, and the other concerns the foundation of the mobile field armies of the fourth century. Lactantius accuses Diocletian of vastly increasing the size of the army, crippling the Empire with the expense, a conclusion perhaps enhanced by the fact that the Diocletianic system of defense involved the creation of two senior emperors with the title Augustus, adopted by himself and his colleague Maximian, and two junior emperors with the title Caesar. These four emperors of the Tetrarchy each had troops at their disposal, so Lactantius perhaps used this as the basis for his calculations. The size of individual army units is not established, but the auxiliary *alae* and cohorts probably remained the same, at 500 and 1,000 strong, at least on paper. It is not possible to calculate the losses during the previous decades of entire units and of individual manpower. The matter of legionary strength is much more fraught, since some sources indicate that the Diocletianic legions were only 1,000 strong. Seston (1946) and Jones (1964) agree that the number of legions rose from about thirty-five to over sixty, so if they were all 5,000 or 6,000 strong there would have been tremendous pressure on recruitment. Vegetius (*Epitoma Rei Militaris* 1.17; 2.2) says that the two legions recruited in Illyricum before Diocletian came to power were 6,000 strong, which could be taken to indicate that when he wrote his military work, this number was abnormal. Some of the legionary fortresses were smaller than those of the earlier Empire, such as El-Lejjun in Jordan, holding a maximum of 1,500 men, but even this does not necessarily imply that all legions were only 1,000 strong, since some of them could have been split up and the various sections housed in outposts. Duncan-Jones (1978) was able to show that in the fourth century, if not under the Tetrarchs, some of the frontier units were divided into small contingents.

Another unsolved problem concerning Diocletian's army is whether or not he laid the foundations of the mobile field army. There had already been a precedent that the ancient historians interpreted as the first mobile cavalry army under Gallienus, who collected together all kinds of horsemen from the units that were still available to him and placed them under one commander, Aureolus. When the Byzantine chronicler George Cedrenus investigated the reign of Gallienus, mobile cavalry armies were very familiar to him, so he stated confidently that Gallienus was the first to use them. The truth is that Gallienus was hard pressed, with enemies to the west, the north, and the east. To make

Portrait of Diocletian on a gold aureus from the Rome mint. As part of his military reforms he created new legions, perhaps only 1,000 strong, and strengthened the frontiers. He may have formed the nucleus of the later mobile field armies, though this is disputed. (Drawing courtesy of Trish Boyle)

matters worse he was denied access to the troops of the western and eastern sectors of the Empire. He needed to be able to move quickly, and to meet the threats he established his headquarters at Milan in the fertile plains of the river Po in northern Italy, where he could move rapidly through the Alps to the north, or to meet threats from Gaul, where the so-called Gallic emperors had declared independence. These usurpers may not have intended to invade Italy but in the search for stable boundaries the legitimate emperor and the self-declared emperors watched each other warily. Gallienus's cavalry army probably did not survive as an independent unit after his assassination, and no direct connection with Diocletian's or Constantine's army can be proven.

Diocletian certainly had with him the *comitatus,* consisting of a variety of mounted men and infantry, and variously interpreted as merely a bodyguard by those who deny that Diocletian instituted the mobile army, or as a mobile central reserve by advocates of a Diocletianic version of the later *comitatenses* of Constantine and his successors. The *comitatus* derives from a well-established precedent dating back to the early Empire, where the companions of the emperor were styled *comites Augusti,* who were described as serving *in comitatu principis.* These men could be civilians from all walks of life, but from the reign of Marcus Aurelius and particularly Severus, when military affairs began to predominate, the *comitatus* was placed on a more official basis and was composed of army officers and administrative personnel who accompanied the emperor on campaign.

Whether Diocletian's *comitatus* really was the nucleus of the field army cannot be answered. The need for a central reserve had become more pressing during the third century, though when Severus placed a newly raised legion, *II Parthica,* at Alba, a mere 20 miles from Rome, it is debatable whether he needed it to rush to the war zone or to protect himself. It was perhaps a combination of these factors, though moving the legion from Rome to the Rhine or Danube would probably take longer than it would to shuttle troops along the frontiers to form a campaign army. This was the time-honored method of assembling an army for a war, by taking units from more peaceful zones and then either sending them back to their bases when the war was concluded or on occasion housing them in new forts in the territory just fought over. The procedure was dangerous in that it left other areas vulnerable, and there was an increasingly obvious need for frontier defenders who remained where they were while the field armies dealt with the major problems. Constantine put this into practice, and at some unknown date the *comitatenses* came into being, consisting of cavalry and infantry, and new units called *auxilia.* These last units were raised either by Constantine or his father, probably from the Rhineland. They were all infantry units and had nothing to do with the old-style auxiliary units (Southern and Dixon, 1996). The cavalry and infantry elements of the field armies were placed under two newly created commanders called *magister equitum* and *magister peditum.* None of the *magistri* of Constantine's reign are known, so their previous careers, rank, and status can only be estimated. Within a short time there were also regional field armies, since one mobile army under the emperor was not sufficient to keep the peace all over the Empire.

With the creation of the field armies, there were changes to the frontier armies, possibly brought about in Constantine's reign (van Berchem, 1952). A law dated to AD 325 distinguishes between three classes of troops: the *comitatenses,* which were the highest ranking, then the *ripenses,* and finally the *alares et cohortales.* There are clear distinctions between the field army (*comitatenses*), and the frontier armies consisting of *ripenses* (sometimes rendered in other documents as *riparienses*) and the old-style *alae* and cohorts. The term *ripenses* covers all the higher-grade frontier troops, whether they are legions or cavalry units. Mounted units called *vexillationes,* probably about 500 strong, had been stationed on the frontiers perhaps after the reign of Gallienus, when the legionary cavalry had been vastly increased in numbers and split off from their parent legions. They acquired the title *vexillationes* toward the end of the third century and are listed in documents as distinct units, with the same rank as legionaries. There were various other mounted units, simply labeled *equites,* or *cunei equitum.* The *alares* and *cohortales* of the frontier armies are ranked as the lowest of all, after legions and cavalry.

The wider term *limitanei* covers all the frontier troops, of all grades, but it is not certain when this label was first applied. It is common in the sixth century but may not have had exactly the same meaning as it did two centuries earlier. The frontier troops of the later Empire are sometimes portrayed as very low

Head of Constantine, originally from a colossal statue of which only fragments remain. During Constantine's reign, the army was split into two sections, frontier troops and the mobile field armies, each with a large cavalry element. (Photo courtesy of David Brearley)

grade, almost worthless troops, because they were supposedly tied to the land and therefore were not much more than a militia. This may be an anachronistic view derived from the sixth-century version of frontier troops. As Jones (1964) has argued, if the troops were tied to the land, then there would be no need to pay them in kind and in cash, and there would be no need to grant land to veterans, but these procedures still pertained in the fourth century. Furthermore, some of the *limitanei* were drafted into the field armies when there was a need and they were given the label *pseudo-comitatenses,* so if their fighting ability and training had lapsed, the emperors would perhaps have looked elsewhere. There were always plenty of the so-called barbarians ready and willing to fight for Rome.

Constantine campaigned against the Franks and Alamanni in Gaul and strengthened the Rhine frontier. He placed a large bridgehead fort at Deutz opposite Cologne, with a potential garrison of 900 men. Bridgehead forts on the

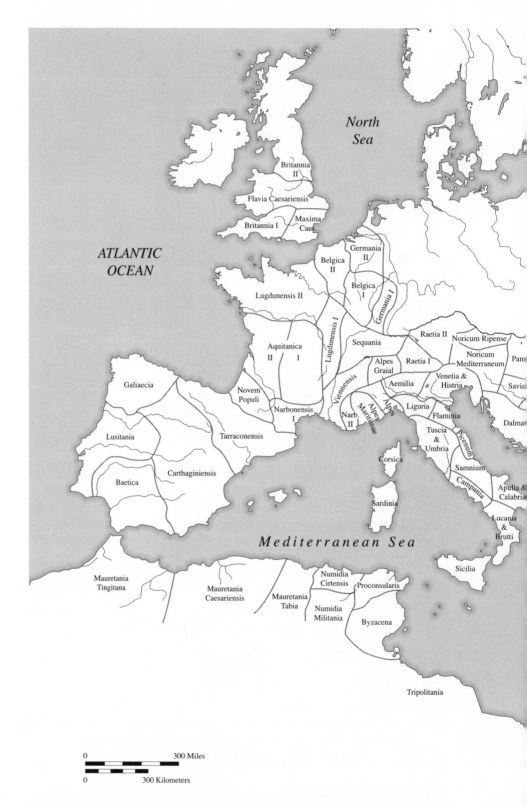

Map of the later Roman Empire reflecting the changes made by Diocletian and his successors. The provinces were split into smaller units, and the frontier commands could extend over more than one province. (Drawn by Graeme Stobbs)

leria

nn.I

Moesia I

evalitana

Dardania

Epirus
Nova

Epirus
Vetus

Macedonia

Thessalia

Achaea

Dacia

Thracia

Haemimontus

Rhodope

Hellespontes

Lydia

Asia

Insulae

Crete

Moesia II

Scythia

Europa

Bithynia

Phrygia
I    II

Caria

Lycia &
Pamphylia

Pisidia

Isauria

*Black Sea*

Paphlagonia

Diospontus

Galatia

Pontus

Armenia
Minor

Cappadocia

Cilica

Mesopotamia

Osrhoene

Augusta Euphratiensis

Syria Coele

Cyprus

Phoenicia

Palestina

Augusta
Libanensis

Arabia I

Arabia II

*Mediterranean Sea*

Libya
Superior

Libya Inferior

Aegyptus
Iovia

Aegyptus
Herculia

Thebais

Danube may owe their origin to him, but the dating is not sufficiently precise. Zosimus accuses Constantine of weakening the frontiers, but he was somewhat biased, an ardent pagan and prejudiced in favor of Diocletian, whereas Constantine promoted Christianity.

After the battle of the Milvian Bridge just outside Rome, when Constantine defeated Maxentius, he abolished the Praetorian Guard. The Praetorian Prefects survived, divested of military command, instead taking charge of the supplies to the army. Since he still needed a bodyguard, Constantine may have established the *scholae palatinae,* which were significantly placed under the direct command of the emperor, removing the possibility that an independent commander would rise to power and attempt to usurp him. Some authorities consider that the *scholae* were established by Diocletian, but Hoffman (1969–1970) favors Constantine.

## COMMAND

The career paths of the generals of the early Empire combined a variety of civil and military posts, so that an aspiring military man from the senatorial order would have absorbed the experience of provincial and sometimes central civil administration, of the legions when they served as tribunes and then as legates, all of which equipped them for provincial commands of their own. The equestrians often gained their military experience from command of the quingenary auxiliary forces, then by serving in a legion as one of the five *tribuni angusti-clavii,* moving on to command of the 1,000-strong auxiliary units. Provincial governors attended to civil and military matters in their provinces, with the help of administrative assistants and army officers. In the second century, perhaps beginning in the reign of Hadrian, the civil and military intermix began to fade. Military specialists had begun to appear who chose to remain in the army rather than follow the civil administrative path, and vice versa civil administrators chose not to go into the army. Hitherto the Romans expected their generals to follow this comprehensive education and experience, which could result in some inappropriate appointments to the army. Gradually, the men with some aptitude for the military posts were selected instead of those whose background and breeding supposedly suited them for the tasks. Marcus Aurelius boosted the careers of some equestrians when he appointed them to military commands because they displayed particular talents, and Severus appointed equestrians to command of legions and some provinces. Gallienus took this a stage further by divorcing senators almost entirely from military command, though some senators survived and followed their normal careers. With Diocletian the civil and military posts were separated. Provincial governors were generally civilians with the title *praeses,* and the commander of the troops was the *dux,* which means

## THE *NOTITIA DIGNITATUM*

This document, literally translated as *List of Offices,* is a list of the civil and military officials of the eastern and western Empires. It includes their respective staffs, units, commanders in the various forts, and garrisons stationed in the two halves of the Empire. Theoretically the *Notitia* should be of great value in studying the late Roman army, but, as usual with ancient documents, there are problems, the date of compilation being one of the most disputed. In very general terms the *Notitia* depicts the late fourth century army, dating perhaps from AD 395, with updates added to about AD 430. The amendments, however, are neither consistent nor complete. The earliest surviving version dates from a copy made in Carolingian times, probably in the ninth century. There are four copies of this Carolingian work, two of them lodged in England—one at Oxford and the other at Cambridge. The other copies can be found in Paris and Munich.

What has come down to us is the western Empire version, in which the information for the eastern Empire is perhaps out of date, not having been amended since AD 395. Someone, or a group of persons, clearly tried to revise the entries for the western half of the Empire but perhaps did not have access to all the facts, possibly because the returns from the offices of the various governors were not being made regularly. The result is a hodgepodge representing the western provinces as they were garrisoned at different dates from the late fourth to the early fifth centuries, with the eastern provinces lagging behind as it was in the late fourth century.

For each half of the Empire, the high officials and their staffs are shown, starting with the Praetorian Prefects, then the *magistri militum,* down to the generals and the provincial governors. Along with the title and rank of each official there is an illustration of his insignia and a brief description of his duties. For each general there is a list of the units under his command, and for the *duces* there is a list of the stations. The document seems to provide a snapshot view of the Empire at one period of time, but this is not the case. Modern scholarship has shown that the *Notitia* includes military posts long since abandoned and units already disappeared. Conversely, in some provinces, forts that are known to have been occupied in the late fourth century are not listed at all. Some of the place names in the *Notitia* within certain areas of command cannot be matched with the sites revealed by archaeology, making it difficult to produce a map of forts and units occupying them.

leader. His full title usually reflected the name of his province, such as *dux Africae* or *dux Aegypti,* but the military command of the *duces* could extend over more than one province, since it was more convenient to give the *duces* control of sectors of the frontier rather than restrict their authority to one small area, and in this case they were usually titled *dux limitis.* Originally, the title *dux* was given to an officer acting in a temporary capacity, commanding a collection of troops to be transported to the war zone, or in temporary command of a complete unit, but the post was standardized in the third century and the *duces* became regular officers. The law codes are specific about the duties of the *duces* (*Cod. Th.* 7.1.9). They commanded the provincial troops, with the exception of the *comitatenses* who were under the *magistri,* and their function was primarily to protect the frontiers, repair the existing frontier works, or build new fortifications should circumstances demand it. They were in charge of recruiting replacements for the army and assigning them to their units, and they were to oversee the collection and distribution of provisions to the troops, sending quarterly reports to the Praetorian Prefects who were ultimately responsible for the administration of the food supply (*Cod. Th.* 11.25).

Developing in parallel with the *duces,* under Constantine the *comites* took on varied roles in administrative and military spheres. The *comes sacrarum largitionum* was a financial official, but *comites* could command troops, in which case they were called *comites rei militaris,* and the law codes also attest to the title *comes limitis.* The commands of the *comites* varied greatly in importance, ranging from a relatively minor frontier posting to a major command. There was considerable flexibility in ducal and comital commands in the late Empire, and their titles and the extent of their authority varied according to circumstances. It is impossible to trace the evolution of the frontier commands since there is not enough information to provide continuity, and the standardization of the earlier Empire did not apply. Appointments were probably made with regard to the needs of the day, but all that survives in the documentary record is a confusing array of different titles from a very long time span. In AD 384, the *dux Aegypti* was replaced by the *comes rei militaris per Aegyptum,* which may or may not mean that the duties had changed. The military titles in the *Notitia Dignitatum,* a late Roman list of officials and their commands, attest *duces* who are not known in any other source, such as the *dux tractus Armoricani et Nervicani,* in command of the troops of five small provinces. The ducal commands of Moesia Secunda and Scythia, listed in the *Notitia Dignitatum* as separate appointments, were later combined into one (*Cod. Th.* 7.17.1). These groupings may reflect either an outbreak of trouble in the region or a shortage of manpower to take command.

## OFFICERS AND MEN

The officers of the late Empire are not as well known as those of the legions and auxiliary troops of the pre-Diocletianic army. Lack of precise dates makes it difficult to assess when titles changed their meaning or went out of use, and there may have been much more variation among the provinces in what the titles meant and the duties that were involved. The most common titles for officers in the late Empire were *praepositus, tribunus,* and *praefectus.* In the early Empire, *praepositus* was not a rank or a regular appointment. The title was applied to officers of various ranks in temporary commands. Legionary centurions called *praepositi* commanded the small units of *numeri* on the frontiers, but in some commands the *praepositi* were tribunes or prefects. In the late Empire, the title *praepositus* covered a similar variety of posts of different grades. *Praepositi limi-*

*tis* commanded sectors of the frontier in Africa, under the *dux Africae*, and elsewhere epigraphic evidence attests *praepositi legionis, cohortis, militum, equitum,* and *auxilii* (*CIL* III 3653; 5670a; 3370; *ILS* 2786).

The highest ranking tribunes served in the *scholae*, and others commanded units of the field army or the frontier troops. Like the title *praepositus*, tribune seems to have covered various grades and ranks. *Praefectus* also covered different posts. The *Notitia Dignitatum* routinely lists *praefecti* as commanders of legions all over the Empire, but the *praefecti alae* are found only in the western Empire.

The junior officers of the late Roman army are imperfectly known, and although the titles of some of them have been preserved, it is possible that they represent chronological or regional variations. The three titles, *a libellis, subscribendarius*, and *regerendarius*, seem to have been used for the same officer, who was probably responsible for record keeping. An officer called *princeps* is found at the head of the offices of the *magistri*, the *duces*, and the *comites*, and it is thought that there would be one of these officers in every army unit. Another high-ranking officer in the army units was the *primicerius*, attested in the *scholae*, and also in the service of at least two of the *duces*. An officer called *senator* seems to rank next highest, followed by the *ducenarius*, serving in the cavalry and infantry units and in the *scholae*. Vegetius says this officer commanded 200 men (*Epitoma Rei Militaris* 2.8). Another officer called the *centenarius* is found in the offices of the *duces*, in cavalry and infantry units, and the *scholae*, but there is insufficient evidence to elucidate the rank or functions of the *ducenarii* and *centenarii*, or how they were related to each other. Two officers, called *biarchus* and *circitor*, may have been concerned with the food supply, and officers called *numerarii*, usually two to each unit, are thought to have been in charge of the finances, collegiality perhaps being an attempt to provide a safeguard against dishonest practices. With the *signifer* and the *draconarius* we are on better ground, the *signifer* being the standard bearer as of old, and the *draconarius* carried the dragon standard, of Sarmatian origin, with a metal dragon's head, open mouthed, mounted on a pole and with a long cloth tube attached to the back of the head rather like a modern windsock. It produced a satisfying roar.

Recruitment to the late Roman army was a constant problem for the emperors and commanders. It may have been Diocletian who passed the law obliging sons of soldiers and some veterans to join if they were physically fit (*Cod. Th.* 7.23.1). Annual conscription was probably also his contribution to filling gaps in the ranks. According to Ammianus (31.4.4), sometimes a money tax took the place of a levy of recruits, which was in any case linked to the land tax and predominantly affected the rural population. Landowners were obliged to produce a number of recruits commensurate with the extent of his holdings, and the smaller landowners joined up in a consortium and took it in turns to provide

## PROFITEERING IN THE LATE ROMAN ARMY

Much like their predecessors, Roman officers of the late Empire were not averse to making profit for themselves. Tales of the exploitation of the civil population illustrate how powerless small communities were when they were up against the military. Requisitioning took the form of stealing under license, and the practice of billeting soldiers on civilians in the cities did not always benefit the citizens.

Officers, not confining their abuses to civilians, were just as ready to exploit their own men. In the early Empire, it is known that centurions demanded bribes from the men to grant exemption from duties or periods of leave, and the later officers did not develope high principles in this respect. Claiming the pay for men who had died was one of the easiest tricks familiar to many another army throughout history, where supervision could not be close and constant. The Emperor Valens tried to correct this and other abuses. He may have succeeded temporarily but the problem arose again in the

sixth century, according to Procopius's tales of officials keeping the names of dead men on the rolls even when there had been large losses in battles (*Anecdotes* 24.5–6), which Jones (1964) says is indicative of conniving between officers, officials, and auditors.

According to Synesius (*Letters* 129) the *dux* Cerialis found yet another way of claiming pay by allowing some of his men very long periods of unpaid leave but not entering the facts in his accounts, thereby taking the cash for himself. Some officers sold the rations for the troops and horses in addition to taking the soldiers' pay, thus leaving some units barefoot and without clothes (Libanius, *Orations* 47.31). Another officer, Cerialis again, engaged in a little illicit trading of his own. Synesius, who clearly had no sympathy for Cerialis, describes how he had the soldiers of the Balgritae lodged with him. They were originally mounted archers, but since Cerialis had sold all the horses, they were now just archers (*Letters* 131).

one recruit. The laws passed by successive emperors reveal what was really happening when recruits were to be found. For instance, Valens insisted that the landowners must provide men from among their registered tenants and not try to pass off onto the army homeless men, so that they could preserve their workforce. The difficulty of recruiting sufficient numbers of soldiers is highlighted by the laws reducing the lower age limit to eighteen (*Cod. Th.* 7.13.1) and probably raising the upper limit to thirty-five years (Jones, 1964). The height qualification was also lowered (*Cod. Th.*7.13.3), indicating that the army was willing to compromise on a larger scale than hitherto about the quality of its recruits.

Another series of laws reveal how desperately men wished to avoid joining the army. First of all, it was declared illegal for potential recruits to cut off their fingers or thumbs. The repetition of such laws reveal that they were powerless to stop the practice. Valentinian lost patience in AD 368 and passed a law (*Cod. Th.* 7.13.5) that condemned self-mutilated draft-dodgers to be burned alive, thus depriving himself of potential recruits altogether. Then common sense prevailed when Theodosius passed another law (*Cod. Th.* 7.13.10) forcing men without thumbs to serve in the army, but if the landowners offered a mutilated man, then they had to find a second one so that the two would equal one fully functional soldier.

Since there was a lack of willing citizens, the army looked elsewhere for its soldiers and found them among the tribesmen from the periphery of the Empire. This was a time-honored practice dating back to the Republic, when tribesmen would be recruited under their own leaders for the duration of a campaign and would serve alongside the army until the end of hostilities. In the Empire the early auxiliary units were recruited from various tribes, predominantly Gauls, Germans, and Thracians, as part of the regular army, receiving citizenship on retirement. Throughout their history, the Romans brought the tribal warriors into their armies and would have been unable to garrison the provinces and fight their wars without them. There were various ways of using barbarian manpower. Tribesmen could be recruited en masse as part of treaty arrangements on the conclusion of peace, and were either distributed among the existing units to fill gaps or were sent to other provinces, such as the 5,500 Sarmatians that Marcus Aurelius sent to Britain. The Goths were defeated by Claudius II Gothicus and recruited into his army, and the Romans came full circle to the practices of the Republic in AD 382, when Theodosius I made a treaty with the Goths, allowing them to fight under their own commanders, just as the troops raised by Republican generals used to fight under native chieftains.

From the late third century onward new methods of recruiting so-called barbarians were established. Settlement of barbarians within the Empire had always been a means of siphoning off pressure on the frontiers, often in large numbers. In the later Empire, it became more common to settle tribesmen inside the Empire in return for contributions to the army. Two groups of people who were brought in on this basis are attested—the *foederati*, literally meaning troops raised in accordance with a treaty (*foedus*), and the *laeti*. The *foederati* were paid in kind by means of food rations (*annonae foederaticae*), which was eventually commuted into an annual payment. It may be the case that when they were first settled they could not provide their own food until their farms were fully established, so the Romans supplied them for the first few years.

A group of tribesmen called *laeti* had been established in Gaul since the Tetrarchy. Although a large number of Frankish tribesmen were settled as *laeti* around Trier, Langres, and Amiens, this does not mean that all the *laeti* were ethnically homogeneous groups. The derivation of the term *laeti* has been variously explained as a group of people who had been captured and returned to the provinces, or more convincingly as a Germanic root word meaning people who were only half free. The latter interpretation accords well with the status of the *laeti* whose settlement within the Empire was dependent on a regular contribution of troops for the army. The law codes mention *terrae laeticae,* the lands of the *laeti,* and Ammianus says that the *laeti* served in Constantius's army. The *laeti* were supervised by officials, perhaps military officers, since a law of AD 366 refers to *praepositi laetorum,* and in the *Notitia Dignitatum* several *praefecti laetorum* are attested in Gaul.

Little is known about the organization of the *laeti* and *foederati,* but it was not an obstacle to a brilliant military career to start out as one of these barbarian troops. The short-lived Emperor Magnentius was a *laetus* but rose to high rank in the army. Many Franks served as Roman soldiers, and at least one of them seemed contented with his dual role, setting up an inscription (*CIL* XIII 3576) that reads *Francus ego cives, Romanus miles in armis*—"I am a Frankish citizen [but] a Roman soldier under arms." Some Frankish officers attained high rank, such as Arbogast, who was appointed *magister militum,* and Richomer who rose to the rank of *comes.* Other barbarians became commanders of the armies, such as the Vandal Stilicho. Without these men of ability and loyalty Rome could not have survived for so long.

## WEAPONS AND EQUIPMENT

Production of weapons, armor, and clothing was a priority in the later Empire, and to meet the needs of the troops, state arms factories were set up, perhaps by Diocletian. They were most likely placed in those areas where production centers were already established (James, 1988), but if there were no preexisting factories then they were established in or near the legionary fortresses, such as Lauriacum, Aquincum, and Carnuntum on the Danube. The *Notitia Dignitatum* lists the factories and their products. Most of the factories were devoted to the manufacture of shields and weapons (*scutaria et armorum*). In the west a major concern was the production of arrows, which in the east were probably made by individuals with a long tradition of home production. There was probably some standardization in state-run arms production, at least on a regional scale, but the archaeological record shows a bewildering variety of armament styles arising from the fact that the native troops used their own equipment.

Textile production was as important as that of arms and armor, and state-operated linen and woollen factories and dye works turned out tunics, cloaks, and blankets. Clothing is depicted on funerary monuments and mosaics, which show soldiers wearing knee-length sleeved tunics. Mosaics show that the tunics were white with purple decoration in the form of roundels at the corners of the hem, two at the front and two at the back. The most common cloak was the *sagum,* reaching to the knees and fastened with a brooch at the right shoulder. Trousers were also worn, introduced by the German tribesmen and the easterners. The cavalrymen of the earlier Empire wore trousers reaching just below the knee, but these were close fitting and designed for horse riding, whereas the Germanic and eastern trousers were baggier. Footwear came in many different styles, comparable to civilian shoes, the hob-nailed military boots (*caligae*) having died out in the second century (Southern and Dixon, 1996).

Military tombstones of the third century tend to portray soldiers in tunics and cloaks, which led some scholars to the conclusion that the use of armor had declined, especially since Vegetius says that after the reign of Gratian the troops did not use heavy armor and helmets (*Epitoma Rei Militaris* 1.20). Coulston (1987) thinks that this only applies to the eastern *comitatenses* after the battle of Adrianople when so many lives were lost and presumably the equipment was lost with them. The archaeological evidence shows that body armor was still in use, though use of the segmented armor typical of the legionaries of the first and second centuries seems to have declined in the mid-third century. Mail and scale armor survived (*lorica hamata* and *squamata*), and a complete mail shirt was found at Dura-Europos, ending just below the waist, with sleeves reaching to the elbow.

The greatest changes in armor are found in helmet design. Instead of the forged types of the early Imperial army, the fourth-century helmets were made in sections, with two halves joined together by a ridge piece, and separate neck guards and cheek pieces added on. The so-called Spangenhelm consisted of four pieces riveted to four bands, with a browband riveted on at the base, and hinged cheek guards. It has been pointed out that the sectioned helmets were probably easier and quicker to make in the arms factories than the old-style versions (James, 1988).

Weaponry remained comparable to that of the earlier Empire. The most common sword type was the long *spatha* used by cavalry and infantry alike. The *pilum* was still used and is depicted on third-century gravestones, but it was renamed *spiculum* according to Vegetius (*Epitoma Rei Militaris* 2.15). The troops still used a great variety of different types of spearheads, ranging from very thin, tapered versions to broad leaf-shaped ones, and the Franks introduced a new weapon, the throwing axe.

The distinguishing mark of a soldier of the late Empire was the military belt. Third-century tombstones show men wearing broad belts, which tended to grow broader in the fourth and fifth centuries. The belts were often highly decorated, with various metal fittings designed for practical use and for display. A set of metal fitments from a military belt was found at Dorchester on Thames in England, consisting of stiffening plates to prevent the belt from doubling over, tubular plates to strengthen the edges, and ring suspension fitments for attaching equipment. The buckle was decorated with animal heads, and the strap end was strengthened with a lancet-shaped metal fitment. Some of the straps were very long and would be wrapped over the belt after passing through the buckle, to dangle over the right hip (Southern and Dixon, 1996).

## FORTIFICATIONS

Although the units of the Roman army were based in permanent forts surrounded by walls and defensive ditches, the soldiers did not expect to be besieged

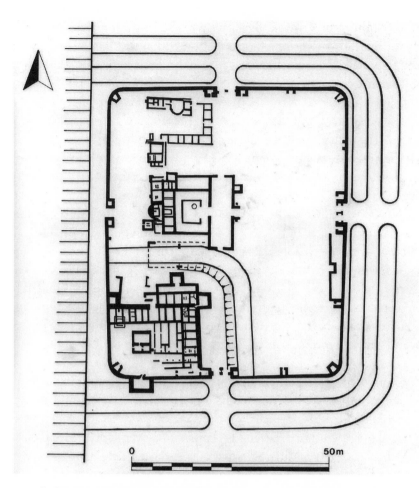

In the later Roman Empire, the military forces were more often on the defensive than the offensive, and forts changed their appearance accordingly. The fort at Eining on the Danube was much reduced in size and separated from the larger fort of the early Empire by a ditch. (Drawing courtesy of Graeme Stobbs)

within their strongholds like medieval castle garrisons. The fort was the administrative base, where the unit records and pay chest were kept, and where the troops were housed when they were not out on exercises and patrols or performing the multiple tasks that are documented in the duty rosters. The soldiers went out to meet threats rather than remaining behind their walls to protect themselves. The army still operated in this way in the third century, but toward the end of the third and the beginning of the fourth centuries fortifications began to look more like the later castles. Existing forts were repaired or extensively rebuilt but with distinctive alterations that signify that the hitherto unchallenged ascendancy of the Romans was waning. While their offensive policy never truly disappeared, they were now more on the defensive than their ancestors.

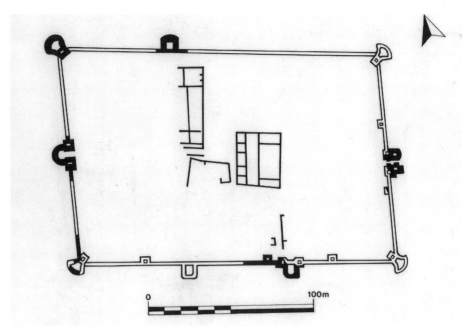

Several forts along the Danube were altered in the late Empire. Three of the four gates at Ulcisia Castra were blocked up and projecting fan-shaped towers were added at the corners to provide defenders with a view along the walls. (Drawing courtesy of Graeme Stobbs)

Older forts often had one or more of their gates blocked, sometimes by the addition of an outward-projecting U-shaped tower joining the original flanking towers. Projecting towers were added to the walls to give a better view of the defenses, and in some areas new fan-shaped towers were added to the corners to afford a greater view of the walls. Some forts were reduced in size, a prime example being the fort at Eining on the Danube, where the late fort fit into a corner of the old one. It was not just the frontiers that required defense. The roads in the interior now had to be guarded by means of road posts and watch towers, fortified stores bases began to appear, and landing stages on river frontiers acquired thick walls reaching down to the water. New forts were not built on the early Imperial pattern like a playing card. They were now four-square with massive walls and crowded interiors. There was no perimeter road inside these forts, the barracks being placed right up against the walls, and often there was only one gate instead of the usual four.

Defensive works also began to appear around cities and towns. Some of them had already been provided with walls during the early Empire, more out of a sense of civic pride than the need for defense, illustrated by the fact that in some cases the walls remained unfinished. These were now completed, existing walls were repaired, or new defenses were built, though it should be pointed out that they were usually built with an emphasis on quality and there are no signs

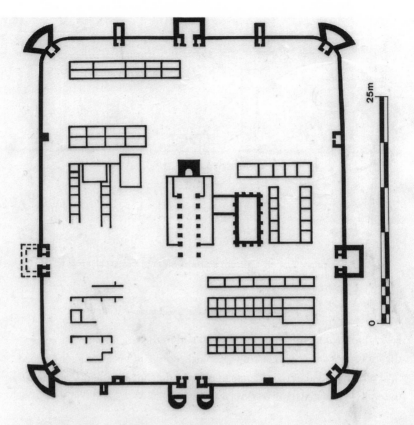

The late Roman version of the fort at Drobeta on the Danube, with blocked gates and extra fan-shaped towers at the corners. (Drawing courtesy of Graeme Stobbs)

of panic-stricken haste (Johnson, 1983). There may have been an Imperial impetus behind the fortification of cities, since Ammianus says that Valentinian included civilian settlements as well as forts in his defense policy. Some civilian sites were moved to more easily defensible hilltop sites, especially in the Alpine regions through which the tribesmen passed on their raids into Gaul and Italy (Johnson, 1983).

These changes were not limited to provincial towns and cities. The ancient city of Rome had been walled in the early Republic, but had long since outgrown the old walls, the urban sprawl extending into the surrounding land without the need for external protection. In the late third century, the Emperor Aurelian decided to build new defenses, enclosing Rome within massive high walls with close-set towers and well-defended gates. For Romans with a sense of history and the eternal destiny of Rome, this no doubt heralded a new era of insecurity and doubt.

## REFERENCES AND FURTHER READING

Coulston, Jon C.N. 1987. "Roman military equipment on 3rd century AD tombstones." In Dawson, 1987, 141–156.

———. 1988. *Military Equipment and the Identity of Roman Soldiers.* Proceedings of the Fourth Roman Military Equipment Conference. Oxford: British Archaeological Reports S394.

Dawson, Michael (ed.). 1987. *Roman Military Equipment: The Accoutrements of War.* Proceedings of the Third Roman Military Equipment Research Seminar. Oxford: British Archaeological Reports S336.

Duncan-Jones, Richard. 1978. "Pay and numbers in Diocletian's army." *Chiron* 8, 541–560.

Hoffman, D. 1969–1970. *Die Spätrömische Bewegungsheer und die Notitia Dignitatum. Epigraphische Studien* 7. Düsseldorf: Rheinland Verlag. 2 vols.

James, S. 1988. "The *fabricae:* state arms factories of the Later Roman Empire." In Coulston, 1988, 257–332.

Johnson, Stephen. 1983. *Late Roman Fortifications.* London: Batsford.

Jones, A.H.M. 1964. *The Later Roman Empire.* Oxford: Blackwell. 2 vols.

Seston, W. 1946. *Dioclétien et la Tétrarchie.* Paris: Boccard.

Southern, Pat, and Dixon, Karen R. 1996. *The Late Roman Army.* London: Batsford.

van Berchem, Denis. 1952. *L'Armée de Dioclétien et la Réforme Constantinienne.* Paris: Geuthner.

CHAPTER 8

# Great Soldiers and Battles

## FAMOUS GENERALS

Throughout Rome's tremendously long military history, the lives of many great generals have been described, and some details of the exploits of ordinary soldiers have been recorded, either in literary form or on career inscriptions. The full biographical background that is usually available for soldiers of more recent armies is unfortunately lacking. Concerning the early Republic, when there was no standing army and the Romans were farmer-soldiers, tales are told of great generals, but history is inextricably combined with legend and has lost nothing in the way of embellishment. One of the most famous Republican generals was Marcus Furius Camillus, who led successful attacks on the Etruscan cities of Veii and Falerii but was then exiled, allegedly for keeping some of the booty to himself. When the Romans faced the onslaughts of the Gauls some years later and were soundly defeated at the battle of the Allia, they remembered Camillus, brought him back from exile, and made him Dictator. At some point, the Gauls captured Rome, but Camillus brought them to battle and won, going on to win more battles and to put an end to civil and political strife in Rome itself. The details of his achievements are somewhat unreliable, combining the fantastic with the feasible, and read like a list of the problems that Rome faced and how solutions were found. Camillus was an early Roman hero, representing all the solid virtues to which political and military men should aspire, and in the absence of contemporary rather than retrospective evidence it is doubtful exactly how much credence can be placed in the legendary stories.

All chief magistrates of the Republic were potential generals, since most tasks, both civil and military, were allocated by lot, except in those cases where clever political intrigue coupled with energetic marshalling of supporters resulted in special appointments like those of Scipio Africanus, Scipio Aemilianus, and Pompey the Great, appointments that transcended all the carefully crafted laws that normally prevented men from reaching commands while still under the specified age and without having progressed through the relevant magistracies. Success as a Roman general did not automatically guarantee a life of ease and repose, or retirement full of honor and respect. Most generals ended badly. Their military achievements began to fade very quickly, and they were brought down, exiled, or sometimes even killed, either as a result of prosecution by their jealous enemies or by their own excesses, such as those that marred the latter years of Gaius Marius. Against this background of deadly Republican politics, Gaius Julius Caesar's ruthless efforts to stay on top are more clearly understood. From Marius onward, generals with soldiers at their backs could overturn the law and the will of the Senate, to which body they were supposed to be subordinate. Toward the end of the Republic, generals who chose not to coerce the state in this way found themselves powerless. Prestige and influence were not sufficient to put into effect their administrative measures or their perfectly reasonable requests for the settlement of their soldiers, and so generals who had been successful abroad gradually became military despots at home. As the Empire rose out of the ruins of the Republic, a system evolved that put an end to the chaos. Under Augustus and his successors, military men were firmly subordinated to the emperor, and given fairly prescriptive instructions when they were sent to govern provinces or fight wars. The period of Republican expansion was almost over, give or take a few Imperial exceptions. Claudius annexed Britain, where for the first hundred years or so there was opportunity for generals to show their mettle, but anyone who showed a little too much initiative in carrying wars beyond the boundaries of his province was usually stopped short. Most Roman wars of the Empire were reactive rather than proactive, and from the late first century AD the emperor himself usually took supreme command. Notable generals arose under this system and received their due recognition and share of honors, but the old Republican rewards for military success, such as the triumphal march through the city displaying booty and captives, became the preserve of the emperors and their immediate families; generals were awarded the insignia of a triumph but not the public display. From Augustus onward all major appointments and all rewards were solely in the emperor's gift, and generals who wished to excel either contented themselves with the arrangement or went down the risky route of attempting to usurp the reigning emperor.

## Generals of the Late Republic

Although the names of several generals are known throughout Rome's early history, it is not until the second Punic War that details begin to emerge that are more or less distinguishable from myth, and some biographical background can be discerned among the eulogistic haze. Modern historians owe a great deal to the fortuitous placement within the Scipio family of one of the Greek captives, Polybius, brought to Rome after the battle of Pydna in 168 BC. Roman military biography surely starts with him, and a separate volume could be filled with the campaigns of the early military men who led Rome to victory from the third century BC to the rise of Marius and Caesar. Although the armies that the early Republican generals commanded were the forerunners of the army of the Empire, for reasons of economy of space in this book, the generals and the battles selected for this section are limited to the period from the so-called reforms of Marius to the second century, covering the formation and the apogee of the Imperial Roman army.

## Gaius Marius (157–86 BC)

Marius was not a member of the old aristocracy, but his origins and early career were not as undistinguished as his enemies liked to proclaim. He married into the nobility by choosing a lady of an aristocratic, though impoverished, family, Julia, whose nephew was Gaius Julius Caesar. Marius began his career in the normal fashion, serving with Scipio Aemilianus at the siege of Numantia, perhaps as military tribune, where he no doubt met the African prince Jugurtha who commanded the Numidian cavalry attached to Scipio's army. Embarking on his political career, Marius was quaestor in 123 and tribune of the plebs in 119 BC, in which post he tried to reduce the power and influence of the aristocrats over the voting populace, and thus made himself very unpopular with the nobility. The Senate made sure that his legislation was never put into effect and that Marius was kept out of politics for a while. He gained no other post until 114 BC when he just scraped in as praetor. As propraetor he went to Spain and suppressed the endemic bandits, who never seemed to stay suppressed for very long.

Since patronage of the more powerful families was vital if a new man like Marius was to rise to prominence, he had associated himself with the influential family of the Metelli, but he was not particularly respectful to his patrons. By 109 BC he was in Africa, serving as legate of Quintus Caecilius Metellus Numidicus against Jugurtha, who had taken over the kingdom of Numidia by force on the death of his uncle, ridding himself of the inconvenient legitimate heirs. His experience of service with the Roman army made Jugurtha a formidable and competent opponent, especially as he was fighting on his own ground and made effective use of it. In 108 BC, Marius asked for leave to return to Rome to stand for the consular elections, with the not too hidden agenda of taking over the African command from Metellus. He argued that Metellus was drawing out the war and that it could be brought to an end much faster, even though he knew that it was a war of attrition that would demand some considerable time before Jugurtha was defeated. Marius was duly elected and given the command in 107 BC, and set about recruiting replacements for the army in Africa. In so

A romanticized portrait of Gaius Marius. (Library of Congress)

doing, he famously lowered the property qualification and accepted the poorer classes as soldiers, setting a precedent for future army recruitment.

Taking Lucius Cornelius Sulla with him as his quaestor, Marius proceeded against Jugurtha, who had forged an alliance with Bocchus, king of Mauretania. After a few Roman victories, Bocchus began to waver in his loyalties, and was persuaded to betray Jugurtha. The surrender of Jugurtha to the Romans, thus bringing about the end of the war, was organized by Sulla, but Marius did not need to argue about who should have all the credit, since another war was brewing in the north of Italy, where Celtic tribes had swept through, causing devastation that reminded the Romans of the terrifying attacks of the Gauls two centuries earlier. In 107 Cassius Longinus and his army were defeated, and two years later the consuls Quintus Servilius Caepio and Gnaeus Mallius Maximus were thoroughly beaten at Arausio (modern Orange). Marius was elected consul with scarcely any opposition, every year from 105 to 101 BC, setting a precedent in some years since he was not even present in Rome to canvass for the post.

For the first couple of years the tribes veered away from Italy, giving Marius time to prepare his army. He owed a debt to Rutilius Rufus, with whom he had served in Africa and with whom he was not on friendly terms. He also recognized that Rutilius's training program had produced good soldiers, so he took over these troops and continued the training. He also perhaps owed a debt to Scipio Aemilianus, whose example he followed of reducing baggage and chasing away camp followers. Encamped on the river Rhone, Marius dug a canal to the sea to facilitate the delivery of supplies. He made alliances with the Gallic tribes who did not welcome the presence of the Cimbri and Teutones in their lands, and he placed Quintus Lutatius Catulus in charge of guarding the passes into Italy through the Alps. When the tribesmen returned ready for an assault on Italy, Marius and his troops were ready, but they did not immediately engage in battle with them. Marius followed them, wishing to choose the right moment and in the meantime to accustom his men to the sight and sound of the enemy.

At Aquae Sextiae (modern Aix-en-Provence), he judged the time ripe for battle. Marius camped near the tribesmen, but the Romans did not have ready access to water. The camp was not completely finished, and a battle seems to have begun accidentally, or at least not in planned fashion, while some of the army slaves were bringing water from the river. They clashed with some of the tribesmen, the auxiliary troops went to help them, and the Romans repulsed the tribesmen, but this was not a satisfactory conclusion. On the next night Marius sent Marcus Claudius Marcellus with 3,000 men to work their way behind the tribesmen and to remain hidden until they heard that battle was joined, using discretion as to when they should emerge. When the main battle began, Marius fought in the front rank, which as Goldsworthy points out (1996) was very rare and reduced the general's chances of directing the battle to virtually nil. In the end the Romans won and the tribes fled, but some of them got through the passes into Italy, because Catulus's men panicked and could not hold them. Marius combined his troops with those of Catulus and finally stopped the tribesmen at Vercellae. This was his finest hour, and had he known how his career was to end, he may have gone into retirement to rest on his laurels.

The rest of his political and military life never reached the heights of his success against the Celtic tribes. Although he was consul for 100 BC, he failed like many another general to arrange for land or pensions for his soldiers. He bought the services of a tribune to push through the necessary legislation, an action that went horribly wrong and resulted in Marius arresting his own tribune. In the Social War Marius held a command in 90 BC without especially distinguishing himself, and then fell foul of his erstwhile quaestor, Sulla. There was opportunity to fight against Rome's enemies in the east, where Mithradates of Pontus had invaded Roman territory and killed many of the Italians whose businesses were based there. Both Sulla and Marius wanted the command, but Sulla gained it after his infamous march on Rome at the head of his troops. In the upheaval, Marius had to flee for his life to Africa, returning to Rome in 87 BC when Sulla had gone to the east. Appointed consul with Cinna as his colleague, Marius entered Rome and butchered his enemies. The carnage ended with his sudden death. It was an ignominious end to a distinguished military career. The ancient historians probably reflected the judgment of many of Marius's contemporaries, that it would have been better if he had died after the battles at Aquae Sextiae and Vercellae, with his reputation shining and untarnished.

### Gnaeus Pompeius Magnus (106–48 BC)

Pompey the Great was an anomaly all his life. His father, Pompeius Strabo, was deeply distrusted and disliked, and when he died, struck by lightning as the story goes, his body was dragged through the streets by the enraged populace until the tribunes restored order. The young Pompey, however, emerged untainted by his father's unpopularity. He never followed the prescribed career of Roman *equites* or senators, and yet he was appointed to extraordinary commands and achieved some spectacular successes. He never lost a war until he fought against Julius Caesar in 48 BC.

Pompeius Strabo reached the consulship in 89 BC, partly as a result of his services in the Social War, when he besieged the town of Asculum, where Italian rebels had massacred Roman officials who had been sent there to try to keep the peace. Pompey was about sixteen years old at the time and served on his father's *consilium*, perhaps even taking part in some of the battles. Also serving in Strabo's army was the young Marcus Tullius Cicero, who developed into one of Rome's greatest orators; the two teenage soldiers probably got to know each other at least on a formal basis in the army.

Strabo's troops were for the most part recruited from among his tenants and those of his associates in Picenum in northern Italy, where the Pompeii held vast estates, the principal source of their wealth, and a fertile recruiting ground for Pompey himself when he started to raise his legions for Sulla, some years later.

Lucius Cornelius Sulla was consul in 88 BC with Quintus Pompeius Rufus as his colleague. The latter was probably a very distant relative of Pompeius

Strabo, whose army he was sent to take over. Strabo had held onto his command, and may or may not have been implicated in the sudden death of Pompeius Rufus shortly after he arrived. While the struggle escalated between Sulla and Marius over the eastern command against Mithradates, Strabo was able to gloss over the murder of the consul. The murder ought to have been a horrendous crime, but the Senate and Sulla were preoccupied, so Strabo stepped back into his command, without declaring his allegiance for Sulla, Marius, or the Senate. Pompey may have learned to play the silent waiting game from his father. When he was older he turned it into an artform, never actually demanding that he should be given commands, and always waiting until he was asked or even begged to take over. Like the Scipios, he presumably worked thorough his clients who agitated on his behalf.

His first military command was obtained on his own initiative, when he raised troops for Sulla as the latter was returning to Rome from the east. Pompey eventually raised three legions from the northern area of Italy, predominantly from Picenum where his family originated. Perhaps he did not manage to raise three legions all at once, but he managed it within a relatively short time. It demonstrates his charisma, the extent of his influence in Picenum, and his administrative and organizational talents, qualities that he retained to the end of his career. As he embarked on assembling troops, he had no idea when Sulla would return, or whether he himself would be wiped out by the armies of the two consuls, Cinna and Papirius Carbo, both confirmed Marians, even though Marius himself was dead. Pompey and his men fought well, survived, and came to meet Sulla in splendid array, with their armor and weapons gleaming. Sulla hailed the young commander as Imperator, a compliment indeed since this was a prestigious title granted to victorious commanders usually by their troops.

As a protégé of Sulla, Pompey was given the command against the fugitive Marians, who had spread out to Spain, Africa, and Sicily. The Sicilian command was Pompey's first task. The provincial governor of Sicily, Perperna, was a known Marian sympathizer, but Pompey had very little to do, since his reputation ensured that Perperna fled, turning up later in Spain with the rebel Marian, Quintus Sertorius. Pompey's troops discovered the consular Papirius Carbo and brought him to their young commander in chains. To put an end to the war in Sicily, Pompey executed Carbo, earning for himself, much later, the title of "boy butcher" from one of his enemies. He settled affairs in Sicily and was appointed to command in Africa against other Marian sympathizers. Here, too, he brought his campaigns to a swift end, displaying the talents that he would use in later life to great effect against the pirates of the Mediterranean and against Mithradates. His administrative and organizational skills matched his capacity to lead soldiers, and he gained his first experience of diplomatic procedures in his dealings with the natives of Sicily and Africa.

Pompey also experienced the potential problems faced by other highly successful generals, in that once his usefulness was outlived in one campaign, he needed to obtain another command, but without being too precocious about it. A display of extraordinary talent could lead to jealousies and even prosecution, so when his troops hailed him spontaneously as Imperator, he tactfully refused and let it be known that he had done so. Later, when the troops protested Sulla's order that he should return to Rome with only one legion, he had to work very hard to convince the men and most of all the outside world, that he was not aiming at rebellion and seizing power.

Outward display that was not too political satisfied Pompey. He added the title Magnus, "the Great," to his name, and demanded a triumph in Rome, to which Sulla reluctantly agreed because the triumph was meant to be reserved for senators, and Pompey was still of the equestrian class, not having held any office and therefore not a member of the Senate. When he was at first refused permission to hold a triumph, Pompey told Sulla that more people worshiped the rising than the setting sun. Perhaps not believing his ears, Sulla asked his associates what Pompey had said. Pompey became the only equestrian to hold a triumph. He was a little disappointed because the elephants that he wished to use to draw his triumphal chariot would not fit through the arches on the route to the Capitol Hill, so he had to make do with horses like other Roman commanders.

When the triumph was all over, he needed employment, and certainly he did not consider humbly taking up one of the junior magistracies in Rome, working his way up to military commands and provincial governorships like other men. He found his opportunity just after Sulla's death, when Marcus Aemilius Lepidus attempted to take over the state, and the Senate needed an army to put an end to the disturbance. Pompey acted with his customary speed and skill, and then innocently kept his troops together, knowing that in Spain the war against the rebel Sertorius was not going very well, and soon a new commander and more troops would be needed to help Metellus Pius.

In 76 BC Pompey went to Spain to eradicate the rebel Sertorius. One of the major problems of fighting in Spain concerned supplies, so Pompey aimed to capture the coastal towns to supply his armies by sea. His next concern was to win over the Spanish tribes and towns in order to deprive Sertorius of assistance, thus drawing the Spanish peoples into a war that had nothing to do with them and was hardly likely to benefit them. One of the towns that turned to Pompey and Metellus was Lauron, so Sertorius besieged it; to his dismay, Pompey was defeated when he came to the rescue. Sertorius positioned himself behind Pompey and neatly trapped him, splitting his forces and holding one part of his army at bay while he massacred the other group. Lauron fell, and Pompey was seen as a commander who could not protect his allies.

In the following year Pompey captured the city of Valencia and defeated the Marian commander Perperna, who had fled from Sicily to join Sertorius. The success was more or less negated by another defeat, because Pompey attacked Sertorius at what he considered to be an opportune moment, without waiting for Metellus to join him with more troops. He was saved the next day when the Sertorians withdrew as Metellus marched up. The war descended into one of small-scale attacks and a constant search for supplies, while the opposing armies chased each other. In the winter Pompey remained close to Sertorius's camp in the mountains, and Metellus took his troops to Gaul, since dividing the forces reduced the problem of feeding them. Pompey wrote an impassioned letter to the Senate, pointing out that he had used up all his own money in supplying his army, and if he did not receive help soon he might have to withdraw. The consuls for 74 BC were Lucius Licinius Lucullus and Marcus Aurelius Cotta, and another war was about to start in the east against Mithradates, whose predatory designs on Roman territory had begun once again. Lucullus had been appointed to the command and realized that disaster in Spain would threaten the success of his own enterprise, so Pompey got his supplies. The trouble was that the Mediterranean pirates had now allied with Sertorius, and so deliveries to the Spanish ports became that much more difficult.

The war was dragging on because throughout 74 and 73 BC Pompey and Metellus did not risk pitched battles, concentrating instead on securing ports, cities, and towns and wresting them from Sertorius's control. War weariness on both sides began to tell on the troops. Sertorius had been fighting specifically against the government of Sulla, who was now dead and whose draconian politics had largely been overturned. Since his troops and the Spanish allies were exhausted, treachery soon raised its head in Sertorius's army. Perperna arranged to have his leader assassinated and took over the army, which he unwisely committed to a pitched battle against Pompey, who set a trap that Perperna walked straight into. Only two Spanish cities still held out and came to an ignominious end, besieged until they starved. Pacification of Spain could begin, though it would take a long time; Roman generals could still cut their teeth and win or lose reputations against the Spanish tribes, as Caesar did in his first independent military command as governor of Further Spain (Hispania Ulterior) in 61 BC.

On his way home, Pompey set up a monument in the Pyrenees, proclaiming that he had conquered 876 cities between the Alps and the borders of Further Spain. Then he hastened back to Italy because the slave army of Spartacus was wreaking havoc and was unexpectedly defeating Roman generals. By the time Pompey reached Italy, Marcus Licinius Crassus had defeated Spartacus, but Pompey met up with about 5,000 of the survivors and routed them, thus robbing Crassus of the complete victory. Pompey said that Crassus had won battles, but he himself had ended the slave war, cutting it out by the roots.

Although Crassus and Pompey persisted in their rivalry throughout their lives, they had to work closely with each other for the following year, since they were both elected consuls for 70 BC. At the end of December 71, still only an equestrian, Pompey held his second triumph; then on the next day he formally entered the Senate as consul. Not having been in the Senate before and therefore not knowing much about senatorial procedure, he had asked his literary friend Terentius Varro to write a handbook for him to explain the protocol. As consuls, Pompey and Crassus finally unraveled the Sullan constitution that had placed power firmly in the hands of the aristocrats. They made the final arrangements to restore power to the tribunes of the plebs, but they were not innovators; they merely finished off what other politicians had started since Sulla's death.

From the end of his consulship in 70 BC until his command against the Mediterranean pirates in 67 BC, little is known of Pompey. He had a family by this time, so perhaps he attended to them and to his estates. He had been married briefly to two women, first as a youth to Antistia, whom he divorced so that he could marry Aemilia, on the recommendation of Sulla. This lady was already pregnant to her first husband, and she died in childbirth. Some time later Pompey married Mucia, who belonged to the clan of the Metelli. Together they produced two sons, Gnaeus and Sextus, and a daughter, Pompeia. It was normal for the Romans to marry into powerful families in order to gain patronage and advancement. Even though Pompey's military reputation was established, he needed support in the political field if further commands were to be obtained.

The pirate menace had enlarged to such proportions that in 67 BC there was agitation for the appointment of a commander to eradicate them. Politically, Pompey stayed in the background while his supporters did the work for him, not wishing to seem too eager for the post. When the command was finally arranged through the good offices of the tribune Aulus Gabinius, Pompey was granted wider powers than anyone before him, admittedly only for a specified duration. He had obviously given the matter some thought and cleared the seas via his legates in a very short time. At the end of the pirate campaign, Pompey wanted the command against Mithradates, which was currently in the hands of Licinius Lucullus, and so more political wrangling began in Rome, culminating in the success of the tribune Gaius Manilius in bestowing the command on Pompey in 66 BC.

The eastern command lasted from 66 to 62 BC, and ultimately encompassed most of the eastern provinces. Pompey was at his peak both as a general and an administrator. The details of the eastern campaigns are not as clear as historians would wish, not least because the chronology is not understood. Pompey took with him writers and philosophers, just as Napoleon took scientists and artists with him to Egypt, but the works of Pompey's literary friends only survive in fragments relayed by later authors such as Plutarch, Appian, and Cassius Dio, leading to some confusion. There seem to be two reports of events in many cases. For example, Pompey pursued Mithradates twice, received two embassies from him, and laid two ambushes for him, all of which are perfectly possible but may indicate that some events have been duplicated.

The salient points of the four-year eastern war revolve around the delicate balance of power between the various smaller kingdoms and Rome's relationship with Parthia. Although the war against Mithradates theoretically concerned only the kingdom of Pontus and the territories invaded by the king, in fact the fighting and the diplomatic activity extended much beyond these areas. The political and military control of Armenia was always disputed between Parthia and Rome, but Armenia was more directly involved in this war because its ruler, Tigranes, had married the daughter of Mithradates, who now chose to take refuge with his son-in-law. Lucullus had achieved early successes against them both, but failed to contain the two kings, who soon won back the territories and the influence that they had lost. At this point Pompey took over, and after lingering for a while trying to win over his troops, an embittered Lucullus went home.

Pompey immediately came to an arrangement with the Parthians under their king Phraates, encouraging them at best to attack Armenia or at worst to refrain from attacking the Romans while the campaign went ahead against Mithradates. Just as he had done in Spain, Pompey needed to isolate Mithradates and persuade his existing and potential allies that cooperation with Rome was more advantageous. He chased Mithradates back to his own kingdom, avoiding pitched battles. Failing to catch him, he turned away from the pursuit into Lesser Armenia, to find supplies for his army, hoping at the same time to lure Mithradates into battle on more favorable ground, but the old king was too well-versed in military tactics to engage. At one point, Mithradates used the old trick of slipping away at night while leaving the campfires burning, but Pompey's scouts reported that he had gone, and Pompey managed to get ahead of the enemy troops and ambush them by gaining control of the high ground flanking a narrow pass. Many of Mithradates's soldiers were killed, but the king escaped. This time, however, Armenia was closed to him, and his son-in-law even put a price on his head to underline his refusal to take him in and risk war with the Romans. Indeed, he was already at war with his own son, also called Mithradates, who had tried to usurp him with Parthian help. Pompey temporarily gave up chasing Mithradates, persuaded the Parthians to withdraw, and turned the squabbles of the Armenian royal house to Roman advantage and profit. He restored the old kingdom within its former limits to the elder Tigranes for an indemnity of 6,000 talents, gave small territories to the younger Tigranes, and dated Roman domination of Syria from this moment when he wrested it from Armenian control. As added security, Pompey placed one of his legates, Lucius Afranius, in Armenia, with a watching brief. The next potential war broke out when Phraates extended Parthian control over Armenia's neighboring territories, attacking Gordyene, but Pompey soon expelled the Parthians and sent Afranius to take over Gordyene.

The states that had been allied to Mithradates attacked Pompey in winter quarters, just before the campaigning season of 65 BC, so he spent some time in restoring peace, principally with the Oroeses, king of Albania (not to be confused with the modern state of Albania) and Artoces of Iberia. By this time, Pompey's troops were spread over most of the east, operating under his legates. Lucius Afranius was still watching Armenia, Aulus Gabinius was in Mesopotamia, some of the troops were guarding communication and supply routes, and some units were patrolling the coasts in case of renewed pirate activity. Pompey took the troops that were not engaged in these activities on an expedition to the Caspian Sea but achieved little military success. According to the Greek author and geographer Strabo, who was born around the time when this campaign took place, the region was infested with poisonous snakes, and also with huge spiders whose bite was eventually fatal, but first made the soldiers hysterical so that they literally died laughing (Strabo, *Geography* 11.4). Nobody knows what kind of poison the spiders injected into their victims, or even if the story is true, but it is interesting to note that the soldiers in Iraq in 2004–2005 also report that there are numerous spiders, not necessarily poisonous, in the desert. Pompey's troops, victorious against most of their two-legged opponents, withdrew in the face of eight-legged adversaries.

In 64 BC, Pompey abandoned the pursuit of Mithradates, turning southward to Syria, Judaea, and Nabataea, where everyone seemed to be fighting everyone else. His legates had already overrun Syria and captured Damascus, and Pompey wasted no time on diplomacy, but annexed Syria in order to put an end to the attacks of the Arabs and the Jews. From there, he went to Jerusalem in order to disentangle the quarrel between Hyrcanus and Aristobulus for the throne of Judaea. He had already met the two contenders in Syria and heard their claims, but he made no judgment, with the result that Aristobulus determined to fight the Romans, and installed himself in Jerusalem where Pompey put him under siege. Although Aristobulus came to Pompey to negotiate, his supporters would not give up, so when the Romans finally won there was a great loss of life. Pompey notoriously entered the inner sanctuary of the temple, probably as an act of curiosity rather than deliberate sacrilege, since he respected most other Jewish religious customs. He made Hyrcanus high priest, not king, in order to lessen the stability of the Judaean state in favor of a strong Roman-controlled Syria.

In the meantime, Mithradates died, and his sons made peace. Pompey was able to concentrate on settling the whole of the east, mostly with reference to Rome's needs, but also with consideration to the natives. His arrangements were fair and feasible, and some of them lasted throughout the Empire until the late third century. He created the Roman provinces of Pontus, Bithynia, Asia, Cilicia, and Syria, all around the coast of Asia Minor and the southern shore of the Euxine Sea, altering the boundaries of Cilicia and Bithynia to take in related areas and to rationalize their populations. He installed garrisons as appropriate, one in Bithynia and two each in Syria and Cilicia.

The greatest general of his day, Pompey returned home in 62 BC and celebrated a magnificent triumph. He gave games and shows and made arrangements to provide Rome with its first stone theater, based on the one he had seen at Mytilene. His popularity and prestige were assured, and he was the most eligible bachelor in Rome, since he had divorced his wife Mucia by means of a letter sent to her while he journeyed home. His standing in the Senate, however, was not so high, and he had made enemies other than Lucullus. When the time came to ratify all his eastern arrangements and to provide for his veterans, he was blocked at every turn. As the months went by, bringing no results, he realized that he needed allies who could forge a path through the political maze. In 60 BC Gaius Julius Caesar returned from Spain, determined to be elected consul for the following year.

### Gaius Julius Caesar (100–44 BC)

There is an unavoidable bias toward Julius Caesar in any account of Roman generalship or political achievement. Of all the generals of the Roman world, Caesar clearly emerges as the most dazzling and energetic, partly because his life story is better documented than that of any other Roman commander, but also because he was a brilliant psychologist who knew how to make men follow him, keep their faith in him, and do what he asked of them. His hallmark was speed, bordering on rashness and impatience, but where speed was not the answer he was shrewd enough to find another way. He lost a few battles but never a war, and though he threatened he did not resort to proscriptions to convert his vision of Rome to reality.

His career began inauspiciously, unlike the glamorous Pompey, who was a soldier and commander from his earliest youth. Although he belonged to an aristocratic family, Caesar was relatively poor, and his father had died young without having reached the consulship. Lack of immediate consular ancestry need not adversely affect the career of a young aristocrat, but Caesar's loyalty to his uncle Gaius Marius, albeit without active participation in the infamous massacres of Marius's last days, almost ensured his early demise. When he came to the attention of Sulla, the nineteen-year-old Caesar was asked to divorce his wife Cornelia in order to marry a lady of Sulla's choosing, in order to bind the young man to the Dictator's cause, but Caesar refused and went into hiding, contracting malaria before he was captured. Sulla was reputed to have remarked that this young man needed careful watching, since he had many Mariuses in him, but he left him alone and did not force through a divorce and remarriage, persuaded to leniency by relatives of Caesar's mother.

Removing himself from Rome, Caesar obtained his first military post on the staff of Marcus Minucius Thermus, a Sullan general and proconsul of Asia, whose task was to round off the eastern war begun by Sulla and keep the peace. One of Caesar's tasks was to persuade King Nicomedes of Bithynia to provide ships for the Roman fleet, a mission that he was supposed to have fulfilled by agreeing to a homosexual relationship with the king. Whether or not this was true or stemmed from malicious rumor cannot be proven one way or the other, but the story was never forgotten, despite the fact that Caesar developed a reputation as one of the greatest womanizers in Rome.

Bringing Nicomedes's ships to join the Roman fleet, Caesar played his part in the attack on Mytilene on the island of Lesbos. His actions were noted, and he earned the *corona civica,* awarded for saving the lives of Roman citizens in battle. Little else is known of him during this period, except that he remained in the east until Sulla's death in 78 BC. The Dictator had resigned in 79, saying that his work was finished, an action that Caesar later described as ludicrous, implying that once he gained power on that level, he did not intend to let it slip.

After the death of Sulla, an attempt at revolution by Marcus Aemilius Lepidus was foiled by Pompey, who was shortly afterward given the command against Sertorius in Spain. In Rome, like other aspiring politicians, Caesar built up a reputation in the law courts, bringing a case against Gnaeus Cornelius Dolabella, who had served in the east and used every opportunity to enrich himself at the expense of the Greek states. Caesar lost his case, but was asked by other Greeks to prosecute Gaius Antonius for extortion. The man was so plainly guilty that he had to appeal to the tribunes of the plebs to pull strings to avoid condemnation. Caesar lost again, but morally he had proved his worth. In 75 BC, he went to Rhodes to study, the Roman equivalent of going to University. This is the context of one of the more fantastic anecdotes about Caesar. He was captured by pirates who operated from the harbors and bays of Cilicia. They held him to ransom, but typically Caesar protested that he was worth a lot more than the figure they had set. He spent a month with the pirates while his colleagues persuaded the coastal cities of Asia to raise the money for him. It is said that he promised the pirates that once he was free he would come back and crucify every last one of them, and he kept his promise. He assembled a small fleet by borrowing ships from the cities that had ransomed him, attacked the pirates, and brought his captives to Pergamum, where he did indeed crucify the lot of them. He was twenty-six years old at the time and held no official post. The fact that he was able to carry out such a mission speaks volumes for the power of Rome and the audacity of the man.

In 73 BC, Caesar was co-opted to the priesthood after his mother's kinsman Gaius Aurelius Cotta died, leaving one of the fifteen posts vacant. This was a significant honor and suggests that Caesar had friends in high places. He was not yet a senator, but his position as one of the college of priests definitely marked the start of his political career. He first entered the Senate in the consulship of Pompey and Crassus in 70 BC, when he was appointed quaestor for the following year in Further Spain. As he was about to depart, his aunt Julia, the wife of Marius, died. So did his wife Cornelia, leaving him a widower with a small daughter, Julia, his only acknowledged child. At his aunt's funeral, Caesar made deliberate reference to his relationship to Marius, contravening the Sullan legislation forbidding the display of images of his former adversary. Then he left for Spain, where next to nothing is known of his activities. One of his principal duties was to pronounce judgment in the courts, providing him with an opportunity to make friends and influence people, or to acquire some financial gain. In 68 BC he returned to Rome and married a lady called Pompeia, no close relative of Pompey the Great, but a granddaughter of Quintus Pompeius Rufus and of Sulla.

The real power in the Roman world was still in the hands of Pompey the Great, and Caesar spoke from the very first in favor of the proposal of Aulus Gabinius that Pompey should be given the command against the pirates. While Pompey was absent, Caesar rose slowly to political independence. He was aedile in 65 BC, responsible for upkeep of public buildings, and policing the streets. In 63 BC, the alleged revolutionary Lucius Sergius Catalina was brought to trial and condemned by the consul Marcus Tullius Cicero. Caesar was marginally implicated in the attempted coup but was not prosecuted; he spoke against execution of the ringleaders, advocating their banishment to different Italian towns, where they should be held under house arrest. This was to no avail, as Cicero had them all killed.

Since Catiline himself had evaded capture, there was still a potential danger, so one of Pompey's adherents proposed that Pompey should be recalled from the east to save the state. As praetor Caesar spoke in favor of the suggestion and came up against staunch opposition from his lifelong adversary, Marcus Porcius Cato. For a short time, Caesar was forbidden to exercise his functions as praetor, but locked himself in his house and waited for popular agitation to restore him to power. As his office came to an end, he was allocated a province and became governor of Further Spain where he had already served as quaestor. It was said that he was in a hurry to leave for Spain because he was in so much debt. His outstanding bills were all paid for him by Marcus Licinius Crassus.

As Pompey returned from the east, Caesar traveled to Spain, but before he departed he divorced his wife Pompeia because during the celebrations in honor of the Bona Dea, a religious festival for women only, held at his house, the notorious rake Publius Clodius had been discovered dressed in women's clothing. This was sacrilege of the highest order, since no male was supposed to witness the proceedings. It was also suspected that Caesar's wife was having an affair with Clodius. "Caesar's wife should be above suspicion" is a phrase that has served in the same political capacity through the ages ever since.

In Spain, Caesar took over ten cohorts and raised more from Spanish allies in order to campaign against the lawless bandits of Lusitania. He rounded them up, but some of them fled to an island off the west coast of Spain, so Caesar gathered ships from Gades (modern Cadiz) and flushed them out. He allowed his soldiers to take a share of the booty that the bandits had gathered, and he sent some of the proceeds to Rome, presumably pocketing the rest. Then he turned to the legal aspects of his post, trying to alleviate the problems still left over from the Roman war against Sertorius. Toward the end of his tenure of Further Spain, Caesar started to lay the foundations of his future career, intent on the consulship for 59 BC. He had been voted a triumph by the Senate for his exploits against the bandits, which meant that he would have to remain outside Rome until he entered the city in procession at the head of his troops. At the same time, it was stipulated that he had to lay down his command and come to Rome in person for the elections. Some of his opponents may have hoped that Caesar would be vain enough to insist on holding the triumph, thus debarring himself from standing for the consulship. Unfortunately for them, Caesar knew how to prioritize. He abandoned the triumph and was duly elected consul for 59 BC.

His colleague was Marcus Calpurnius Bibulus, but before the year had progressed very far contemporary wits had labeled it the consulship of Julius and Caesar. Bibulus, backed by Cato, tried to oppose Caesar but was either simply ignored or discouraged by force and eventually gave up. The most important legislation that Caesar passed concerned the land bill to solve several problems at once, not only alleviating the population pressure at Rome by settling men on farms, but also providing for Pompey's veterans who had already been waiting for a few years while their leader was blocked at every turn by his enemies in the Senate. Caesar's first attempts to have this bill passed were reasonable. He had examined all other land bills of the past years and had been careful to circumvent all the objections raised to them, but when he still met with opposition he resorted to force. In acting reasonably himself, he exposed the opposition as unreasonable. His other legislation concerned taxation, extortion in the provinces, and the ruler of Egypt. The tax gatherers of the province of Asia had put in a bid for the contract but found that the profits were not as high as they had anticipated, so Caesar finally adjusted the situation and warned the tax gatherers to be more cautious in future. His laws on extortion formed the basis of fair dealings with the provinces for the next centuries, ensuring that provincials could bring about a prosecution at Rome against governors who had overstepped the rules. He procured Roman recognition for Ptolemy Auletes as ruler of Egypt and earned considerable profit for himself and Pompey out of the deal, setting the scene for Pompey's flight to Egypt after the battle of Pharsalus.

The matter of the provinces to be allocated to the consuls of 59 BC was something that Caesar did not intend to leave to chance. He secured a long-term command in Gaul, where he knew that he could make a military and political reputation for himself to equal that of Pompey the Great. At this time, he and Pompey were not rivals, and perhaps he did not even foresee a time when they would be in conflict with each other. Since they worked together politically, Caesar had suggested that they tighten the bonds in the familiar Roman way by a marriage. Pompey had divorced his wife Mucia in 62 BC when he returned to Rome, and was still free, so he married Caesar's daughter Julia. Even contemporaries recognized this as a love match as well as a political expedient, and Pompey and his young wife enjoyed five years together until she died in childbirth.

After his consulship Caesar desired greater glory and found it in his first independent long-term command. The several tribes of Gaul conveniently fought other Gallic tribes with monotonous regularity and made it possible for Rome to interfere in favor of one tribe against another. The Aedui appealed to Rome for help against the Sequani, who in their turn called in Germanic tribes from across the Rhine, under their leader Ariovistus. Gaul was in turmoil. Displaced peoples wanted to move into the territory of other tribes. For instance, the Helvetii, who were originally from beyond the Rhine, had moved into what is now Switzerland but threatened to move once again. Just as the Mediterranean pirate problem required a commander with wide powers for a longer term than was normal, the Gallic problem demanded wide-ranging powers and continuity if Rome was to be free of the threat of invasion that had occurred in the fourth century BC and not very long ago when Marius was elected consul for several years in succession.

Originally, Caesar was granted command of Cisalpine Gaul and Illyricum with three legions, to be held for five years. In addition, after a proposal put forward by Pompey, he was also granted command of Transalpine Gaul, loosely interpreted as all the rest of the country beyond the Alps, with one legion. This was the start of Caesar's ten-year conquest of Gaul. Specifically, his five-year command should have ended on 1 March 54 BC, and the Transalpine command had to be renewed every year.

An account that would do justice to all Caesar's military exploits in Gaul would require several chapters, if not volumes, and the tale has been told before, not least by the man himself. There are several secondary sources that analyze his campaigns and trace them through modern France. Lack of space here precludes anything but a synopsis. Caesar's first campaign prevented the Helvetii from settling in Gaul, and he records how he erected a fortified line stretching for 16 miles to block one of their routes. The tribe was pushed back into their newly adopted homeland in Switzerland, resettled, and given the task of guarding against inroads by the German tribes. In the same campaigning season, Caesar attacked Ariovistus and the Suebi, brought into Gaul by the Sequani. The Suebi had taken more land than the Sequani had intended, and now they were powerless to stop their advance. Caesar tried diplomacy and then moved to the capital of the Sequani, Vesontio (modern Besançon) to prevent Ariovistus from occupying it. He offered battle, but it was only on the seventh day that Ariovistus attacked—so quickly and ferociously that the Romans did not have time to throw their *pila* and went straight in with their swords. At the end of the battle, the Germanic tribe dispersed, and the tribesmen who had been hoping to cross the Rhine and settle in Gaul turned back.

Titus Labienus was left in charge of the army for the winter, and Caesar retired to Cisalpine Gaul. There were civil matters to attend to in his province, and also from the southern Alps he could keep an eye on political developments in Rome. In the following year, 58 BC, Caesar moved against the Belgic tribes of northern Gaul and then the Veneti on the western coast and the Aquitani in the southwest. Of all the tribes in the Belgic federation, the Nervii feature the most in Caesar's account. He was merciless against them, until they were almost obliterated, and then he made fairly lenient terms. They retained their lands, and other tribes were warned not to harass them.

In 57 BC, Pompey resurfaced and was granted a commission to secure the corn supply of Rome, with wide-ranging powers for five years and a staff of fifteen legates. Caesar's command was approaching its end with less than three years to run, so Pompey was likely to be the man of the moment once again. In the spring of 56 BC, Caesar met with Licinius Crassus and Pompey at Luca in northern Italy, the most southerly point that he could approach while still in command in Gaul. The conference between the three men may not even have taken place with all of them together, but whether he saw them singly or together, agreements were clearly arrived at. Caesar needed allies at Rome if his command was to be extended sufficiently to allow him to complete the conquest of Gaul. The other two men also derived what they wanted, the consulship for 55 BC being one of their aims. The modern term for this informal pact is the First Triumvirate, but Caesar would not have recognized it as such. It is modern historians who recognize that this meeting of three men foreshadowed the official one after the murder of Caesar, between Octavian, Mark Antony, and Lepidus, whose title was "*Tresviri rei publicae constituendae*" or three men charged with protecting the state. Caesar's arrangement in 56 BC was more personal and had no official sanction. His main aim was to ensure that his enemies did not remove him from his command before it expired and to extend it for another term, all of which Crassus and Pompey could arrange for him while he was absent from Rome.

The displacement of tribes had not ceased after the defeat of Ariovistus and the Suebi, and in 55 BC Caesar had to repel the Usipetes and the Tencteri who wanted to cross the Rhine and settle in Gaul. He negotiated with the friendly Ubii, who had submitted to Rome, for lands for the Germanic tribes to settle on, but the matter was resolved by fighting. As Caesar drew closer and closer, the Germans stalled for time, and battle started almost accidentally when some of their cavalry attacked Caesar's Gallic allies. A conference with the tribal leaders was called, but Caesar took them all prisoner and routed their warriors. They were pursued until they recrossed the Rhine, and Caesar followed them,

Idealized portrait of Gaius Julius Caesar, who campaigned in Gaul for ten years, purposefully building up a formidable military reputation to equal Pompey's. He relied on his troops to keep him in power and to subdue all his rivals, and to defeat Pompey when the civil war broke out between them. (Photo by Walter Sanders/Time Life Pictures/Getty Images)

hastily and impressively building a timber bridge to allow his troops to cross. It was only a demonstration but an effective one.

Britain became the focus of Caesar's attention in the remaining campaigning season of 55 BC when he reconnoitred the island and then attacked again in 54 BC. His excuse was that the Britons were sending help to the Gauls of the northwest, which may even have been true, but mostly the campaigns contributed to the glorious reputation of Gaius Julius Caesar. He almost met with disaster, since, having failed to appreciate the action of the tides, he lost some of his ships. The years from 54 until his command expired were troubled by rebellions among the Gauls. Ambiorix, the leader of the Eburones, destroyed several Roman cohorts in the winter of 54 BC, and most of the next year was spent eliminating resistance in the northwest of Gaul. In 52 the epic struggle against Vercingetorix began, with Gallic resistance running into the following year, even after Vercingetorix had surrendered.

In that same year, the politicians at Rome began to agitate for Caesar's recall, and the foundations of the civil war with Pompey were laid. The political wrangling was prolonged until 49 BC, with Caesar hanging on to his command with great tenacity and preparing to win the consulship for 48 BC, so that he could progress seamlessly from military command to political power as he had done when he returned from Further Spain. In blocking him, the Senate leaned toward Pompey, whose role was characteristically ambivalent until almost the last moment. Pompey had arrived at considerable power while Caesar was absent. In 52 BC, when rioting between rival political factions came to a head, he was "sole consul," which was a contradiction in terms because the very nature of the consulship was collegiality, but it was a compromise instead of appointing him Dictator. As well as his anomalous consulship, Pompey held a command in Spain while still in Rome, exercising his functions as governor and commander via his legates. This arrangement foreshadowed the provincial system under Augustus when governors of the Imperial provinces acted as legates for the supreme commander, the emperor.

Pompey rapidly ended the violence in Rome and shored up his own position by prolonging his command in Spain, still without leaving the city. Though civil war was by no means inevitable at this stage, Pompey seemed to be working against Caesar's interests through his legislation. Caesar had been granted permission to stand for the consular elections *in absentia,* but a new law of Pompey's consulship stated that candidates had to be present at Rome. Pompey inserted a special clause exempting Caesar. Another law imposed a five-year gap between holding a magistracy in Rome and a promagistracy in a province. It was designed to prevent candidates from running up huge debts that they knew they could settle by exploiting the provincials as soon as they reached their provinces. It was also meant to prevent magistrates from accumulating power and continuous command of armies.

Caesar's enemies started to agitate for his recall. It is much disputed exactly when his command should terminate, but 1 March 50 BC seems to be the crucial date. Caesar proposed to stand for the elections for the consulship of 49 BC while still in command of his troops. His enemies tried to bring him home earlier so that he would be vulnerable to anyone bringing a prosecution. Compromise was suggested to avoid confrontation between the two most powerful men in the Roman world. It was decided that Pompey should go to Spain, or he should be dispatched to the east where the Parthians seemed likely to cause trouble. It was suggested that both men should relinquish their commands, but then there was squabbling over who should be the first to do so. The problem was that by this time neither of them felt safe enough to face their enemies and each other without the support of an armed force.

When civil war came, Pompey was not ready. He had underestimated how quickly he could raise troops against Caesar's experienced men, so as Caesar crossed the Rubicon, Pompey went south to Brundisium to evacuate Italy and go to Greece, where he could train his army. Caesar chased after him and besieged Brundisium, but by brilliant tactics Pompey foiled Caesar's attempt to capture him. He embarked the heavy-armed troops in strict silence, leaving the light-armed troops on the walls until he was ready, and then he gave the signal for them to withdraw. Caesar's men quickly climbed over the walls, only to find that trenches had been dug across the streets, and there were pits with sharp stakes set in them, disguised by hurdles. In addition to these obstacles, there were barricades in other streets, and huge palisades guarded the route to the harbor. By the time Caesar's men had worked their way around all the hazards, Pompey was at sea.

Caesar did not follow Pompey to Greece but dealt with administration at Rome and then went to Spain to knock out the armies there under Pompey's legates, Lucius Afranius and Marcus Petreius in Nearer Spain, and Terentius Varro in Further Spain. Caesar said he was going to fight the army without a leader and would then go to Greece to fight the leader without an army. At the battle of Ilerda (modern Lerida), Caesar defeated Afranius and Petreius, and being a man of sense, Varro surrendered. Returning to Rome, Caesar was made Dictator. He hurried through some legislative and administrative measures and then set off to face Pompey, without sufficient ships to take all of his army. He embarked with 15,000 legionaries and about 500 cavalry, sending the ships back for Mark Antony to bring the rest. This did not happen immediately since part of the Pompeian fleet blockaded Antony. Impatiently waiting in Greece, Caesar tried to set sail in a small boat to return to Italy and hasten the embarkation of his troops. He declared to the reluctant captain: "You carry Caesar and his fortune." But after fruitlessly putting to sea, he had to admit that his usual luck had run out and he needed favorable winds as well to carry him across. Antony eventually broke out and brought the army to join Caesar.

Pompey and Caesar raced their troops toward Dyrrachium on the coast, where Pompey seized the higher ground south of the town and dug a fortified line around his camp, protected on the western side by the sea. His navy was supreme, so he could therefore be supplied relatively easily. Caesar retaliated by building another fortified line around Pompey's works, hemming him in. Pompey had not lost any of his talents for warfare and was still a worthy opponent for Caesar. He sent a deserter to Caesar offering to betray the town of Dyrrachium, and Caesar walked into the trap. Caesar was very nearly killed and almost lost his army since the Pompeians attacked his camp in three places, and were driven off only after bitter fighting and losses. On another occasion, exploiting information about Caesar's unfinished fortifications at the southern end of his lines, Pompey attacked and very nearly succeeded in routing the Caesarians, who fought long and hard and drove the Pompeians off.

The campaign now revolved around supplies. Caesar's men were on the verge of starvation, and he was forced to move off to find food, followed by Pompey. The two armies camped at a place where there were abundant supplies, called Pharsalus. There Pompey fought his last battle, riding off the field before it was over and taking ship for Egypt. Caesar knew that he had to follow Pompey as quickly as possible. Some years earlier, Pompey had been instrumental in putting Ptolemy Auletes back on the Egyptian throne—for a price—and some of his Roman soldiers were still in Egypt, helping to shore up the shaky Ptolemaic dynasty, now represented by Auletes's son Ptolemy and his daughter, Cleopatra. Since they owed their position to Pompey, it would be legitimate for him to ask for money and soldiers to continue the war against Caesar. Unfortunately for Pompey, the young Ptolemy's advisers decided that the best way to avert a Roman civil war on their territory was to remove Pompey, so that when Caesar arrived in Alexandria in pursuit of him, there would be no one to fight. Thus when Caesar disembarked, he was presented with a jar containing Pompey's head. "Dead men do not bite," said one of Ptolemy's tutors.

Caesar had four more years to live, years that would be filled with frantic activity. The Egyptian Royal House was divided by civil war, and it was important for Roman interests to establish the right candidate on the throne. Caesar chose Cleopatra over her brother Ptolemy XIII and had to fight the Egyptian army to place her in a position of unequivocal power, famously burning the great library of Alexandria when he set the Egyptian fleet on fire. Before he could return to Rome, he fought against Pharnaces, the son of Mithradates, to stop his advance into the Roman territories of Bithynia and Pontus. At the end of this war, which was rapidly concluded, Caesar summed up his achievements very succinctly in a letter to his friend Gaius Matius, saying "*veni, vidi, vici*" (I came, I saw, I conquered).

Pompeians remained in North Africa, led by Cato and Pompey's father-in-law Metellus Scipio. Another war was inevitable if Caesar was to retain his hold on power in Rome, but his troops were tired and restless, and a mutiny broke out before he could embark for Africa. Many of the soldiers camped outside Rome, waiting for Caesar to hear their demands, which they made at a time when they knew that he needed them for the coming campaign. If he was desperate, he might be persuaded to give them all sorts of rewards, but he listened to them and then addressed them not as he usually did, *Comilitones* (comrades in arms) but as *Quirites* (citizens), implying that they were discharged. He said he would grant all their demands, after he had returned from Africa, where he would fight using other troops. His gamble paid off, and the men went with him to fight the Pompeians.

The African campaign ended at the battle of Thapsus, where Caesar deliberately allowed the Pompeians to believe that they had entrapped him with their troops deployed to the north and south of his camp, which lay in a narrow strip of land between the sea to the east and a lake to the west. By sending some of his troops on board ship to land on the coast behind his main adversary Metellus Scipio, Caesar managed to entrap the Pompeians between two forces of his own. The survivors of Thapsus fled to join Cato at the town of Utica, but all was lost and Cato famously committed suicide rather than live out his life as proof of Caesar's studied policy of *clementia* (mercy). The other Pompeians were hunted down and killed, but Pompey's sons and Titus Labienus fled to Spain where they assembled another army. In 45 BC, Caesar went to fight them in Spain.

The Pompeian fleet and all the surviving troops from Africa were welded into another fighting force by Gnaeus and Sextus Pompey, augmented by Spanish allies loyal to the Pompeians. Sextus held the town of Corduba, where Caesar besieged him to try to draw Gnaeus to the rescue and then into battle, but Gnaeus did not take the bait. Caesar raised the siege and concentrated on another town, Ategua, 20 miles southeast of Corduba, where there were valuable food stores. The town fell, and Gnaeus, unable to do anything to help the garrison or the inhabitants, drew off, chased by Caesar. The two armies stopped at Munda where they fought the last battle. Gnaeus had chosen his ground well. There was a stream and a marsh between the two armies, which the Caesarians had to cross when the battle started, almost accidentally: Caesar was about to break camp and move off, when he noticed that the enemy had drawn up and decided to attack. Details are lacking, but at one point Caesar dashed to the front to rally the troops, and then the Tenth legion started to push back the Pompeian left wing. Labienus was ordered to move from his position on the right wing to shore up the left, but he met Caesar's ally King Bogud of Mauretania, who drove him off. The battle fizzled out and the Pompeians fled. Gnaeus was captured and executed, but Sextus joined the fleet, surviving for another decade and proving a thorn in the flesh of Octavian and Antony, supreme at sea. The battle site of Munda has not been positively identified, but it probably lay near Urso, where Caesar founded a colony after the war ended.

Returning to Rome, Caesar remained outside the city on one of his estates, preparing to enter the city in triumph. While he was waiting, he wrote his will. He left money to all the citizens in Rome and to the men who would shortly assassinate him. More importantly, in a codicil to the will he adopted his great nephew Gaius Octavius as his son, naming him as his chief heir. When the assassins struck on the Ides of March 44 BC, they did not know of the terms of the will and had made no plans beyond ridding the world of Caesar the Dictator. Perhaps no one could have foreseen that the sickly teenager named as Caesar's heir would take up his inheritance with such masterly patience and determination, to be transformed only seventeen years later into Augustus, master of the whole Roman world with a firmer grip on it than Caesar ever had.

## Imperial Generals

### Tiberius (42 BC–AD 37)

For much of his early life, Tiberius was with the armies, either on diplomatic missions in the east or experiencing long and bitter fighting on the Rhine and Danube. He was born on 16 November 42 BC and named like his father Tiberius Claudius Nero. His mother was Livia Drusilla, who later married Octavian before he had earned the title Augustus, bringing her two sons Tiberius and Drusus into the Imperial family. During the political upheavals and civil wars following the murder of Julius Caesar, as an infant Tiberius accompanied his parents in flight to Sicily and then to Greece, returning to Rome in 39 BC.

His mother Livia divorced her husband to marry Octavian when Tiberius was four years old, and five years later when his real father died, Tiberius delivered the funeral oration for him. Though he was not marked out for the succession, Tiberius was still a prominent figure among the Imperial family. At Augustus's triumph in 29 BC, Tiberius rode the left trace horse drawing the triumphal chariot, while Marcellus, Augustus's nephew rode on the right. Two years later Tiberius put on the *toga virilis,* in a ceremony signifying that Roman youths had become men, and in 26 to 25 BC, he saw his first military service in Augustus's wars against the Cantabrians. Next he went on a combined military and diplomatic mission to restore King Tigranes to the throne of Armenia in 20 BC and brought home from Parthia the standards that had been captured in 53 BC from the defeated army of Marcus Licinius Crassus (Tacitus, *Annals* 2.3).

Augustus bestowed praetorian rank on him and sent him to govern part of Gaul, called Gallia Comata (long-haired Gaul) in 16 BC, and during the following year Tiberius fought against the Raeti and Vindelici of northern Italy, where Roman control had not yet been fully established (Dio 54.20.4). Tiberius reached the consulship in 13 BC, but this honor was offset a year later when Augustus's closest associate, Marcus Vipsanius Agrippa, fell ill and died. From earliest childhood Tiberius had been betrothed to Vipsania, the daughter of Agrippa by his first wife, Caecilia, and the eventual marriage was a happy one. The couple had one son called Drusus. Since his dynastic needs always overrode personal happiness, Augustus decided that this marriage should be dissolved and that Tiberius should be bound closer to him by marrying Julia, Augustus's daughter by his wife Scribonia, whom he had divorced in order to marry Livia. Tiberius obeyed with great reluctance, and it is said that when he saw Vipsania in public he burst into tears. It probably did not help that Julia, a pawn in Augustus's dynastic schemes, was the widow of Vipsania's father. Tiberius's later reputation for misery and debauchery may have stemmed from this period of his life.

For the next six years, Tiberius was dispatched on one military mission after another on the northern edge of the Roman world. In 11 BC he was awarded a new kind of honor, *ornamenta triumphalia,* for his defeat of the Breuci and the Dalmatians in Pannonia. This was a substitute for an actual triumphal procession through the streets of Rome, which was confined to Augustus himself and members of his household, and then to the emperor alone. Other generals, acting as legates of the emperors had to be content with the insignia and the honor rather than a parade.

From 10 to 9 BC, Tiberius commanded armies on the Danube in wars against the Pannonians and the Dacians, and was hailed as Imperator by the troops. This was a significant honor and a title that was soon to be the monopoly of the emperors themselves, and not their generals. A terrible personal tragedy for Tiberius occurred in 9 BC when his brother Drusus died, while campaigning in Germany at the head of a large army, like Tiberius. As the wars were coming to an end, Drusus had fallen from his horse. The injuries eventually proved fatal, but he clung on to life long enough for Tiberius to make an arduous and lengthy journey in record time to see him. Three years after losing his wife through divorce, Tiberius had now lost his beloved younger brother.

Transferring his scene of operations to the Rhine, Tiberius spent most of 8 BC in Gaul where he settled 40,000 Germanic tribesmen after they had surrendered (Suetonius, *Augustus* 21). His reward was a second consulship in 7 BC and tribunician power for the next five years. Tribunician power, or the power of the tribunes, was more wide ranging and flexible than the powers of the consuls. Tribunes could veto any proposals in the Senate, convene meetings, or bring proceedings to a halt. Augustus eventually managed to separate the power of the tribunes from the office, so he could exercise the functions without actually being elected tribune. The tribunician power was the real basis of the executive authority of the emperors. However, Tiberius chose to withdraw from public life and went to Rhodes, where he stayed for eight years, from 6 BC to AD 2 (Suetonius, *Tiberius* 10.2–11.1). It may be that behind the tales of rivalry within the Imperial family and Tiberius's demands for a rest, there was a subtext concerning a watching brief on the eastern provinces and Parthian activities. Agrippa had withdrawn from Rome some time before, remaining like Tiberius on an island within reach of the east, and the story that had been circulated was likewise one of intense competition between Agrippa and Augustus's heirs.

During the long reign of Augustus, his careful plans for the succession were continually thwarted. When his first choice, his sister's son Marcellus died, he adopted as his own sons Gaius and Lucius, the offspring of Agrippa and Julia and therefore his grandchildren. They were both young and apparently healthy, and no one could have foreseen that they would both die while still young, leading some ancient authors to speculate that Livia must have had a hand in the matter to remove all rivals to her own son Tiberius. Since food hygiene and medical care in the Roman world left much to be desired, the deaths of Gaius and Lucius may have been purely accidental, but it was one more stage on the road to the accession of the Emperor Tiberius. He returned to Rome and was formally adopted by Augustus, on condition that he in turn adopted his nephew Germanicus, the son of his brother Drusus. By AD 4, Tiberius was again at war in Germany across the Rhine, pushing as far as the river Elbe in a campaign that Tacitus dismisses as fairly routine. Whatever the ultimate Roman plans may have been for Germany, they were not fulfilled, since revolt broke out in Illyricum and Pannonia in AD 6, and the foremost general of the day, Tiberius, was chosen to quell it. The task occupied the next three years, until Tiberius was satisfied that he had done the job properly. He commanded as many as fifteen legions and accompanying auxiliaries, a vast enterprise for one man, but his thoroughness and careful planning won the day. He was recalled but would not return to Rome until he had stamped out the last shred of rebellion.

If he hoped for some respite from fighting in the northern climate, hot in summer and bitterly cold in winter, struggling to bring in adequate supplies and to keep control of so many legions, Tiberius was to be disappointed. Just as the rebellion was crushed, terrible news came from Germany, where in AD 9 the General Quinctilius Varus was utterly defeated, with the loss of three legions in the forests beyond the Rhine. The Romans had miscalculated, thinking the Germans subdued and ripe for settlement and Romanization. Varus was more of an administrator and lawyer than a military man and was chosen to supervise the inception of Roman government. The disaster came as a shock: rough and uncultured tribesmen, who were not considered capable of unified action or of following orders, had surrounded and annihilated Roman troops. Many armies since then have made the same mistake about the capabilities of supposedly unsophisticated enemies.

Augustus was deeply despondent, and needed a tried and trusted general to repair the damage. Tiberius took on the task with tremendous caution. He was concerned that there should be no mistakes or disasters caused through rashness or misunderstanding. He took no decisions without first consulting his circle of officers and friends, inspected everything himself, sat on the ground like the soldiers did when taking his meals, slept without a tent, and issued all his orders in writing with the instruction that anyone who did not understand them should come at any time of day or night to ask for clarification. The description comes from the pen of Suetonius (*Tiberius* 18), and even after 2,000 years it is almost possible to hear Tiberius grimly gritting his teeth and getting down to the task before him. After about a year, in AD 11, he was ready to take the campaign across the Rhine. Like many another rigorous commander before him, he instructed the soldiers to take only the most essential baggage, but Tiberius stood by as the Rhine crossing was made, personally checking the wagons and pack animals to see that they were not overloaded.

The campaign that he had started was finished off by his adopted son Germanicus, who joined him in AD 11. Two years later, as the elderly Augustus's health began to fail, Tiberius returned to Rome, leaving Germanicus in command. When Augustus died in AD 14, Tiberius reluctantly became emperor, using a Greek proverb to describe his situation. He said that controlling the Roman world was like holding a wolf by the ears; if he once let go, he knew he would be savaged. He never went on campaign after he became emperor and was noted for leaving his governors in their provinces for many years, depriving them of the varied careers that their predecessors and successors enjoyed. His reign saw little military activity compared to those of later emperors, and he seems to have taken to heart Augustus's advice not to extend the Empire. There were no major conquests or wars of aggression, perhaps because he himself had fought rebellious elements to a standstill and perhaps, too, because he felt that he had endured enough fighting for one lifetime.

### Germanicus (15 BC–AD 19)

Tiberius's brother Nero Claudius Drusus married Antonia, the daughter of Mark Antony, and produced two sons, Germanicus and the future Emperor Claudius. During the lifetime of Germanicus and for some years afterward, his brother Claudius who walked with a limp and spoke with a prohibitive stammer, was kept in the background, debarred from military or political service and devoted to intensive study. Germanicus, on the other hand, was a military hero, and two centuries after his death, his birthday was still celebrated in the calendar of religious festivals, at least in the eastern armies.

When Tiberius was adopted by Augustus, Germanicus was in turn adopted as the son of his uncle Tiberius, who now had two sons, Drusus and Germanicus. The marriage of Germanicus and Vipsania Agrippina, the daughter of Julia and Agrippa, was to prove very fruitful—nine children in all. It may have seemed to Augustus that there were enough heirs to secure the succession. In the event, it was neither Drusus nor Germanicus who succeeded Tiberius, but Germanicus's youngest son, who accompanied his father and mother on campaigns in Germany, sometimes wearing his miniature military uniform. The soldiers nicknamed him Caligula, from *caliga,* the military boot.

Germanicus served with Tiberius in the Pannonian campaign from AD 6 to 9, and in the last year of the fighting he was instrumental in bringing about the surrender of Bato, the leader of the Breuci. For these exploits Germanicus was awarded *ornamenta triumphalia*. By AD 11 he was back with Tiberius and the army in Germany, and in AD 13 when Tiberius had returned to Rome he was given the command of the armies of Upper and Lower Germany, with proconsular power. The death of Augustus in AD 14 sparked off mutinies in the armies of Pannonia and the Rhine. Drusus and the Praetorian Prefect, Aelius Sejanus, were sent to deal with the Pannonian troops, and Germanicus hurried to the Rhine from Gaul where he had been conducting the census, registering property for tax purposes. The troops of Upper Germany, consisting of four legions and auxiliaries under Gaius Silius, were relatively calm, but two of the four legions under Aulus Caecina in Lower Germany, *legio XXI* and *legio V*, were stirring up trouble among the rest of the army. The other two legions, *I* and *XX*, were less turbulent. Tacitus blames the recruits from the city of Rome who were not used to hard work, and Caecina seems to have done nothing to stop the rioting, in which many of the centurions were attacked and beaten.

The legionaries could not really be blamed for discontent, since their centurions bullied them and got rich on the bribes they demanded for more lenient treatment and a relief from fatigues. Some of the men had served for many years and were wearily demanding their discharge. When Germanicus arrived to confront them, one or two men seized his hand, thrusting his fingers into their mouths so that he could see that they had no teeth! The first interview with the troops was ineffective, and there was a complication in that they encouraged Germanicus to declare himself emperor. He refused in the traditional way by threatening to kill himself, but not all the legionaries despaired for him. Tacitus records that at least one of them, Calusidius, offered him his own sword, saying that it was sharper (*Annals* 1.35).

Since there was a danger that the troops might break out and start to plunder the nearby provinces of Gaul, Germanicus decided to discharge the men who had served for twenty years. Those who had served for sixteen years were to be kept on for a further four years, excused from heavy duties but obliged to fight enemies if the occasion arose. Money grants were promised, but the soldiers did not trust either him or the government and demanded the cash there and then. Thus, Germanicus paid out of his own funds and those of his entourage. These measures quelled the mutiny for a short time, and Germanicus administered the oath of loyalty to the troops of Lower Germany. The legions of Upper Germany were easily persuaded to take the oath, with only *legio XIV* holding out for a while.

All the goodwill was almost wiped out when the commission arrived from Rome to confer proconsular *imperium* on Germanicus, who was in Cologne at the time, while Caecina and the two mutinous legions remained in camp. The soldiers who were with Germanicus thought that they had been betrayed, and the senators were about to revoke all Germanicus's concessions. One or two of the senators were lucky to escape with their lives. Once everything was explained the troops calmed down, but Germanicus decided that the current mood of the army threatened the safety of his wife and children, so he sent them away, along with the wives and families of some of the officers. The sight of the women and children, especially Agrippina and Caligula, moving off without a military escort, softened up the soldiers, who submitted to a dressing down by Germanicus. They were reminded of how Julius Caesar had once quelled a mutiny by calling the men citizens instead of comrades in arms.

It remained to convince the two legions that had started it all, *legio V* and *legio XXI:* Germanicus let it be known that he was coming in force and would fight them if necessary, if they did not round up the ringleaders of the mutiny. This put an end to the troubles and enabled Germanicus to turn the pent-up aggression to good use by attacking the German tribes across the Rhine. He advanced against the Marsi. Tacitus says that he reached the boundary marked out by Tiberius in the forest, but it is not known precisely either where this was or where the homelands of the Marsi lay. After he laid waste the territory for a 50-mile radius all around the Marsi, Germanicus led the army back, attacked by other tribes that tried to cut him off. He marched in square formation with the cavalry and ten auxiliary cohorts leading, then *legio I* and the baggage, flanked on the left by *legio XXI* and on the right by *legio V* with *legio XX* in the rear. The Germans launched their main attack at the rear, but after hard fighting, in which Germanicus took an active part in rallying the troops, he drove off the tribes. He was voted a triumph in AD 15, while he was still in command.

His next campaign was against the Chatti, a tribe that was better organized and more cohesive than many others in that they were able to plan ahead and follow orders. They were potential allies of Arminius, who had defeated Varus only a few years before and had never been captured. Therefore, the Chatti were doubly dangerous to Roman ambitions. Germanicus took the field with four legions and 10,000 auxiliaries, and Caecina commanded another four legions and about half as many auxiliaries. Movement into Germany was swift because there had been a severe drought and the streams were easily fordable. Germanicus left Lucius Apronius behind with troops to build bridges and make roads, because when the floods came the troops would be hindered in getting back to the Rhine.

News came from Segestes, a German chief loyal to Rome, that he had been attacked by Arminius, so Germanicus went to the rescue, for which he earned the title Imperator at the request of Tiberius. Along with Segestes and his family was his daughter, who was married to Arminius and was pregnant with his child. Still searching for Arminius, who was among the Cherusci inciting them to war against Rome, Germanicus sent his troops to the mouth of the river Ems.

Four legions under Caecina took the land route, and four with Germanicus himself boarded ships sailing through the lakes and estuaries to meet them. One of the officers, Lucius Stertinus, attacked a village of the Bructeri and found there the eagle of *legio XIX,* which had been annihilated in Varus's disaster in AD 9. This prompted Germanicus to look for the battle site, which they found, and there they buried the remains of the soldiers who died, marking the spot with a funeral mound.

Arminius attacked a cavalry force in the forests but called off the action when Germanicus arrived and drew up the legions. It was too late in the season to launch another attack to track Arminius down, so Germanicus withdrew, without leaving behind any garrisons or attempting to occupy the area that had just been overrun. He carried some of the troops on board ship round the coastal areas and back to the Rhine, while Caecina marched overland. These troops were almost trapped in a marshy area where the bridges had not been repaired. Hard pressed by the Germans, Caecina made camp, protecting the builders from attack and also the parties sent to make new bridges. The next day he marched in square formation and made another camp under the same difficult circumstances. This camp was surrounded and attacked by the Germans, but Caecina anticipated the attack and formed up his men ready to burst out of all the gateways at once, and the Germans were driven off. Caecina led his troops home. At headquarters on the Rhine at Vetera (modern Xanten), a rumor had started that the Germans were approaching with a large force. As a result, the panic-stricken troops very nearly destroyed the Rhine bridge and were only prevented from doing so by Agrippina's determined stance, placing herself in front of the panicking men and bringing them to their senses.

The pursuit of Arminius continued into the next season, AD 16, with Germanicus preparing in earnest before he launched the attack. He planned to ferry the bulk of his army around the coast and land in Germany at the mouth of the river Ems. Gaius Silius and Aulus Caecina were ordered to construct several different naval vessels for operations around the lower Rhine and the river Waal. Some were designed with flat bottoms to be run aground without damage, others had rudders at each end so that they could be drawn off quickly as soon as the rowers started to pull, and still others had floored decks for the transport of artillery, equipment, and horses. In the meantime, Silius was sent into the territory of the Chatti to raid their settlements, though he was prevented from achieving very much because of the heavy rains. Germanicus heard that one of the forts on the river Lippe was under siege, so he took six legions to the rescue. However, there was no battle, since the Germans drifted back into the forests as he arrived. They had destroyed the funeral monument recently set up for the troops of Varus, as well as an altar that had been dedicated to Drusus.

After this sideshow, the campaign began in earnest. Germanicus had the two armies of the Upper and Lower Danube at his disposal, consisting of eight legions and attendant auxiliaries. Joining the fleet, he took his army to the river Ems, but landing on the western bank he lost time in building a bridge to carry the troops across to the eastern side. The Romans advanced to the river Weser, where Arminius and his warriors faced them on the opposite bank. Tacitus includes a story that Arminius asked to see his brother Flavus, who had joined the Roman auxiliary forces and remained loyal. The meeting probably did occur, but Tacitus uses the interview to illustrate the Roman and the German point of view.

Arminius marched away to form up near the river Weser, in a forest sacred to one of the German gods, with higher ground behind him where he placed some of his warriors in reserve. Scouts reported his position to Germanicus, who followed, marching in battle-ready formation, with auxiliaries and archers in front and then four legions and two cohorts of the Praetorian Guard, where Germanicus stationed himself. Next came a picked force of cavalry, the remaining four legions and auxiliary infantry and mounted archers for the rearguard. When turning into battle, this would place the legions in the center with the Praetorians and the cavalry, and the auxiliaries on the wings. When the battle started, it appears that the German reserve forces on the high ground engaged too soon and were mown down in a flank attack by the Roman cavalry. Gradually, the Romans pushed the German forces back. Some of them drowned as they tried to escape across the Weser, and the rest melted away, to reemerge and attack the army as it marched back to the river Ems. As a result of Germanicus's victories, Tiberius was hailed as Imperator by the troops. From the reign of Augustus onward no general in the field dared to claim the title Imperator for himself, because it hinted at usurpation, so the titles given to an emperor sometimes denote wars fought by his commanders and do not necessarily imply that the emperor campaigned personally in the war zone. Despite the titles and self-congratulation on this occasion, however, Germanicus had won an incomplete victory, since once again the Romans had failed to capture Arminius, who rode off, wounded but still able to fight another day.

Knowing which routes the Romans would have to take, the Germans arranged an ambush, near to an earthwork that the Angrivarii had built as a boundary line between their lands and those of their neighbors. Deciding that attack was the best form of defense, Germanicus divided the army into two, taking one force himself to attack the tribesmen behind the earthwork and the other to clear out the woodlands nearby. He used slingers and light artillery against the defenders sheltering behind the earthwork and eventually broke through into the wooded area where fighting was fierce but not conclusive. Some of the legionaries were drawn off to make a camp, and the battle came to an end.

Upon Germanicus's return to the Rhine with the fleet, a serious storm scattered and wrecked the ships, with heavy Roman losses. Although it was late in the season, Germanicus mounted a few raids on the Chatti and the Marsi to off-set the disaster, in case the Germans thought that he was weakened beyond repair. In the lands of the Marsi, the Romans found another eagle standard from the army of Varus.

The German campaigns were finished for the time being, but it would require further wars under more generals before the Romans settled on the Rhine as the frontier. Although Germanicus would have liked to have stayed for more campaigning to complete the subjugation of the German tribes, Tiberius recalled him at the end of AD 16. There was a splendid triumph in Rome, and Germanicus's popularity was underlined when all the Praetorian cohorts came out to meet him instead of the two that had been ordered to do so. Tacitus continually harps on the jealousy that Tiberius felt for his adopted son, which may or may not be true. Tiberius certainly knew how to impose discipline and respect, but he did not have the knack of making the soldiers love him. At any rate, either because he was the best man for the job or because Tiberius wanted him out of the way, Germanicus was sent to the east, basing himself in Syria to ensure that the Parthians did not attempt to take over Armenia. Friction arose when Gnaeus Calpurnius Piso was sent out as legate to govern Syria, and within three years of leaving Germany, Germanicus was dead. It was said that Piso had been ordered to watch and hinder Germanicus, and when he died, perhaps of food poisoning, it was also said that Piso and his wife had poisoned Tiberius's only serious rival. Piso was accused of the crime and tried in the Senate, but committed suicide when it was clear that he was to be found guilty. No one has ever solved the mystery, and it has remained a useful tool for historical novelists ever since.

### Gnaeus Domitius Corbulo

The hallmarks of Domitius Corbulo were harsh discipline, determined intransigence, and careful planning. His reputation in this respect has perhaps been exaggerated by Tacitus, who portrayed in Corbulo the embodiment of the old Roman virtues that he admired in the generals of the Republic. Corbulo fought for Rome under Claudius and Nero, when the Empire was still young and the Republic was still a vivid memory. He was suffect consul in AD 39 and was given a command in Lower Germany in AD 47, though the area was not yet a province—that was a development of Domitian's reign.

The coasts of Gaul and the lands of Lower Germany were continually raided by a band of men commanded by a renegade tribesman of the Canninefates, called Gannascus, who had served as a Roman auxiliary. He had assembled a fleet and resorted to piracy, and was accused of inciting the Chauci to revolt. Corbulo responded by bringing up triremes and other ships of shallower draught to operate in the coastal areas and estuaries. Soon he flushed out Gannascus, though without capturing him, which left him free to cause further trouble among the tribes beyond the Rhine. In order to preempt this, Corbulo started to toughen up his troops, putting them through their paces and exercising strict discipline. All tasks, including sentry duty, outpost routines, and digging the ditches for the camps were to be performed fully armed. To underline the point, Corbulo executed two men—one for wearing only a dagger while he used his spade and the other for not wearing his side arms at all (Tacitus, *Annals* 11.18).

The Frisii of the Lower Rhine were so impressed by his preparations for war that they submitted to him without a fight, settling on the lands that he designated for them. To ensure their future cooperation, Corbulo stationed some of his troops in their lands and prepared to attack the Chauci across the Rhine. He sent embassies to try to persuade them to surrender, and secretly to find Gannascus and kill him. The death of Gannascus enraged the Chauci, but just as Corbulo was ready to take them on, orders came from the Emperor Claudius to withdraw to the left bank of the Rhine. Germany beyond the Rhine had been a sensitive area since the disaster of Varus, and Claudius perhaps reasoned that an expedition was likely to require long years of fighting and lots of manpower— or he could simply have been jealous. He had recently added Britain to the Empire, so he did not want to commit more soldiers to a campaign and he did not want to be eclipsed. Corbulo obeyed, allegedly commenting that the generals of the Republic were more fortunate. In order to employ the troops that he had prepared for war, he dug a canal to join the river Rhine to the Meuse near the coast so that shipping did not have to risk the uncertain temper of the North Sea when sailing from one to the other. He was awarded *ornamenta triumphalia*, the closest that the generals of the Empire came to holding a triumph, since Augustus reserved such displays for members of the Imperial house.

Corbulo's next appointment was under Nero, in the east, where he campaigned for an unusually long time, over ten years, with different titles and duties, but primarily in command of the armies. The king of Parthia, Vologaeses, had installed his brother Tiridates on the throne of Armenia, and it was imperative to restore Roman influence, if not domination, in Armenia. The teenage Emperor Nero ordered troops to be moved up closer to the Armenian border. His advisers recommended the appointment of Corbulo as legate of Cappadocia and Galatia.

Corbulo served in the east for over ten years, from AD 55 to 66 or perhaps 67, but the chronology of his campaigns is not clear. He probably spent the first two to three years preparing for the campaign, spending his first winter in Armenia in AD 58 to 59. All the suggestions for the dates of Corbulo's campaigns meet with difficulties at one point or another. The first problem that Corbulo faced when he arrived in his province was control of the troops in the east. Half of them were to remain with Ummidius Quadratus, governor of Syria, while the other half with its attendant auxiliary infantry and cavalry was already wintering in Cappadocia. As a preemptive measure against Parthian attacks on any of the eastern provinces and neighboring states, the various allied rulers were told to take their orders from either Corbulo or Ummidius Quadratus, according to the location of the emergency. This could only lead to squabbling. In this situation, one supreme commander was called for, but Nero and his advisers presumably did not want to risk giving so much power to one individual.

Vologaeses agreed to furnish hostages, but the Roman commanders both sent officers to receive them. Rather than argue in public, these officers allowed the hostages to choose whose camp they would go to, and they chose Corbulo (Tacitus, *Annals* 13.9). The pending war did not break out for two years or more after Corbulo's arrival. The chronology is not clear, even though Tacitus relates events in annalistic fashion. The emphasis is on Corbulo's training regime for his troops, who were said to have become very lax in their eastern postings, some of them never having built a camp or seen any fighting. First, Corbulo weeded out the unfit, the old, and the infirm, and then he levied troops in Galatia and Cappadocia. A legion was transferred to him with its auxiliary troops from Germany. To accustom the legionaries to hardship, Corbulo put them into winter camp under canvas, where stories were told of men freezing to death on sentry duty, and one man's hands dropping off as he tried to put down his bundle of firewood (Tacitus, *Annals* 13.35). Desertions began, and just as quickly ceased, because Corbulo instituted the death penalty for the first offense, not for the second or the third as other commanders had done. While all this was going on, to set the example, Corbulo went about wearing only light clothing and with no head covering.

The auxiliary units were dispersed at various points, with instructions to watch the enemy but not to engage in battle. One of the commanders, however, a senior centurion called Paccius Orfitus, was persuaded by the firebrands among his troops and offered battle. He was defeated, and he and his surviving men were ordered to camp outside the ramparts, until the other soldiers prevailed upon Corbulo to relent.

Instead of attacking the Romans directly, Tiridates began to attack the Armenian cities loyal to Rome. Corbulo retaliated, divided his forces to follow Tiridates, and attacked those states loyal to the Parthians. King Antiochus of Commagene was encouraged to attack neighboring states on Rome's behalf. The Parthians asked for a conference but insisted that, while Tiridates should be accompanied by 1,000 horsemen, the Romans could bring as many men as they wished provided that they did not wear armor. Since the Parthian horsemen were renowned archers, Corbulo did not fall for this ploy, for his men could be mown down very quickly if things went wrong. Instead he suggested that the conference should take place in sight of the two armies. He drew up with the auxiliaries on the wings and *legio VI* with about half of *legio III* in the center, but under only one eagle so that it seemed that he had only one legion. The ruse was unnecessary, since the Parthians did not offer battle and withdrew.

Corbulo secured his communications and supply routes so that the Parthians could not cut them, and he went on attacking the Armenian citadels loyal to Parthia. He chose one of the most important, Volandum (which may be the modern Igdir), for himself and left the legionary legate Cornelius Flaccus and the camp prefect Capito to subdue other strongholds. After a very short time—one day for Volandum—the towns fell, and Corbulo was ready to attack the capital, Artaxata. Typically cautious, he marched toward it in square formation, with *legio III Gallica* on the right flank, *legio IV Ferrata* on the left, the baggage in the center with some of *legio X Fretensis,* and 1,000 cavalry to guard the rear. On the wings he placed the rest of the cavalry and the foot archers. The rearguard was given strict orders not to pursue the Armenians, who pretended to flee in order to draw the Romans off, but Corbulo's men did not give chase. There was no siege, since Artaxata opened its gates without a fight. Corbulo, judging it to be too large for him to hold and defend, burned it.

By this time, the Parthians were faced with troubles in their own kingdom, so the war was virtually at an end. Corbulo decided to aim for the stronghold of Tigranocerta, marching through difficult terrain in a very hot climate with hardly any food and water, but was again spared the rigors of a siege. Tigranocerta also opened its gates, and this time he did not put the city to the torch. Returning to Syria, he took over from Ummidius Quadratus and put the province in a state of defense against the next incursions of the Parthians, which were sure to come as soon as the troublesome elements had been quelled. Corbulo asked the emperor to send another governor to control the regions he had just overrun, and Caesennius Paetus was dispatched as legate of Cappadocia and Armenia. Corbulo divided his troops with Paetus, retaining three legions and the garrison of Syria for himself.

Soon afterward Corbulo had to return to Armenia and rescue Paetus, who had gotten into difficulties and was besieged in his camp. Corbulo took care over his supplies, using trains of camels to carry his grain and hay. Tacitus used Corbulo's own commentaries of his eastern campaigns and says that the Parthians had no supplies and were about to leave, but Paetus surrendered, needlessly as it turned out. There may have been some sour grapes on Corbulo's part, because his recent work in Armenia was almost negated by Paetus's actions. After an interlude during which Corbulo diplomatically warded off Parthian attacks and demands that the Romans should abandon the installations across the Euphrates, a new governor was appointed for Syria, and Corbulo returned to Armenia with a brief that allowed him to make war if he thought it necessary. Given another legion from Germany, he started to mount an expedition into Armenia. He assembled a large force consisting of four legions, accompanied by vexillations from the legions of Egypt and the Danube and a large number of auxiliaries. The size of this force and the reputation of its commander were sufficient to bring the Parthians to terms. Armenia was to be ruled by a king whom the Romans chose and supported, and the Parthians were for the moment restrained from further depredations against the eastern Roman provinces. If Corbulo had been able to follow his instincts, he would probably have carried the war into Parthia itself. The reality, however, was that he was not a Republican general with considerable freedom of action, but a legate of the emperor, and as such he had to obey orders.

Corbulo's ultimate fate did not reflect his achievements, and he was not allowed to return to Rome as the savior of the east and to go onto other commands. In the AD mid-60s a conspiracy was discovered against the Emperor Nero, in which Corbulo was implicated because his son-in-law Lucius Annius Vinicianus was one of the accused. When the ringleaders had been punished, Nero left Rome to tour through Greece, and on arrival in AD 66 or 67, he invited Corbulo to meet him. The shrewd general who had done so much for Rome knew what the invitation implied and committed suicide. His daughter Domitia would become the wife of the future Emperor Domitian.

## HEROES FROM THE OTHER RANKS

Only a very small proportion of the vast numbers of soldiers who served Rome throughout her history are known by their names, mostly derived from inscriptions commemorating special occasions or more commonly recording their deaths. For information about the soldiers who distinguished themselves in Roman military service, historians must rely on the few sources that record the men and their achievements. In this regard, the surviving literature and inscriptions represent an arbitrary selection of heroic acts or consistently high achievement.

Contemporary records would have been much more abundant. The army kept records of its personnel from Republican times, with details of when they enlisted and their various duties. It is clear that the officers also noted the characteristics, good and bad, of the men. According to Appian (*Civil War* 3.7), when Mark Antony wanted to identify the troublemakers in his army, the tribunes produced a list for him from their files. When soldiers had performed particularly well in battles or on campaigns, their names were similarly recorded and written up in reports, from which the commanders could compile lists when rewards were to be handed out. Soldiers appreciated the presence of their generals or the emperor in battles because they were more likely to be noticed if they had a chance to excel. In Dacia in AD 88 before the battle of Tapae, Domitian's general Tettius Julianus ordered his men to inscribe their own names and those of their officers on their shields, so that anyone who performed particularly well would be more easily recognized and their exploits recorded (Dio 67.10).

The recognition and rewards meant a great deal to the recipients, not purely from the point of view of monetary gain or the promotions that often followed a significant act of bravery. Great ceremonial attached to the giving of rewards, as evidenced by the special parade organized by Titus for his army in Judaea, reported by Josephus (*Jewish War* 7.13–15). The names of all men who had performed well during the war were read out, and as each man came forward, Titus himself presented the various decorations appropriate to the deed and the rank of each soldier, accompanied by gifts of silver, gold, and clothing.

Some soldiers attached sufficient importance to their decorations to record them on inscriptions, or their heirs recorded the details for them. A second-century inscription from Spain (*ILS* 2661) documents the career and rewards of Lucius Aemilius Paternus, who had served as centurion in several legions and then in the Urban Cohorts and the Praetorian Guard. He accompanied Trajan on his expeditions to Dacia and Parthia, and was decorated by the emperor three times, twice in the Dacian Wars and once in Parthia. Another much decorated officer was a commander of auxiliary troops, an equestrian officer called Gaius Julius Corinthianus. He died while serving in Dacia, at the age of thirty-nine, having risen to the rare command of a milliary *ala*. During his career he earned several decorations, including the *corona muralis,* for storming a city. The fact that these men and several others specifically listed their awards indicates the importance that they attached to them, but with regard to the historical record, it simply proves that the men had performed great exploits in battle and offers no information with which to reconstruct what they did to earn them. There can be no certainty about which campaign or campaigns they served in, much less the exact location.

Conversely, in at least one incident, the campaign, the location, and the exploit are known, but not the names or ranks of the men who carried it out. Tacitus (*Histories* 3.23) relates that at the second battle of Cremona in the civil war of AD 69, the soldiers of Vitellius had mounted their artillery on raised ground and were causing great damage to the troops fighting for the cause of Vespasian under Antonius Primus. The operators of one particularly large ballista were hurling huge stones into the Flavian ranks, so two soldiers took shields from the dead men around them, crept up to the machine, and put it out of action by cutting the cords that formed the torsion springs. They were both killed, and no one recorded their names. In the same battle, a centurion called Atilius Verus was killed after rescuing the eagle of the Seventh legion, recently raised by Galba.

Rather than relying upon the historians to record their actions, some self-declared heroes set up inscriptions to commemorate them. Tiberius Claudius

Maximus set up a stone while he was still alive to bear witness to his career (Campbell, 1994; Speidel, 1970). He held various appointments but did not advance to high rank. He was a legionary cavalryman in *legio VII Claudia,* decorated in the Dacian Wars by Domitian, and promoted by Trajan to *duplicarius* in *ala II Pannoniorum.* He served under Trajan in Dacia and in Parthia and earned decorations for bravery, but he considered that his greatest achievement was bringing the head of the Dacian king Decebalus to the emperor. On the inscription, he insists that he captured Decebalus, but what he does not mention is that the king committed suicide. However, Claudius Maximus presumably found and recognized the king, dead or alive, and detached his head. For this act, Trajan promoted him from *duplicarius* to decurion of the Pannonian *ala.*

Another soldier serving under Hadrian in Pannonia performed a spectacular feat in peacetime, with the emperor in attendance. His success is documented on an inscription (*ILS* 2558). The soldier belonged to a Batavian unit, famous for its expertise in swimming, and while in full armor he swam across the Danube, a considerable achievement in itself, but he also shot two arrows, breaking the first one in two with his second arrow. The inscription states that no one was ever able to compete with him in javelin throwing, and no archer could outdo him in firing arrows. The one vital fact that does not appear in the inscription is the soldier's name.

Historians have derived the most information about heroic acts performed by officers and men from Caesar's commentaries. Some of these notices concern single episodes where individual soldiers distinguished themselves. An anecdote included in the description of the siege of Cicero's camp concerns two rival centurions, Lucius Vorenus and Titus Pullo. They were both anxious for promotion, having reached quite high rank, and they vied with each other as to which of them would be the first to achieve the post of senior centurion. They spurred each other on to perform a brave but not very effective act, by bursting out of the camp to engage the Gauls surrounding it. Pullo went first, asking Vorenus what he was waiting for. He threw his *pilum* and then used his shield to ward off missiles, but one of them struck his belt in such a way that he was prevented from drawing his sword, so Vorenus came to his aid, fighting several Gauls at once, only to fall into a dip in the ground, requiring assistance in his turn from Pullo. The two men fought their way back to the camp, having performed a spectacular feat and no doubt increasing their reputations, but Caesar does not say that he rewarded them or promoted them (*Gallic War* 5.44).

A few of Caesar's officers are mentioned in more than one battle situation. One of these is the senior centurion (*primus pilus*), whose name is variously given as Publius Sextius Baculus in the Loeb translation of Caesar's *Gallic War,* or elsewhere as Sextus Julius Baculus. He first came to Caesar's attention during a battle against the Nervii, when he was severely wounded but carried on fighting until he could not stand up (*Gallic War* 2.25). He survived, and Caesar relates how the same man helped to save the day, along with the tribune Gaius Volusenus, when the winter quarters of *legio XII* under Servius Galba was attacked by the Gauls (*Gallic War* 3.4–5). The situation was so bad that the under-strength legion did not have sufficient men to defend the ramparts, and the Gauls had managed to get close enough to begin to fill in the ditch and to demolish the earthen walls. Baculus and Volusenus urged the commander to make a sortie, since attack was the best form of defense. The legionaries erupted from all the gates, killed a third of the Gauls, and drove the rest off. A similar occasion at a different camp gave Baculus a chance to demonstrate his courage later on, when he was supposed to be recuperating with the wounded and sick men, and the camp was attacked while five cohorts were outside gathering food. All the gates needed defending, and despite the fact that he was wounded and had not eaten for five days, Baculus dashed out to one of the gates, seized arms from the nearest man, gathered the centurions of the cohort left to guard the camp, and stood firm in the gateway, providing the necessary breathing space for the troops to form up. He was badly wounded again, and had to be dragged back to safety. Caesar does not tell us that he died, so perhaps this irrepressible soldier survived to fight more battles.

Caesar names Lucius Aurunculeius Cotta as a heroic officer who was killed in tragic circumstances. Cotta was in winter quarters with Quintus Titurius Sabinus when the revolt of Ambiorix broke out. The camp was besieged, and after a parley, Ambiorix offered safe passage for the Romans to leave camp and join either Cicero or Labienus in their winter quarters, something over 50 miles away. This would be at least two days' journey, weather permitting, and Cotta advised against leaving. Here Caesar manages to insert a moral lesson, summarizing and perhaps inventing Cotta's speech in the military *consilium* with Sabinus and the officers. The main points raised by Cotta were that no orders to evacuate had come from Caesar, the battles of the past days had shown that the entrenched camp was strong enough to withstand assaults, good stores of food had been brought in, and Caesar would come to their relief when he heard of their plight. Sabinus, on the other hand, feared a long siege and starvation, and thinking that Caesar had left for Italy, he concluded that there would be no relieving column. He chose to trust Ambiorix and accepted what he thought would be a safe passage, and eventually the other officers agreed. The troops left the camp the next day. Cotta went up and down the column, but it was too long for him to control, so he eventually ordered the men to abandon the baggage and form a square for better protection on the march, which as Caesar says was the correct decision but instilled fear into the men. They probably had little chance however they had marched, because Ambiorix had prepared an ambush. During the fighting, Cotta was hit in the face by a sling bullet but carried on fighting, refusing to join Sabinus in an attempt to negotiate with Ambiorix. He died still fighting, and Caesar's judgment of him was that he had done his duty as a commander by encouraging the men and as a soldier by fighting among them (*Gallic War* 30–37).

One of the most famous anecdotes of Caesar's wars concerns the siege of Pompey's camp at Dyrrachium in the civil war. When Pompey mounted three simultaneous attacks on Caesar's lines, there was fierce fighting, with the Caesarians pinned down in one section of the ramparts by arrow fire. Thirty thousand arrows were collected after the battle at this point alone, and four centurions from one cohort lost their eyes. Another centurion of the eighth cohort, Cassius Scaeva, was more fortunate. He survived, and his shield was displayed before Caesar with 120 holes in it. He was rewarded on the spot, with a gift of 200,000 sesterces and promotion to the first centurion of the first cohort, that is, *primus pilus,* since it was largely by his actions that the day had been saved at that particular point of attack.

Another of Caesar's officers, Gaius Caninius Rebilus, can be traced throughout the Gallic Wars right through to the end of the civil wars, and his promotion is clear both from Caesar's commentaries and from the nature of the tasks he was given. He started as one of Caesar's legates, not necessarily in command of one specific legion but as a deputy assigned to different tasks. During the struggle with Vercingetorix and the siege of Alesia, Caninius and another legate called Gaius Antistius Reginus, commanded a two-legion camp. When the siege was over and Vercingetorix had surrendered, Caninius was sent with one legion to winter in the territory of the Ruteni (*Gallic War* 7.83; 90). He is next heard of in charge of two legions, which he took to the relief of one of Rome's staunchest allies, the Gallic chief Duratius, who was blockaded in his stronghold of Lemonum (modern Poitiers) by other Gauls under Dumnacus. With only two legions at his disposal, Caninius dug in and erected an entrenched camp, which withstood the attacks of the Gauls, giving him time to send a message to another legate, Gaius Fabius, who brought his troops to assist, but before he arrived Dumnacus raised the siege and left. Fabius engaged him in separate cavalry actions and finally routed the Gauls (*Gallic War* 8. 24–30). Next, two Gallic rebels, Drappes and Lucterius, occupied Uxellodunum, where Caninius arrived as soon as he heard the news. He divided his forces and built three camps on high ground, joining them up with a rampart to blockade the town, but he did not complete the circuit because he did not have enough men to defend the whole perimeter. Some of the Gauls slipped out to find food supplies and started to bring them in by night, but the Roman sentries heard them, Caninius sent out troops, and the whole Gallic force was killed. Drappes was captured. When Gaius Fabius joined him with more men, Caninius completed the ramparts and blockaded the town. Caninius sent dispatches to alert Caesar, who rode with all the cavalry forces to Uxellodunum, leaving the legions to follow under the command of Quintus Calenus. Caesar cut off the town's water supply, brought about the surrender of the Gauls, and as an example to other tribes, he cut off the hands of all those who had carried arms against Rome. Caesar was approaching the end of his proconsulship, so he could not afford to settle for half measures in case the other Gallic tribes rose in revolt, undoing the work of the past decade.

Caninius accompanied Caesar at the outbreak of the civil war with Pompey the Great. Since Caninius was a personal friend of one of Pompey's naval officers, Scribonius Libo, Caesar asked him to approach Libo, who in turn was asked to persuade Pompey to come to the conference table. The mission failed (*Civil War* 1.26). By the time of the war in Africa, Caninius had reached proconsular rank and was put in charge of the siege of Thapsus with three legions (*African War* 86). When the war was carried to Spain, Caninius was sent to garrison the town of Hispalis while Caesar camped nearby with the main force (*Spanish War* 35). Caninius Rebilus was not strictly a military hero; he did not achieve great acts of courage in battle, but he was a loyal and intelligent officer whose career demonstrates the initiative and freedom of action that Caesar allowed his legates, and how promotions could be earned from good steady service.

## FAMOUS BATTLES AND CAMPAIGNS

There were so many famous battles between Rome and her enemies throughout the Republic and the Empire that an account of them would fill a whole volume. Accordingly, a representative selection must be made, leaving out several battles even though they ended wars or changed the course of history. For many of the known battles, all that can be described is the name with sketchy detail of who fought whom and why. It is rarely possible to reconstruct exactly what happened. Sometimes, even when armed with more detail, it is not known exactly where the battle site lay, except that the place names can narrow it down to the vicinity of a town or city. Some of the most famous battles described by the ancient historians cannot even be located as precisely as this. No one knows where Boudicca met defeat at the hands of Suetonius or where Agricola faced the northern Britons. In Dacia in AD 88, Tettius Julianus defeated the army of Decebalus at Tapae, and some years later Trajan's army met the Dacians in the same vicinity, but the battlefields have not been precisely identified. Archaeological discoveries may one day reveal these sites, as the hitherto unknown location of the defeat of Varus was revealed in recent years. At the end of the nineteenth century, Theodore Mommsen proposed Kalkriese near Osnabrück as the Varan battle site, and after long and patient searching, an Englishman, Major Tony Clunn of the Rhine army, assembled enough evidence to convince archaeologists that this was indeed the place where three Roman legions were wiped out in AD 9 (Clunn, 1999).

## Pharsalus, 48 BC

When Caesar moved off from his blockade of Pompey at Dyrrachium, his prime purpose was to find food and fodder. He marched into Thessaly where the crops were just ripening. Although it was August by the Roman calendar, the months and the seasons no longer matched, so in reality it was early summer. Caesar's camp was in the vicinity of Pharsalus, but he does not describe precisely where he was in his commentaries. Historians therefore have to choose between two separate sites about 7 miles apart, Pharsalus and Old Pharsalus, on the river Enipeus (Kutchuk Tcharnali). Pompey followed him and camped close by, on a hill in a strong defensive position that could be attacked only with great difficulty, and there he remained, steadfastly ignoring Caesar's attempts to entice him into a pitched battle. The opposing armies drew up each day facing each other, but Pompey's troops remained near their camp high up the slope. Pompey's strategy was to wait and wear Caesar down without risking a confrontation, but his subordinates were eager to annihilate the Caesarians once and for all, and nagged him into fighting. He might have succeeded, except for a quirk of fate. Caesar had decided to strike camp and move away, but on that very morning when the soldiers were packing up and about to set off, Pompey's army drew up in battle order much further down the hill than their normal position. It was an opportunity not to be missed. Caesar hastily countermanded his orders and brought his army out in battle order.

Pompey rested his right wing on the river Enipeus and strengthened his left wing by placing his huge cavalry force there, very much enlarged since he had recruited many horsemen from his native allies. He may have siphoned off about 600 cavalry and stationed them near the river on his left, but no source except Frontinus says this (Goldsworthy, 2003b). Announcing his plans at his *consilium* during the previous night, Pompey explained that he intended to demolish Caesar's right wing with an onslaught of his horsemen under the command of Titus Labienus and then force a way around the flank and rear to close the trap. The plan was sound, especially as the Pompeians knew that Caesar was outnumbered in both infantry and cavalry, with only eight legions that were not up to full strength, to face Pompey's eleven legions, and a mere 1,000 cavalry against Pompey's 7,000. Since he could never hope to overcome such large numbers of horsemen with his own meager forces, Caesar had to strengthen his right wing. He entrusted the command of the left to Mark Antony, facing Pompey's general Lucius Afranius, and the center to Gnaeus Domitius Calvinus, opposite Pompey's father-in-law Metellus Scipio. On the right, facing Pompey himself, he placed in command Publius Sulla, the son of the Dictator, and remained there himself. His cavalry force was also on the right flank, and his famous *legio X* was positioned to the right of the line of infantry, so he knew he could rely on them to hold firm. He also formed up a fourth line by withdrawing one cohort from the third line of each legion and placed it out of sight as a reserve, in case the right wing should start to crumble or disaster struck elsewhere in the whole line. One other factor was perhaps instrumental in Caesar's eventual victory: he ordered his troops to strike at the faces of the Pompeian soldiers, judging that the psychological impact would spread fear and panic.

The battle opened with a Caesarian charge, which the Pompeians received without moving, since Pompey did not want his men to be winded before they fought. Caesar thought this a mistake, in that the men who charged forward had the advantage and did not have time to work up their fear while watching an army coming toward them. Once battle was joined, Pompey's right and center held out and fought hard, and so Labienus ordered the cavalry to attack and envelop the Caesarian right. However, they failed to work their way round rapidly and decisively, and were scattered by an attack on their own flanks by the troops that Caesar had concealed. The removal of the horsemen opened up the Pompeian left to further attack by Caesar's reserve fourth line, and he also sent in the third line to help the first and second. The battle was lost at that point. Pompey rode off the field and back to the camp, which ought to have been defended by the seven cohorts that he had left there, but he neglected to make any arrangements for the defense and rode away as Caesar's men approached. He took a few attendants with him and went to the city of Larissa, where he told the inhabitants of his defeat and advised them not to resist Caesar. Then he made for the coast, and ultimately Egypt, where he was killed. One of the main protagonists was removed, but the civil war was not yet over. Caesar did not learn of Pompey's fate until he arrived in Alexandria, but Pompey's sons and many of his legates were still at large and could not be allowed to build up their power. Perhaps if Pompey had been spared in Egypt and Caesar could have negotiated with him, the war may have been ended less bloodily, but in 48 BC the victor of the battle of Pharsalus had merely completed the first stage. Four more years of war and two major battles at Thapsus and Munda were to follow before Caesar could shake off the Pompeian threat.

## Philippi, 42 BC

The legacy of the civil war between the Caesarians and the Pompeians was another series of wars between Caesar's successors and his assassins. The men who called themselves the Liberators accomplished their aim of bringing down Caesar in March 44 BC, but seem to have imagined that their contemporaries would applaud their deed and revert to the old system without so much as a hint of a plan. They had underestimated the strength of feeling among Caesar's circle of clients and associates, but fortunately, for a short and tense interval just after the murder, Mark Antony as consul managed to restore order, reconciling the Liberators to the Caesarians and avoiding an immediate bloodbath in Rome. It was short lived. The Liberators fled to the east and started to raise troops, and the tide turned against Antony, who was declared an enemy of the state. He left Rome for his province of Gaul, facing troops sent against him by the Senate, stirred up by the polemical oratory of Cicero.

In the midst of this turmoil, Caesar's nineteen-year-old great-nephew Gaius Octavius arrived in Rome. He had been in Macedonia with the army, awaiting Caesar's arrival for a campaign on the Danube and had returned to claim his inheritance as Caesar's heir. He called himself Gaius Julius Caesar Octavianus, though the latter part of his name that has descended to the modern world was not the name by which he advertised himself. He recruited Caesar's *clientelae*, and trod very carefully, seeming to ally himself with Cicero against Mark Antony, accepting a command to fight Antony in northern Italy. It was all a facade, and he soon allied himself with Antony to turn on the anti-Caesarians and build up his own power. He gained the consulship at the head of his soldiers, and in an officially recognized junta of three men that is known as the Triumvirate, he carved up the Roman world with Antony and Lepidus. When the time came, and they were strong enough, Antony and Octavian declared war on the conspirators who were led by Brutus and Cassius in the east.

The first difficulty was to ferry the troops to the east, because the conspirators controlled the seaways, but Antony succeeded in sending troops under Decidius Saxa and Norbanus Flaccus across the Adriatic to Macedonia, where they landed safely and marched down the Via Egnatia toward Thessalonika. They camped near Amphipolis and awaited Antony and Octavian who arrived at Dyrrachium as soon as there were favorable winds to take them across the Adriatic, and as soon as Staius Murcus and Domitius Ahenobarbus, the lieutenants of Brutus and Cassius patrolling the coasts, drew off for a while. When the two halves of Antony's army joined up, it was known that Brutus and Cassius had encamped near Philippi, so the troops marched there with a small reconnoitring party in advance to sound out the defenses of the conspirators. They had chosen their ground very well, utilizing all the defensive aspects of the terrain to form two separate camps, Brutus in the northern camp, straddling the road with mountains protecting his flank, and Cassius in the southern camp, protected by a marsh. They had also erected defensive earthworks to prevent the approach of attackers.

Antony made camp to the west of the conspirators, joined by Octavian who had fallen ill at Dyrrachium and been left behind. No battle was likely to occur unless Antony could force the conspirators out of their defenses, so he decided to cut their supply line by building a causeway across the marsh, around the southern defenses of Cassius's camp, toward the Via Egnatia to the east. His troops built quite a long section of this causeway in secret, while each day

Antony drew up the rest of his army to offer battle and to distract attention from the building works. When Cassius discovered what was happening, he started to build a line of defenses north of Antony's causeway. The first battle of Philippi began with a skirmish over these defenses, when Antony sent out some of his men across the causeway and Cassius attacked them. The fighting escalated as Antony poured more men into the struggle, and Brutus's army joined in, thinking that they could take Antony in the flank and crush him. The outcome was not decisive. Although Antony took Cassius's camp, Brutus took Octavian's, so that the two armies swiveled round through 90 degrees, still facing each other and neither side victorious. What tipped the balance and prepared the way for final victory for Antony was that Cassius misunderstood what he saw. He had been driven out from his camp, and he assumed that Brutus had likewise been defeated, so he committed suicide.

Now alone, Brutus repaired the damage, entrenching himself even more firmly behind defenses, prepared to wait until lack of supplies forced Antony to move. Perhaps like Pompey at Pharsalus, he succumbed to the firebrands among his officers who considered Antony weakened and therefore easily defeated. Brutus offered battle, and Antony hastily accepted. His first move was to try to outflank Brutus, which made the latter send in his reserve, and then Antony switched to an all-out attack on the center. It may be that he deliberately feigned an attack on the flanks to make Brutus commit his reserve, and once that was out of the way, he then launched his assault on the center. Alternatively, as some scholars have pointed out, he may simply have seen an opportunity and attacked the center at the right moment. Whichever it was, Antony's maneuvers won the day. Brutus fled, with four legions, leaving Antony master of the battlefield. During the pursuit, an officer pretended to be Brutus and gave himself up, but when he was brought to Antony the ruse was discovered. As for Antony's feelings, he may have been glad that it was not Brutus, because then he would have been forced to execute him. In the end Brutus committed suicide, so Antony could be generous and grant him an honorable funeral, but he allowed Octavian to cut off the conspirator's head and take it to Rome to throw it down at the foot of Caesar's statue. Since Antony had nailed Cicero's head and hands to the Rostrum in the Forum, he was not in a position to refuse on ethical grounds.

Despite the presence of Octavian, the victory at Philippi was Antony's. The troops hailed him as Imperator, and when the provinces were carved up once again between him and Octavian, Antony won control of Cisalpine and Transalpine Gaul with about seventeen legions, and all of the east. It was the lion's share, and for about a decade Antony was the most important man in the Roman world. At the naval battle of Actium, in 31 BC, his supremacy passed to Octavian, and he committed suicide, dying in the arms of Cleopatra, as Alexandria fell in the following year.

## Britain in AD 60: Suetonius Paullinus and the Defeat of Boudicca

Suetonius Paullinus was a contemporary of Corbulo, and Tacitus (*Annals* 14.29) says that in military skills he was a worthy rival to Corbulo, having conquered a national enemy. Suetonius reached the consulship in AD 41 (some sources indicate AD 43). He campaigned against tribesmen in the Atlas Mountains of Africa before his appointment as governor of Britain, from AD 58 or 59 to AD 61. His first task was the subjugation of north Wales, where he mopped up resistance and finally arrived on the coast opposite the island of Anglesey, the stronghold of the Druids. Just as he was about to finish off the war, the rebellion of Boudicca flared up behind him in the more peaceful and advanced areas of the province, so he hurried back to London with whatever troops he could muster.

The story of the rebellion is told by Tacitus (*Annals* 14.30–38). On the death of King Prasutagus of the Iceni tribe, who lived in what is now East Anglia, the kingdom was left jointly to the king's wife Boudicca and to the Emperor Nero. Unfortunately, the procurator Catus Decianus forcibly took over the kingdom using the troops at his disposal while Suetonius was in Wales, and in the ensuing fight Boudicca was flogged and her daughters were raped. Declaring revenge and with nothing to lose, Boudicca gathered her own tribesmen and persuaded other tribes to join her in avenging the insults done to them and to drive them out. The newly founded Roman towns of Camulodunum (modern Colchester) and Verulamium (modern St. Albans) were ferociously attacked and burned to the ground by the combined tribes under Boudicca's command. A detachment of *legio IX Hispana* under Petillius Cerialis was badly mauled and had to withdraw with great losses, perhaps to the camp at Longthorpe, rather than the fortress at Lincoln, which would have been too far distant for him to attack and withdraw.

Suetonius did not underestimate the power of the British forces, and he knew that he could not defend London with the troops at his immediate disposal. He abandoned it and its inhabitants and moved off to meet the troops coming from Wales, sending a message to Poenius Postumus, the camp prefect of *legio II Augusta* in the southwest, to march to join him. Infamously, Postumus refused the order on the grounds that there was too much unrest in his own area to risk leaving it.

Suetonius was left with depleted forces from *legio XIV* and *legio XX* and his auxiliary troops, to meet the onslaught of the Britons. He chose his ground at an unknown location, probably near Mancetter in the Midlands. To his rear was a narrow defile ending in a wooded area, which he scouted thoroughly to ensure that no Britons were hiding there and a plain in front where the battle was fought. He drew up in standard formation, with his legions in the center flanked by the light-armed troops and the cavalry on the wings. He held the troops back, not throwing their *pila* until the Britons were very close, so that there was more certainty of hitting the target and not wasting missiles. Then the Romans charged in a wedge-shaped formation, scattering the enemy, but the Britons had brought their wagons and placed them behind their army, and this impeded their escape. The end result was a massacre, and a thorough search for any survivors that lasted for some time. The ultimate fate of Boudicca herself is unknown. The force of the rebellion and the damage caused can be estimated from the numbers of replacements that Nero sent to Britain from Germany; 2,000 legionaries, 8 cohorts, and 1,000 cavalry.

Suetonius was recalled soon after the victory because he allegedly made difficulties for the civilian procurator, Julius Classicianus, who replaced Catus and treated the Britons more leniently. This may be true, but Suetonius did not suffer disgrace. He became consul in AD 66, and when the civil wars of AD 69 broke out he declared for Otho.

## Britain in AD 83/84: Gnaeus Julius Agricola and Mons Graupius

If Agricola's daughter had not married the historian Tacitus, all that would be known of Agricola in Britain is that he was governor when the water supply was laid down at the fortress of Deva (modern Chester), where he is named on the lead piping, and that his name appears on an inscription from Verulamium (modern St. Albans). As it is, Tacitus provides a fairly eulogistic biography of him that tells us a great deal but hides so much detail that archaeologists and historians will probably still be debating the finer points for centuries to come.

Agricola was born in AD 40 at Forum Julii (modern Fréjus) in Gaul. His military career was unusual in that, unlike other officers who usually served in different provinces, he served three times in Britain: as military tribune during the rebellion of Boudicca, then later as legionary legate of *legio XX*, and then as governor of the province. He was relatively young for such a prestigious command, and he held it for seven years, whereas the normal tenure was three to four years. He reached the consulship in AD 76, and may have arrived in Britain as governor in AD 77 or 78, replacing Sextus Julius Frontinus, who had subdued the tribes of South Wales. The dispute about the exact dates of his term as governor makes it impossible to discern whether he fought at Mons Graupius in AD 83 or 84.

Tacitus says that it was late in the season when he took over, and his first campaign was in North Wales against the Ordvices. His second season was spent rounding off the conquests of Petillius Cerialis in northern Britain, and not until his third season did he meet with "new tribes" as Tacitus describes them (*Agricola* 22). He campaigned as far north as the river Tay, and then in his fourth season he stopped to consolidate his gains, establishing a string of fortifications across the Forth-Clyde isthmus, which archaeologists have identified in part.

In the fifth season, Tacitus describes naval operations on the west coast of Scotland. Agricola drew up his troops somewhere facing Ireland, which he said he could have subdued with only one legion. Perhaps it is fortunate that he never tried, since many another military leader has seriously underestimated the land and people of Ireland. In the sixth season, he nearly won a victory, but it eluded him, and he brought the tribes to battle in the seventh. His real success is not that he won the battle but that he managed to persuade the tribesmen to unite and fight. In Scotland it is usually the invader who gets into difficulties and starves, while the tribes retreat into the mountains and wait, but the combined naval and land operations of the sixth season perhaps wasted their lands and harassed them to the point where they had nothing to lose. They chose a leader called Calgacus, which means the Swordsman, and faced the Romans. Tacitus uses the fabricated prebattle speeches of both leaders to put forward the opposing points of view of the Britons and the Romans.

The final battle was at a place called Mons Graupius. Speculation as to where this was has filled many an article in journals and still occupies scholars today. The site requires a hill, of which there is no shortage in Scotland, and a Roman camp nearby. Both are present in Aberdeenshire at Durno, with the hill of Bennachie in the background, but this is only one likely location for this elusive battle. The tribesmen formed up on the slope, relying on the momentum of their initial charge to break the Roman ranks. Agricola put his legions just in front of his camp, with the auxiliary forces in the front line, infantry in the center, and cavalry on the wings. This formation with legions in the rear was not unusual in the late first century. Agricola kept four cavalry units in reserve to throw into the battle wherever it should be necessary, probably to counter the necessity of extending his line further than he would have liked to avoid being outflanked.

Agricola had his horse taken away before battle was joined in order to lead from the front, which meant that he had to rely on his officers to make the correct responses to whatever the Britons did in areas where he could not personally direct developments. In the event, he did not have to employ his legions. The auxiliaries withstood the charge when the Britons closed, and the reserve *alae* broke the British ranks and worked around to the rear, trapping them between the two forces. The Britons fled, widely dispersed, and next day the Roman scouts could not find anyone to fight. The tribesmen were defeated in this battle, but resistance was not eradicated. The natives were contained by a line of forts blocking all the mouths of the glens, controlling access between the Highlands and the Lowlands, but if the Romans had remained in Scotland it is likely that there would have been more hard fighting against bands of rebels before Romanization could begin.

Agricola sent his fleet all around the island after the battle, thus proving that it was not attached to another land mass, and he made a point of returning to the south in a very leisurely manner, demonstrating Roman sovereignty. He had conquered the rest of Britain after his predecessors had subdued Wales and the north of England, and could look forward to another prestigious appointment. This he never achieved, and to make matters worse, only a few years after Mons Graupius, Domitian faced serious trouble on the Danube, where he lost two armies fighting the Dacians, and he withdrew the troops from the far north of Britain. Coin evidence shows that the army had gone by AD 87, if not earlier, and a few years later Trajan made a boundary line on the road joining Corbridge to Carlisle, more or less on the line that Hadrian would choose to build his wall.

## Trajan and the Dacian Campaigns

When Trajan became emperor in AD 98, he inherited an unsatisfactory peace treaty that Domitian had arranged with the Dacians after the victory at Tapae in AD 88. The Romans paid indemnities and sent engineers to help the Dacian king Decebalus to build fortifications, which kept the peace for the time being. Domitian knew that another war was necessary, but he had first to deal with an attempted coup in Germany and he wanted to prepare for the next Dacian War in great detail. He was assassinated in AD 96 before he could embark on another war, and his successor Nerva did not pursue it.

Trajan, concerned about the amount of money leaving Rome for the coffers of the Dacian king, could not allow the growing power of Decebalus to threaten Roman interests, so in AD 101 he set off for war. The sources for the two major campaigns in Dacia are the pictorial narrative of Trajan's Column and the account written many years later by Dio. Reconciling the two is problematic, and equating both sources with the archaeological evidence is more difficult still.

The sources can only hint at the massive scale of preparations for the war. On Trajan's Column there are representations of stores dumps, baggage trains, pack animals, and all kinds of transport, but it cannot give any impression of the vast numbers of animals and vehicles that would be necessary to transport the men and equipment of nine legions or parts of legions and accompanying auxiliaries to the war zone. Nor do the sources illuminate how communications were guarded or where garrisons were left, or how individual columns under subordinate commanders operated independently on specific missions. Dio hints at this when he says that Lusius attacked in other areas while Trajan marched with the main army. This general was Lusius Quietus from North Africa, who served in the wars with his horsemen.

The first episode of the war as depicted on Trajan's Column concerns a crossing of the Danube on a bridge of boats. Once inside Dacian territory, the objective was probably the Dacian stronghold of Sarmizegethusa in the Carpathians, but no source states this specifically. According to Dio (68.8), the

This scene from Trajan's Column shows the Roman troops boarding ships. (Archivo Iconografico, S.A./Corbis)

Romans fought a battle near Tapae, but the site is not known. Dio merely states that many enemies were killed and Romans wounded, and when the bandages ran out, Trajan gave orders to tear up his clothes. This is a strange assertion, which implies that there were very many wounded and that someone had not prepared well enough by checking the medical stores. Trajan erected an altar on the site to the Roman dead.

Decebalus sent envoys but did not come in person even when a meeting was arranged with Roman officers, so Trajan pressed on, seizing the fortified heights on the route to the Dacian capital. In one of these mountain strongholds, the Romans found an eagle captured from the legions of Cornelius Fuscus, Domitian's Praetorian Prefect who had been defeated in the years before a third army had been raised under Tettius Julianus. The panels of Trajan's Column suggest that there was considerable military activity, gradually destroying the Dacian food supplies and fortified bases, until Decebalus agreed to terms imposed by the Romans. He agreed to surrender his artillery, dismantle his fortifications, hand over his prisoners and deserters, withdraw from conquered territory, and have the same friends and enemies as the Roman people. With the benefit of hindsight, Dio says that Decebalus had no intention of keeping to these terms but was biding his time until he could rebuild his strength. Trajan no doubt knew this too. He placed garrisons at strategic points, including Sarmizegethusa, celebrated a triumph, and took the title Dacicus. Significantly, he did not annex the territory, and while Decebalus was still alive there was always a threat that he would extend his power base and start to take in other lands once more.

By AD 104, Decebalus had rearmed and was intent on taking over the lands of his neighbors the Iazyges. In 105, Trajan embarked on another war, this time building a bridge to cross the Danube at Drobeta. Dio waxes lyrical about the dimensions of this bridge, with twenty piers of solid stone, rising to 150 feet above the foundations in the fast flowing river, with arches spanning a gap of 170 feet between each pier. The army marched into Dacia over this bridge, and Dio says that the war was conducted with prudence rather than haste. Trajan was a good administrator and organizer and had no intention of wrecking his chances of winning this war by neglectfulness or rashness. The scenes on Trajan's Column again illustrate battles and skirmishes but without enabling us to decide where and when they took place, and Dio adds little in the way of literary support. By AD 106 the war was over, ending with the suicide of Decebalus and the presentation of his head to the emperor by Tiberius Claudius Maximus. Dacia was turned into a province and garrisoned by two legions and auxiliary troops, not without profit to Rome since the emperor could now build up the treasury by means of the precious metals from the mines in the Carpathians. The Dacians had proved formidable opponents of the Romans, requiring four campaigns to subdue them—two fought under Domitian after the initial invasion of Moesia, and two under Trajan, resulting in the final annexation of the territory.

Trajan's next campaign was in the east, fought like most eastern wars over the control of Armenia and the threat of Parthian domination. Dio says that Trajan merely sought after glory. In fairness, however, no emperor ever solved the Parthian problem satisfactorily, though several of them tried. Trajan thought that the answer lay in annexing the northern part of Mesopotamia between the Euphrates and the Tigris Rivers, protecting the northeastern border of Syria, but on his accession in AD 117 Hadrian abandoned it. Other emperors tried again. Marcus Aurelius sent his Imperial colleague Lucius Verus to the east in the 160s. Verus did not take the field personally but through the agency of his generals, chiefly Avidius Cassius, Mesopotamia was taken over once again. The Parthians saw this as a threat, and so there could never be a true peace. The Emperor Septimius Severus, drawn to the east in the civil war against his rival Pescennius Niger, tackled the problem again.

## Severus and the Eastern Campaigns

In AD 193, the Emperor Pertinax was assassinated after a reign of less than three months. Several contenders arose to take over the Empire, among them the governor of Upper Pannonia, Septimius Severus, a native of Leptis Magna in North Africa. His rivals were Didius Julianus who succeeded in buying the Empire by bribing the Praetorians and persuading the Senate to accept him, and two other provincial governors, Clodius Albinus from Britain and Pescennius Niger in the east.

Severus marched on Rome, eliminated Didius, disbanded the Praetorians, and formed a new and larger guard of his own. He chose to march against Niger first, placing his closest associates in command of sections of his army to perform specific tasks. The campaigns occupied him from AD 194 to 196. Marius Maximus besieged Niger in Byzantium, while Tiberius Claudius Candidus was allotted the task of eliminating Niger's general Aemilianus who was watching the coastal towns and ports of Asia Minor. Candidus won the battles and captured Aemilianus, who was executed, but the remnants of Aemilianus's troops fled to Bithynia, where the city of Nicaea assisted them. Following after them, Candidus brought them to battle in a pass where the road from Nicaea to Cius ran by Lake Ascania. Some of his troops were on the heights, showering the Aemilian soldiers with their javelins, stones, and any missiles they could find, but the troops massed in the plain were assailed by arrows fired by the enemy bowmen who had seized boats and sailed on the lake to fire at Candidus's men. At some point Niger himself appeared, having escaped from Byzantium and gotten through the siege lines. His presence spurred on his troops, who started to push the Severans back until they broke and ran. Candidus leapt into action, seized hold of the standard bearers and swiveled them round to face the enemy, berating his troops for turning tail, and managed to rally the army to repulse Niger. The pursuit ended when night fell, and Niger reached the safety of the city of Nicaea.

After this battle, Candidus was sent into the province of Asia to operate on land and sea, harassing the enemies of Rome, and Severus appointed Publius Cornelius Anullinus to command the campaign army, to chase Niger into Galatia and Cappadocia. There were a few indecisive encounters, but the final battle was fought at Issus, where Alexander the Great defeated Darius. Anullinus and Niger faced each other in a pass where cliffs descended into the sea at one side, and forested mountains protected the other side. Anullinus sent a detachment under one of his officers, Valerianus, to find a way through the trees on the mountains to come up behind Niger. At first, the Severans were very hard pressed, to the extent that they held their shields above their heads to form the *testudo,* or tortoise, to enable them to close with the enemy. They would probably have been severely mauled but were saved by a tremendous thunderstorm that suddenly broke out "from a clear sky" (Dio 75.7.6), driving wind and rain into the faces of Niger's men but doing little harm to the Severans since the main force of the storm was at their backs. When Niger's troops started to break up and retreat, they suddenly met Valerianus coming up from their rear. They panicked, not knowing which way to turn, sandwiched between the two Severan generals. It was a complete rout. Niger fled to Antioch but was captured and killed. His remaining troops moved into Osroene and Mesopotamia, where they were pursued by the army under Severus, aiming for the city of Nisibis. On the way there, the soldiers suffered from lack of fresh water but would not drink what was on offer until Severus himself drank some of it. As Birley (1988) points out, Severus would be used to water from desert wells.

Like Caesar in Gaul, Severus sent several commanders to different locations to quell the enemy and the natives. Lateranus, Candidus, and Laetus were dispatched to devastate the lands of the tribesmen, and later the army was divided into three groups under Anullinus, Laetus, and Probus. Their objectives and the way in which they operated are not elucidated, but between them Severus and his generals brought peace for a while to the east. Severus installed his friends as governors of the provinces and the command of the legions, and departed to eliminate his western rival, Clodius Albinus.

In AD 197, Severus was back in the east. While he was absent in Gaul, the Parthians had attacked Mesopotamia and besieged Nisibis. Severus mounted another expedition, crossing the sea to Asia Minor with his family and his Praetorian Prefect Plautianus. The party moved to Syria where Severus marshaled his troops. He had raised three new legions, *I, II,* and *III Parthica,* perhaps for the first eastern campaign or at the end of it, but the date is no known. He left *II Parthica* at Albano near Rome and took the other two on his new expedition. The king of Armenia made peaceful overtures and offered help, and in return was recognized by the Romans; King Abgar of Edessa, installed by Severus in the previous campaign, sent money and soldiers.

The besieged city of Nisibis was relieved by Julius Laetus, and as Severus himself drew near, the Parthians retreated, so the first operations against them were successful. Not satisfied with this demonstration, Severus now determined to penetrate deep into Parthian territory. In his entourage was the brother of Vologaeses, the Parthian king, his presence indicative of the rift in the Parthian Royal household, and a factor in Severus's decision to mount the next campaign in AD 198. He retired to Syria to prepare. He had boats constructed to ferry some of his army down the Euphrates while the rest marched on land parallel to the river. Parthian resistance was nonexistent. When the Romans approached Babylon, they found it abandoned, and crossing from the Euphrates to the Tigris, they discovered that Seleucia was also empty of troops. Severus moved on to the capital, Ctesiphon, which was also given up without a fight. The Romans sacked it but did not occupy it, and made no attempt to annex the lands they had just overrun. Dio says that Severus had problems with supplies and had to return by a different route up the Tigris because all the food and fuel were used up on the way to Ctesiphon.

Severus's next project was to besiege the city of Hatra, which had given aid to Niger. Trajan had not succeeded in reducing this city, and Severus did no better. He had to draw off after losing many men and some of his siege engines. The soldiers began to grumble and lose faith, making relations between the men and the emperor somewhat strained. The Praetorian Prefect Plautianus added fuel to the flames and was probably the instrument behind the execution of Julius Laetus, who had served well in the previous eastern campaign, in Gaul, and in relieving Nisibis. He was far too popular, and the soldiers would not move unless he commanded them. He was executed before he could accumulate too much authority. Some time later another loyal officer, Tiberius Claudius Candidus, was also removed.

Since he had not managed to reduce Hatra the first time, Severus tried again, having prepared more thoroughly this time in laying in stores and having siege engines built by an engineer from Nicaea called Priscus. During the assault, the Romans broke through the outer defenses built of earth and were ready to attack the inner walls, but Severus called them off and the impetus was lost. The inhabitants of Hatra rebuilt the outer wall during the night. The Roman troops were furious, no doubt because the prospect of loot was snatched away. Birley (1988) suggests that Severus had achieved what he wanted—the submission of Barsemius, the ruler of Hatra. At any rate, the Romans moved off, and Severus eventually retired to Palestine, though perhaps not as precipitately as Dio suggests.

The campaign was not noted for its military success since the enemy had not put up much of a fight, but it resulted in the adjustment of boundaries and the creation of new provinces. Severus divided Syria into two provinces and strengthened the defenses of both. He annexed Osroene and moved the borders, adding part of it to the province of Mesopotamia, more or less reconstituting the old Trajanic province. Nisibis became the capital of Mesopotamia, which was garrisoned by the two new legions, *I* and *III Parthica*. For the time being Severus considered that he had solved the eastern problem. Short of conquering and annexing the whole of the Parthian Empire, which was hardly possible for the Romans, the creation of stable borders was the next best solution. The warlike Trajan had decided on almost the same plan, but his acquisitions were abandoned by Hadrian. Although Severus advertised to the Roman world that he had made a bulwark for Syria by annexing Mesopotamia and Osroene, critics were not so certain that it was such an advantage. Dio (epitomized by Xiphilinus, 75.3) complained that the provinces brought no profit but required vast expense to keep them peaceful, and what is more, the Romans were drawn into the wars of their new neighbors. This was the perpetual dilemma of the Roman Empire, wherever the boundaries lay.

Temple of Saturn and Triumphal Arch of Septimus Severus (right), Rome, Italy. (Library of Congress)

### REFERENCES AND FURTHER READING

Birley, Anthony R. 1988. *Septimius Severus: The African Emperor.* London: Routledge.

Campbell, J. Brian. 1984. *The Emperor and the Roman Army 31 BC–AD 235.* Oxford: Clarendon Press.

Clunn, Tony. 1999. *In Quest of the Lost Legions: The Varusschlacht.* London: Minerva Press.

Fuller, J.F.C. 1965. *Julius Caesar: Man, Soldier, Tyrant.* London: Eyre and Spottiswood.

Goldsworthy, Adrian K. 1996. *The Roman Army at War 100 BC–AD 180.* Oxford: Clarendon Press.

———. 2003a. *The Complete Roman Army.* London: Thames and Hudson.

———. 2003b. *In the Name of Rome: The Men Who Won the Roman Empire.* London: Weidenfeld and Nicolson.

Lepper, Frank, and Frere, Sheppard. 1988. *Trajan's Column.* Gloucestershire: Alan Sutton.

Seager, Robin. 1979. *Pompey: A Political Biography.* Oxford: Blackwell.

Shotter, David. 1992. *Tiberius Caesar.* London: Routledge.

Southern, Pat. 1998. *Mark Antony.* Stroud, Gloucestershire: Tempus Publishing.
———. 2001. *Julius Caesar.* Stroud, Gloucestershire: Tempus Publishing.
———. 2002. *Pompey the Great.* Stroud, Gloucestershire: Tempus Publishing.

CHAPTER 9

# Current Assessment

## MAJOR PROBLEMS IN THE STUDY
## OF THE ROMAN ARMY

The most serious problem in studying the Roman army is that the assembled evidence derives from widely dispersed parts of the Empire and from very different periods of time, and the synthesis of these individual pieces of evidence may possibly represent a somewhat distorted view of the whole. Although there is considerable information about the organization of the legions and auxiliary units of the Roman army, one of the simplest questions cannot be answered: no one can state categorically how many men there were in a legion or whether there was in fact a standard figure for all the legions all over the Empire at all times. For this reason, the numbers given in books on the Roman army vary between 5,000 and 6,000 men. These figures refer to paper strength, since probably no unit in the Empire maintained a constant unvarying complement throughout its life. The problem of legionary size becomes particularly acute for the Diocletianic legions, which may have been only 1,000 strong. Some scholars make a distinction between the older pre-Diocletianic legions and the new ones raised from the end of the third century onward. The question is not finally resolved even when archaeologists investigate a late Roman legionary fort that seems to have contained only 1,000 men, because it is possible that a legion could have been split up into smaller outposted units, with their headquarters stationed elsewhere.

The strength of auxiliary units is better documented, predominantly by papyrus evidence that reveals that the numbers of personnel varied from year to year. The major problem involved in the study of the auxiliaries is whether their pay was inferior or equal to that of the legionaries. It used to be accepted that there was a varying scale of pay for legionary cavalry, ordinary legionaries, auxiliary cavalry, and auxiliary infantry, but more recently it has been argued that there was little difference in pay scales (Alston, 1994; Speidel, 1992). These theories are based on sound evidence, but none of it is yet comprehensive enough or conclusive enough to be certain.

A fairly extensive picture of the day-to-day activities of the army can be pieced together from papyrological evidence and from the Vindolanda tablets, affording a glimpse into the enormously wide-ranging tasks of the peacetime army. The documents and letters from the eastern provinces, supplemented by those from Vindolanda, can also reveal much about the social interaction of the soldiers with the civilians, about the attitude of the military forces to the natives, and vice versa, the opinion of many civilians about the soldiers. With the passage of time, the distinctions between natives and troops was blurred by the recruitment of locals, but there was perhaps always a divide between the army and the provincials. As the pressures on the frontiers increased and the army units became less static, moving around the Empire to fight various wars, this divide may have increased. In the later Roman Empire, the appeals to the emperors for justice and the small-scale litigation in some of the provinces shows that the soldiers were oppressors and bullies. In Egypt, for example, a woman lamented that her son had gone to join the barbarians, by which she meant that he had joined the Roman army. The impression given by the current evidence may only represent the worst scenarios, without presenting the balancing information that the army was in general doing its job and was appreciated by the people it was supposed to protect. In modern life bad news is reported more often than good and makes more of an impression. Until documents come to light praising the army and individual soldiers, our view of its performance will remain somewhat derogatory.

Study of the Roman army at war has been the subject of several books examining either the whole history of Rome or limiting the study to the Republican army, the Imperial army, individual campaigns, or the lives and achievements of famous generals (Gilliver, 2000; Goldsworthy, 1996, 2003a, 2003b). Despite the wealth of Greek and Latin literature, only a handful of reliable sources inform us how the army operated in battle and on campaign. There were many military manuals in existence in Roman times, but they have not all survived; in any case they only deal with optimum practice and not reality. Conversely, the accounts of the historians that purport to deal with reality are always subject to misconceptions and distortions. Many generals wrote commentaries recording their campaigns, such as Suetonius Paullinus, Domitius Corbulo, and the Emperor Trajan, but we have only Julius Caesar's invaluable works with which to construct a picture of the army in wartime. In future years, it may be possible that one or two of these commentaries will come to light, perhaps as a result of a discovery such as the library at Herculaneum.

One of the most tantalizing features of the deployment of the army derives from the lack of knowledge of the emperors' aims and objectives. Most of the facts can be established as to where and against whom the army fought, but the purpose and the policy decisions behind the wars are not elucidated. Scholars speculate on how far Augustus originally intended to go in Germany, assuming that his objective was to reach the river Elbe and make a tidy frontier, but this is modern thinking superimposed on the ancient evidence of troop movements and siting of fortifications. Some historians think that Claudius invaded Britain purely for the military glory and that the acquisition of minerals and metals, slaves, and hides was simply a fortuitous adjunct to conquest and could have continued, as the geographer Strabo asserts, without the bother of administering the province. After twenty centuries, modern scholars cannot really hope to understand how the emperors conceptualized the Empire or what they wanted to gain from wars of conquest or retribution.

A major source of controversy arising from lack of knowledge of Roman Imperial policy revolves around the establishment and the maintenance of the frontiers. Luttwak (1976) summarizes Imperial strategy, and Mattern (1999) provides a fresh overview, but it cannot be proved one way or another whether there was an overall plan, continuously developed and amended to meet the various problems as they occurred, or whether there was only a reactive response tailored to each event. Hadrian closed off the Empire and put an end to the idea that territorial expansion could go on and on, unchecked except by arriving at distant oceans. He thereby incurred the displeasure of many of his subjects, some of whom equated expansion with opportunities for exploitation. Although there were some minor adjustments to the frontiers, the principle was never reversed. The greatest extent that the Empire ever reached was attained under Trajan, and immediately after his death, Hadrian abandoned some of the recent conquests. Occasionally, warlike emperors adjusted boundaries and added parts of outlying territory, but in general Roman expansion ceased in the second century AD. For some scholars, this represented stagnation and decline (Mann, 1974), despite the fact that the Empire carried on for three more centuries until the barbarian kingdoms were established in the west.

Study of the frontier works of the Empire naturally started with an examination of the remains—the stone wall of Hadrian and the turf wall of Antoninus Pius in Britain, the timber palisade and the earthworks in Germany, the stretches of stone walls and forts in Africa, and the various roads and lines of towers in Dacia and the east. The problems of dating the successive repairs and rebuilding have not been fully resolved, but much progress has been made. Yet, the lack of knowledge of policy and purpose still limits the study of the frontiers, which is continually complicated by the tendency to try to relate archaeological finds to established historical events, not always successfully. More recently, attention has turned to the functions of the frontiers, their impact on the inhabitants within and outside the provinces, and their social and economic aspects (Elton, 1996; Whittaker, 1994).

Study of the frontier works such as forts, fortlets, and the various towers also began with an examination of the physical remains, revealing considerable uniformity throughout the Empire, while the differences in design and execution could illuminate not only changing fashions, but the needs of the terrain, the nature of the enemy, and how the Romans perceived the threats posed by the peoples that they faced in different regions. Not all forts were attached to frontiers, so their functions perhaps differed in the hinterland and on the frontier itself, but groundplans and artifacts cannot tell the full story of how they worked. Nor is it possible to relate how the smaller installations functioned, or whether the milecastles of Hadrian's Wall and the Kleinkastelle of the German frontier housed soldiers whose prime duty was to patrol, either along the frontier line or beyond it. The so-called watch towers or signal towers are even more problematic because no contemporary source explains what they were designed to do. The fact that descriptive names such as signal towers and watch towers are assigned to these installations signifies the lack of certainty about their purpose. Consequently, modern scholars can argue that they were used to send messages along the frontiers, or that the soldiers in the towers simply watched for activity and reported on it. But in both cases it cannot be known what was communicated to whom, nor exactly how it was communicated, and what happened after the message had been received.

The examination of forts and fortresses extended to the areas outside the installations, to the civil settlements and surrounding fields, but only small amounts of evidence allow us to reconstruct the lives of the inhabitants of these settlements and the way in which they interacted with the military authorities. Archaeological examination of the surroundings of a fort are hampered by lack of upstanding remains and in most cases by the fact that the fort sites are now covered by modern cities and towns. Thus, only a small section of a fort or its *vicus,* cemetery, and agricultural lands can be examined. It is known that meadows and cultivated fields were laid out around a fort, but how they were used has not been fully established. One of the most intriguing factors is that we do not know where the Romans kept their cavalry horses and pack animals, since picket lines, corrals, and compounds do not show up well in archaeological terms (Dixon and Southern, 1992; Wells, 1977).

## FURTHER DIRECTIONS OF RESEARCH ON THE ROMAN ARMY

Students of the Roman Empire owe a great debt to the scholars of the nineteenth century who embarked on the prodigious tasks of assembling and recording the corpus of inscriptions and sculpture from all around the Empire, tasks that ran on into the twentieth and twenty-first centuries and are still ongoing. In the late nineteenth century, Hermann Dessau published an assemblage of a wide selection of inscriptional evidence from all over the Empire (*ILS*), usefully classified into subject groupings so that the military material can be sampled all together. In the mid-twentieth century, all the inscriptions of Roman Britain were published (*RIB*), arranged by place of origin so that the military material is identifiable by site.

Certain areas of the Empire have been very well covered while the others lag behind, so there is a need for further collection and publication for those provinces that have not been studied as extensively as Britain, Germany, and some of the Danube regions. Another pressing need, not foreseen by the scholars who reproduced the texts of inscriptions in the original Latin and Greek, is for translations of these vast collections, for the benefit of the majority of students who have no knowledge of these ancient languages. The optimum circumstance would be a collection with not only translations but also detailed commentaries about the context and meaning of inscriptions. Some of this work has been done, to quote a few examples such as Campbell (1994) who collected the major source material for the Roman army; Ireland (1986) who brought together all the sources including literary, epigraphic, and numismatic evidence, for the study of Roman Britain; Dodgeon and Lieu (1991) who document the eastern frontier in the third century; and Loriot and Nony (1997) who put together the sources for the crisis of the Empire beginning with the assassination of Severus Alexander. The current problem is that publication still tends to be devoted either to reproduction of the original texts or to translations of the sources. What is really needed, however, is a combination of both, like the parallel texts of the Loeb editions of Greek and Roman works, where the translator not only translates but establishes a standard text with notes, some of them quite detailed, as in Whittaker's translation of Herodian. A translation of an inscription, however carefully done, is in part an interpretation, and it would be convenient to see the original as well, for use with a dictionary if not with prior knowledge of the original language.

Some areas of research for the Roman army can only be taken forward by means of extensive excavation and survey, with the results collated and synthesized over a long period of time and throughout several regions of the Empire. Increased study of the different types of military installations all over the Empire would make it possible to build up a comprehensive idea of how the occupants of the fortresses, forts, and fortlets lived and worked, and would serve to highlight the developments in the army over time. The forts of the later third century reflect the changed priorities of the army, with more cramped accommodation and the greatly increased strength of the defenses compared to those of earlier periods. It would be helpful to establish when and where the innovations started, in response to which events, all of which is probably impossible to achieve by archaeological means alone.

Archaeology is not the only means of studying forts and frontiers. Reconstruction of buildings, regarded with great circumspection by some scholars, not only serves to interest the general public and tourists, but highlights the technology behind Roman construction, bringing architects and builders face to face with the problems that the Romans encountered and overcame. In order to bring Roman buildings to life, either by drawing, painting, model making, computer-generated images, or full-scale reconstruction, it is necessary to make educated guesses and sometimes make mistakes. However, the efforts of artists and builders in this enterprise can only be praised and encouraged, provided that the results are not advertised for all time as the Truth. Each generation needs to make additions and subtractions to their knowledge, and questions must be constantly asked. For instance, most reconstructions of the buildings inside forts are represented as single-storey constructions, but it has been questioned whether they may have had two or more storeys, with a ladder to reach the upper floors that would not leave any archaeological traces.

The same principles apply to the various reenactment societies that have grown up in the past decades, whose enthusiasm in reproducing Roman armor and equipment is related to academic research and refined by experiment. They have found out, among other useful things, where and how the helmets, boots, and belts hurt and cease to be comfortable, and what can be done to improve them. Once again, in their attempts to design authentic material, mistakes may be made, but this does not detract from the contribution that reenactment societies can make to the study of the army because only practical experiments can show how effective armor and weapons could be.

One development of recent decades is the formation of international congresses to study particular aspects of the Roman army. The frontier congresses began in Durham just after World War II and still contribute greatly to the study of the legions and auxiliary units and their forts, as well as many other aspects of the frontiers such as civil-military relations, the supply system, and military communications. Another series of international conferences deals with the production and distribution of arms, armor, and equipment. Occasional seminars and conferences are arranged to discuss particular aspects of the army. All these meetings of minds advance knowledge, reexamine accepted norms, and raise further questions for research.

Another welcome development that needs to be taken much further is that efforts have been made to overcome the mutual exclusivity of the study of the Roman army of the late Republic and early Empire on the one hand and that of the Iron Age tribes of the northern and western areas of the Empire on the other. Shared knowledge in each of these specialist fields can only be beneficial, since the two different societies that met on the frontiers of the Empire interacted and influenced each other and produced adaptive changes in both realms. The idea of frontiers as exclusive and impermeable barriers has probably been made redundant, but there is some way to go in understanding the interaction of Romans, provincials, and non-Romans. Similarly, in the eastern provinces, study of the natives and the Romans has begun to meld to a greater degree than hitherto, but access to some of the erstwhile provinces can be difficult or restricted for western archaeologists and historians.

The ethnicity of Roman soldiers has received more attention in the last few years, but more work needs to be done on the origins of the soldiers and the recruitment patterns of the legions and auxiliary units on the basis of the thousands of inscriptions and archaeological finds from various forts. The so-called irregular troops, the *numeri,* have been surveyed (Southern, 1989), but more work needs to be done on the date of their creation, their functions, and the great diversity of units with the title *numerus,* in particular those of the later Empire as listed in the *Notitia Dignitatum.*

Many of the directions for further research require the impossible or near impossible: more extensive excavation, the discovery of more records, inscriptions, papyri, or wooden tablets. Most of all, scholars need informed speculation, lateral thinking, and reexamination of the existing evidence and received opinion. Occasional discoveries that change opinions or simply add to knowledge are not completely out of the question, which means that the fascination of investigating the Roman army will never die, and the definitive study will never be written. We can simply make interim statements, with updates from time to time.

### REFERENCES AND FURTHER READING

Alston, Richard. 1994. "Roman military pay from Caesar to Diocletian." *Journal of Roman Studies* 84, 111–123.

Campbell, J. Brian. 1984. *The Emperor and the Roman Army 31 BC–AD 235.* Oxford: Clarendon Press.

———. 1994. *The Roman Army 31 BC–AD 337: A Sourcebook.* London: Routledge.

Dixon, Karen R., and Southern, P. 1992. *The Roman Cavalry from the First to the Third Century.* London: Batsford.

Dodgeon, M.H., and Lieu, S.N.C. 1991. *The Roman Eastern Frontier and the Persian Wars (AD 226–363): A Documentary History.* London: Routledge.

Elton, Hugh. 1996. *Frontiers of the Roman Empire.* London: Batsford.

Gilliver, Catherine M. 2000. *The Roman Art of War.* Stroud, Gloucestershire: Tempus Publishing.

Goldsworthy, Adrian K. 1996. *The Roman Army at War 100 BC–AD 200.* Oxford: Clarendon Press.

———. 2003a. *The Complete Roman Army.* London: Thames and Hudson.

———. 2003b. *In the Name of Rome: The Men Who Won the Roman Empire.* London: Weidenfeld and Nicolson.

Ireland, S. 1986. *Roman Britain: A Sourcebook.* London: Croom Helm.

Loriot, Xavier, and Nony, D. 1997. *La Crise de L'Empire Romain 235–285.* Paris: Armand Colin.

Luttwak, Edward. 1976. *The Grand Strategy of the Roman Empire from the First Century AD to the Third.* Baltimore, MD: Johns Hopkins University Press. Reprinted London: Weidenfeld and Nicolson, 1999.

Mann, John C. 1974. "The frontiers of the Principate." *ANRW* II.I, 508–531.

Mattern, Susan P. 1999. *Rome and the Enemy: Imperial Strategy in the Principate.* Berkeley: University of California Press.

Southern, Pat. 1989. "The *Numeri* of the Imperial Roman army." *Britannia* 20, 80–140.

Speidel, M.A. 1992. "Roman army pay scales." *Journal of Roman Studies* 82, 87–106.

Wells, Colin M. 1977. "Where did they put the horses? Cavalry stables in the early Empire." In J. Fitz (ed.), *Limes: Akten des XI Internationalen Limeskongresses, Szekesfehevar,* 1976. Budapest: Akademiai Kiado, 659–665.

Whittaker, C.R. 1994. *Frontiers of the Roman Empire: A Social and Economic Study.* Baltimore, MD: Johns Hopkins University Press.

# APPENDIX

# Rank Structure in the Roman Army

## OFFICERS

### *Legatus Augusti pro praetore*

Commander in chief of all the armed forces in a single province. A senator who had reached the consulship, with experience of civil administration posts and army commands in different parts of the Empire. Responsible for the civil government and the defense of his province, commanding up to four legions, and several auxiliary units. Promotion and next post: the governor of a garrisoned province was at the zenith of his career. He could hope for a second consulship and a post as governor of a larger province such as Britain or Syria, the two most prestigious appointments of the Empire.

## LEGIONS

### *Legatus legionis*

Commander of a legion. A senator who had served as a military tribune and had experience of civil posts. Legionary legates were appointed by the emperor and usually served for about three years, commanding 5,000 to 6,000 men. Promotion and next post: as propraetor, or governor of an unarmed province for two or three years, with predominantly civilian administrative duties, then election to the consulship.

### *Tribunus laticlavius*

"Broad stripe" tribune, second in command of a legion. A young man of the senatorial class, but not yet a senator, in his first important military post, usually held for one year, but some officers served longer; for instance, the future Emperor Trajan remained in this post for a few years. Promotion and next post: enrollment in the Senate, and a succession of junior magistracies such as the quaestorship, a posting to different provinces performing mostly civil administration, and then a post as legionary legate, granted by the emperor.

### Praefectus Castrorum

Camp prefect, third in command of a legion. The camp prefect was from the equestrian order, an experienced officer, a long-serving centurion who may have been appointed directly to the army as a centurion, who then worked his way up to the post of *primus pilus,* the first centurion of the first cohort of a legion, or much more rarely he may have risen from the ranks to reach the post of centurion and acquired equestrian status. Some camp prefects had served as *primus pilus* twice, in different legions. Promotion and next post: a few camp prefects gained further promotion, sometimes going on to posts in the Praetorian Guard, and some of them were appointed as procurators in the provinces.

### Tribunus angusticlavius

"Narrow stripe" tribune, five in each legion. Equestrian officer with some previous military experience, usually as a *praefectus* commanding a quingenary auxiliary cohort. The duties of the *tribuni angusticlavii* varied, mostly comprising staff work, but they could take command of detachments of legionaries from time to time, to perform specific tasks or to convey groups of men to selected destinations. Promotion and next post: the most common posting was as *praefectus* of a quingenary auxiliary *ala.* The more prestigious posts as tribunes of the milliary cohorts and *alae* were reserved for the successful few who wished to pursue a military career. The milliary cohorts were fewer in number than other auxiliary units, and there was never more than one milliary *ala* in any province, so the number of legionary tribunes and auxiliary prefects exceeded the number of posts.

## OTHER RANKS

### Centurions

The *primus pilus* was the senior centurion of a legion, being the first centurion of the first cohort, which usually contained five double-strength centuries of

160 men. The five centurions were ranked in order with titles that reflected the organization of the Republican army: *primus pilus, princeps, princeps hastatus, hastatus,* and *hastatus posterior.*

The remaining nine cohorts each contained six centuries, with 80 men per century, making a total of 480 men in each cohort. Within each individual cohort, the centurions ranked in seniority as illustrated by their titles, again reflecting the Republican army: *pilus prior, pilus posterior, princeps prior, princeps posterior, hastatus prior, hastatus posterior.* It is disputed whether there was a strict gradation of posts, starting with the centurions of the tenth cohort as the most junior, rising in seniority to those of the second cohort and then the prestigious first cohort, or whether the centurions of all the cohorts were regarded as equal in rank. Promotion was usually on merit to the more senior cohorts, but could on occasion be granted in dramatic circumstances, as happened to Cassius Scaeva in one of Caesar's legions, promoted immediately after a battle from centurion of the eighth cohort to *primus pilus.*

## Junior Officers

The officers below the centurions were called *principales* and received either double pay (*duplicarii*) or one and a half pay (*sesquiplicarii*). The *aquilifer,* who carried the eagle standard of the legion, and the *imaginifer,* who carried the image of the emperor, ranked as officers. The first three junior officers in each century were the *optio* (orderly, second in command to a centurion), *signifer* (standard bearer, carrying the *signum* of the century), and *tesserarius* (a clerical post, keeper of the watchword). There were also junior officer posts such as the *librarius* and *cornicularius* who worked as headquarters staff, keeping unit administrative and financial records and dealing with the clerical work of the unit. A combination of these posts was usually held in succession but not necessarily in the same order, so there is not enough evidence to discern a rank structure that applied to all legions. The *optiones* could aspire to a centurion's post, as indicated in the title *optio ad spem ordinis.*

## AUXILIARY UNITS

### *Tribunus* (Tribune) of an *Ala Milliaria*

An equestrian in the highest military post in the auxiliary arm, commanding 1,000 cavalry. An officer of this rank would have served as prefect of a quingenary unit, then as *tribunus angusticlavius* in a legion, or on occasion in more than one legion. It was common to serve as prefect of a 500-strong cavalry unit after leaving the legion. Only a few of the equestrian officers would ever reach this post in a milliary *ala,* and with luck and opportunity he could go on to higher equestrian posts, culminating in one of the great Prefectures in Rome.

### *Tribunus* (Tribune) of a *Cohors Milliaria*

Equestrian commander of a 1,000-strong infantry unit, on the fourth rung of his military career (*quarta militia*). He would have served as commander of a quingenary auxiliary infantry cohort, then as *tribunus angusticlavius* in a legion and perhaps as a prefect of a 500-strong cavalry *ala.* As commander of a milliary cohort, he would rank below the tribune of a milliary *ala.*

### *Praefectus Alae,* Prefect of a Quingenary *ala*

Equestrian officer on the third rung of his career path, commanding 500 cavalry and serving for three to four years. He would usually have started out as a prefect of a quingenary infantry cohort and then served in a legion as *tribunus angusticlavius.* His next post would be as commander of a milliary unit, or since there were never enough of these posts to go around, he might choose to take up civil administrative posts.

### *Praefectus Cohortis,* Prefect of a Qingenary Cohort

This post was the most junior of the equestrian career opportunities, commanding 500 auxiliary infantry for two or three years before going on to serve as one of five *tribuni angusticlavii* in a legion.

### Junior Officers

The auxiliary infantry units were divided into centuries, as were the legions, and each century was commanded by a centurion in charge of eighty men. Very little is known about the rank structure below the auxiliary centurionate, except that *duplicarii* and *sesquiplicarii* are attested, so it is assumed that the junior officers were modeled on those of the legions.

In the cavalry units, the troops were divided into *turmae* of about thirty men with two officers in command, the chief one being the *decurion.*

# GLOSSARY

*ACETUM:* sour wine

*AD SIGNA:* deduction from military pay to the burial club

AEDILE: city magistrate originally responsible for supervision of the *aedes,* or the temples of the plebs. During the Republic there were two aediles subordinate to the tribunes of the plebs (*TRIBUNUS PLEBIS*), and later two more aediles were elected from among the patricians (*aediles curules*). In the Empire the main duties of the aediles were caring for the city, keeping public order, and attending to the water supply and markets. They were also in charge of the public games (*ludi*) until Augustus transferred this duty to the praetors. All the municipalities of the Empire employed elected aediles fulfilling the same purposes as those in Rome.

*AERARIUM MILITARE:* military treasury set up by Augustus in AD 6 to provide pensions for veterans

*ALA* (plural *ALAE*): a military division, squadron, or wing of an army

*ALA MILLIARIA:* auxiliary cavalry unit of approximately 1,000 men

*ALA QUINGENARIA:* auxiliary cavalry unit of approximately 500 men

*ANNONA MILITARIS:* provisions for the army

*AQUILA:* eagle standard of a legion, instituted by Marius in the first century BC

*AQUILIFER:* standard bearer carrying the eagle standard of the legion

*ARMILLAE:* decorative armbands awarded for distinguished service

*ARTABA:* Egyptian corn measure, one-third of a Roman *modius* (q.v.)

*AS:* lowest denomination Roman coin, made of bronze

*AUCTORITAS:* a measure of the reputation and social and political standing of Roman senators and politicians. The literal translation "authority" does not convey its true meaning. *Auctoritas* could be earned and increased by political or military achievements and lost after disgraceful conduct.

*AUREUS:* Roman gold coin, worth twenty-five *DENARII*

*AUXILIA:* literally "help troops," the term used by the Romans to describe the units recruited from non-Romans. They were generally organized as *ALAE* and *COHORTES* during the Empire.

*BALLISTA:* artillery engine firing either arrows or stone projectiles

*BENEFICIARIUS* (plural *BENEFICIARII*): the *beneficiarii* were usually legionaries with long experience, on the staff of a provincial governor and stationed at important places on the frontiers or within the provinces. They may have undertaken police work and perhaps were responsible for intelligence gathering.

*BUCELLARII:* literally "biscuit eaters," used of the private armies formed from the retainers of the powerful landowners of the late Empire

BUCINA: horn sounded to change the guard or used during military ceremonies

BUCINATOR: hornblower

BURGUS: watch tower or fortified landing place on a river

CAMPIDOCTOR: drill-instructor

CANABAE: the civilian settlement outside a legionary fortress. *See also* VICUS

CAPITATIO: a poll tax

CAPITUM: fodder; in the later Empire when payments to the soldiers were made partly in kind, *capitum* and *annona* were the terms used for food for the horses and the men

CAPSA: bandage box; alternatively a box for storing documents

CAPSARIUS: medical assistants

CARROBALLISTA: light field artillery BALLISTA carried on a cart usually pulled by mules

CATAPHRACTARII: heavy armored cavalry, perhaps armed with lance and shield

CENTURIA: a century, or a division of a cohort. Nominally a *centuria* consisted of 100 men, but, in practice, a *centuria* typically consisted of 80 men.

CENTURION: commander of a century, or CENTURIA

CERVESA: Celtic beer

CIBARIUM: non-grain foodstuffs, but applied to the food supply in general

CINGULUM: military belt of leather, with metal attachments for the sword and other equipment. The use of this term was not common until the third century AD.

CLIBANARII: slang for heavy armored cavalry. It is derived from *clibanus,* meaning oven. It is not certain whether these troops were the same as CATAPHRACTARII or whether they were armed and fought in a different way.

COHORS (plural COHORTES): a cohort. A division of a legion containing six centuries, or an auxiliary infantry unit consisting of either 500 (*quingenaria*) or 1,000 (*milliaria*) men.

COHORS EQUITATA: part-mounted auxiliary unit, consisting of either 500 strong (*quingenaria*) or 1,000 (*milliaria*) men

COLONUS: tenant of a landowner

COMES (plural COMITES): the entourage of an emperor consisted of his friends (*comites*) on an unofficial basis at first, but Constantine gave the title *Comes,* usually translated as count, to his military commanders and provincial governors. There was originally no connotation of rank in the title, but with the passage of time three grades were established called *ordinis primi, secundi,* and *tertii.*

COMITATENSES: collective name for the units of the late Roman field army, comprising cavalry and infantry

COMITATUS: derived from COMES, *comitatus,* by the fourth century, denoted the field army

COMMEATUS: a term used to describe either the food supplies or periods of leave from the Roman army

CONSUL: senior magistrates of the Republic. Consuls were elected annually in pairs and were responsible for civil duties and command of the armies. During the Empire the consuls were still elected annually, but they had reduced military responsibilites and were subordinate to the emperor.

*CONSTITUTIO ANTONINIANA:* act passed by Caracalla in AD 212, making all freeborn inhabitants of the Roman Empire citizens

*CONSUL ORDINARIUS:* during the Empire there were often more than two consuls in the year. The *ordinarii* were the officially elected consuls, who might hold office for a month or two. They then gave way to the *CONSULES SUFFECTI.* The *ordinarii* were the eponymous consuls, giving their name to the year.

*CONSUL SUFFECTUS:* the suffect consuls were those who held office after the *ordinarii,* gaining experience and rank before going on to other appointments

*CONTARII:* cavalry units of the later Roman Empire, carrying the *CONTUS*

*CONTUBERNIUM:* a tent party or the soldiers sharing one barrack room, normally consisting of eight men

*CONTUS* : a long, two-handed lance, used by the *CONTARII*

*CORNICEN:* hornblower playing the *CORNU*

*CORNICULARIUS:* clerical assistant, adjutant to a senior officer, or attached to the provincial governor's staff

*CORNU:* large horn, curved around the hornblower's body and held by a cross piece

*CUIRASS:* armor protecting the upper body. The Roman army used several types, including mail, plate, or scale. *See also entries under LORICA*

*CUISSE:* armor usually used by cavalrymen to protect the thighs

*CUNEUS:* wedge shaped battle formation. During the late Empire the term was used to describe cavalry units.

*CURIALES:* members of the city councils

*CUSTOS ARMARUM:* literally guard of the arms and armor

*DECURIO:* cavalry officer commanding a *TURMA*

*DENARIUS* (plural *DENARII*): Roman silver coin worth four *SESTERTII*

*DILECTUS:* the levy, and used of recruitment generally, from the verb *diligere,* meaning to value or favor

*DIOCESE:* administrative grouping of several provinces, instituted by Diocletian in the late second or early third century AD

*DIPLOMA:* literally, in Latin, a letter folded in two; used by modern scholars to describe the pair of bronze tablets issued to discharged auxiliaries and the men of the fleets—not the term that the soldiers would have used for the tablets

*DONA MILITARIA:* military decorations

*DRACO:* dragon standard, perhaps introduced into the army by the Sarmatians, tribesmen of the Danube area

*DRACONARIUS:* standard bearer carrying the *DRACO*

*DROMEDARIUS:* camel rider

*DUPLICARIUS:* soldier on double pay; second in command of a cavalry *TURMA*

*DUX* (plural *DUCES*): literally, leader; the term used for equestrian military officers in command of troops in the frontier regions, usually with the title *dux limitis.* Their commands sometimes covered more than one province. *Duces* were raised to senatorial status by Valentinian in the fourth century AD.

*EQUITES LEGIONIS:* cavalry of a legion, initially thought to number 120 men but increased by the Emperor Gallienus to over 700 men in the mid-third century AD

*EQUITES SINGULARES:* cavalry men usually seconded from the *ALAE,* acting as bodyguards to a provincial governor, usually in units 500 strong. The *equites singulares Augusti* were the cavalrymen guarding the emperor.

*EXPLORATORES:* scouts; initially individuals or small groups of men sent out to reconnoitre, later specific units

*FABRICA:* workshop

*FOEDERATI:* literally those who are allied in war; derived from *foedus,* a treaty, and denoting troops raised according to the terms of a treaty. To be distinguished from the sixth century *foederati,* which were regular troops.

*FRUMENTUM:* grain, but often used of the food supply in general

*GENTILES:* non-Romans; applied to free tribes beyond the frontiers and also tribesmen settled within the Empire

*GLADIUS:* short thrusting sword, probably originating in Spain. It was used by the Roman army from the third century BC to the third century AD.

*GREAVE:* leg armor, usually of metal, covering the lower leg from knee to ankle

*HASTA:* general term for spear, covering a variety of sizes and types

*HIBERNA:* winter quarters

*HIPPIKA GYMNASIA:* cavalry tournament of the Imperial period in which the men and the horses displayed their skill and expertise. They typically wore highly decorated clothing and equipment.

*HONESTA MISSIO:* honorable discharge from the Roman army

*HORREA:* granaries

*IMAGINIFER:* bearer of the *imago,* or image of the emperor

*IMMUNES:* soldiers exempt from fatigues because they performed special tasks

*IMPEDIMENTA:* the baggage train

*IN NUMEROS REFERRE:* phrase used for entering the names of recruits in the military records

*INTERVALLUM:* space between the rampart of a Roman fort or camp and the internal buildings, or tents

*IUGUM:* a unit of land for tax purposes, not always a standard measure since the type of land and the crops grown were taken into consideration by the assessors

*IUMENTA:* baggage animals, specifically mules

*LAETI:* tribesmen settled by treaty inside the Empire, with obligations to provide men for the army

*LEGION:* the term *legio* originally meant the choosing, or the levy, and was eventually applied to the main unit of the Roman army. Around 5,000 strong, the legion was an infantry unit but also contained some cavalry. Legions of the late Empire were smaller, newly raised units being only about 1,000 strong.

*LIMES:* frontier

*LIMITANEI:* frontier troops of the late Roman army

*LORICA HAMATA:* mail armor made from iron rings interlinked

*LORICA SEGMENTATA:* armor made from overlapping metal plates

*LORICA SQUAMATA:* scale armor

*MAGISTER EQUITUM:* master of horse; in the Republic this title was given to the second in command to a Dictator; in the late Roman army it was an important military post in command of the cavalry units

*MAGISTER MILITUM:* master of the soldiers, i.e., the whole army in the late Roman period

*MAGISTER OFFICIORUM:* late Roman head of the secretarial offices

*MAGISTER PEDITUM:* master of the infantry of the late Roman army

MANIPLE: a unit of the Republican army consisting of two centuries

*MEDICUS:* doctor

*MEDIMNUS:* Greek measure for grain used by Polybius; estimates of modern equivalents vary considerably

*MODIUS:* Roman corn measure

*NUMERUS* (plural *NUMERI*): meaning "unit" in a very general sense, but from the late first or early second century applied to small, so-called ethnic units commonly found on the German and Dacian frontiers and in Africa

*OPTIO:* second in command to a *CENTURION*

*PAENULA:* soldier's cloak, something like a duffel coat with a hood

*PALUDAMENTUM:* officer's cloak worn around the shoulders with the end draped over the left arm

*PHALERAE:* military decorations worn on the breastplate

*PILUM:* missile weapon used by legionaries consisting of a long thin metal shank with a pyramidal tip, attached to a wooden shaft. There were various different sizes and types of *pila.*

*PRAEFECTUS:* prefect, a title given to several different officials and military officers; most commonly a commander of an auxiliary *ALA* or cohort

*PRAEFECTUS CASTRORUM:* camp prefect, third in command of a legion during the Empire

*PRAEIURATIO:* first stage of the military oath (*SACRAMENTUM*) in which the first man repeated the entire oath and the rest declared "the same for me" (*idem in me*)

*PRAEPOSITUS:* title given to an officer temporarily in command of troops, such as the *NUMERI* of the German and Dacian frontiers, or vexillations of troops brought together for a war. It is not strictly a rank, and soldiers of different grades could be appointed as *praepositi* for very varied tasks of high or low importance.

*PRAESES* (plural *PRAESIDES*): provincial governor of equestrian rank, common from Severan times onward

*PRAETENTURA:* part of a Roman fort in front of the headquarters (*PRINCIPIA*), as opposed to the area behind it known as the *retentura*

*PRAETOR:* the praetorship had a long history. Originally the praetors were the chief magistrates in early Republican Rome but were eventually superceded by the consuls. When the consuls were absent the praetor was in charge of the courts, acted as president of the Senate, and had the right to command armies.

*PRAETORIUM:* commanding officer's house in a Roman fort, usually with rooms arranged around a courtyard, to house his family and servants

*PRATA:* literally, meadow. In the military context this area was probably where the unit's animals were grazed around a fort.

*PRIMUS PILUS:* the most senior CENTURION in a legion, commanding the first century of the first cohort

*PRINCIPIA:* headquarters of a Roman fort where the standards were laid up and the administrative offices were situated

*PROBATIO:* preliminary examination of recruits and horses for the army

*PROTECTORES:* a title used by Gallienus for his military entourage, not simply a bodyguard, but perhaps the foundation of a staff college formed from officers loyal to the emperor

*PSEUDO-COMITATENSES:* late Roman troops taken from the LIMITANEI or frontier armies to serve in the field army

*PTERUGES:* leather straps attached to armor

*QUAESTOR:* originally the lowest ranking magistrates of the Republic appointed to assist the consuls in financial matters. The office was held by young men at the start of their career before they had entered the Senate. As the Empire expanded more quaestors were created to deal with provincial administration. Quaestors acted as deputies to consular governors and could hold commands in the army. Sometimes in modern versions of ancient works, quaestor is translated as quartermaster, which is not strictly accurate.

*RIPENSES:* troops serving on river frontiers in the late Roman army

*SACELLUM:* chapel of the standards in the headquarters of a Roman fort

*SACRAMENTUM:* the military oath of obedience and loyalty to the emperor; during the Republic soldiers swore to obey their commanders, usually the consuls

*SAGITTARIUS:* archer

*SAGUM:* cloak worn by soldiers

*SCHOLA:* late Roman cavalry guard unit; *scholae palatinae* were the emperor's guard

*SESQUIPLICARIUS:* soldier on one and a half times normal pay; third in command of a cavalry TURMA

*SESTERTIUS:* Roman silver coin; four *sestertii* equalled one DENARIUS

*SIGNIFER:* standard bearer

*SIGNUM:* military standard of an individual century, consisting of various metal emblems on a pole, frequently topped by a hand with the palm facing forward

*SINGULARES:* bodyguards of various Roman officers, chosen from their original units, either cavalry or infantry. *Equites* and *pedites singulares consularis* formed the guard of a provincial governor, chosen from the units in the province and *equites singulares Augusti* formed the bodyguard of the emperor, chosen from units all over the Empire.

*SPATHA:* long sword, used by infantry and cavalry from the second century AD onward, and predominantly by the cavalry of the late Roman army

*STIPENDIUM:* military pay, also applied to a period of service

*TERRITORIUM:* in the military context, land belonging to the army marked by boundary stones and perhaps used to grow crops

*TESTUDO:* literally tortoise or turtle, a formation where soldiers raised their shields above their heads and overlapped them at the front and the sides to advance in almost complete protection.

*TIRO* (plural *TIRONES*): recruit

*TRIBUNUS PLEBIS:* officials drawn from the plebeian classes (plebs) to represent their interests at meetings of the Senate. Tribunes were allowed to veto any proposals made by senators if they were considered detrimental to the plebs.

TRIUMPH: a triumph was granted by the Senate to victorious generals, who valued this opportunity to show off their captives and the spoils of war by processing along the Via Sacra in Rome to the Temple of Jupiter. The *triumphator* rode in a chariot with his face painted red. Beside the *triumphator* stood a slave constantly reminding him that he was mortal. The *triumphator* was then supposed to approach the temple on his knees to dedicate the spoils. Augustus recognized the inflammatory nature of the triumph and took steps to limit it to members of the Imperial family. Other generals were denied the procession and were granted triumphal ornaments instead (*ornamenta triumphalia*).

*TUBA:* a long straight trumpet

*TUBICEN:* soldier who blew the *TUBA* to transmit signals

*TURMA:* smallest unit of an *ALA* or the mounted contingent of a *COHORS EQUITATA*, commanded by a *DECURIO* and probably containing thirty-two men

*VALETUDINARIUM:* hospital

*VELITES:* light-armed infantry of the Republican army

*VETERINARIUS:* veterinarian, used for civilian practitioners as well as soldiers; also listed as *medicus veterinarius*

*VEXILLARIUS:* bearer of the *VEXILLUM*

*VEXILLATIO:* a detachment of troops, often drawn from different units to fulfill a temporary purpose

*VEXILLATIONES:* late Roman cavalry units, possibly instituted by Gallienus. Their strength is disputed, perhaps consisting of 500 men, but some scholars argue for about 1,000.

*VEXILLUM:* military standard of fringed cloth, usually red or purple, hung from a cross bar on a lance

*VIATICUM:* traveling money, given to new recruits who had passed their *PROBATIO* to help them on the journey to the units to which they had been assigned

*VICARIUS:* governor of a *DIOCESE,* answerable to the Praetorian Prefects

*VICUS:* a rural village or an area within a town. In the military context it refers to the civilian settlement outside a Roman auxiliary fort. *See also* CANABAE

*VIGILES:* the fire brigade of the city of Rome, organized in military fashion by Augustus

# BIBLIOGRAPHY

## ABBREVIATIONS

*AE*          *Année Epigraphique*

*ANRW*        *Aufstieg und Niedergang der Römischen Welt.* Ed. H. Temporini. Berlin: de
              Gruyter.

*BAR*         British Archaeological Reports

*BJ*          *Bonner Jahrbücher*

*BMC*         *Coins of the Roman Empire in the British Museum*

*BRGK*        *Bericht der Römisch-Germanisch Kommission*

*CIL*         *Corpus Inscriptionum Latinarum*

*CJ*          *Codex Justiniani*

*Class. Jnl.* *Classical Journal*

*Cod. Th.*    *Codex Theodosianus=The Theodosian Code and Novels and the Sirmondian
              Constitutions.* Translated by C. Pharr. New York: Greenwood Press.

*Ep. Stud.*   *Epigraphische Studien*

*HA*          *Historia Augusta = Scriptores Historiae Augustae*

*IGR*         *Inscriptiones Graecae ad Res Romanas Pertinentes.* Paris: Leroux,
              1902–1927.

*ILS*         *Inscriptiones Latinae Selectae.* Ed. H. Dessau. Berlin. 3 vols.

*JRA*         *Journal of Roman Archaeology*

*JRMES*       *Journal of Roman Military Equipment Studies*

*JRS*         *Journal of Roman Studies*

*OCD*         *Oxford Classical Dictionary.* Eds. S. Hornblower and A. Spawforth. Oxford:
              Oxford University Press, 1996, 3rd ed.

*P. Dur*      *Excavations at Dura-Europos: Final Report V Part I: The Parchments and
              Papyri.* Eds. C.G. Welles, R.O. Fink, and J.F. Gilliam. New Haven, CT:
              Yale University Press, 1959.

*P. Grenfell* *New Classical Fragments and Other Greek and Latin Papyri.* Eds. B.P.
              Grenfell and A.S. Hunt. Oxford, 1897.

*P. Lond.*    *Greek Papyri in the British Museum.* Eds. F.G. Kenyon and H.I. Bell.
              London, 1893–.

*P. Mich.*    *Papyri in the University of Michigan Collection.* Eds. C.C. Edgar et al. Ann
              Arbor: University of Michigan Press, 1931–.

*P. Oxy.*     *The Oxyrhynchus Papyri.* Eds. B.P. Grenfell et al. London, 1898–.

*P. Ryl*      *Catalogue of the Greek Papyri in the John Rylands Library, Manchester.* Eds.
              A.S. Hunt et al. Manchester, 1911–1952.

343

| PBSR | Papers of the British School at Rome |
| PIR | Prosopographia Imperii Romani saec. I. II. III. Berlin: de Gruyter, 1932–. |
| RIC | Roman Imperial Coinage (1923–) |
| RIU | Die Römische Inschriften Ungarns Vols. 1–4. Budapest: Akadémiai Kiado; Vol. 5. Bonn: Rudolf Habelt. |

## ANCIENT SOURCES

Unless otherwise stated, the ancient works in this list appear in the original Latin or Greek with an English translation in the Loeb editions published by University of Harvard Press.

Ammianus Marcellinus
Caesar. *Civil War*
Caesar. *Gallic War*
*Digest.* Trans. A. Watson. University of Pennsylvania Press, 1985.
Dio. *Roman History*
Herodian. *History of the Empire*
Hyginus. *De Metatione Castrorum.* Leipzig: Teubner, 1977
Lactantius. *De Mortibus Persecutorum.* Trans. J. L. Creed. Oxford: Clarendon Press, 1984.
Livy. *History of Rome*
Orosius. *Adversus paganos Historiarum.*
Pliny. *Natural History*
Plutarch. *Parallel Lives*
Polybius. *The Histories*
*Scriptores Historiae Augustae*
Strabo. *Geography*
Suetonius. *Twelve Caesars*
Tacitus. *Agricola*
Tacitus. *Annals*
Tacitus. *Germania*
Tacitus. *Histories*
Tertullian. *Apologeticus.* Ed. A. Sauter. Aberdeen: Aberdeen University Press, 1926.
Tertullian. *De Anima.* Ed. J. H. Waszink. Amsterdam: J. M. Meulenhoff, 1947.
Vegetius. *Epitoma Rei Militaris.* Ed. A. Önnefors. Stuttgart: Teubner, 1995.
Velleius Paterculus. *Compendium of Roman History*
Vitruvius. *The Ten Books on Architecture.* Trans. M.H. Morgan. New York: Dover Publications.

## MODERN WORKS

Alston, Richard. 1994. "Roman military pay from Caesar to Diocletian." *JRS* 84, 111–123.

———. 1995. *Soldier and Society in Roman Egypt: A Social History.* London: Routledge.

Austin, Norman J.E., and Rankov, N. Boris. 1995. *Exploratio: Military and Political Intelligence in the Roman World from the Second Punic War to the Battle of Adrianople.* London: Routledge.

Bell, H.I., et al. (eds.). 1962. *The Abbinaeus Archive: Papers of a Roman Officer in the Reign of Constantius II.* Oxford: Clarendon Press.

Birley, Anthony R. 1988. *Septimius Severus: The African Emperor.* London: Batsford. 2nd ed. Reprinted by Routledge, 2000.

———. 2002. *Garrison Life at Vindolanda: A Band of Brothers.* Stroud, Gloucestershire: Tempus Publishing.

Bishop, Michael C., and Coulston, Jon C.N. 1993. *Roman Military Equipment from the Punic Wars to the Fall of Rome.* London: Batsford.

Bowman, Alan K. 1983. *The Roman Writing Tablets from Vindolanda.* London: British Museum.

Bowman, Alan K., and Thomas, D.J. 1983. *Vindolanda: The Latin Writing Tablets.* London: Society for the Promotion of Roman Studies. Britannia Monographs Series No. 4.

Brand, Clarence E. 1968. *Roman Military Law.* Austin: University of Texas Press.

Brauer, George C. 1975. *The Age of the Soldier Emperors: Imperial Rome 244–284.* New Jersey, NJ: Noyes Press.

Braund, David C. 1984. *Rome and the Friendly King: The Character of Client Kingship.* London: Croom Helm.

Breeze, David J. 1971. "Pay grades and ranks below the centurionate." *JRS* 61, 130–135.

Brunt, Peter A. 1950. "Pay and superannuation in the Roman Army." *PBSR* 18, 50–75.

———. 1971. *Social Conflicts in the Roman Republic.* New York: W.W. Norton.

———. 1975. "Did Imperial Rome disarm her subjects?" *Phoenix* 29, 260–270.

———. 1981. "The revenues of Rome." *JRS* 71, 161–172.

Campbell, J. Brian. 1984. *The Emperor and the Roman Army 31 BC–AD 235.* Oxford: Clarendon Press.

———. 1987. "Teach yourself how to be a Roman general." *JRS* 77, 13–29.

———. 1994. *The Roman Army 31 BC–AD 337: A Sourcebook.* London: Routledge.

———. 2002. *War and Society in Imperial Rome 31 BC–AD 284.* London: Routledge.

Cheesman, George L. 1914. *The Auxilia of the Roman Imperial Army.* Oxford: Clarendon Press.

Cherry, David (ed.). 2001. *The Roman World: A Sourcebook.* Oxford: Blackwell.

Chevallier, Raymond. 1976. *Roman Roads.* London: Batsford.

Connolly, Peter. 1998. *Greece and Rome at War.* London: Greenhill Books. Rev. ed.

Cornell, Tim, and Matthews, John. 1982. *Atlas of the Roman World.* Oxford: Phaidon.

Davies, Roy W. 1969. "The *medici* of the Roman armed forces." *Ep. Stud.* 8, 83–99.

———. 1971. "The Roman military diet." *Britannia* 1, 122–142.

Develin, R. 1971. "The army pay rises under Severus and Caracalla and the question of the *annona militaris.*" *Latomus* 30, 687–695.

Devijver, H. 1989. *The Equestrian Officers of the Roman Army.* Vol. 1. Amsterdam: J. Gieben.

———. 1992. *The Equestrian Officers of the Roman Army.* Vol. 2. Stuttgart: F. Steiner.

Devijver, H. (ed.). 1976–2001. *Prosopographia Militiarum Equestrium Quae Fuerunt ab Augusto ad Gallienum.* Leuven: Universitaire Pers Leuven.

Dilke, Oswald A.W. 1985. *Greek and Roman Maps.* London: Thames and Hudson.

Dixon, Karen R., and Southern, Pat. 1992. *The Roman Cavalry from the First to the Third Century AD.* London: Batsford.

Duncan-Jones, Richard. 1982. *The Economy of the Roman Empire.* Cambridge: Cambridge University Press. 2nd ed.

———. 1994. *Money and Government in the Roman Empire.* Cambridge: Cambridge University Press.

Durry, Marcel. 1938. *Les Cohortes Prétoriennes.* Paris: de Boccard.

Elton, Hugh. 1996. *Frontiers of the Roman Empire.* London: Batsford.

Feugère, Michel. 2002. *Weapons of the Romans.* Stroud, Gloucestershire: Tempus Publishing.

Fink, Robert O. 1971. *Roman Military Records on Papyrus.* Cleveland, OH: Case Western Reserve University for the American Philological Association.

Frayn, Joan M. 1979. *Subsistence Farming in Roman Italy.* Fontwell, Sussex: Centaur Press.

Gabba, Emilio. 1976. *Republican Rome, the Army and the Allies.* Oxford: Blackwell.

Gardner, Jane F. 1993. *Being a Roman Citizen.* London: Routledge.

Garnsey, Peter, et al. (eds.). 1983. *Trade in the Ancient Economy.* London: Chatto and Windus.

Gilliver, Catherine. 2000. *The Roman Art of War.* Stroud, Gloucestershire: Tempus Publishing.

Goldsworthy, Adrian K. 1996. *The Roman Army at War 100 BC–AD 200.* Oxford: Clarendon Press.

———. 2000. *The Punic Wars.* London: Cassell and Co.

———. 2003a. *The Complete Roman Army.* London: Thames and Hudson.

———. 2003b. *In the Name of Rome: The Men Who Won the Roman Empire.* London: Weidenfeld and Nicolson.

Goodman, Martin. 1997. *The Roman World 44 BC–AD 180.* London: Routledge.

Grenfell, B.P., et al. 1898–. *The Oxyrhynchus Papyri.* London: Egypt Exploration Society for the British Academy.

Hopkins, Keith. 1980. "Taxes and trade in the Roman Empire, 200 BC–AD 400." *JRS* 70, 101–125.

*Inscriptiones Graecae ad Res Romanas Pertinentes.* 1906–1927. Paris: E. Leroux. Reprinted 1975. Chicago: Ares. 4 vols.

Johnson, Anne. 1983. *Roman Forts.* London: A. and C. Black.

Johnson, Stephen. 1976. *Roman Forts of the Saxon Shore.* London: Elek. 2nd ed.

———. 1983. *Late Roman Fortifications.* London: Batsford.

Jones, Arnold H.M. 1974. *The Roman Economy: Studies in Ancient Economic and Administrative History.* Oxford: Oxford University Press.

Kent, John P.C. 1978. *Roman Coins.* London: Thames and Hudson.

Keppie, Lawrence. 1984. *The Making of the Roman Army.* London: Batsford. Reprinted with additions by Routledge, 1998.

Le Bohec, Yann. 1994. *The Imperial Roman Army.* London: Batsford. Republished by Routledge, 2000.

Lee, A.D. 1993. *Information and Frontiers: Roman Foreign Relations in Late Antiquity.* Cambridge: Cambridge University Press.

Lepper, Frank, and Frere, Sheppard. 1998. *Trajan's Column: A New Edition of the Cichorius Plates.* Gloucestershire: Alan Sutton.

Levick, Barbara. 2000. *The Government of the Roman Empire: A Sourcebook.* London: Routledge. 2nd ed.

Lewis, Naphtali, and Rheinhold, Meyer. 1955. *Roman Civilization: Sourcebook II: The Empire.* New York: Columbia University Press.

Lintott, Andrew. 1993. *Imperium Romanum: Politics and Administration.* London: Routledge.

———. 1999. *The Constitution of the Roman Republic.* Oxford: Oxford University Press.

Luttwak, Edward. 1976. *The Grand Strategy of the Roman Empire From the First Century A.D. to the Third.* Baltimore, MD: Johns Hopkins University Press. Reprinted London: Weidenfeld and Nicolson, 1999.

MacMullen, Ramsay. 1963. *Soldier and Civilian in the Later Roman Empire.* Cambridge, MA: Harvard University Press.

———. 1974. *Roman Social Relations 50 BC to AD 284.* New Haven, CT: Yale University Press.

———. 1980. "How big was the Roman army?" *Klio* 62, 451–460.

Mann, John C. 1974. "The frontiers of the Principate." *ANRW* II.I, 508–531.

Marsden, Eric.W. 1969. *Greek and Roman Artillery: Historical Development.* Oxford: Clarendon Press.

Mattern, Susan P. 1999. *Rome and the Enemy: Imperial Strategy in the Principate.* Berkeley: University of California Press.

Mattingly, Harold, and Carson, R.A.G. (eds.). 1923–1964. *Coins of the Roman Empire in the British Museum.* London: British Museum. 6 vols. Reprinted 1976.

Maxfield, Valerie A. 1981. *The Military Decorations of the Roman Army.* London: Batsford.

Millett, Martin. 1990. *The Romanization of Roman Britain: An Essay in Archaeological Interpretation.* Cambridge: Cambridge University Press.

Mitchell, Richard E. 1990. *Patricians and Plebeians: The Origins of the Roman State.* Ithaca, NY: Cornell University Press.

Parkin, Tim G. 1992. *Demography and Roman Society.* Baltimore, MD: Johns Hopkins University Press.

Pflaum, H.-G. 1955. "Deux carrières equestres de Lambèse et de Zana." *Libyca* 3, 123–154.

Pharr, Clyde (trans.). 1952. *The Theodosian Code and Novels and the Sirmondian Constitution.* New York: Greenwood Press.

Potter, Tim. 1987. *Roman Italy.* London: British Museum Press.

Robinson, Harold R. 1975. *The Armour of Imperial Rome.* London: Arms and Armour Press.

Robinson, O.F. 1997. *The Sources of Roman Law: Problems and Methods for Ancient Historians.* London: Routledge.

Rostovtzeff, Michael I. 1957. *Social and Economic History of the Roman Empire.* Oxford: Clarendon Press. 2nd ed.

Roth, Jonathan P. 1999. *Logistics of the Roman Army at War (246 BC–AD 235).* Leiden: Brill (Columbia Studies in the Classical Tradition Vol XXIII).

Roxan, Margaret. 1978. *Roman Military Diplomas 1954–1977.* University of London, Institute of Archaeology Occasional Publication no. 2.

———. 1985. *Roman Military Diplomas 1978–1984.* University of London, Institute of Archaeology Occasional Publication no. 9.

———. 1986. "Observations on the reasons for changes in formula in diplomas circa AD 140." In W. Eck and H. Wolff (eds.). *Heer und Integrationspoltik: die Romischen Militardiplome als Historische Quelle.* Cologne and Vienna: Böhlau.

———. 1994. *Roman Military Diplomas 1985–1993.* University of London, Institute of Archaeology Occasional Publication no. 14.

Roxan, Margaret, and Holder, Paul. 2003. "Roman military diplomas." *Bulletin of the Institute of Classical Studies.* Supplement 82.

Saddington, Dennis B. 1982. *The Development of the Roman Auxiliary Forces from Caesar to Vespasian, 49 BC–AD 79.* Harare: University of Zimbabwe Press.

Salway, Peter. 1965. *Frontier People of Roma Britain.* Cambridge: Cambridge University Press.

———. 1991. *Roman Britain.* Oxford: Clarendon Press.

Scheidel, Walter. 1996. "Measuring sex, age, and death in the Roman Empire: explorations in ancient demography." *JRA:* Supplementary Series no. 21. Ann Arbor, MI.

Shelton, Jo-Ann. 1998. *As the Romans Did: A Sourcebook in Roman Social History.* Oxford: Oxford University Press. 2nd ed.

Sherwin-White, Adrian N. 1973. *The Roman Citizenship.* Oxford: Clarendon Press.

Shotter, David. 1994. *The Fall of the Roman Republic.* London: Routledge.

Sommer, C. Sebastian. 1984. *The Military Vici in Roman Britain.* Oxford: BAR 129.

Southern, Pat. 1989. "The *Numeri* of the Roman Imperial army." *Britannia* 20, 81–140.

———. 2002. *The Roman Empire from Severus to Constantine.* London: Routledge.

Southern, Pat, and Dixon, Karen R. 1996. *The Late Roman Army.* London: Batsford.

Speidel, Michael A. 1992, "Roman army pay scales." *JRS* 82, 87–106.

Speidel, Michael P. 1973. "The pay of the *auxilia.*" *JRS* 63, 141–147.

———. 1994. *Riding for Caesar: The Roman Emperor's Horse Guard.* London: Batsford.

Sutherland, Carol H.V. 1974. *Roman Coins.* London: Barrie and Jenkins.

Sydenham, Edward A. 1952. *The Coinage of the Roman Republic.* London: Spink.

Talbert, Richard J.A. 1984. *The Senate of Imperial Rome.* Princeton, NJ: Princeton University Press.

Wacher, John (ed.). 1987. *The Roman World.* London: Routledge. 2 vols.

Watson, Alan (ed.). 1998. *The Digest of Justinian.* Philadephia: University of Pennsylvania Press. Rev. ed.; 4 vols.

Watson, George R. 1969. *The Roman Soldier.* London: Thames and Hudson.

Welles, C. Bradford, et al. (eds.). 1959. *Excavations at Dura-Europos: Final Report V, Part I: The Parchments and Papyri.* New Haven, CT: Yale University Press.

White, Kenneth D. 1970. *Roman Farming.* London: Thames and Hudson.

Whittaker, Charles R. 1994. *Frontiers of the Roman Empire: A Social and Economic Study.* Baltimore, MD: Johns Hopkins University Press.

Woolliscroft, David. I. 2001. *Roman Military Signalling.* Stroud, Gloucestershire: Tempus Publishing.

# INDEX

A note on Roman names: the Romans did not use their last names a surnames but proclaimed their families usually by their second name. For example, Marcus Tullius Cicero belonged to the family of the Tullii. His own personal name was Marcus. Lucius Cornelius Sulla belonged to the Cornelii. In accordance with normal practice, most persons listed in this index are listed under their family names with reference from their last names. Emperors are indexed under the names in most common usage.

# ABOUT THE AUTHOR

Pat Southern studied for her BA Honours degree in Archaeology and Ancient History at the University of London External Department and went on to gain a Masters in Roman Frontier Studies at the University of Newcastle upon Tyne, where she also worked for several years as librarian in the Department of Archaeology. She has published several books on Roman themes, including The Roman Cavalry and The Late Roman Army, both co-authored with Karen R Dixon. She then produced biographies of the Emperor Domitian, Augustus, Mark Antony, Cleopatra, Julius Caesar, and Pompey the Great, followed by her latest book examining the problems of the third century AD in The Roman Empire From Severus to Constantine (Routledge 2001). She still works as a librarian and is a committed Roman army enthusiast.

# Mr. Bell and the Telephone

## by Carolyn Clark

## Table of Contents

# Who Was Alexander Graham Bell?

You have probably seen lots of different kinds of telephones. But have you ever seen the very first telephone?

You might be surprised that this telephone looked so different from the telephones you know. The first call ever made was made in 1876. It was made on a large machine like this.

In 1876, the telephone was a brand-new invention. ➲

⌂ Alexander Graham Bell

The telephone was **invented** by
Alexander Graham Bell. He was a
teacher and a scientist. He was curious
to learn about how things worked.

Alexander Graham Bell was born in Scotland in 1847. He lived in a house with his parents and his two brothers. Even as a boy, Alexander was curious and liked to read to learn new things.

⏶ Here is Alexander Graham Bell at age 16.

As a teacher, Alexander taught his students to talk.

Alexander liked to sit by his father as he worked. His father taught people who could not hear. He worked hard and taught them how to speak. When Alexander grew up, he would become a teacher like his father.

# What Happened in the United States?

When Alexander was 16, his family moved from Scotland. They settled in Boston, Massachusetts, in 1871.

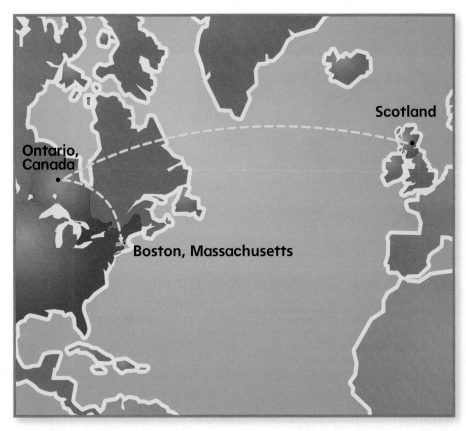

Scotland

Ontario, Canada

Boston, Massachusetts

↰ Alexander and his parents first moved to Canada and then to the United States.

At that time in the United States, people would visit a **telegraph** office to send messages. Their message would be sent in code on a telegraph machine. It would go to a telegraph office far away.

telegraph machine ⊃

⇧ This drawing shows a busy telegraph office where messages were sent or received.

Only one message could be sent at a time. Bell knew he wanted to invent a telegraph that could send more than one message. He needed a helper and asked Thomas Watson to work with him.

This painting shows Bell and Watson in Bell's office.

While working on his idea for a new telegraph, Bell had another idea. Bell and Watson knew that **electricity** could make sound travel over a wire. They wanted to send words over a wire, too.

# What Was Bell's New Invention?

On March 10, 1876, an amazing thing happened. Bell said, "Mr. Watson—come here—I want to see you."

Watson, who was in another room, heard him. The sound of his voice came through over the wires. They were the first words spoken over an electric telephone. Bell's call to his friend Mr. Watson was the first telephone message.

⌂ Bell and Watson show the first telephone.

The telephone was a hit! Everyone wanted to have one. Soon even the White House in Washington, D.C., had its first telephone. Guess which friend the President called first? Alexander Graham Bell, of course!

⚲ This is President Rutherford B. Hayes with the First Lady in 1878.

As the years went by, different scientists invented new and better kinds of telephones.

This time line shows some of the later telephones.

**Time Line of Telephones**

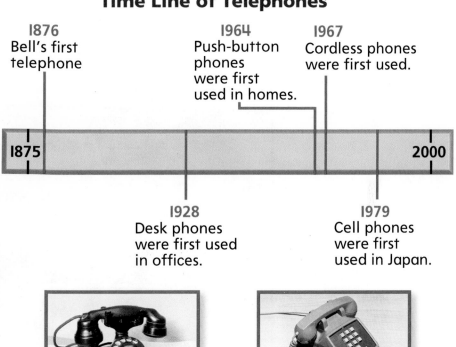

1876
Bell's first telephone

1964
Push-button phones were first used in homes.

1967
Cordless phones were first used.

1875 — 2000

1928
Desk phones were first used in offices.

1979
Cell phones were first used in Japan.

Desk phone, 1928

Push-button phone, 1964

Telephones have changed a lot since Alexander Graham Bell invented the first one. What do you think Mr. Bell would say if he saw a cell phone that takes pictures? He would probably be glad to see that his idea keeps getting better and better.

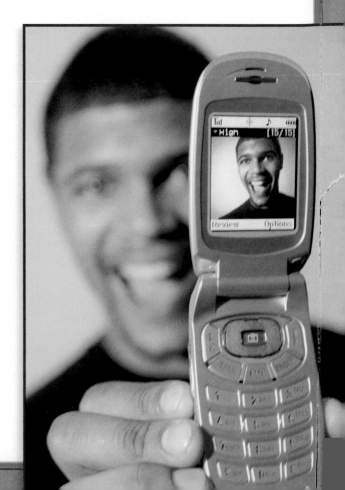

This cell phone can take a picture. ➲

# Glossary

**electricity** *(i-lek-TRIS-uh-tee)* a kind of energy used to make heat, light, and sound *(page 9)*

**invented** *(in-VENT-id)* made something for the first time *(page 3)*

**telegraph** *(TEL-uh-graf)* a machine that sends messages over wires by a code *(page 7)*

---

# Index

# Comprehension Check

## Retell

Use a Make Inferences Chart to make an inference about what you read. Then tell a partner what you learned from this book.

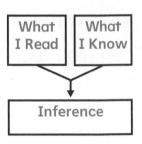

## Think and Compare

1. Why do you think President Rutherford B. Hayes called Alexander Graham Bell first?

2. What is your favorite way to send messages to your friends?

3. Why is it important for people to try to invent new things?